COMPUTERS

and LIFE

An Integrative Approach

COMPUTERS
and LIFE

An Integrative Approach

JEFFREY FRATES
Los Medanos College

WILLIAM MOLDRUP
Merced College

PRENTICE-HALL, INC., Englewood Cliffs, New Jersey 07632

Library of Congress Cataloging in Publication Data

Frates, Jeffrey.
  Computers and life.

  Bibliography: p. 355
  Includes index.
  1.-Computers and civilization. 2.-Electronic
data processing. I. Moldrup, William. II.-Title.
QA76.9.C66F7 1983   303.4'834   82-9832
ISBN 0-13-165084-X   AACR2

Editorial production/interior design: Margaret McAbee
Cover design: Kenneth J. Alexander
Manufacturing buyer: Edw. O'Dougherty

Printed in the United States of America

10 9 8 7 6 5 4 3 2 1

PRENTICE-HALL, INTERNATIONAL INC., *London*
PRENTICE-HALL OF AUSTRALIA PTY. LIMITED, *Sydney*
PRENTICE-HALL CANADA, INC. *Toronto*
PRENTICE-HALL OF INDIA PRIVATE LIMITED, *New Delhi*
PRENTICE-HALL OF JAPAN, INC., *Tokyo*
PRENTICE-HALL OF SOUTHEAST ASIA PTE. LTD., *Singapore*
WHITEHALL BOOKS LIMITED, *Wellington, New Zealand*
EDITORA PRENTICE-HALL DO BRASIL LTDA., *Rio de Janeiro*

Dedications

To SUE, ERIN, JASON, LISA, AND JASON

While the actual preparation of this manuscript was the responsibility of the authors, there are many people behind the scenes without whose assistance a work such as this would be impossible. I would most sincerely like to express my love and appreciation to my wife for her support and assistance during the preparation of this book. I would further like to thank our production editor, Margaret McAbee, whose editorial talents turned our manuscript into a finished product. I would also like to thank those who reviewed manuscript, and those companies who supplied photographs which enhance the quality of the text. Finally, I would like to thank Ken Alexander of Los Medanos College, for the cover design, part opening art, and cartoons.

JEFFREY FRATES

To my family and friends

My appreciation and gratitude to all who have given their support, encouragement, and understanding during the production of this book—especially my family, friends, colleagues, and students. Since I performed all of my manuscript typing on a word processor, I wish to thank Muse Software, Inc. for their valuable and courteous assistance. I would also like our reviewers, especially Professor Jack Dineen of Middlesex Community College, for the comments and criticism which helped to improve our book. We take full responsibility for any mistakes that might remain. Finally, to the editorial staff at Prentice-Hall, especially Margaret McAbee, I am greatly indebted for their patient and friendly guidance.

WILLIAM MOLDRUP

CONTENTS

PREFACE
TO THE INSTRUCTOR

In our years of teaching we have found that selecting one suitable text for a computers and society course is difficult. Many texts contain too much emphasis upon hardware or not enough, too much on social issues or not enough, too much about future trends or not enough, too much programming or none at all. And, when a text is found that has the proper balance in one of these areas, rarely are the other areas equally well balanced.

We have attempted to overcome this difficulty in two ways: first, by focusing on a balance that is suitable to several approaches without imposing constraints on the instructor, and second, by incorporating a totally unique approach to the subject that should eliminate many of the traditional problems associated with computer and society texts. Although we bring more than thirty years of computer experience into this book, we each contribute from a very different perspective: one from a business and hardware orientation, the other from a social science, humanities, and software approach. Most important, we share the viewpoint equally that human beings are *the* most important component of any computer system—and it is this perspective which permeates all of our writing.

AN INTEGRATIVE APPROACH

Simply stated, an integrative approach unites within each chapter the applications, their social impact, hardware components, and possible future directions of this technology. Therefore, in each applications chapter we focus on a particular field, such as medicine or education, discuss the numerous ways in which computers are used in this particular area, the positive and negative effects of these uses, the typical hardware configurations used, and the future developments that are likely to occur over the next decade.

We organized the material in this fashion to demonstrate how computer applications, the hardware from which such systems are constructed, and the social implications of these systems are interrelated. By synthesizing these three elements in each chapter, we hope to overcome the difficulty experienced by both instructors and students when using texts that present these topics in a fragmented manner as if they were separate and unrelated areas.

We wanted to write a book that would be relatively easy to teach and learn from; we felt that a structure closely paralleling real life—where hardware, systems, and social effects are integrated—would facilitate teaching and therefore learning. For, other than in textbooks, one does not encounter computer hardware, applications, and their social-economic impact as separate entities.

In addition to clarifying the interaction between hardware, systems, and implications, this integrative approach emphasizes the human factor. In each chapter we have explained how *people* use computer systems and equipment, and how *people* are affected by their use. Consequently, the crucial role of humans, in a variety of situations, is a recurring theme. To provide a broad perspective on the applications under discussion, we have woven quotations from several sources into each chapter discussion. We have made no attempt to posit a causal relationship between computer systems and their social impact. Rather, in the Social Implications sections of each chapter we objectively present several advantages and disadvantages of computers in the field under discussion—this underscores our belief that computer applications and their impact can change rapidly and, that it is the students who must resolve ultimately such issues for themselves.

TEACHING SUGGESTIONS

We designed this book for use in a single term introductory course on computers and society. In the instructor's manual that accompanies this text, we present specific suggestions for teaching each chapter as well as discussion topics and appropriate test questions. There should be no difficulty for you, the instructor, to relate different aspects within each chapter since all of the transitions and interrelationships are explicitly clarified with an overview at the beginning of each chapter.

The chapters form a continuous progression of information, with references to specific chapters made when a topic has been discussed previously or when it is to be discussed in a later chapter. However, the progression is not seamless and can be separated into five distinct areas: Chapters 1-3 (FOUNDATIONS) are introductory (history, hardware, and software); Chapter 4 is pivotal in that it introduces the social issues that reappear throughout the book and it makes the transition from hardware/software into the applications. Chapters 5-16 cover twelve major applications; Chapter 17 (Policy, People, and Employment) synthesizes several themes and projects them into the future. And finally Appendices provide introductions and programming examples for the BASIC and Pascal languages.

In the APPLICATIONS section (Chapters 5-16) the format for each chapter consists of six parts in the following order:

1. *Perspective*—an overview of the rationale for the use and expanding use of computers in the field under discussion in the chapter.

2. *Computers in . . .*—an exposition of how computers are actually being employed now within the applications area.

3. *Social Implications*—the pros and cons, both advantages and disadvantages of computer usage in the field, are discussed.

4. *Hardware*—descriptions of typical small, medium, and large computer systems that provide the appropriate capability for use in the application discussed in the chapter.

5. *A Look Toward the Future*—major trends that are expected in the applications area within five to ten years.

6. *Study and Review*—questions for study, class discussion, and preparing for tests.

WHAT YOUR STUDENTS CAN GAIN

In addition to covering the major topics required in a one-term computers and society/computer literacy course, this text aids students in understanding the interdependence between human beings, computer systems, and the hardware from which such systems are constructed. And, unlike most texts, hardware vocabulary and concepts are not dropped or forgotten after the first few chapters—each chapter reviews the important concepts that were introduced in the FOUNDATIONS chapters. Students are informed of the fact that all systems have impact and that people comprise the most important element within an interactive system such as a computer system. Students are introduced, via numerous applications, to the job opportunities that exist in data processing and related computer technology fields. For those students who do not plan to pursue a career in data processing, an in-depth approach is provided so they can acquire a suitable measure of 'computer literacy' which is becoming prerequisite for entering any business or institutional field. By learning to treat computer concepts, applications, and implications as related topics, students can come to understand the importance of computer technology as these devices create social change in the next generation much as the automobile and television did on past generations.

PREFACE
TO THE STUDENT

You are about to begin studying a subject that is unfamiliar to most people. In fact, computer science and data processing actually scares some people. But as modern societies become increasingly computerized, it is essential for people to understand computer technology in general terms.

To get an office job in today's market, most workers must have some understanding of data processing and computer concepts, or be willing to learn them. Workers who do understand data processing concepts are considered valuable and are more likely to be promoted. But even beyond jobs and careers, some understanding, or "computer literacy" is essential. Almost every aspect of our personal lives, from banking to trucking, from entertainment to consumer products, is influenced by computer technology in some manner. To know of these changes and use them to our benefit, everyone should become computer literate.

This textbook will not make you an expert in computer science; it will explain the concepts, facts, and theories that relate to what a computer is, how it is used, and what the social implications of its uses are. To do this, the subject matter is divided here into three parts: 1) the facts that explain what a computer is and how it works, 2) the various uses or applications of computer technology, and 3) the social implications of expanding computer use.

This book provides you with a brief, yet firm understanding of the basic computer concepts which are important in order to more fully understand the various applications that are described.

STRUCTURE OF THE BOOK

The text is divided into three parts, each intended to be a logical extension of the previous one. In part one, three chapters introduce the fundamental concepts of what computers are, how they work, and what they are and are not capable of doing.

The second part, chapter 4, is a transition discussion which provides an overview of the major sociological positive and negative implications of computer technology. Because these major implications recur in different forms in the applications chapters that follow, their presentation collectively in one chapter early in the book enables one to better understand the social effects of this new technology when business and industry computer applications are described.

The third part, beginning with chapter 5, describes in great detail the uses of computers and electronic data transfer in a wide variety of fields. These chapters establish the broad perspective on the uses and implications of computer technology in many of our major institutions.

STRUCTURE OF THE CHAPTERS

Each chapter in this book begins with a theme and a quotation from some piece of literature that relates to the subjects presented in the chapter. The first 3 chapters in the book provide a straightforward presentation of technological facts about computers and presents these in as concise and nontechnical a way as possible. The fourth chapter provides a bridge or transition from the technology to the applications in commerce and life.

Chapters 5 through 17 are structured similarly. After the opening quotation, the PERSPECTIVE section provides background about the application to be discussed. The uses of computer technology within that specific area are then described. At the end of the chapter the section entitled: SOCIAL IMPLICATIONS presents both pro and con arguments regarding the uses of computer technology within that specific area. Many of the topics presented in this section amplify certain points which may have been originally discussed in chapter 4. The next section, HARDWARE, describes typical types of computer systems which are likely to be used in those applications described in the chapter. The final section in each chapter, A LOOK TOWARD THE FUTURE, projects current trends within that specific application on into the future, in an attempt to predict the changes in that area expected in five to ten years.

Finally, questions at the end of each chapter serve as a personal review and as a means of assuring that you have understood the major concepts presented in the chapter.

HOW TO USE THIS BOOK

Naturally your instructor is your guide through the subject matter presented herein. However, you can develop your own method for reading the book to derive the maximum benefit from the material. The first four chapters must be read in sequence, as there is a logical flow from one chapter to the next. The remaining chapters may be read in any sequence, as they do not follow one another in terms of presentation of information: they are independent of one another. Read the sections at the end of the chapters carefully as they not only present new information, but act as a summary and review as well. After you have read each chapter, answer the questions at the end of the chapter to reinforce your understanding of the material.

WHAT YOU WILL GAIN

This book will inform you of important facts about computer science today and the implications this technology has on the general quality of life around us.

When you finish this book and the coursework, you may decide to study computer science in greater detail, consider it as a possible career choice; or use your knowledge of computer science to enhance your ability to perform special duties in another career. Whatever the purpose of your study in this course, an increased understanding of computers and their implications can aid you in the future, no matter what your occupational goal.

COMPUTERS
and LIFE

An Integrative Approach

Part 1

FOUNDATIONS

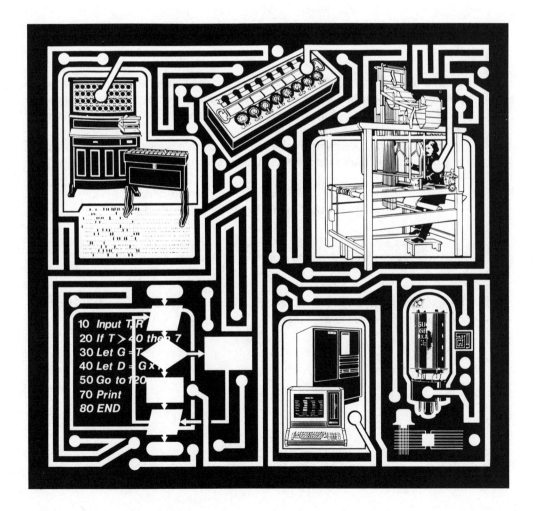

No other technology known to humans has advanced at such a rapid pace as has computer technology in the space of the last 30 years. This technology is almost beyond the understanding of the average individual; even trained professionals require continuous updating of technical skills to stay current.

The following comments, made by two notable authors, reflect the attitude of many people about the advancements in today's technology.

> *For the average individual, any sufficiently advanced new*
> *technology is basically indistinguishable from magic.*
> *(Arthur C. Clarke, 1979)*

> *If we really understand it, it must be obsolete.*
> *(James Burke, 1979)*

The first part of this book should provide the reader with a solid, basic understanding of this rapidly advancing technology.

1

THE INFORMATION/COMPUTER REVOLUTION

PERSPECTIVE

Few of humanity's inventions have created more controversy than the computer. This device, which is able to store large amounts of information and make complex arithmetic calculations and logical comparisons in fractions of a second, has stirred the imagination and emotions of many people. Few can claim that the computer does not already affect their business transactions or the quality of life around them. Yet, for as wide an effect as computers have on society, they seem to be among the most misunderstood facets of technological advancement. As the following quote indicates, while we don't fully understand the impact of computers, we must prepare ourselves to deal with them in the future.

> We probably cannot predict the precise social consequences of the computer revolution any more than the early auto-makers could have predicted Detroit's . . . position in our economy today. What we can do, however, is lay the groundwork for the planning and management of the inevitable changes. We should be ready to control the impact of universally available information and manage the effects of a cash-less society. Otherwise we might end up with the computer equivalent of smog, highway blight or worse.
>
> *(INFOSYSTEMS, 1978)*

Many people feel that we have evolved into a society that is—or soon will be—controlled and directed by computers. For years, discussions of business ethics and the modern corporate structure have centered on the faceless, impersonal nature of

3

our business organizations. Now this concern has been amplified by the increasing use of computers and computer networks. The computer has become so powerful and so widely used that it is beginning to take on an identifiable personality—a personality many people are beginning to believe should be legally controlled and held accountable for its errors.

Computers are not even fully understood by the individuals they serve. If the job that a particular executive is working on goes wrong, he or she can say, "The computer blew it!" and probably will be absolved of guilt. Unfortunately, this attitude has made the computer a scapegoat. It's easy to blame the computer because it can't fight back; yet few people are willing to accept the fact that computers are merely tools of human beings. Hammers, crowbars, screwdrivers, and other devices are tools used to amplify man's existing physical capabilities. They can do nothing unless directed by a human being. The same is true of computers—which leads us to the realization that much of what we might like to blame on the computer can be directly attributed to some human action.

As powerful as computers are, they appear to have as much potential to be abused and misused in ways that can have negative effects on society as they do to advance technology and have positive effects on life.

Most people are aware of one computer horror story or another: they know a friend who had problems with a computer; they read a story in the newspaper; or they experienced problems with a computer themselves. But no matter what the source, their immediate reaction often is to blame the computer instead of the person behind it.

Tell your computer to have its
silicon chips checked!

A major part of the general public's attitude toward the computer is the product of a lack of knowledge about computers and what they do. Consequently, a blind trust is placed in the relatively few people who are knowledgeable about computers; unfortunately, sometimes the public's confidence is placed in those who would take advantage of that trust to use the computer for personal gain. When a computer is used in a way that causes loss to other individuals or business firms the belief that computers themselves are evil and uncontrollable is reinforced.

Because the use of computers is expanding, it follows that the average person should learn more how they work, even if only as a defensive measure. Since computers also have an enormous potential for benefitting society, a person should learn about them in order to contribute to the computers' influence on society. In either case, this book is designed to familiarize readers with basic computer concepts, to identify areas of potential misuse, to illustrate the positive aspects of computer applications, and to enable readers to formulate educated opinions about computers and their role in the society of the future.

VIEWPOINTS ON COMPUTER USE

As viewed by people from various backgrounds, the computer takes on different perspectives.

The Computer Manufacturer   may consider the computer to be a divine gift; a device of infinite benefit to mankind; a machine to be constantly improved, made faster, expanded; a source of increasing profits.

The Computer User   may consider the computer to be a source of trouble; not fast enough; too expensive; lacking reliability; the object of too many people expecting electronic miracles.

The General Public   may consider the computer to be a box of magic; an amazing electronic brain that can do anything with a single, simple command: "Compute!"; the source of wrong credit card billings and mistakes in bank balances; a device that intensifies the feeling of loss of privacy.

The Social Scientist   may consider the computer to be a device dedicated to the invasion of individual privacy, a volatile filing cabinet that contains all sorts of private information ready to be spewed forth at the touch of a button; a device sure to be used to subvert the masses.

The Courts   may consider the problems and the computer manipulations so incomprehensible that cases are thrown out of court. Or various issues emerge. What are the individual's rights to privacy? Who owns the facts or information about a person: the person the information pertains to, or the organization that spent the money to collect it?

The Computer Thief   may consider the computer as a storehouse full of prizes, a giant electronic safe to crack and rob; a source of proprietary information, confidential lists, and a challenge to devious ingenuity.

The reasons for all of these viewpoints are numerous and varied. Many of these notions may be justified, but then many may not. They do, however, point to one fact: There is no common belief about what computers are, how they work, what they can do now, what they can do in the future, and, finally, how they should be directed for the betterment of life instead of the destruction of liberty.

To understand the computer fully requires more than the completion of a single course in school or the reading of a single book. But a curious person can easily acquire enough information to analyze and evaluate the computer arena today. For there exists a set of basic concepts and terminology that provides a framework for understanding the complex workings of a computer. When some of these concepts are explained and become clear, the computer may not be so mysterious after all.

THE INFORMATION AGE

The age in which we now live is quite different from that of our parents or any other generation. It is characterized by rapid change in technology, life styles, and values. Such rapid change is difficult to understand or predict, and can result in disorientation, confusion, and uncertainty about what the future holds for us. In the early 1970s, writer Alvin Toffler termed this experience "future shock." Now, as we experience the 1980s, another new term explains one major force that is shaping our future—the "information explosion." Some sociologists claim that we are moving from an industrial age into a post-industrial "information age."

Since civilization began, societies have collected, stored, and transferred information. Never before has the amount of complex information, and its ease of collection, storage, and rate of growth matched that of the 1970s, however. For example, by 1800 the amount of new information, or knowledge, doubled about every 50 years. By 1950, it was doubling every 10 years, and it is estimated that today it doubles every $2\frac{1}{2}$ to 3 years. If we are not to be overwhelmed by its magnitude, techniques must be developed to allow us to utilize this valuable information resource easily and economically. The various ways in which governments, businesses, and individuals use computers to meet the challenge of the information explosion are discussed in this and subsequent chapters.

Recent statistics indicate how dramatically the information systems are affecting modern society. Each year a larger share of the world's gross national product (GNP)—the total value of annual output of goods and services—is claimed by information industries—or, as they are sometimes called, the knowledge industries. These industries include education, data processing, management consulting, publications of all types, radio and television, and scientific research. As a management consultant wrote:

> The "knowledge industries," which produce and distribute ideas and information rather than goods and services, accounted in 1955 for one-quarter of the United States gross national product. This was already three times the propor-

tion of the national product that the country had spent on the "knowledge sector" in 1900. Yet, by 1965, ten years later, the knowledge sector was taking one-third of a much bigger national product. In the late 1970's, it accounted for one-half of the total national product. . . .

From an economy of goods, which America was as recently as World War II, we have changed into a knowledge economy.   *(Drucker, 1979)*

This shift in our GNP is reflected in a shift in employment with a larger percentage of employees moving into service work, while the percentage employed to produce goods has declined steadily since 1965.

Finally, the amount of money spent on data processing equipment in industries such as aerospace and petroleum is currently more than $600 per year per employee. A government survey completed in the early 1980s indicated that more than 33 percent of spending for new plants and equipment by U.S. industries was going into data processing machinery—up from just 10 percent in 1970.

INFORMATION REVOLUTION

Today computer products and services make up the fastest-growing major industry in the world. Computer sales have increased from an estimated $339 million in 1955 to more than $60 billion per year in the early 1980s. Clearly the computer has become the information machine of our age—a machine that has actually created new industries.

As media theorist Marshall McLuhan suggested, the computer has become the central nervous system of our society. The computer has certainly expanded man's general capacity to manage the information available in our complex world, because when the computer was devised to lend structure and organization to existing information, it was found that the device could also be used to synthesize that information in ways that sometimes create additional information. Therefore, the computer designed originally to organize information has actually evolved into a device that can be used as a source of information itself.

How has this evolution occurred? If we assume that the computer came into being as a tool to handle information in an expanding technological society, then we should be able to trace and identify the factors that have contributed to the rapid growth of computers. Certainly an expanding population that generates an increasing number of facts about people, places, and things is a principal factor in an information explosion. However, the following pressures have also reinforced the desire of specific organizations—and society in general—to use the computer as a tool to increase the efficiency of communications and the capability to handle information:

The Explosion of Knowledge. In the age of specialization there are now detailed studies conducted in fields which ten to fifteen years ago received little atten-

The data processing manager would like your approval for $18,841,533 to acquire distributed processing capability with remote intelligent terminals and clustered input stations with hierarchical storage to improve throughput.

tion. Scientists of all types are studying new subjects and generating volumes of information that must be recorded, verified, and cross-referenced to existing knowledge.

Growth of Organizations. In an era of an expanding economy, more organizations come into existence. Both commercial and governmental groups consume existing information and generate new information. Furthermore, the interaction of organizations within society creates more data.

Technological Complexity. The products manufactured by our industrial society have become more numerous and more complex. This increases the need to describe products, provide information about their use and repair, and produce information that allows people to know that each product exists.

Diversification. More organizations, both governmental and commercial, are engaging in a wider variety of activities than ever before. The government is looking for ways to provide better services for the general population, and businesses are looking for activities that will increase their profits. Both generate more data.

Responsiveness. Organizations need to be able to respond to changing conditions in order to make positive changes, or simply to forecast future trends. Organizations must have up-to-date information on which to base decisions on future courses of action.

Consequences of Action.   Organizations need a means of predicting the outcome of activities based on specific courses of action. Actual construction of working models or the blind selection of a course of action and observance of results is too expensive and time-consuming. Organizations need efficient, inexpensive means of testing hypotheses without actually physically carrying out a course of action.

Cost Trends.   The productivity of human labor has not increased proportionately with cost. There are certain physical limits to any person's ability to produce. Increased wages will not necessarily result in greater production.

INFORMATION, DATA, AND DATA PROCESSING

Data processing is a term that may bring to mind images of sterile air-conditioned rooms full of expensive-looking equipment. Spinning tape reels, flashing lights, and futuristic-looking machinery characterize the average individual's conjecture about the meaning of data processing. This may well be an accurate mental picture of what data processing represents in many instances, but data processing does not necessarily include only the computer. **Data processing**, more generally and accurately defined, simply means the organization of data to achieve a desired result. Viewed from this perspective, the computer is only one of many ways to arrange data. To provide an additional dimension to the term data processing, the word **system** can be added. A system is simply an organized way of doing something. Thus, a data processing system (see Fig. 1.1) is an organized way of manipulating data to achieve a desired result. From here, then, it should be clear that the computer is but one method of data processing.

Computers, as a method of data processing, are tools that can produce powerful effects. Many apparent changes can be expected in any organization and society where computers are utilized. The reason computers are used so extensively today is that they produce information that organizations and segments of society find indispensable. While many individuals may complain about the use of such information, they cannot dispute that the computer is the most efficient organizer of information in existence. To this end we should examine more closely some basic information concepts, and how the computer or any data processing system is able to produce usable information.

Information can be thought of as the end result of some data manipulation ac-

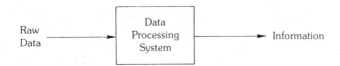

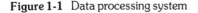
Figure 1-1 Data processing system

tivity. Data—which means facts—are the raw materials from which information is made. Data are facts about people, places, things, and their activities. These unorganized facts, or raw data, are transformed by some process into an arranged, ordered, usable form called information. In a stricter sense, data may consist of numbers and letters that can be restructured by a data processing system in a way that will increase their usefulness.

The processing or restructuring of data into usable information may take place in many ways. However, raw data are not randomly manipulated and then formulated into usable information. Instead, data are arranged according to a predetermined plan to achieve a desired result. To achieve this desired result, the data being manipulated or processed go through a cycle of steps: collection, input, data processing, and data output (see Fig. 1.2).

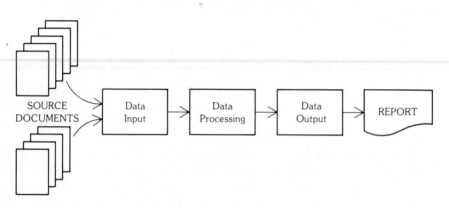

Figure 1-2 Data processing cycle

Data Collection.   As a transaction occurs, or as data originates, it is usually written onto a source document. The source document becomes a written record of the original transaction.

Data Input.   The data are then translated or coded into a format more acceptable as input to a specific data processing system. This coding may take the form of numbers written in specific locations on a particular form, or the preparation of punched cards or magnetic tape for input into a computer.

Data Processing.   Once the data are input to a data processing system, the data are organized into a more usable format. The arrangement that takes place at this point may be sorting, classifying, or some form of numeric computation. After the data is processed, it may then be stored for use at a future time.

Data Output.   When usable information has been created, it must be communicated to the people in an organization who will benefit most from it. Data output is the process of preparing the information in a form most beneficial to the user. The output can take on many forms—as will be discussed in future chapters—but most frequently takes the form of a printed report.

The specific activities detailed above can be carried out by different methods in different data processing systems, but the general order of activities does not change.

Methods of Data Processing

Three specific systems for processing data exist: (1) manual systems that rely on human physical organization of information; (2) mechanical systems that augment a person's physical capacities with a machine such as a calculator, a typewriter, or the forerunner to computerized data processing—an electromechanical punched card data processor; and now (3) electronic systems, such as the computer, that manipulate information with a minimum of human intervention. Regardless of the system used, however, the steps performed according to the data processing cycle remain the same (see Fig. 1.3).

Manual And Mechanical Processing   Manual data processing techniques are still used in modern organizations and, even with the large number of computer systems in existence, are still the dominant methods of data processing. Every step in the data processing cycle can be completed by using tools that have been available for hundreds of years: pens, pencils, paper, ledgers, worksheets, trays, files, and other manual devices.

The invention of such "tools" as accounting pegboards, document control registers, and edge punch cards, has improved the efficiency of manual methods. And a variety of mechanical and electronic office machines are still used with manual systems of processing data and as part of newer, more complex, technological systems. The most commonly used office machines are typewriters, adding machines, calculators, and cash registers. Although these devices are primarily mechanical and require manual direction, technological advancements have made them more versatile components of more complex systems such as electronic computers. Many manual-mechanical devices can be equipped with special devices that allow them to be hooked up directly to a computer system or store data in some form, such as magnetic tape, that can be entered into a computer system at a later time. Cash registers in use today have come a long way from the old cash register that simply printed a paper receipt. The modern electronic cash registers can record much more information about a transaction, and either transmit it directly to a computer or store it on magnetic tape for later entry into a computer system.

Punch Card Data Processing   The origins of the punch card and machines that handle the cards dates back to the late 1800s. The use and refinement of this equipment was slow until the 1940s when the potential of this method began to be realized, and the use of punch card equipment grew dramatically. Even when the computer system became a more expedient form of data processing, many techniques from punch card processing, including the use of punch cards themselves, continued to be used.

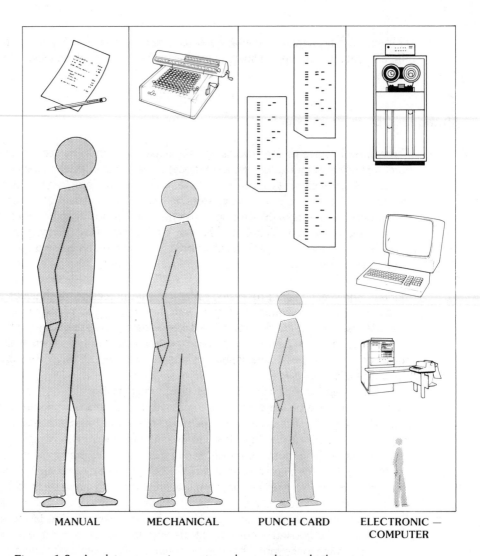

| MANUAL | MECHANICAL | PUNCH CARD | ELECTRONIC — COMPUTER |

Figure 1-3 As data processing systems have advanced, the amount of human labor needed to handle larger amounts of data has diminished.

Punch card data processing was the first mechanical process that performed the basic data processing operations automatically. A punch card data processing system was made up of individual mechanical components or machines. The fact that they were mechanical limited the speed of processing due to the movement of the mechanical parts. In addition, because each machine in such a system performs only one special function, the processing is not continuous but sequential, in a string. Cards must be transferred from one machine to another in order to perform the next operation.

With the development of faster, more integrated computing systems, punch card machines are becoming extinct. Of the punch card machines once in wide-spread use, only three—the card punch, the verifier, and the sorter—remain in use with computer systems, and their use is dwindling rapidly. The card punch is used to record data from source documents onto the punch cards that will be fed into a computer. The verifier is used to determine that the data on the punch cards is accurate. The sorter is used to arrange cards in numeric and/or alphabetic order, or by some other classification. All other functions performed on punch cards can be done more efficiently by computer. For this single, high-speed device does not require that the punch cards be handled more than once—for input.

Electronic Data Processing   The most significant development in data processing technology results from the integrated electronic circuits that enable the computer to operate at incredible speed. The amazing speed of a computer can be attributed directly to the fact that data can be transformed into electrical impulses and moved around within a computer, rather than by the movement of mechanical parts. The fact that instructions, which the computer can execute itself, can be entered and stored within the computer means that many complex calculations can be performed in seconds rather than hours of time.

Computers can perform all of the operations in the data processing cycle automatically, with little or no human intervention. Because most of the actual operations that take place happen inside a computer, there are no visible flourishes of activity.

The major advantages of a computer data processing system are:

1. The speed is faster than in any other form of data processing.

2. A single computer can perform a wide variety of activities as directed by a set of instructions (program).

3. After data and instructions are fed into a computer, processing is continuous with a minimum of human intervention.

4. Data and programs may be stored inside a computer indefinitely and be retrieved quickly.

5. Accuracy is greater than in any other system.

Although the computer is by far the best method of processing data, it may not be appropriate for every application. Amounts of data to be processed and cost of a processing system are also considerations when choosing the best data processing system for a particular application.

HISTORY OF COMPUTING DEVICES

People, both primitive and modern, have always had a need to count. The crudest form of counting aid, of course, is the use of fingers and toes. The limitations on how far one could count with only these aids was easily overcome by the discovery that pebbles and other small objects could be grouped and used for counting.

The problem of handling groups of pebbles conveniently was solved about 5,000 years ago when the forerunner of the abacus was devised to help organize the pebbles. This device, referred to as a counter, was simply a clay board with a number of grooves in which the pebbles could be placed. The board enabled the pebbles to be moved from side to side to facilitate counting. The abacus, in its present form, is believed to have originated in China about 2600 B.C. The abacus consists of several rows of beads strung on wires, mounted in a rectangular frame. (Figure 1.4a) Although simple in appearance, in the hands of a skilled operator an abacus can be used for many computing needs. The abacus is still widely used in many parts of the world.

Numbering Systems

Although not in everyday use, Arabic numerals were known well before Columbus discovered America. Mathematics was a developing science. Navigation, with its need for complex calculations to discover a ship's position at sea, was an area in which Roman numerals were difficult to use. To support these applications, mathematical and trigonometric tables were created. One of the more important of these early tools was a table of logarithms, first published by John Napier in 1614. Based on the ideas underlying logarithms, Napier developed a primitive form of slide rule called Napier's bones, a mechanical arrangement of strips of bone on which numbers were painted (see Fig. 1.4b). When brought into combination, these strips would perform direct multiplication. A few years later, in 1620, Edmund Gunter put together two logarithmic scales on two strips of wood and fashioned a device similar to a modern slide rule (see Fig. 1.4c). The slide rule, which is perhaps the first analog computer, performs multiplication and division by adding and subtracting.

Mechanical Calculating Devices

Trigonometric and logarithmic tables are created by solving long and complex mathematical formulas. In early times, these tables were created by hand and had many errors. Many individuals dreamed of a machine to do this work. Leonardo da Vinci made some drawings of a machine to do such calculations but he never built a working model. The first person actually to develop a working model of an adding machine was a French philosopher-mathematician named Blaise Pascal who, in 1642 at the age 19, invented a device to assist in adding long columns of figures at his father's tax office in Rouen, France (see Fig. 1.4d). Pascal's gear-driven machine, the size of a shoe box, consisted of a row of wheels with teeth numbered from 0 to 9. It was a simple device, like an odometer on an automobile, however, it incorporated two principles that were utilized in later developments: the "carry-overs" could be automatic, and multiplication could be performed by repeated addition.

In 1666, Sir Thomas Morland used a series of disks to replace Napier's bones and developed an operational multiplier. In 1673, Gottfried Leibnitz improved upon Pascal's device by making a machine that was capable of performing multiplication by means of repeated addition (see Fig. 1.4e).

Throughout the 1700s, numerous attempts were made to produce a satisfactory calculating machine. The first really successful calculating device was that of Charles Thomas who, in 1820, invented a calculator that improved on Leibnitz' machine. This calculator is considered to be the predecessor of all present-day desk calculators.

One of the more interesting computer pioneers was Charles Babbage. Babbage dreamed of a machine to compute and print mathematical tables and, in 1830 with support from the British government, he began constructing his "difference engine" (see Fig. 1.4f). By 1834 Babbage abandoned plans for his difference engine and began a more ambitious project: an "analytical engine."

Babbage's device parallels the design of modern computers closely although it was conceived more than 100 years before the first computer was built. The analytical engine had four basic units: a store for holding data and intermediate results; a mill for performing arithmetic computations; a system of gears for transferring data between the store and the mill; and a separate device for putting data into the analytical engine and getting answers out.

Although ambitious, Babbage was never able to build his machine, although the design was later proved to be workable. There were two reasons for his failure: First, the technology of the 1830s was not capable of producing gears and levers precise enough to build something as complex as the analytical engine. The second, and perhaps paramount, reason was that there was no real demand for such a machine in the mid-1800s. Babbage was ahead of his time.

In 1887, Doré Eugene Felt patented a key-driven adding machine known then as a Marconi Box and now as a Comptometer (see Fig. 1.4g). About the same time, William Burroughs, a bank clerk, constructed a machine to assist with bookkeeping, completed it in 1884 and successfully marketed it in 1891.

The Monroe calculator was introduced in 1911 (see Fig. 1.4h). This was the first rotary keyboard machine to achieve success.

The first accounting machine used in U.S. banks was developed by the National Cash Register Company in 1909. However, large-scale development of the machine did not occur until after the close of World War I. By means of a moving carriage, this cash register could sort data into columns and perform the functions of recording, calculating, and summarizing (see Fig. 1.4i).

Electrically activated machines came into general use about 1920. Electric action provided greater speed in the use of calculating machines. However, all these machines were limited in two ways: First, they were manual instead of automatic, requiring some form of action by an operator; second, they functioned independently of other units. Both limitations were overcome by punch card equipment, in which a series of machines were connected into a system that uniformly processed a set of data automatically. Although each machine was capable of performing only one operation on a set of data, at least transferring that data from machine to machine was a more exact process through the use of the punch card.

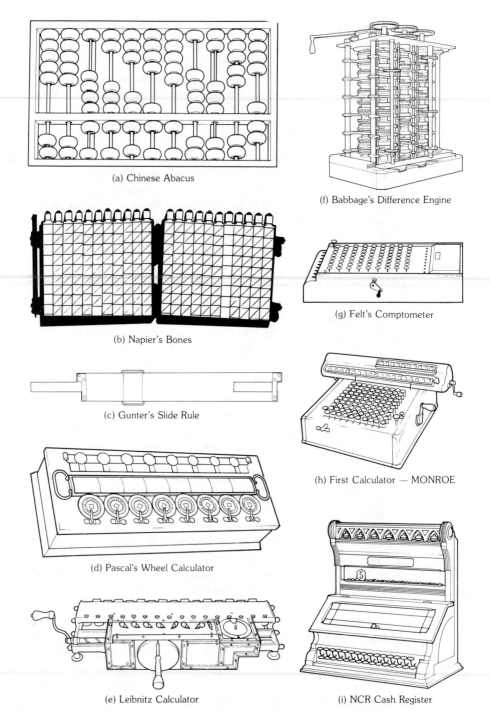

(a) Chinese Abacus

(f) Babbage's Difference Engine

(b) Napier's Bones

(g) Felt's Comptometer

(c) Gunter's Slide Rule

(h) First Calculator — MONROE

(d) Pascal's Wheel Calculator

(e) Leibnitz Calculator

(i) NCR Cash Register

Figure 1-4 Early computer tools

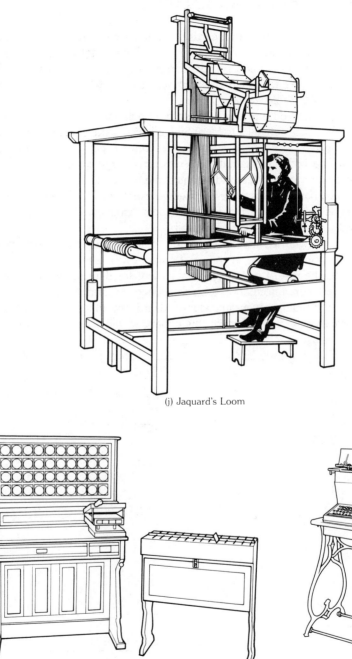

(j) Jaquard's Loom

(k) Hollerith's First Punch — Card
Accounting Machine

(l) First REMINGTON
Typewriter

HISTORY OF PUNCH CARD MACHINES

Although the use of punch cards for data processing was new in the late 1800s, it had been used earlier for other purposes. Most notable was the automatic weaving loom of Frenchman Joseph Jacquard in the mid-1750s (see Fig. 1.4j). In his automatic loom, weaving was directed by a card in which holes provided instructions that controlled the weaving process.

The first data processing use of punch cards was to compile the statistics of the 1890 U.S. census. Dr. Herman Hollerith, a statistician with the Census Bureau, developed a mechanical system of recording, computing, and tabulating census data. The 1880 census data was written on large cards that had to be hand sorted into desired categories and counted manually. The cards were sorted again and again by hand to select the required information. The 1890 census, which involved millions more people, might not have been completed by the end of the decade if the hand sorting process had been used.

Through the early 1900s, many companies adopted punch card equipment for data processing uses. In the 1920s and 1930s several advancements further expanded the use of punch card equipment for data processing. First, punch cards that held more information were developed. Second, machines that could add, subtract, and multiply were introduced. Third, machines that could handle alphabetic information were developed; this expanded the scope of jobs that the equipment could be used for.

From the early 1920s until the early 1960s, punch card data processing or unit

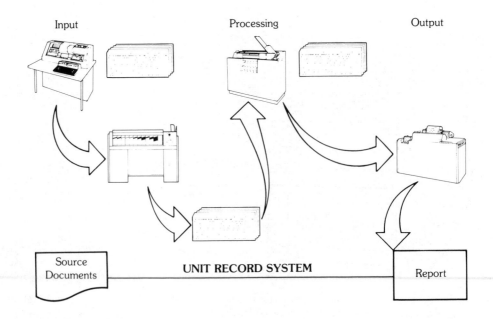

Figure 1-5 Unit record system

record equipment was the major method of data processing for large companies. Although still in limited use today, it has largely been replaced by the computer.

As mentioned before, regardless of the data processing systems used, they all in some manner perform the basic steps in the data processing cycle. The machines that perform the steps in different systems may vary, but what they do doesn't. Figure 1.5 represents how the basic data processing cycle is performed, using punch card data processing for the unit record system to be described here.

In the unit record system (punch card data processing), data pertaining to individual items are maintained on separate records or cards, instead of on lists, rosters, or in journals or ledgers. Data from source documents are punched into cards. These punched cards are then fed through a series of machines for further processing. The actual processing involves the physical movement of cards through machines to sort, merge, and perform calculations. The output, or reporting of processing results, takes place on an accounting machine that prints out data on a sheet of paper.

This system operates on the unit record principle that requires that each punched card or record contains information about one transaction. Each record may contain more than one piece of data, but all must refer to the same item.

HISTORY OF ELECTRONIC COMPUTERS

In 1937, Howard Aiken of Harvard University conceived the idea of wiring together the components of a unit record system and controlling them by a roll of paper punched tape; Aiken completed the Mark I, the first successful computer, in 1944. Aiken's Mark I was far from the computer we know today. It was not an electronic computer, but an electro-mechanical computer in which mechanical registers were used to store numbers. These mechanical registers are like switching relays in telephone switching systems.

During World War II, Dr. John Mauchly and Prosper Eckert created the first truly electronic computer. Their computer, designated Electronic Numerical Integrator and Calculator (ENIAC), used vacuum tubes instead of relays and was controlled—or programmed—by wires, much the same as unit record equipment.

Both of the computers mentioned so far were controlled externally. It was necessary to wire or read detailed instructions into the machine as work progressed. Because the computer processes data according to instructions, its operations were not flexible. To increase the computer's capacity to process data, programmed instructions had to be stored inside the computer. This would give the computer access to the instructions as fast as they were needed.

In 1945, John von Neuman proposed the internally programmed computer. The Electronic Discrete Variable Automatic Computer (EDVAC) would accept and store a set of instructions. This meant that (1) the computer could be programmed by a set of cards before processing started; (2) a program could be written and tested before it was run with actual data; (3) the machine could be self-directing, requiring no human operator to guide each step.

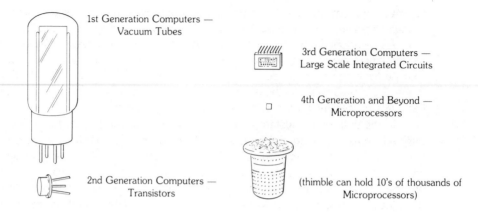

1st Generation Computers —
Vacuum Tubes

3rd Generation Computers —
Large Scale Integrated Circuits

4th Generation and Beyond —
Microprocessors

2nd Generation Computers —
Transistors

(thimble can hold 10's of thousands of
Microprocessors)

Figure 1-6 The shrinking computer

Mauchly and Eckert, who developed the ENIAC, later designed and built the first commercial computer, Universal Automatic Computer (UNIVAC). The UNIVAC was the first computer to be sold to private business. It was also one of the first machines to use magnetic tape for the input and output of data.

Since then there have been many significant advancements in the developing technology of computers. Those already mentioned here represent the highlights of the early years of computer development. Generally, the advancements of computer technology can be classed into four chronological categories called generations; these are summarized in Fig. 1.6.

First Generation—1946

Early computers mainly used vacuum tubes in their circuits. They were bulky, used great amounts of power, generated a great deal of heat, and were not very reliable. Some machines had the ability to store programs internally, and they received their input data from paper tape or punch cards (see Fig. 1.7).

Second Generation—1959

Technical advancement in the fields of electronics resulted in the second generation of computers. Solid-state devices, such as transistors, replaced the vacuum tube, allowing for smaller, faster, more powerful computer systems. The application of solid-state electronics to computer design focused on modularity or block-building concepts. Various units of a computer were built as individual units, allowing systems to be expanded easily without having to replace the entire computer. Other improvements included faster input-output units, better programming abilities, greater capacity and faster storage, as well as the ability to transmit data to other computers at great distances over telephone lines.

Figure 1-7 An early IBM computer in use during the 1950s (Courtesy of International Business Machines Corporation)

Third Generation—1965

This era is characterized by the advanced miniaturization that began during the second generation. Electronic circuitry was etched, rather than wired, and tiny crystal structures replaced vacuum tubes and transistors. This further miniaturization of circuits, which were called integrated circuits, made possible the development of computer systems that were smaller and greater in capacity, with operating speeds measured in billionths of a second. Other related developments, such as optical scanners, magnetic ink character readers, and larger, faster storage devices, took place to advance even further the computer's ability to handle data.

Although the use of programming languages had been developing at the same time, the third generation was the first in which the process of programming computers underwent a major change. More languages were developed as well as multi-programming that allowed the simultaneous processing of programs to take place inside the computer. Remote processing was also introduced. This allowed data inside the computer to be accessed by a typewriter-like device, called a terminal, located across the street or across the nation. Another significant advancement during the third generation was the advent of minicomputers and time sharing, which enabled many users to share one computer simultaneously.

Fourth Generation—1970

The early 1970s saw the introduction of computers that were smaller, faster, yet more powerful than their predecessors. The use of Large-Scale Integrated circuits (LSIs) allowed even smaller computers to be designed. These more densely packed circuits made possible the manufacture of microprocessors—entire computers on one tiny, integrated circuit chip. Microprocessors, which are discussed in detail in the next chapter, hold great promise for the future. The functions of many day-to-day products are changing as these small, inexpensive microprocessors are used to control their operations.

Few accurate speculations can be made about what will happen in the computer field in the years ahead. Surely, microprocessors will play an increasingly important role. More computers in the home, more hobbyist computer users, and certainly easier ways to communicate with computers will continue to expand the acceptance of computers along with television, radio, and other electrical conveniences.

STUDY AND REVIEW

1. What is information? What is the difference between data and information? What takes place that changes data into information?

2. Throughout time, people have feared the advancement of mechanization and automation. With the coming of the electronic computer, do you think these feelings have become more intensified? Why?

3. Increased computer use has been primarily promoted by increased amounts of information generated by society. What specific factors can be cited as having contributed to the information explosion? Do you believe the statement that computers themselves have evolved into sources of original data that add to the information explosion? Why?

4. Computers are often blamed for foul-ups in organizations. Is it fair to say, "The computer blew it!" or are there other factors that have a greater bearing on the results a computer produces?

5. Do you believe that citizens can influence the ways that computers are used? If so, in what ways?

6. Do you believe computer usage threatens your personal freedom in any way? If so, in what ways?

7. Distinguish between the three basic types of data processing systems.

8. What were 4 of the major mechanical calculating devices that preceded the widespread use of electronic computers?

9. Since their introduction in the 1940s, computers have undergone revolutionary changes described as "generations." What are the four historical computer generations? What features distinguish each?

2

BASIC
COMPUTER CONCEPTS

PERSPECTIVE

Not long ago, computers were mysterious objects that few people understood. Today, although most people are still unfamiliar with this electronic marvel, computers are playing major roles in all facets of life around us. As the following quote indicates, there is no reason to expect that the expanded use of computers will diminish. On the contrary, computers will become a greater part of our lives.

> *Computer scientists see intelligent machines as causing an evolution of sorts. Whereas the first phase of the technical age, engineering such things as the automobile, the jet, and a host of appliances, the next phase, they say, is the improvement of man's mental comfort. By relieving man of dull, repetitive tasks, by readily providing him with information and solving problems, the computer of the future will be a "steam engine" as applied to the mind.* (Brand, 1973)

Years ago, most people felt that computers were used only in commercial organizations such as banks and department stores, and in government. Today computers are playing important roles in such far-ranging fields as education, transportation, and medicine. The use of computers generally—for processing data—has significantly increased the ability of individuals to use information to support various activities and promises to grow as advancements in technology lower the costs involved.

Before discussing some of the actual uses of the computer in fields mentioned here, we present some basic concepts about what a computer is and how it works.

Although the theme of this chapter could easily be expanded into an entire book, we limit the presentation to developing a framework for understanding how the computer can be used in the applications to be discussed throughout the remainder of this book.

THE ELECTRONIC COMPUTER

The term computer is sometimes applied to any device that calculates, however, as the term is used in this book, a more restrictive definition is needed. A **computer** is defined here as an electronic device that accepts input, stores large amounts of data, executes complex instructions that direct it to perform mathematical and logical operations with a minimum of human intervention, and outputs the answers in a form readable by humans.

Basically, a computer system is comprised of the five components or machines shown in Fig. 2.1. Each component performs a specific task, but is interconnected with the other four components to form a computer system. The five components are: (1) input, (2) output, (3) control, (4) arithmetic-logic, and (5) storage. In describing each component, a comparison is made with a human system, so as to clarify the role of each component in the computer system.

> *input.* The input unit of a computer system takes coded data, possibly in the form of punched cards or magnetic tape, and translates them into electrical impulses that are fed into the control unit where they can be processed. Comparing this action with a human system, when a person receives information it usually comes in two forms: (1) oral, or spoken input; and (2) visual, or written input.

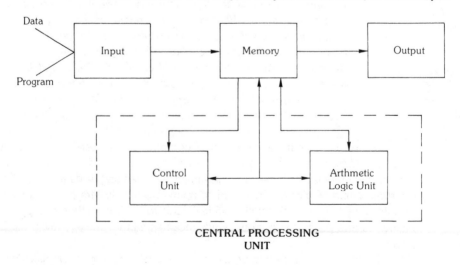

Figure 2-1 A central processing unit

Regardless of the method, eyes and ears translate the perceived information into a format that can be transmitted to the human control unit, the brain.

Control.   The control unit of a computer is contained within the central processing unit, or CPU, and is comparable to the human brain. The control unit does no actual processing, but by reading and interpreting the instructions of a program, the control unit directs other machine units to execute program steps.

Arithmetic-Logic.   This unit, also contained within the CPU, performs all calculations, comparisons, and decisions made by a computer. Data is moved from temporary storage within the CPU to the arithmetic-logic unit where all processing takes place. As a parallel, our brain acts as an arithmetic-logic unit when we take the components of a problem from paper, compute results, and return the answer to paper.

Storage.   This component, the equivalent of human memory, is responsible for storing information so that it can be retrieved at high speed by the CPU when it is needed. The data are stored in electronic form on such devices as magnetic tapes and magnetic disks.

Output.   The output unit in a computer system usually takes the processed information from the CPU and prepares it in a format easily read by a human. The equivalent in a human system would be either speaking or writing the answer to a mental calculation. The most common type of computer output is a high-speed printer.

To summarize briefly, all input (instructions and data) is entered into memory through the CPU by an input unit. When the CPU is ready to begin processing, the instructions are moved one at a time to the control unit where they are interpreted. The interpreted instructions then tell the computer what data are to be moved to the arithmetic-logic unit and what operations are to be performed on that data. When all of the instructions have directed the processing of data in the arithmetic-logic unit, they will direct the computer to output the results of the processing and perhaps even store the results back in the memory for future use.

The electronic equipment that actually performs the processing is referred to as the **hardware;** the various instructions called **programs** that are written to direct the operation of the hardware are generally called **software**.

HARDWARE

The electronic hardware used to make up a computer system may be selected to fit the exact requirements of a particular use. Newer generations of computers are built around modular concepts which allow the specific components of a computer system to be selected and assembled much the same as one might select different engine, wheel, and transmission accessories to affect the performance of a new car. The central processing unit, or CPU, which is the actual heart of a computer, does all of the actual processing, and also controls the operations of the other components connected to it. The CPU is sometimes referred to by manufacturers as the **mainframe**. Other parts in the computer system—the input, output, and storage units—are called **peripherals** and offer a wide variety of methods, speeds, capacities, and cost (see Fig. 2.2).

Input Devices

The primary function of input devices is to convert data into the electronic impulses that a computer can work with inside the CPU. Because a computer is not capable of reading data in the same manner we are, before the data can be input to a computer they must be converted to a form that the computer can use. When data are converted into a form for entry into a computer, the form that the data take is usually called the **input media.** Input media commonly includes punched cards, punched tape, and magnetic tape, and documents with data printed in magnetic ink or a special optical character type font. After the data are coded or recorded on these media, they can then be entered into the computer through an input device. Many different devices are used to provide input data to computers.

Punch Card Reader   This input device reads the holes in punched cards and converts the card code to electronic impulses. Standard punch cards contain 80 characters of information and can be read by punch card readers at speeds varying from 100 to 2,000 cards per minute.

Punch Tape Reader   Punch tape is also used as an input medium. The punch tape

Figure 2-2 Several examples of small, microprocessor-based microcomputers (Courtesy of Tandy/Radio Shack)

reader converts the hole code on a continuous strip of paper tape into the electronic impulses communicated to the storage unit of the central processor. Speeds of these units range from 100 to 2,000 characters per second.

Magnetic Tape and Disk　Special devices known as key-to-disk and key-to-tape machines can be used to record data directly onto the surface of magnetic tape or a magnetic disk through the use of a keyboard. When recorded on disk or tape, the data can be read into the computer at high speeds.

Optical Scanner　The optical scanner, or optical character reader, reads data directly from a document that is printed in a special type font. This special type font may be machine printed on the document or, in some cases, may actually be handwritten onto the document.

Keyboard Terminal　Data can be manually entered into a computer through a keyboard terminal. As the operator types, the typewriter converts the key-strokes into electronic impulses that are fed into the central processor. Usually this device—which can be either an electric typewriter that produces readable hard copy, or a cathode ray tube (CRT) display where images are shown on a television screen—is located at a distance from the computer, but is connected to it by cables or by data transmission lines. The keyboard terminal is used mainly when there is not a great deal of input data or when the computer must be asked questions (see Fig. 2.3).

Several other types of input devices are not considered to be major methods of input, but are used in some instances. Such devices include light pens, bar code readers, and point of sale (POS) terminals (electronic cash registers). In addition, there are devices capable of input that are not connected directly to a computer. It is

Figure 2-3 Terminals used as input/output devices for computer systems (a) Courtesy of Hewlett-Packard (b) Courtesy of Texas Instruments

possible to communicate with computers, or input data to computers, over great distances by connecting the equipment with telephone lines. Such activity is known as teleprocessing. The equipment or hardware that allows input devices to be connected to a computer over telephone lines is referred to as a telecommunications device. Almost any input device that can be used with a computer can be hooked up to telecommunications equipment to transmit data over telephone lines.

Central Processor and Data Storage

The central processor is the device or unit that actually processes the data. The central processor is composed of three parts: (1) the storage (memory) unit, (2) the arithmetic-logic unit, and (3) the control unit. All three may be contained in one cabinet, or they may be separate pieces of equipment connected by a cable.

Storage Unit   One important characteristic of a computer is that it can store large amounts of data and rapidly retrieve them when directed to do so. The three types of storage used by a computer are:

1.   Internal Storage. Internal storage (also known as primary or main storage) is linked directly to the central processor of the computer. Instructions and data are fed in by input devices and stored in internal storage. Three traditional types of storage used by a computer are: (1) magnetic core, (2) magnetic film, and (3) monolithic memory chips. Newer forms of internal storage that promise to increase storage capacity and decrease access time and cost are magnetic bubble memories and charged-looped couplers.

2.   Auxiliary Storage. Auxiliary storage (also called secondary on-line storage) devices are located outside the central processor, but are connected to it. Although access time for auxiliary storage is much slower than for internal memory, this type of memory is larger and less expensive than internal storage. The common types of auxiliary storage are magnetic disks, magnetic tapes, magnetic drums, and magnetic mass storage systems.

3.   External Storage. External storage devices, like auxiliary storage devices, are located outside the central processor, but are not connected to the central processor. External storage is used to store data to be processed, or processed data that will be used again. Common types of external storage are punched cards, paper tape, magnetic tape, and magnetic disks.

Arithmetic-Logic Unit   The arithmetic-logic unit of the central processor performs a variety of computing and decision-making functions. All computations are performed in this unit. The arithmetic-logic unit is capable of comparing two numbers and determining the lesser and greater. The computer can also be instructed by a program to take alternative courses of action based on the results of the comparisons.

The arithmetic-logic unit includes registers, adders, and counters. A register is capable of receiving data, holding it, and transfering it as directed by the control unit. An adder receives data from two or more sources, performs the arithmetic, and sends the results to a register. A counter counts the number of times an operation is performed.

Control Unit   The control unit automatically directs and coordinates all units of the computer. It tells the input devices what data to put in storage and where to store them. It tells the storage unit where to store data and the arithmetic-logic unit where to find data, what operations to perform, and where to store results. And finally, it tells the output devices what information to record and where to record it.

The control unit operates according to the stored program receiving and executing its instructions one at a time until the entire program has been executed (see Fig. 2.4).

Output Devices

Output devices convert the processed information that the central processor has created into a more useable form. Most frequently, that form is a printed report that can be read by a person. The output from the central processor, however, can be in a form that allows it to be stored on some media that can be used as input to some future processing task.

Devices that convert the electrical impulses of the computer into human read-

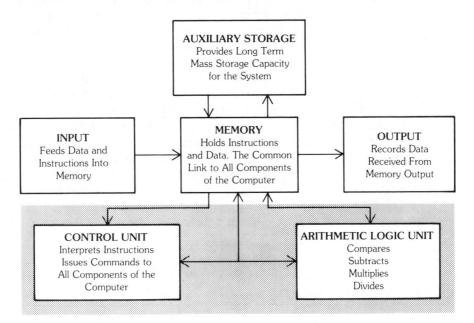

Figure 2-4 Functional relationship of a computer system

able form are: (1) high-speed printers that usually print an entire line at a time, and (2) keyboard terminals (both hard copy and cathode ray tube—CRT) that print a character at a time and are thus much slower. Most of the media previously mentioned for both input and auxiliary storage can also be used for output. Paper tape, punched cards, magnetic tape, magnetic disks, and the like, can accept output from the central processor. Figure 2.5 shows the variety of devices that can be used for both input and output.

COMPUTER PROGRAMMING: SOFTWARE

Computers are capable of making complex calculations and working with large amounts of data, but the actual organization of these capabilities into a system that works toward meeting specific objectives depends on computer programs or software. **Software,** as distinguished from hardware, refers not only to the set of programs that make a computer run, but also to the data those programs use, all the documentation that must exist to describe how those programs are to be used, and how the operating personnel should proceed when using the whole computer system.

Programs, or sets of instructions for performing computer operations, are usually designed to solve particular problems. That is not necessarily always true, however. There are actually two separate types of computer software: (1) applications software, which are programs designed and written to solve specific user-oriented problems, and (2) systems or operations software, which help programmers and users make better use of computer systems. All computer software includes programs. Within these programs, the programming people must specify exactly what the computer is to do step by step. Because we do not speak any computer language, several non-verbal programming languages have been developed. These allow people to express their intention to the computer in a form (or language) that a computer can translate into a machine language that it can understand and act upon. Various levels of languages, from machine languages to assembly languages and high-level symbolic languages, exist to be used in writing specific types of programs. Systems or operations programs are usually written and stored in machine language form, while applications programs are written in high-level symbolic languages that are easier for programmers to use in expressing the solutions to specific problems. Both systems and applications software will be discussed in the next chapter.

COMPUTER CLASSIFICATIONS

No industrial standards have been adopted to classify computers; however, computers are commonly classified by purpose, type, and capacity.

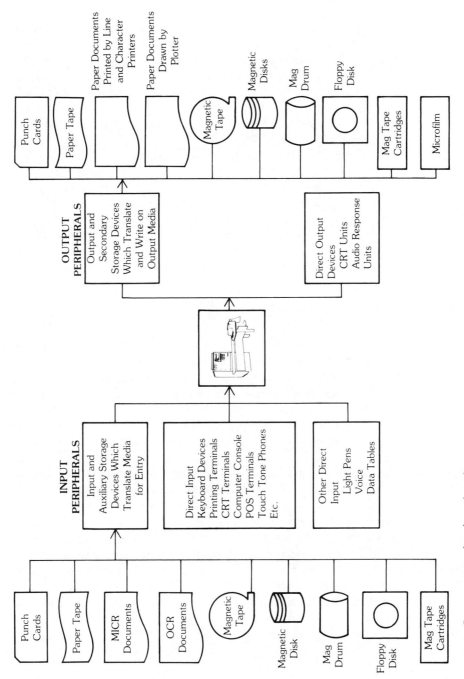

Figure 2-5 Computer peripherals and media

Purpose

Computers are considered to be either special purpose or general purpose systems. Special purpose computers are usually designed and built to do a very limited set of operations. The instructions to do these operations and the actual capabilities of the machinery are built into a computer as it is constructed. After it is constructed, installed, and operating, what the computer can do cannot be altered. Navigation computers, transportation system control computers, or manufacturing process control computers, all of which are dedicated to one task or process, are examples of special purpose computers.

General purpose, sometimes referred to as programmable, computers are capable of working in a wide variety of applications. These computers are directed in a specific application by a set of instructions known as a program. Programs may be written and stored inside a computer to direct it to perform a wide variety of operations. These programs may be altered as the computer uses them to change the way a computer performs a specific operation, or they may be discarded entirely and replaced by a new program designed to direct the computer in a new application. These general purpose computers are limited only by their physical size and speed.

Type

Computers are usually analog or digital types. The distinction is made by how the computer represents data. Analog computers are usually special purpose and represent data by setting up physical situations that are analogous to data in digital or mathematical form. Analog computers usually work with data such as pressure, temperature, revolution, speed, or voltage. An analog computer is basically a measuring device, capable of converting a physical property into a symbolic representation (numbers) that we may use to describe a physical condition. A car speedometer is a good example of an analog computer. The speedometer is capable of measuring the speed of a vehicle and converting it to a numerical form that we then use to describe the vehicle's speed. Analog computers usually have no memory. Information is obtained from them by reading dials or similar types of registers. Analog computers are used most often as controlling devices in some continuous process.

Digital computers are the main topic of this book and are not capable of obtaining data by measuring, but operate on data fed into the computer in some coded form. Digital computers have a memory and are capable of performing complex calculations on the data fed into them. Digital computers are also capable of working with alphabetic as well as numerical data, which makes them ideal for processing data.

Some computer systems are combinations of digital and analog. The analog part measures and creates a numerical representation of data that is then fed into the computer for further processing.

Capacity

Each generation of computers has provided increased capacity over the previous generation. This capacity is not strictly the physical size of the computer, but rather it is circuit reliability, circuit speed, circuit size, and memory size.

Current electronic circuit technology includes large-scale integration (LSI), monolithic system technology (MST), and solid logic technology (SLT). These technologies increase the number of circuits that can be built into a computer, and reduce the number of connections made to a chip (small silicon electrical circuits containing thousands of electrical components) which, in turn, reduces the distance between chips and increases speed (see Fig. 2.6).

As mentioned earlier, the size of computers is constantly changing as a result of advancements in microelectronic circuit technology. Exact size and capacity classifications are difficult to make because of this fact. We can form three broad categories, however, as long as we realize that there is much latitude even within each of these categories. The three categories are: microcomputers, minicomputers, and large computers. Microcomputers range in price from several hundred dollars to $20,000. Minicomputers (usually known as time-sharing computers) can range to

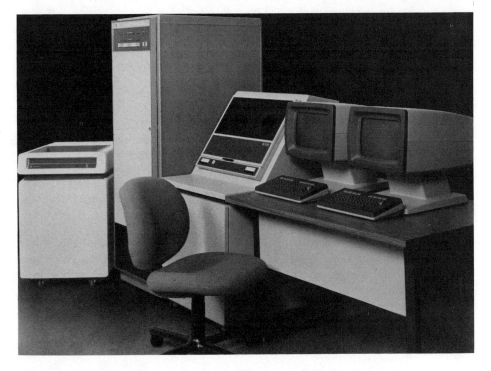

Figure 2-6 A time-share minicomputer (Courtesy of Hewlett-Packard)

Figure 2-7 A full-scale, large-batch computer system
(Courtesy of International Business Machines Corporation)

$200,000. And large computers have prices that range into millions of dollars. As computers increase in size and cost, their speed or access time decreases, memory size increases, and input-output speed increases. Some of the larger, more expensive systems are leased from computer companies rather than purchased (see Fig. 2.7).

COMPUTER APPLICATIONS

The application of a computer is determined by each specific user. Applications need not be grouped by types of users, because each application may be different in business and scientific work.

File Maintenance

This was a common use of computers in the 1970s and is becoming an even more important use in the 1980s. In a file maintenance application, the computer is used to maintain a large master file of information that is kept current by making changes, additions, and deletions as needed. This process of altering a file is usually known as updating.

Data Summarization

This application is sometimes called data reduction or report preparation. In this application, large amounts of detailed data are condensed into a concise, more usable form. Data summarization usually takes either the form of tabulation in which the number of transactions in a particular category is compiled, or the totals of times or amounts in other categories.

Numerical Computation

Such computations are usually the evaluation of mathematical formulas. Operations such as payroll, sales extensions, and so forth, have precise mathematical formulas for arriving at the answers. Numerical computation involves the application of these formulas to specific sets of data to arrive at the correct result.

Data Arrangement

This application alters the sequence of a set of data according to a specific rule. A typical application would be sorting an employee payroll file into employee number sequence or name alphabetic sequence.

Simulation

In simulation, the computer is used to approximate the performance of something. These items are sometimes physical such as performance of an automobile or plane, or sometimes conceptual such as a mathematical model of a country's economy. Simulation is used to discover the consequences of various courses of action on the item being simulated without the expense or hazard of testing on real life objects.

Process or Operations Control

Production operations in all phases of manufacturing require precise control. Many times, while monitoring processes, various modifications must be made as a process continues. Requirements for this application are for continuous, precise monitoring of a process as well as the ability to detect deviations from accepted standards, and either alter the process or signal that an alteration is needed.

Information Retrieval

In information retrieval, the computer usually searches a large quantity or file of data for a particular item. These applications are not considered file maintenance applications because individual items in the file that are found, or accessed, are not subject to change but are retrieved only for informational purposes.

Other classes of computer applications exist, but are far less frequent than those mentioned here. Most other applications are subdivisions of those listed.

CAPABILITIES AND LIMITATIONS

On a very broad basis, who uses computers and what they are used for has already been explained. How computers can do all of these applications for different groups of users is of somewhat less concern than those specific factors that allow computers to be applied in the ways already described. Listed below are the computer's basic capabilities and limitations.

Capabilities

1. Speed: The computer can perform complex calculations in small fractions of a second.

2. Accuracy: When given correct data and programs, the computer's results are virtually error free.

3. Reliability: The computer can work for unlimited lengths of time with great accuracy and little human supervision. After a program is written and fed into the computer, it will accurately execute the program over and over again, without any additional direction.

4. Universality: The computer can theoretically solve any problem that can be expressed in mathematical terms and written as a set of computer instructions.

5. Memory: The computer can store immense amounts of information to which it can gain access in fractions of a second.

Limitations

Despite these wonderful capabilities there are some limitations:

1. Complexity: New problems require time and money to prepare for use of the computer. Programs that are written and used only once are not very cost-effective.

2. No intelligence: While capable of accomplishing very complex tasks, the computer can do nothing unless instructed to by a human in the form of a program.

3. Cost: Although computers have been getting cheaper, they are still expensive and not all potential users can afford the computer's great benefits.

COMPUTER SYSTEMS

In this section we describe several basic types or configurations of computer systems that meet the requirements of different applications. No one computer system can be considered best for all possible uses. Capabilities of different systems must be matched with the requirements of specific applications. The four basic types of computer systems described in this section are: batch, time sharing, teleprocessing, and networks. The final section of this chapter discusses microprocessors and microcomputers and their role with other computer systems and in their own applications.

Batch Computers

As the commercial use of computers expanded in the late 1950s and through the 1960s, computer installations usually consisted of a large centralized facility that served an entire company. Individuals or departments who wished to use the computer submitted their request to the personnel in the facility, and in time were scheduled for computer use. If the workload of the facility was heavy when a job request was submitted, it could take some time before the request was acted on, and thus the information produced might not be as timely or relevant as it could have been were it produced when initially requested.

Each individual application would have its own program and related set of data. The program and its data form what is known as a job for the computer, which is capable of executing only one job at a time. If several jobs are to be done, they must be put into a sequence of order, or queue, in which the computer can execute them one at a time. After completely executing one job in the queue, the computer takes the next job in order. This is known as **batch processing** or using a batch computer (see Fig. 2.8a).

While batch computers normally have relatively fast input and output devices, the speeds at which the input and output devices work are nowhere near as fast as the internal processing speed of the central processing unit. Thus, much of the time that a batch computer spends working is usually spent on inputting data and outputting data while the central processor stands idle, waiting for the input or the output of data to finish before moving onto the next job.

The principal characteristic of batch computers is that groups or batches of similar data, such as payroll information, sales transactions, or inventory records, will be collected and processed together in a batch.

Although there appear to be many drawbacks to the use of batch computers for applications that require large amounts of data to be processed, they represent the most efficient method. Newer types of computer systems have been devised to take greater advantage of the computer's tremendous speed. These systems are being used to make computer time and power available to a wider group of individuals and provide them with the information that they need to react more rapidly to changing conditions with their jobs.

Time Sharing

Time sharing is a term used to describe a processing system that has a number of independent online (connected to the computer) data entry stations that are capable of using a single central processor simultaneously (see Fig. 2.8b). The speed of the central processor allows the CPU to switch from entry station to entry station (usu-

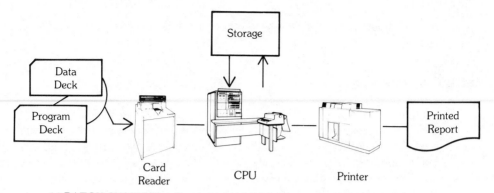

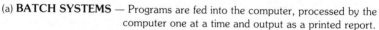

(a) **BATCH SYSTEMS** — Programs are fed into the computer, processed by the
computer one at a time and output as a printed report.

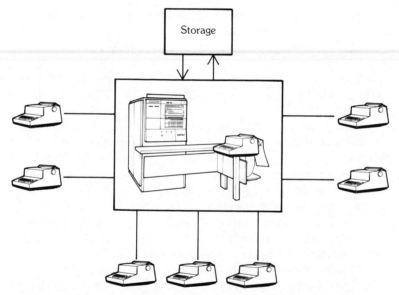

(b) **ONLINE REAL TIME TIMESHARING** — CPU accepts programs or requests
for information from many different
I/O devices simultaneously. Data
and programs are entered directly
into the CPU by a user through an
I/O device such as a terminal.

Figure 2-8 Computer systems

ally a terminal) and perform the processing required by each. The speed is so great
that usually individual users have the feeling that they have sole use of the CPU.
Time-sharing systems may be designed to serve the needs of a single organization,
or, as in the case of computer service bureaus, may provide computer services to
subscribers who, for a fee, may have access devices in their businesses hooked to
the central processor of the service bureau by telephone lines.

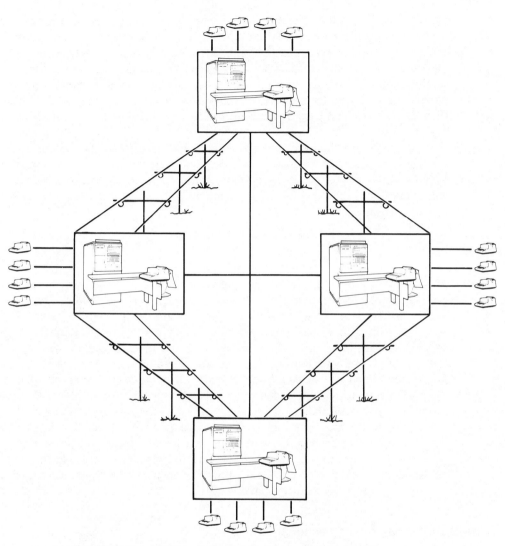

(c) **NETWORKS** — CPU's are linked together by communications links such as telephone lines to form networks which may span a great geographic
distance. Systems within the network may then share programs,
information and processing capabilities.

Figure 2-8   (continued)

Teleprocessing

Typical data processing installations of days past had input-output devices, or
access devices, located close to the computer and connected directly to it. In the advanced computer systems now in use, access devices are not necessarily located in

the same vicinity as the computer, but may be in an entirely different location. By connecting access devices from remote locations to the computer by some form of communications link, computers become teleprocessing systems. Teleprocessing is the result of the combined technologies of electronic data processing and electronic communications methods. In a **teleprocessing system,** data are transmitted between a central computer and remote access devices through communications links such as telephone and telegraph circuitry, radio wave transmissions, or microwave transmissions.

Although what we have begun to describe here is a single input-output device connected to a remote computer, teleprocessing techniques can be expanded to create a computer system in which one central computer is accessed by input-output devices in a number of remote locations. This is often referred to as **distributed processing.**

Networks

An extension of time sharing and teleprocessing involves connecting central processing units by telecommunications lines to form computer networks. These networks may then share data, software, and other information processing resources.

These **computers networks**, more commonly referred to as distributed processing networks (see Fig. 2.8c), allow a large number of computers to share significant resources among a large group of users. These networks may be used in a single organization, or may tie together many independent organizations. The use of computer networks, or distributed processing, is characterized by three types of uses: (1) single organization or company networks which may have small computers located in branch offices to handle local processing and reports to district or home office systems; (2) independent organization networks that may provide computing resources to various users on a fee basis; and (3) independent organization information sharing networks that connect computers containing information resources to be shared by many independent agencies.

Data Base Management Systems

Computers of all sizes and types are increasingly used in organizations to replace paper-based filing systems. This new electronic application utilizes what is known as a database management system. First, a **data base** is assembled from all of an organization's information resources and stored inside a computer. A **data base management system** is the entire collection of software and procedures designed to use the information in the database. Such electronic information bases and their systems greatly increase the efficiency of an organization. Faster, easier access to more timely information can be provided, and the manipulative powers of the computer can be utilized by nontechnicians through the use of English-like query languages.

By using teleprocessing, networks, and data base systems, organizations can provide access to a great amount of information to employees, regardless of their physical location.

THE MICROPROCESSOR REVOLUTION

As time passes, computers become more powerful, less expensive, and smaller. Much of this is attributable to advancements made in microelectronics. Today's computers are constructed with technologies that are capable of building circuits hundreds, even thousands, of times smaller than their counterparts ten years ago. At the heart of this revolution is the **microprocessor,** a 1/4-inch-square-chip of silicon that is capable of holding the 100,000 or so electrical components of a CPU. In this section, we explore microprocessors, microcomputers, and microcomputer systems.

Microcomputers: What Are They?

A **microcomputer** is a system based on an assembly of microprocessors. A **microprocessor**, the heart of a microcomputer, is a programmable, large-scale integrated circuit chip that contains all the elements required to process data. Microprocessors differ from conventional central processing units by occupying only a single tiny chip capable of performing the basic arithmetic, logic, and control functions of a computer (see Fig. 2.9).

Figure 2-9   Thousands of electrical components can be packed into a silicon chip which can fit through the eye of a needle. (Courtesy of International Business Machines Corporation)

Frequently called a "computer on a chip," microprocessors have a wide range of actual and potential applications. They may become the heart of more "intelligent" computer systems or they may perform control functions for automobiles, household appliances, and industrial machinery.

Although the terms microprocessor and microcomputer are often used interchangeably, there are distinct differences in the two. Microprocessors are used to form microcomputers. While microprocessors have all the capabilities for processing data, only after they are connected, or integrated, into microcomputer systems are they capable of inputting, outputting, and storing data (see Fig. 2.10).

Microprocessor Applications

The uses of microprocessors can be divided into three broad categories: (1) data processing uses in which microprocessors are used as parts of larger computer systems; (2) microcomputers in which one microprocessor forms the heart of a small-scale computer system; and (3) as a device used to control the operation of a piece of equipment that is not used as a data processing machine (see Fig. 2.11).

Figure 2-10 An enlarged view of a ¼-inch square silicon chip that is capable of storing 64,000 characters of information. (Courtesy of Intel Corporation)

Figure 2-11 A silicon chip is embedded in an epoxy "pin package" which can be integrated into a microcomputer or other piece of electronic equipment. (Courtesy Intel Corp.)

Data Processing Uses Microprocessors are used in large-scale computers as part of minicomputer CPUs and in many other computer peripherals, including intelligent terminals, I-O devices, and external memory devices. Probably the most significant result of the use of microprocessors in data processing equipment is the increase in distributed processing capabilities. Single computer systems that are made up of microprocessor controlled components can distribute large amounts of processing responsibility to individual components within a system, allowing the large central CPU to devote itself to larger more important processing tasks. Microprocessors are used in many of the components of a large-scale computer so that, if certain components fail, tasks can be reassigned to other units that are still operating.

Microcomputer Systems With the capability offered by microprocessors, almost any organization can afford the efficiency of an electronic data processing system. Microprocessors have become the heart of small, inexpensive yet powerful computer systems that are available at prices ranging from $500 up. These small micro-

43

computer systems, while certainly revolutionizing the data processing capabilities of many organizations, have also created a hobbyist and personal computing field. Such microcomputers are now being interconnected into local networks.

Other Equipment Uses The capabilities of microprocessors have been recognized by the manufacturers of almost every type of machinery or device. Microprocessors are increasingly being used to control the operations of virtually every type of equipment. The low cost, associated with the capability of complex programming abilities, allows manufacturers to integrate microprocessors into equipment designed for purposes other than data processing tasks (see Fig. 2.12).

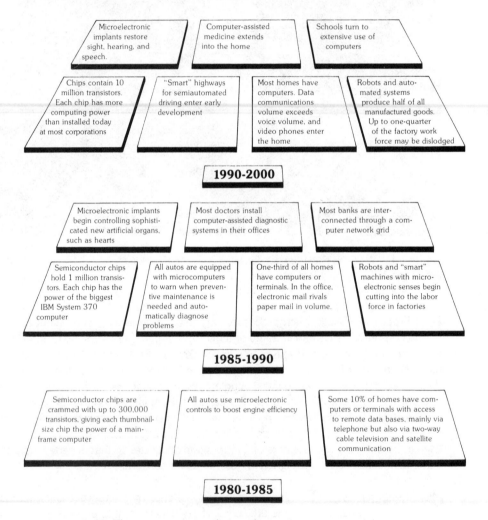

Figure 2-12 The coming impact of microelectronics

STUDY AND REVIEW

1. Describe the three ways that computers are classified.

2. The capabilities of a computer allow it to be used in a variety of applications for different users. What are the types of applications of computers?

3. Discuss the capabilities and limitations of computers.

4. Describe the major components in a computer system.

5. What is programming and why is it necessary?

6. What is teleprocessing?

7. Describe a computer network.

8. What are some of the major ways in which telecommunications will be used in business organizations in the near future?

9. What do you see as some of the advantages and disadvantages of large-scale networks?

3

SOFTWARE:

Programs and Languages

PERSPECTIVE

While most of us are probably amazed at the ability of a computer to solve apparently impossible problems, it is important to remember, as indicated in the following quotation, that computers are incapable of doing anything unless directed to do so by a person.

> Computer software includes the instructions which enable the computer's physical equipment (hardware) to do the work. Without it, most computer hardware (a few special hardwired computers excepted) is just a mass of inanimate wire and metal; with software, the machine comes to life and begins to produce its output. (Wessel, 1974)

A human operator, or computer programmer, may spend hours analyzing and defining a problem to prepare a set of instructions that a computer can follow to solve a particular problem. To be able to prepare that set of instructions, however, the programmer must have a complete understanding of the problem and, in effect, already know the steps necessary to solve the problem without the computer.

The set of instructions that a computer will follow to solve a problem is called a **computer program.** The instructions in a program must be detailed, sequential, and structured according to the way that the computer functions. Hundreds of individual programs are needed to give an electronic computer the capabilities to solve a variety of problems. Some programs direct the internal operations of the computer such as those which control the input and output devices or manage the storage areas within the computer, while others direct the computer to solve specific user problems such as payroll preparation or scientific computation. After these programs are written and stored inside the computer, they may be used over and over again by the computer with a minimum of human intervention.

Collectively, the group of programs that a computer needs to function is known as software. This chapter focuses on the different types of software used by a computer, and the communications methods, or languages, used to write programs that are part of a computer's software.

COMPUTER SOFTWARE

Computer software is an essential complement to computer hardware (see Fig. 3.1) in that the hardware is incapable of doing anything unless there are programs to direct it. The individual programs that make up the computer software are prepared by computer programmers who use a wide variety of programming languages designed to allow humans to communicate with computers. The software programs fall into one of two categories: (1) **systems software**—those programs designed to control the execution of other programs and utilize the hardware efficiently; and (2) **applications software**—those programs designed to use the capabilities of the computer to solve specific user-oriented problems.

How the Computer Executes Programs

Certain programs that the computer uses are stored internally, while others are entered as they are needed. Usually, systems software programs are stored inside the computer. Certain components of systems software are always in use because they direct the computer's activities. As an applications program is entered into the computer through an input unit, a number of activities take place. First, the systems

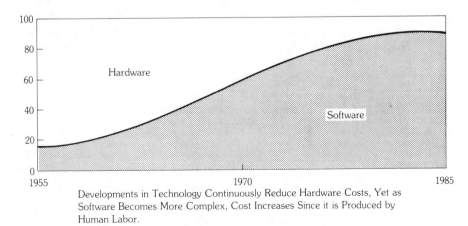

Developments in Technology Continuously Reduce Hardware Costs, Yet as Software Becomes More Complex, Cost Increases Since it is Produced by Human Labor.

Figure 3-1 Cost trends for computer systems

software directs the computer to translate the program into a language it can understand (machine language), and then the program is stored in working storage. The systems software then directs the computer to move one instruction at a time from working storage to the control unit (within the CPU) where it is executed and then returned to working storage. Some instructions will require that the computer move data into the arithmetic-logic unit for manipulation. Applications programs may also be stored in auxiliary storage and recalled into the CPU when needed. In this case, the steps in the execution of a program are the same as those when a program has been entered through an input device. The difference, however, can be that a program stored inside the computer can be stored in translated form.

Systems Software

The principal element of systems software is the operating system. Programs that comprise the operating system are different from computer to computer, but serve the same purpose. As computers become more technologically complex, so do the operating system programs. The goal of computer manufacturers, however, is to make computers "friendlier," or easier for nonprogrammers to use. This is accomplished by writing software that in effect allows the computer system to take care of itself. If systems software is designed properly, those who use the computer can communicate with it in a simple nontechnical manner, using a query language. A **query language** is usually a series of single word commands that enable the operator or programmer to activate certain capabilities of the computer without having to write a program.

The Operating System   An operating system is a complex group of programs which enables the computer to schedule work in the most efficient manner. Operating systems control the flow of programs and data through the computer, control input and output devices, and manage the storage facilities of the computer by storing data and programs and retrieving them when needed. As the operating system supervises the many internal operations of the computer, the programmer is free to concentrate on the solution to a specific user problem, rather than concentrating on how the computer is carrying out every single task internally.

As an example of the role of systems software, we discuss one of its components and how it eases the job of the programmer.

A computer program can be divided into three segments: (1) input—entering data into the computer; (2) processing—the internal manipulation of data; and (3) output—reporting the results.

A very large portion of each applications program that a programmer may write is involved with the input and output of data. The part of the operating system known as the input-output control system (IOCS) relieves the programmer of all equipment and timing considerations involved with input and output, allowing the programmer to concentrate on the programming portion of the program. The IOCS consists of a group of programs that control the reading of input and the writing of output data. The ability of the IOCS to perform these functions reduces the programmer time necessary to produce a working program.

Overall, operating systems reduce the amount of human intervention required to process data by computer. Small computers, capable of executing a single program at a time, have operating systems called monitors. Time-shared computers, network computer systems, and other complex computer systems require increasingly complex operations software.

There are many other components of systems software that are too complex to describe in any great detail here. Some of these other components include: compilers and assemblers for translating programs into executable form, and utility programs for handling routine housekeeping chores for the computer.

Applications Software

After a computer has been given the ability to perform a variety of tasks, these abilities must be coordinated in a specific manner to meet the objectives established by the needs of a particular application. **Applications software** are programs written in one of several types of programming languages to use the capabilities of the computer to solve specific problems for the user. **Systems software** might be considered the computer's basic intelligence—much the same as people have basic intelligence consisting of a variety of items they draw upon when the need arises. For example, when someone gives us the instruction, "Cook an egg" (applications software), we call upon our systems software that allows us to perform the necessary tasks to cook an egg. The single instruction "cook an egg" does not actually tell us everything to do, the same as each instruction in an applications program may not tell the computer every individual step to perform to accomplish a particular task. The applications program then, in effect, coordinates the abilities of the computer and directs it to solve a particular problem.

PROGRAMMING LANGUAGES

Because humans basically cannot speak or write in computer language, and since computers cannot speak or write in human language, an intermediate language had to be devised to allow people to communicate with computers. These intermediate languages, known as programming languages, allow a computer programmer to direct the activities of the computer. These languages are structured around a very exact set of rules that dictate exactly how a programmer should direct the computer to perform a specific task. With our powers of reasoning and logic, we as humans are able to accept an instruction and understand it in many different forms. Since a computer must be programmed to respond to specific instructions, instructions cannot be given in just any form. Programming languages standardize the instruction process. The rules of a particular language tell the programmer how the individual instructions must be structured and what sequence of words and symbols must be used to form an instruction.

Instructions   Each program is made up of individual instructions. These instructions must be precise, simple, and must follow the rules of the programming language. Since each instruction in a program is executed sequentially, it must provide the computer with the exact information needed to execute the instruction.

A typical instruction in a programming language consists of two parts: an operation code (or op code) and a series of operands. The op code tells the computer what to do—add, subtract, multiply, divide, and so forth. The operands tell the computer what to do it to. The operands in an instruction may consist of the actual data that the computer may use to perform an operation, or the address in storage where the data is located.

Some computers use several hundred types of operation codes in their instruction formats and may provide several methods for doing the same thing. Other computers use fewer operation codes, but have the capacity to perform more than one operation with a single instruction. While all instructions will not fall into a single class, there are four basic types of instructions: (1) input-output instructions; (2) arithmetic instructions; (3) branching instructions; and (4) logic instructions:

> *Input-Output Instructions.*   Input instructions direct the computer to accept data from a specific input device and store it in a specific location in storage. Output instructions tell the computer to move a piece of data from a storage location and record it on the output medium.

> *Arithmetic Instructions.*   All of the basic arithmetic operations can be performed by the computer. Since arithmetic operations involve at least two numbers, an arithmetic operation must include at least two operands.

> *Branch Instructions.*   Branch instructions cause the computer to alter the sequence of instruction execution within the program. There are two basic types of branch instructions: (1) unconditional branch statements that branch regardless of existing conditions; and (2) conditional branch statements that branch only when certain conditions exist.

> *Logic Instructions.*   Logic instructions allow the computer to change the sequence of instruction execution, depending on conditions built into the program by the programmer. Typical logic operations include: shift, compare, and test.

Types of Languages

Effective utilization and control of a computer system is primarily through the software of the system. As we have stated, there are different types of software that are used to direct the computer system. Systems software directs the internal operations of the computer, and applications software allows the programmer to use the computer to solve user oriented problems. The development of programming techniques has become as important to the advancement of computer science as the developments in hardware technology. More sophisticated programming techniques and a wider variety of programming languages have enabled computers to be used in an increasing number of applications.

Programming languages, the primary means of human-computer communication, have evolved from early stages where programmers entered instructions into the computer in a language similar to that used in the application. Modern programming languages fall into one of three categories, each of which is discussed: (1) machine language; (2) assembly language; and (3) high-level symbolic language.

Machine Language The earliest forms of computer programming were done by using languages that were structured according to how the computer stored data internally—that is, in a binary numbering system. Programmers had to construct programs that used instructions written in binary notation (1s and 0s). Writing programs in this fashion is a tedious, time-consuming process, and is somewhat inpractical. For this reason, machine language programs that are written today are often written by using octal or hexadecimal numbers.

Each instruction in a machine language program consists, as mentioned before, of two parts: an op code, telling the computer what to do, and the operand, telling the computer what to do it to. An added difficulty in machine language programming is that the operand of an instruction must tell the computer the address within storage where the piece of data to be worked with is located. The programmer must designate storage locations for both instructions and data as part of the programming process. Furthermore, the programmer has to know the location of every switch and register that will be used in executing the program, and must control their functions by means of instructions in the program.

A machine language program allows the programmer to take advantage of all the features and capacities of the computer system for which it was designed. It is also capable of producing the most efficient program as far as storage requirements and operating speeds are concerned. Few programmers today write applications programs in machine language, but most systems software used by computers is written in machine language.

Assembly Language Because machine language programming proved to be a difficult and tedious task subject to much human error, a symbolic way of expressing machine language instructions was devised. In assembly languages, the operation code is expressed as a combination of letters rather than numbers, sometimes called mneumonics. This allows the programmer to remember the operations codes easier than when expressed strictly as numbers. The address, or location in storage of the operands, is expressed by using a symbol rather than the actual numeric address. After the computer reads the program, operations software are used to establish the actual locations for each piece of data used by the program.

Because the computer understands and executes only machine language programs, the assembly language program must be translated into machine language. This is accomplished by using a systems software program called an assembler. The assembler accepts an assembly language program and produces a machine language program that the computer can actually execute. Although assembly language programming offers an improvement over machine language programming, it is still an involved process, requiring the programmer to write programs based on a particular computer's operation codes. (The difficulty of programming and the time required to program computers in assembly languages and machine languages led to the development of high-level symbolic languages.)

Symbolic Language   The symbolic languages, sometimes referred to as problem-oriented languages (POLs), reflect the type of problem being solved rather than the computer being used to solve it. Machine and assembly language programming is machine dependent—each computer must have its own machine or assembly language—while POLs are machine independent, allowing one high-level language to be used on a variety of computers.

While the flexibility of POLs is greater than with machine and assembly languages, there are close restrictions in exactly how instructions are to be written and formulated. Only a specific set of numbers, letters, and special characters may be used to write a high-level symbolic program; special rules must be observed for punctuation. High-level language instructions do resemble English language statements; the mathematical symbols are, for the most part, the symbols used in ordinary mathematics. Several of the most significant types of high-level programming languages are discussed in a later section of this chapter.

Characteristics of Programming Languages

Table 3.1 shows a simple program in machine language, assembly language and symbolic language. Each program instructs the computer to input three numbers, add the first two numbers together, and output the result. You may note that even without much programming experience, as we move from machine language instructions to assembly language instructions to high-level symbolic language instructions, simply reading the program becomes easier. Notice that the machine and assembly language programs contain nine instructions each, while the high-level language (BASIC) contains only four. One statement, or instruction, in a high-level programming language is often used to generate several machine instructions; a fact that is significant for several reasons. First, it reduces the amount of time that a programmer must spend writing the program, because the number of instructions required to designate processing activity is reduced; second, it reduces the possibility of errors on the part of the programmer.

HIGH-LEVEL PROGRAMMING LANGUAGES

There are hundreds of high-level or problem-oriented programming languages. In this section, a few of the most widely used languages are discussed. Programmers writing in high-level languages use special coding sheets that are helpful to the pro-

TABLE 3.1 CATEGORIES OF PROGRAMMING LANGUAGES

Machine Language	Assembly Language
020021	INPUT A
020022	INPUT B
020023	INPUT C
030021	ADD A
030022	ADD B
040023	SUB C
050024	STORE D
060024	OUTPUT D
070000	HALT

High Level Language (Basic)
INPUT A, B, C
LET D = A + B − C
PRINT D
END

grammer in preparing instructions according to the specifications of the particular language (see Fig. 3.2).

There exist two basic applications of data processing namely: business data processing, which involves relatively simple calculations performed on large amounts of data; and scientific data processing, which performs complex calculations on relatively small amounts of data. Particular languages are structured to meet the needs of these specific applications. Languages, such as FORTRAN, are scientific languages that allow a programmer to express mathematical calculations in simple form. Other languages, such as COBOL, allow a programmer to write programs that handle input and output efficiently. The four high-level languages discussed here are FORTRAN, COBOL, BASIC, and PASCAL.

FORTRAN

FORTRAN is the oldest high-level programming language in existence. The language was developed and a compiler written to convert FORTRAN programs into machine language in the mid-1950s. Over the years several different forms of FORTRAN have been used, but in 1966 the organization known as American National Standards Institute (ANSI) produced a standardized version of FORTRAN that programmers could use to write programs that could then be run on any computer having a FORTRAN compiler.

The name of this language comes from FORmula TRANslator. At the time that the language was developed, computer users consisted primarily of scientists,

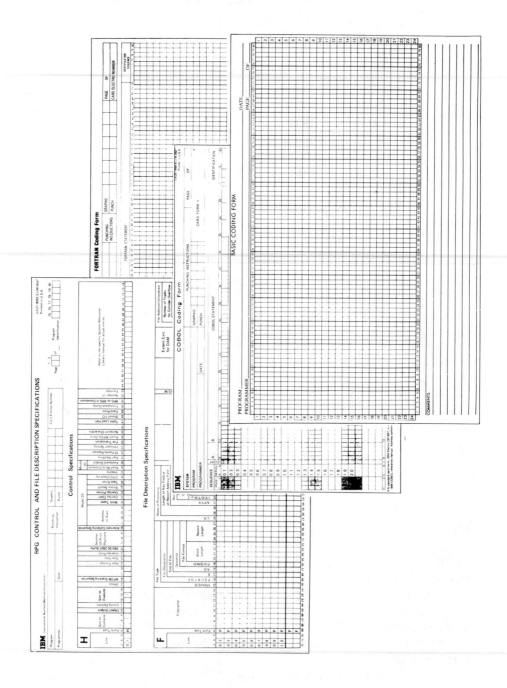

Figure 3-2 Typical coding sheets for several popular languages

engineers, and mathematicians; therefore, the language was developed to meet the needs of the type of applications they generated.

In FORTRAN, the basic instruction is called a statement. FORTRAN consists primarily of mathematical notation. The rules for forming mathematical expressions in FORTRAN are similar to those used to form expressions in algebra. Individual mathematical values are expressed in the language by using symbols known as variables. These variables can be single alphabetical characters, but most often are words that describe what they represent. Variables are used to form the mathematical expressions. When the program is actually executed, exact numeric values are substituted into the mathematical expressions in place of the variables, and the calculation is made.

Although FORTRAN was originally designed as a scientific language, it can be used to solve business problems. However, because certain nonnumeric data cannot be expressed in FORTRAN, it is not well suited to certain common business applications such as data file manipulation.

COBOL

COBOL, or COmmon Business Oriented Language, was introduced in the late 1950s. A group of representatives from private industry and the federal government met and devised this language that could be used to process alphabetic or alphanumeric data as well as numeric data. This language was primarily for use in business applications. COBOL instructions are written in a language or structure that allows the reader of a COBOL program to determine what the program is designed to do without having to become involved with all the technical details usually associated with a programming language. For this reason, COBOL programs are considered somewhat self-documenting. The program itself, by the language and structure used, can describe to the reader what the program is directing the computer to do.

The structure of a COBOL program is comparable to that of a book. Whereas in FORTRAN the basic instruction is called a statement, in COBOL it is called a sentence. The next level up from a sentence in COBOL is a paragraph, followed by sections and divisions.

Four divisions are used in COBOL programs: (1) identification—which identifies the entire program by a name; (2) environment—which describes the type of computer that will compile and execute the program; (3) data—which describes all the data to be used by the program; and (4) procedure—which contains the processing steps to be performed during program execution.

While COBOL uses a language that is easily understood and is somewhat self-documenting, it is not an easy language to write programs in or to learn. However, COBOL is easier than writing programs in machine or assembly languages, and is the most widely used language for business applications.

BASIC

With the popularity of interactive time-share computing, languages have been developed to allow the user both the ease of learning programming and the ease of entering the programs into the computer. One of these languages is BASIC. BASIC is a conversational language in which a program can be entered directly into the computer from a terminal, and the compilation will take place at the same time that the program is executed.

BASIC programs make use of four types of instructions: input instructions; calculation or "LET" instructions; control or branch instructions; and output or "PRINT" instructions. The structure of a BASIC program is very similar to that of a FORTRAN program, except that the data may be entered into the computer and retrieved from the computer more easily by using BASIC than FORTRAN.

BASIC allows the programmer to write a simple program, enter it into the computer, and receive the result immediately. While initially developed as an interactive language that could be used to teach students how to program, the simplicity of BASIC has gained wide acceptance as an applications language used by individuals with relatively little data processing experience. BASIC is also being used extensively on the new generation of microcomputers.

PASCAL

PASCAL is considered the BASIC of the future. The high-level language clarifies the problem-solving programming process through its block-structure design. It is hoped that PASCAL will bring some standardization to the programming of microcomputer systems. Although most microcomputer systems available now use BASIC, there are so many different versions of BASIC that available software packages will work only on a narrow group of systems, thus causing much extra effort and expense to develop software for every microcomputer system.

The description of languages provided here is brief. A wide variety of other languages are used with computers, but those discussed here can probably be considered the most used.

THE PROGRAMMING PROCESS AND METHODS

Any program written to direct the activities of a computer system is the result of much more than a programmer writing a set of instructions on a piece of paper and then copying them into the computer through an input device. Before writing a program in any programming language to solve a particular problem, the programmer must have a thorough understanding of the problem, as well as an approach to solving it. This section discusses several concepts that facilitate the development of a working program.

To create an efficient and useful program programmers should:

1. Define the problem.
2. Plan the solution to the problem.
3. Select a programming language.
4. Code the solution (write the program).
5. Test the solution (program).
6. Document the program.

Each of these tasks is usually performed in sequence, each task being a logical progression of the previous one. In most instances, these tasks or steps are the responsibilities of several individuals: the individual requesting the program, a systems analyst, and finally the programmer. While each performs a separate but necessary function in the solution of a specific problem, the programmer has the ultimate responsibility for writing the instructions the computer will follow (see Fig. 3.3).

1. PROBLEM ANALYSIS. The problem is studied and defined. Input and output specifications are made. A method of computer solution is developed.	
2. ALGORITHM AND FLOWCHARTING. The programmer reduces the problem to discrete steps. Charts are prepared that graphically illustrate the flow of data. Desk debug.	
3. & 4. SELECT AND CODE. Each step of problem is reduced to an instruction or group of instructions in a language such as FORTRAN. Coding sheets and language manuals aid the programmer. Desk debug.	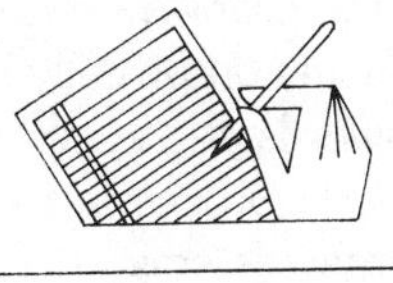
5. RUNNING AND DEBUGGING. The program is taken to a computer to compile and execute. If it doesn't, bugs must be removed so it will run. Consultation with others may uncover causes of trouble. Program testing.	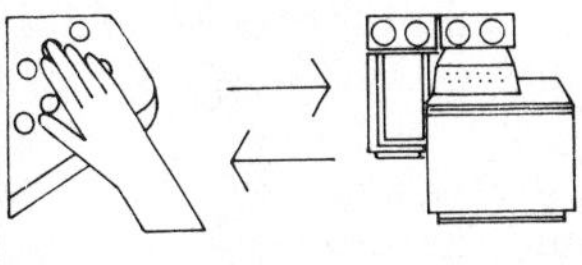
6. DOCUMENTATION. A write-up is prepared on the program, explaining program logic. Flowcharts, instructions, and details are included to help others use the program or for later modification.	

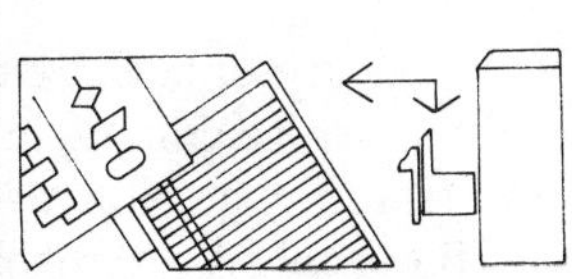

Figure 3-3 Summary of the programming process

As each step in the programming process is accomplished, the solution to the problem becomes clearer and clearer. When all the preliminary steps in the programming process are completed, the actual writing of the program becomes nothing more than converting the solution into the exact instructions of a program according to the syntax rules and structure of a particular programming language.

Defining The Problem

The task of problem definition is usually one of determining what has to be done. The first event that leads to the use of a computer is the recognition of the need for information. Frequently, the need for information is the result of a management decision determining that important information is necessary to help the organization function more effectively. In any process, after the decision is made to use the computer to solve a problem and produce information, the programming process is initiated.

The initial definition of the problem is often the responsibility of data processing personnel other than the programmer. A systems analyst initially perceives the needs of the individuals requesting information and determines how the computer can be used to produce it. A systems analyst is to a programmer what an architect is to a builder. The architect determines the needs of the individual who will eventually occupy the building to be designed, and then draws plans that the builder executes to produce the actual building. In the same manner, the systems analyst determines the needs of the individual requesting the services of a computer, then draws up a set of plans the programmer can use to write the specific programs to produce the information desired.

The written material produced at this point in the process is not a program, but rather a series of specifications outlining the information needed and how it is to be produced. Most of these specifications are in the form of a pictorial representation of the problem and its solution, known as a flowchart. The flowchart, simply, represents graphically how data will be processed (see Fig. 3.4). Using a combination of words and symbols, the flowchart shows how data will flow through all parts of the data processing system. There are two distinct types of flowcharting: one used by the systems analyst in the problem definition stage of program development, and the other used by the programmer to help plan the solution to the problem and write the program.

Flowcharting

The type of flowchart developed and used by a systems analyst uses the symbols that we saw in Fig. 3.4. This type of systems flowcharting shows the passage of data through all parts of the data processing system. More specifically, a **systems flowchart** is a symbolic representation of the procedures used to convert raw data into information that can be used by those requesting it. The systems flowchart shows each work station through which the data will pass, but little is shown on a

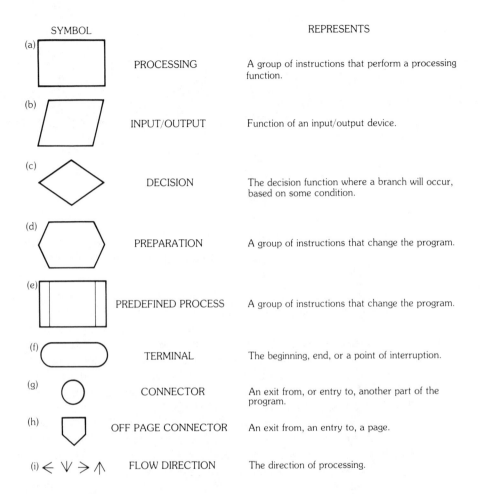

SYMBOL		REPRESENTS
(a)	PROCESSING	A group of instructions that perform a processing function.
(b)	INPUT/OUTPUT	Function of an input/output device.
(c)	DECISION	The decision function where a branch will occur, based on some condition.
(d)	PREPARATION	A group of instructions that change the program.
(e)	PREDEFINED PROCESS	A group of instructions that change the program.
(f)	TERMINAL	The beginning, end, or a point of interruption.
(g)	CONNECTOR	An exit from, or entry to, another part of the program.
(h)	OFF PAGE CONNECTOR	An exit from, an entry to, a page.
(i)	FLOW DIRECTION	The direction of processing.

Figure 3-4 System flowcharting symbols

systems flowchart about how the computer will process the data. (Figure 3.5 shows a sample systems flowchart.) The role of the computer as part of a systems flowchart is often represented by a single symbol. What actually takes place inside the computer is the concern of the programmer and will be developed further in the program flowchart created by the programmer.

Planning the Solution

After the specifications for producing information have been established by the systems analyst, the programmer must determine the role of the computer in producing the desired information and plan how the computer will accomplish the conversion of the data into information.

In this stage of the process, the programmer will use a problem statement pre-

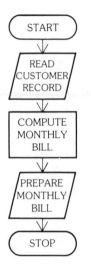

Figure 3-5 A systems flowchart

pared by the systems analyst as a basis for establishing the actual procedures that the computer will follow to arrive at a solution to the problem. The problem statement that the programmer may work with may be similar to what a mathematics student may work with while trying to solve a word problem. While the programmer may use many tools to describe the sequence of steps that the computer will follow to arrive at the solution to a problem, the most commonly used programming tool is the program flowchart. A program flowchart may use the symbols shown in Fig. 3.6. This is similar to a systems flowchart, except that the program flowchart describes the activities that take place inside the computer to arrive at the solution to a problem. By constructing a program flowchart, the programmer can analyze the structure of the solution and determine if the logic within the flowchart represents a reasonable plan for the solution of the problem (see Fig. 3.7).

Selecting A Language

Once the solution of a particular program has been planned, before actually writing the program a programmer must select a specific language to use in writing the program. The procedures for the solution of a problem may differ, depending on the type of language used.

Two important factors to consider in selecting a specific programming language are the time spent writing the program, and the amount of time the computer may take to actually compile and execute a program. Programs that are written in a machine language are easier and faster for the computer to understand and process because they are written in a language close to how the computer works with data internally. However, machine language programs are harder to write and, therefore, take more programmer expertise and time. Programs written in any of the symbolic

60

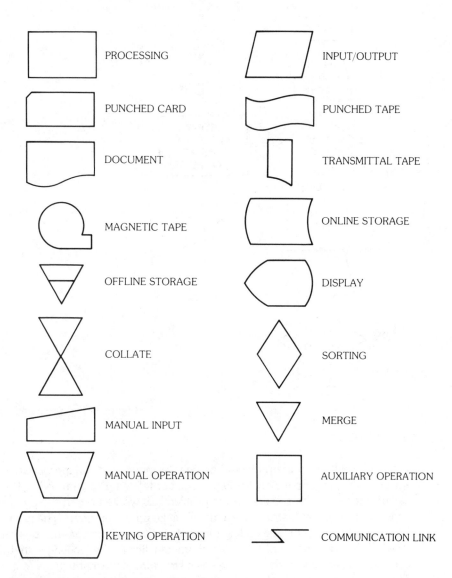

Figure 3-6 Program flowcharting symbols

programming languages are much easier for programmers to create, but they require more computer time to compile and execute.

If a programmer decides to write a program in a high-level symbolic programming language, there are many available. Many symbolic programming languages are designed to simplify the programming process in specific types of applications.

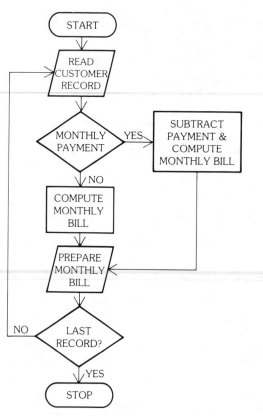

Figure 3-7 A program flowchart

Coding the Solution

After the solution to the problem has been planned, and an appropriate language selected, the program may actually be coded or written. Program coding is the process of translating the solution of the problem, as worked out in the program flowchart, into the exact instructions that will make up the program. The program may be written on programming coding forms that offer the programmer several advantages. They show some of the basic characteristics of the languages that they are designed for, as well as showing the basic structure of the instructions to be written. The use of coding forms also reduces clerical errors that may be made while writing the program. They also simplify the process of entering the program into the computer. Finally, they serve as documentation for the program, assisting in its organization and identification.

Testing the Solution

No program should be put into use until it has been thoroughly tested and all errors have been eliminated. This step of the programming process is often called testing and debugging.

Programs seldom execute successfully the first time. Often, no matter how simple or complex, the program contains at least a few errors. There are two levels of debugging: (1) desk checking or debugging, which is locating as many errors as possible before the program is entered into the computer; and (2) compilation, in which the computer translates the program into the binary language the computer understands and works with. The compilation process may generate diagnostics or error messages that may show the programmer sources of errors and faulty logic within the program.

When the programmer is reasonably assured that the program is correct, it should be tested. The purpose of testing is to determine whether a program produces the expected results. Normally, a program is tested by executing it with a set of inputs for which the results are already known. Because a program may contain many segments, or modules, the programmer must select data that will test all parts of the program. If the program produces the correct results, then the programmer may move on to the next step in the process before actually putting the program into use.

Program Documentation

Providing the documentation for the program is the last step in the process before putting the program into use. Program documentation provides a written description of each step in the programming process. Documentation should include a clear statement of the original problem and what the program is designed to accomplish. Documentation should then describe the program logic; this includes flowcharts, the input data to be used, and the output to be produced.

After the background material for the program has been provided, the documentation next should provide a user's directory, or operator's manual, that supplies procedure instructions to the operator who will actually execute the program on the computer.

Since programming methods differ from programmer to programmer, documentation is important to ensure that each programmer, operator, or systems analyst who works on the program in the future has some documentation enabling them to trace the procedures that were initially used to prepare the program.

In comparison with equipment costs, programming costs have risen dramatically—to the point where software is now more expensive than the hardware. The computer industry is looking for ways to reduce programming costs, and one direction is the development of more complex but friendlier operating systems that allow easier use by nontechnicians. Another direction is to reduce the number of diverse languages that are used to program computers. This can be accomplished by standardizing existing languages, or by developing more powerful new languages and encouraging more people to use them.

To achieve more widespread use of computers, they must become easier to use. People need to be able to unlock the power of a computer without having to undertake an extensive education program. The only way that this can take place is for programming languages to become more powerful, yet simpler and easier to use.

Those who design the hardware and develop the software to utilize the hardware will have to keep in mind that the most good can be done for the most people by making computers easier to use.

STUDY AND REVIEW

1. What is programming?

2. What are the two types of computer software?

3. What is a programming language?

4. Describe the following: (1) operating system, (2) compiler-assembler.

5. What are the three major types of programming languages? Discuss major features of each.

6. Describe the steps taken in developing a successful program.

7. Explain the difference in the two types of flowcharting, and describe how one relates to the other.

4

COMPUTERS,
PUBLIC OPINION,
AND ISSUES

PERSPECTIVE

Now that you have acquired a basic understanding of computer concepts and terminology, you are about to embark on a fascinating tour through the world of computers. However, before beginning this journey, it is important to become familiar with some of the terminology and concepts pertaining to the personal and social issues that arise from the widespread use of computers. The purpose of this chapter is to explore, discuss, and clarify the principal issues that accompany computer applications. With this knowledge you will gain a deeper understanding of the impact computers have on people and institutions. We use this chapter, therefore, to focus on the issues in depth so that they will be easier to recognize and discuss as they recur in future chapters. As the following quotation indicates, we want our readers to be prepared for the future.

> *Certainly our way of life is going to change drastically as a result of computers. Equally certain, we need new laws, new education, and new attitudes to cope with this revolution. Can we acquire these in time? Or is the changing environment coming too quickly?*
>
> *(Martin and Norman, 1970)*

This chapter provides the foundation for understanding the impact of computer use, just as the previous chapters provided the foundation for understanding the hardware and software concepts underlying computer applications. Accordingly, we have designed the applications chapters so that a brief mention of hardware concepts will be made in each chapter along with a short discussion of pro and con social issues. Consequently, you may find it beneficial to refer to Chapters 1-3 occasionally for further classification of hardware and software concepts, or to this chapter for clarification of the social issues. By reading this book in this fashion, you will continually be reminded of the close and interdependent relationship between computers and people—and how this relationship often has far-reaching social implications. However, before discussing the issues, you should first understand the importance of your current beliefs and attitudes toward computers.

THE CRUCIAL ROLE OF ATTITUDES

> *Man is disturbed not by things but the views he takes of them.* *(Epictetus, A.D. 95)*

> *It is very obvious that we are influenced not by "facts" but by our interpretation of facts.* *(Adler, 1924)*

As indicated by these quotations, our attitude toward something is heavily influenced by our beliefs and interpretations of facts. In Chapter 1 we saw that the "information explosion" naturally leads to expanded use of and need for the computer. However, whether we perceive these uses as beneficial or harmful depends on our beliefs about computers; they are not an inherent nature of computers. The purpose of this book is not to give "the correct attitude" toward computers, which you can merely accept without question, but rather to provide a balanced framework of accurate information so you can develop your own perspective.

Beliefs, Perception, and Behavior

Often when we acquire information from friends, parents, television, or even a textbook on computers, we are not aware of the impact this information has on our lives. However, it is a well-documented fact that information affects our beliefs, beliefs affect how we perceive things, and how we perceive things affects how we behave. A simple example illustrates this interrelatedness. A young child perceiving a small bottle on a shelf proceeds to pick it up, take off the cap, and smell its contents. The liquid smells sweet, looks like syrup, and the child is about to drink from the bottle when a parent enters the room. The parent immediately tells the child to put down the bottle and begins to explain that the interesting symbol on the bottle's label (a skull and crossbones) indicates that the substance is a poison and will cause death if consumed. This information not only provides the child with a new belief about liquids, but also alters the child's perception so that the "interesting symbol" now becomes a warning or a danger sign. As a consequence, the child's behavior is also changed in that he or she will no longer attempt to drink from containers so marked. Whether we are concerned with how children learn about poisons or how adults learn about computers, this example helps to underscore the basic relationship between information, belief, perception, and behavior that is common to all human experience. Our beliefs play a crucial role in forming attitudes that guide and direct our actions; if our beliefs are inaccurate, our behavior will be misguided.

Beliefs about Computers   Practically all members of society hold certain beliefs and attitudes toward computers. These attitudes fall into two general categories: attitudes based on working knowledge and/or formal training/education concerning computers, and attitudes that have no basis in experiences of this type. Although *you* may have experience with computers, it is important to realize you are in the minority—the majority of people have no such knowledge. The prevailing views of this much larger group represent the public's opinion about computers—the opinions that shape so many lives. At this point it must also be stressed that the truth or falsity, accuracy or inaccuracy, of this public opinion is not really important. What is important is the role these beliefs have in forming either positive or negative, realistic or unrealistic, attitudes toward computers. We must keep in mind that it was widespread opinion, not facts, that inhibited world trade and exploration when people argued that the earth was flat. And it was prevailing attitude, not facts, that permitted mentally handicapped individuals to be killed because they were thought to be possessed by "evil spirits."

Most public opinion about computers is shaped primarily by the mass media: radio, television, movies, newspapers, and magazines. Fortunately, the mass media is now providing a more factual and documentary type of information about computers than in the past. However, generally speaking, much of the information imparted by the media in the past has relied heavily on sensationalism, news stories, and computer "horrors" in order to market its broadcasts and publications. Other major sources of beliefs about computers come from the movies and literature. It is primarily the science fiction element that discusses computers the most. Because relatively few nonfiction accounts (other than textbooks in computer science) have influenced public opinion about computers, it is not surprising how much influence has been exerted by fictional portrayals. Unfortunately, it is this type of information that not only shapes attitudes and beliefs, but also heavily influences our behavior—the extent to which we understand, accept, or reject the computer.

Changes in Attitudes   Although this rather narrow spectrum of information has exercised a disproportionate effect in forming public opinion in the past, there are positive indications that its influence is gradually diminishing. This significant change can be attributed to three main factors.

First, the dramatic increased usage of computers that was brought about by phenomenal cost reductions in computing. Not only are more people using computers, but the variety of uses is expanding into different disciplines (such as in the arts, humanities, and the social sciences) that previously made little or no use of the computer. As more people from different backgrounds use the computer, the dif-

Figure 4-1 Using a home computer to compose music (Courtesy of Micro Music, Inc.)

fusion of accurate information throughout different segments of our society becomes possible. Thus the stereotype of the computer as merely a tool for the mathematician, scientist, or business manager is slowly being replaced with a broader view.

Second, the development of the microprocessor (discussed in Chapter 15), the basis for personal home computers, computerized appliances, automobile systems, and numerous other applications, created a revolution. Now that millions of individuals can directly benefit from and use computer technology daily in their own homes, many of the myths about computers are being replaced by accurate, first-hand experience.

Finally, because of the widespread use and popularity of the computer mentioned above, there is now a demand for accurate, factual, nonfictional accounts. It is not uncommon now to see hour-length documentaries on television about computer uses in medicine, transportation, artificial intelligence, and many other topics, or brief news coverage of a new or extremely beneficial use of computers. But most important is the contribution you can make. Even though you may never write a news story or produce a documentary film about computers, you can make a significant contribution to the public's understanding of the computer through your conversations with family, friends, and fellow students/employees. Your ideas and opinions play a very important role in developing an accurate perception of computers for those who have had no such exposure. As Robert Lee, an IBM executive, wrote more than 15 years ago.

> *In the long run, it will probably be the youngsters who have grown up in a world of computers who will more truly understand the new relationship of man and the machine. They will not be handicapped by older concepts, they will not feel a sense of ego threat, and they will not be in some sort of identity crisis in relation to machines. Instead, I believe they will be eager to understand the new tools, to use them to extend their knowledge and to extend their freedom to build the kind of future they want. And, out of this, I think a new concept of man will develop—a concept of man which includes and which accepts his ability to amplify the powers of his mind.* (Lee, 1966)

THE MAIN ISSUES

In order to clarify computer impact issues, and facilitate our understanding, we have separated them into several distinct categories. We must caution you that, when these issues are confronted in real life, they are not as clearly defined and distinct as we have presented them here. Rarely are the issues isolated from many other factors that both obscure and complicate a situation. The real issues do not have clearly defined boundaries and, when issues do arise, they are intertwined with human beliefs, attitudes, and the social context in which they occur. Nevertheless, being familiar with the issues in their "pure" form as presented here should alert you to their main characteristics and, thus, facilitate your identification and discussion of them.

Privacy

> *We're living in the decade of 1984, and if we don't quickly start to implement mechanisms for defining and protecting privacy, it will be gone by the end of the 1980s.* (Trubow, 1981)

Strictly speaking, computer systems, like other tools people have invented, do not have inherent disadvantages or flaws. Problems arise, however, when computer systems are used without careful planning or consideration of the total impact the system is likely to have on organizations and individuals. One predominant problem associated with computers is the invasion of privacy issue. During the past two decades numerous congressional hearings have been held and many books written about computers and privacy. The main theme connecting these different perspectives is the right to be left alone, a right first advocated in the now famous article by Warren and Brandeis entitled "The Right to Privacy" that appeared in an 1890 *Harvard Law Review*. Now, almost 100 years later, federal and state legislation is beginning to acknowledge and incorporate the individual's right to privacy into law and policy. The right to privacy in relation to computers arises mainly in the context of computer data banks and how information about individuals is collected, stored, and exchanged. In this setting, the right to privacy is usually understood as the right to control information about oneself.

Three Points on Privacy   First, concern about personal privacy is older than the computer—people have been trying to protect their privacy, through law and social customs, for hundreds of years.

Second, because of the enormous collection of information about individuals, particularly within the last 50 years, it became necessary to store most of this information in computer data banks. It has become too costly, too time consuming, and too inconvenient for organizations and the people they serve to handle this information in any other way. These data must be collected in order to provide benefits and services for the public. For example, education, banking, insurance, credit, drivers' licenses, and employment all depend on information collected from individuals. Because this information is sometimes incorrect, not up to date, or is used for purposes other than those for which it was originally intended, many people erroneously conclude that the computer is to blame for these problems.

Third, since privacy is not invaded by the computer, what is the real problem? The answer is: record keeping practices and personnel guidelines. The amount of information collected, the number of people who use the information, and the speed at which it can be exchanged have all grown dramatically; unfortunately, record keeping policies have changed little in the last 100 years. The type and extent of data collected have never really been examined carefully to determine what is relevant to an organization's needs. Often useless or frivolous information is retained simply because it was collected in the past. Fortunately, many organizations, both public and private, are now starting to resolve these problems by asking questions such as: What is the bare-minimum amount of information needed in order to provide the services we grant? Not only does this approach reduce privacy problems, but it also reduces the costs of collecting unnecessary data, which are often passed on to the taxpayer/customer.

Possible Solutions   In 1975, the Privacy Act of 1974 was enacted and, for the first time in our history, imposed standards and safeguards to protect individual privacy. Although this bill applies only to federal data banks, it requires registration of all data banks; the establishment of rules and procedures for collection and dissemination of information; criminal penalties for violation of any part of the Privacy Act; and methods by which a person can view his or her files and correct inaccurate information. A privacy protection commission also was formed by the Privacy Act to investigate abuses, oversee implementation of the act, and make suggestions. Reports from this commission have made strong recommendations for reform, particularly in the private sector.

An even more comprehensive approach is now being taken by Congress to develop a national information policy, a policy that would concern itself with privacy, security, and the uniform regulation of all information technologies: radio, cable television, electronic banking, computer telecommunications, libraries, and others.

> *While the spectacular growth of computer technology and communications technology in the last thirty years has been notable, what is even more significant is the rapid way these technologies are merging . . . Computer and communications technology are not only merging but are also converging with related technologies such as printing and photography. When all these elements are fully integrated, the resultant capability for information transfer and exchange could create a form of national information interdependence.* (National Information Policy, 1976)

Current Trends in Privacy Although legislation governing federal data banks has been operative for several years, there are still demands for extensive legislation in the private sector. However, the absence of a unified government policy and clear conception of informational privacy seems to be the current barrier preventing enactment of the comprehensive legislation needed to cover all the relevant technologies. Both national and international conferences dealing with privacy acknowledge the need for control—particularly self-administered control—but fear that there may be economic burdens if overly strict legislation is adopted. At the international level, information flow from one country to another (transborder data flow) could be impeded if there is no uniform agreement regarding privacy among different countries.

Perhaps most important, at all levels of public and private organizations, a deep regard for personal privacy already exists. In fact, many large firms and state governments that are not affected by present federal privacy laws have already implemented privacy policies that in many cases exceed the federal requirements. Though the solutions to both the national and international privacy policy are not clear, it is clear that all segments of our society that deal with personal information and the emerging communications technologies are attempting to resolve and eliminate difficulties before they turn into serious threats to our privacy.

Automation

We are finally entering the age of automation. Up to now we've just been talking about it.   *(Noble, 1980)*

The fear of being displaced or unemployed because of the high level of computer automation is probably the second greatest problem related to computers. However, the numerous studies regarding automation and unemployment are, at best, inconclusive at this time. Statistics indicate that people who lose their jobs because of a computer system usually find other jobs after a short period, and that the number of jobs eliminated by computers is offset by the number of new jobs created in the computer-related fields. Because of the complexity of this topic, we discuss it further in Chapter 17—after you have had an opportunity to evaluate the many different ways in which the computer affects our lives.

One factor that makes the assessment of the effect of computers upon employment difficult is that many "new" segments of our society are now seeking employment. More women and younger (college-age) people are entering the job market than ever before, and there is a movement to increase the retirement age from 60 or 65 to 70 years of age. And, even though the number of jobs is increasing dramatically in the computer fields, it is still too soon to estimate the effect that the widespread use of low-cost micro- and minicomputers will have on business and industry in the 1980s and 1990s. The optimists claim the ever-expanding computing industry will create more jobs and new industries, keeping unemployment low. The pessimists say society will soon be ruled by a white collar elite, with large-scale automation, widespread unemployment, and associated social problems far worse than the depression of the 1930s.

Many social scientists point out that the question of radically changing employment trends has never been carefully examined. This is partially due to the fact that many of the prophets of doom of the 1960s, who predicted increased automation and severe unemployment during the 1970s, were not accurate in their proclamations. The absence of high unemployment during the 1970s led many to believe that automation may never cause large-scale unemployment. This position, though, is currently highly contested. Critics remark that although the use of computers has created many new jobs, these tend to require higher levels of education and create white-collar managerial positions. Furthermore, unions have offset much of automation's negative effects by requiring industries that are becoming computerized, such as typesetting and automotive assembly, to retain displaced workers in other capacities until they retire, quit, or die.

It will still be several years, therefore, before we can measure the actual effects of automation. In the meantime, there are some measures that can be taken to alleviate employees' fears of being either replaced or displaced by the computer. For example, the British Department of Industry has developed guidelines (similar to those in American business) for managers who would like to introduce computers and other advanced technologies. The recommendations are:

Consult with your staff from the very beginning when you are considering the feasibility of new systems.

Your actions should clearly demonstrate that you are concerned with the interests and requirements of the users and that their interests will be integrated into the design of any new system.

Be sure to explain clearly and honestly the likely consequences of the system and plan with your staff how to anticipate and overcome problems.

Perhaps this type of careful planning and consultation can reduce the amount of fear associated with changes in the working environment. One thing we can be sure of: automation is well on its way and irreversible. The question is how it will be handled.

Human-Machine Interface

Although many individuals who work in a computer environment have overcome the fear of being replaced by a computer, another problem, more subtle but unsettling, remains. This difficulty sometimes results in people quitting their jobs or not applying for a position where they must work with a computer. This is the issue of human-machine interface—how people and computers work together.

> *People fear losing their jobs at first, but even if they're not displaced, their fear can continue. They fear they won't be able to handle the pressure of working with the new technology and that their job performance will begin to suffer; they fear that when things start moving too swiftly, they won't be able to hang on.*   (Buchanan, 1980)

The issue of human-machine interface takes several different forms. For workers, it is most commonly experienced as "shock." For managers, it creates awesome decision-making situations. For society, it has enormous impact upon our values.

Computer Shock   The age in which we now live is quite different from that of our parents or any other generation. It is mainly characterized by rapid changes in technology, life styles, and values. Often these changes are difficult to understand and predict, resulting in disorientation, confusion, and uncertainty about what the future has in store for us. One writer in the early 1970s, Alvin Toffler, termed this experience "future shock." Now, as we experience the 1980s and move closer toward the 1990s, another term has been introduced to explain one major force shaping our future, the "information explosion." In fact, some people claim we have already moved from an industrial age into a postindustrial "information age."

However, there is a need to introduce an even newer term, "computer shock," which is a special type of future shock and an integral part of the information age. Computer shock occurs when you are not able to comprehend or effectively participate in a particular computer environment—mainly due to the complexity of the situation. This might happen at your job, as a customer in a bank, retail store, or supermarket—even in your own home! Whenever an individual does not understand how equipment operates, how a response or instruction should be given to a computer, how the software operates, and so forth, computer shock is likely to take place. And the incomprehensible system does not have to be a large multimillion-dollar computer. This incomprehensibility can exist in all types of new microprocessor technology. Microwave ovens, digital wrist watches, all electronic automobile ignitions, and numerous household applicances are but a few examples of the new technology that creates a bigger gap between humans and machines. You can no longer take apart and repair this new wave of computer technology products—you cannot even open these products and look inside to see their workings. Parents can no longer explain to their children (nor employers to their employees) how these devices operate. All these minor side-effects eventually accumulate to produce a disproportionate feeling of confusion and alienation. When combined with larger systems in banks, supermarkets, and one's place of employment, the results can be very far-reaching and overwhelming.

Figure 4-2 Humans and machines working together in a design environment (Courtesy of International Business Machines Corporation)

This problem of human-machine interface can result in an individual feeling confused, frustrated, threatened, and intimidated, or experiencing similar emotional responses. These feelings, unfortunately, also bring with them a negative, combative attitude toward computers in general, which often leads to resistance to all types of change. What can be done?

Possible Solutions   First, there must be an awareness of the problem by designers and manufacturers of computer technology (both hardware and software) and the organizations that use the products. Essentially this aspect of the issue has already been achieved. However, there is always a time lag between the time the problem is identified and when it is corrected. Businesses that manufacture or use computers generally understand the importance of "friendly" computer systems—systems that people can easily understand and use effectively, systems that are specifically user oriented.

Second, and perhaps most important, there must be better education and distribution of information to the users (consumers, employees). For small appliances and other consumer products this could best be accomplished through well-written pamphlets, advertisements, and instruction manuals—information that clearly explains the underlying "mysteries" of the product. For organizations there must be better planning (similar to the suggestions in the guidelines developed by the Department of Industry in England, discussed earlier) before the computer is introduced or its current use expanded.

Not only should this planning involve the participation of *all* users of the system during the design and implementation stages, but it should also include on-going training/education for all those who come in contact with the system—managers, clerical help, and customers. Often multimillion-dollar systems are installed and the only education that accompanies these systems are a few demonstrations by equipment manufacturers along with a day or two of on-the-job training for supervisors and a few of the clerical help. Also, the brochures and operating manuals that are distributed to the employees are often incomprehensible to the uninitiated, filled with jargon and technical terms. Appropriate preparation increases the cost of the system, but it is absolutely necessary if the system is to be effective and the users satisfied. Humans must be clearly informed of their crucial role so they are not computer "shocked"—so they do not feel they are merely a cog in the wheel of a large, impersonal machine.

Finally, a more direct and immediate approach must be taken to correct current inadequacies because the two plans discussed above will take several years to implement properly. Because time sharing, networks, and microcomputers have permitted such rapid increases in the number of computer users, there are many important indications that users are going to play an even larger role in determining the success or failure of systems in the future. Programming languages and query-type database languages are being developed that will permit interactive conversations with the computer in something very close to English. For example, at one international computing conference, experts urged that special consideration be given to the "naive" user—a person who has no computer background or who is unfamiliar with special equipment—in the future design of computer systems. Because of the diverse backgrounds and requirements of the users of large systems, the computer must be able to communicate in a variety of ways in a manner that would be "natural" for the user, and at a conceptual level appropriate to the user's needs and abilities. In the interim, however, before the increased sensitivity to the user is reflected in new software and hardware, there are certain steps that can be taken to make the transition smoother. By adapting "cosmetic" programming techniques, systems can use existing software and hardware to enhance the human-machine relationship and make the systems more "friendly." Some of the suggestions that have been made for making the environment more comfortable for the user are:

> Communicate in the user's terms—do not use jargon or technical language. For example, rather than displaying the message "A603 LOAD MODULE DOES NOT EXIST," a "friendly" system might respond with: "Are you sure you typed that name correctly? Please enter it again."

> Be responsive to the user—do not keep the users waiting longer than five seconds without informing them why there is a delay or what activity is taking place.

> Have accessible, responsive human backup to answer questions and help resolve difficulties.

Yet, despite all the efforts being made to allow humans and machines to interact effectively, progress is slow and the actual benefits are difficult to measure because so many other factors influence the computer's public image. Nevertheless, the above suggested solutions should eventually significantly reduce "computer shock."

Decision Making

Another main issue in which human-machine interface is extremely important, and under scrutiny as a potential problem area, is decision making. With the advent of database management systems and management information systems that now operate in real time (see Chapter 8), the effectiveness of the decision maker is crucial. Some managers, who may not have formal training with these new systems, may be unable to utilize systems effectively or to implement the necessary changes in their organization to optimize their system's capabilities. As leaders in both private and public sectors become increasingly dependent on information systems to make top-level decisions, their knowledge (or ignorance) of the systems becomes critical. However, just as employees and customers sometimes experience difficulties in comprehending and integrating with the computer, so can managers. Not only must managers make decisions that depend on how well they understand the system, they must also make decisions on how the computer should be used. That is, not only must productivity and profits be considered, but so must the human dynamics of the organization—particularly in relation to the computer. (More will be said about this in Chapter 17.)

There was a time when purely quantitative factors such as output, capital expenditures, gross and net profit, and so forth dictated managerial decisions. But, in an age where productivity (which has been declining) and other key indicators of business well-being are closely linked with employee satisfaction and morale, these qualitative aspects of the working environment must also be considered. Managers who understand how to use a computer system, and know how to integrate employees with the system effectively, will be the leaders in the 1980s and 1990s. Again, awareness of this issue and continuing education for both managers and employees are key steps toward improving both decision making and employee morale.

Changes in Values. Without exaggeration, it is safe to say that even more profound effects have resulted from the human interface with technology. The alienation, fear, and apprehension that can occur in computer environments is also taking place in our society as a whole. Technology and computers, in particular, have radically changed the ways in which we live, work, and communicate with each other. The structures of organizations, employment patterns, families, and even the nature of friendships have changed in response to the effects of technology. Accompanying these structural changes are changes in our values. Philip Zimbardo, a social psychologist at Stanford University, has been researching the issue of human isolation for many years and has coined a term, "The Age of Indifference," to signify this current trend in social/personal relationships. As Zimbardo stated:

> The Devil's strategy for our times is to trivialize human existence in a number of ways: by isolating us from one another while creating the delusion that the reasons are time pressures, work demands, or anxieties created by economic uncertainty; by fostering narcissism and the fierce competition to be No. 1; by showing us the personal gains to be enjoyed from harboring prejudices and the losses from not moving out when the current situation is uncomfortable. Fostering in us the illusion of self-reliance, that sly Devil makes us mock the need for social responsibility and lets us forget how to go about being our brother's keeper—even if we were to want to.   (Zimbardo, 1980)

Some of the factors ushering in this age of indifference, according to Zimbardo, are: the rise of middle-class affluence, upward economic mobility, geographic mobility, breakdown of the family, and youthful cynicism. However, who is the Devil? Is it technology? We do not believe that it is; rather, it is a lack of understanding of technology, an inability to appreciate the impact technology has on society and the individual. If we become isolated from our working and living environments due to their incomprehensibility, it becomes very easy to be isolated from family and friends. Our self-image can be lowered due to a feeling of helplessness from not being able to understand and effectively control the environments in which we live and work. What can be done?

Possible Solutions   In order to overcome the resulting indifference, managers, teachers, government leaders, and parents must emphasize and demonstrate the importance of mutual responsibility. Not only must employees be loyal to the employer, but the employer must appreciate and be sensitive to the needs of employees. There must be effective, two-way communication in all environments so that all parties involved can participate in the decisions that affect their lives. We must change our values so that the human, personal factor is always most important. This is a long-term goal, but there are many intermediate actions that can start immediately, such as the suggestions given in the two preceding sections regarding computer shock and decision making. Most of the issues discussed in this section have been acknowledged by business, government, and education; the future will reveal whether or not the issues are understood and acted upon.

Abuse and Misuse

Sometimes the claim is made that the mere existence of computers opens the possibility for their misuse, resulting in abuse or harm to individuals. It is not uncommon to hear and read stories in which people are falsely arrested or detained because of incorrect computer printout information, or of people being incorrectly billed, sent unordered merchandise, denied benefits because a computer "claimed" they were dead, or some other such annoying problem. Often these types of events lead to an antagonism toward computers and the organizations that use them. However, when it is understood how these and associated problems arise, the belief that the computer is the perpetrator can be corrected and clarified. Part of this clarification is presented in the next section when we discuss the sources of computer system errors. Meanwhile, we can eliminate much of the frustration and misunderstanding by making an important distinction between *intentional* and *unintentional* abuses. As a philosopher once quipped, "Even a dog knows the difference between being kicked and being tripped over."

Intentional Abuses   This type of abuse results from utilizing the computer or computer information in some way that harms an individual, organization, or some other entity, such as a mass transit system or other computer controlled system. This type of misuse is carried out in a premeditated way, with "forethought and malice." These types of acts are more accurately called computer crimes, and are discussed in depth in Chapter 16. It will suffice to say at this point that most of the annoying problems mentioned above are not due to intentional abuses. These serious intentional offenses, such as using a computer to embezzle funds, or stealing computer information to blackmail someone, are relatively infrequent. Unfortunately, because someone is usually harmed and a computer is involved, news stories and headlines tend to sensationalize the occurrence.

Unintentional Abuses   This is the category into which most computer grievances fall. When one finds a computerized statement difficult to comprehend, has problems trying to correct an inaccurate bill, or receives 30 issues of the same magazine each week, often the response is, "Why is the computer doing this to me?" Again, the computer is not the villain. The confusion, harrassment, bewilderment, or inconvenience is usually due to some specific *human* oversight—completely unintentional. We will now examine how these errors get into computer systems.

Sources of Computer System Errors

Although monumental advances have been made during the last 30 years to allow computers and people to communicate more easily with each other, there are still times when this communication fails, resulting in problems. However, it is difficult to tell which is more problematic: the failure of human-machine communication, or the failure of the media to present the problems accurately. Although press reports of computer "errors" are becoming more accurate, there have been at least 25 years of general misrepresentation of the nature of these "errors." By examining more closely how these "errors" originate, we will better understand how to discuss and, perhaps, eliminate or reduce the frustration and confusion surrounding this topic.

Computer "error" blamed for massive overpayments by Social Security Administration.

Probers are looking into a monumental overpayment by the Social Security Admin. in its Supplemental Security Income (SSI) program. The nearly $403.7 million overpayment is being blamed on a "computer error," and the Administration's Bureau of Data Processing has come in for sharp criticism . . . .   (Infosystems, 1975)

When we read headlines that a computer error caused some catastrophe or are told by a clerk that a billing or bank statement error was caused by the computer, we tend to form the belief that the computer is somehow responsible. The purpose of this section is to clarify the nature of these "errors" so you can decide or find out exactly who or what is responsible. The authors are indebted to James Martin and Adrian R.D. Norman for a lucid presentation of this topic in their book, *The Computerized Society.* Although it is difficult to document precisely the number and extent of errors caused by each of the six categories in Table 4.1, the order in which they are listed roughly represents their influence, from more to less impact.

TABLE 4.1 SOURCES OF COMPUTER SYSTEMS ERRORS

Source	*Possible Solution*
1. *Data Input:* keypunch error, initial recording of transaction error, etc.	Verify by building data range tests into programs.
2. *Questionable System Philosophy:* poor design of system, too inflexible, not enough human backup to resolve unpredictable problems; for example, overbooking airlines reservations or disconnecting utilities based on computer output, not direct human contact.	Do not allow important actions to be taken without human intervention; do not make the system inflexible or unresponsive to human feedback; do not base design on inadequate data.
3. *Application Program:* program that is not fully debugged, does not operate as designed; for example, machine does not compute interest correctly, omits information when outputting results; does not calculate overtime pay.	Do more complete testing before implementation; break down larger, more complicated programs into easier to test modules.
4. *Operator Errors:* operator not following program directions to operator or not following correct operating procedures; taking shortcuts, using wrong tape, disk, cards, etc.	Have operator engage interactively with program instructions to operator and document all procedures on operator's console; have operator tests built into program; require verification of tape, disk identification, etc.
5. *Software:* bugs in manufacturer supplied software such as language translators, operating systems, etc.; more likely in new, complex systems, such as large timesharing, real-time networks.	Not too common now since extensive testing can be done by other computers; also many of these errors only affect the installation, not the customer.
6. *Hardware:* malfunction of computer circuitry or input-output transmission errors, especially in telecommunications.	With the new technology and built-in error detection and correction capability, potential problems are usually detected before errors occur; sometimes just upgrading to newer equipment will eliminate errors.

If any of the above sources could be labeled a "computer error," it would have to be item six, *Hardware,* which is the least significant of all the errors listed. In the 1950s and 1960s, hardware errors were common and troublesome, often giving the impression the computer was at fault for all errors. But with the new microcircuits and extremely accurate quality control, errors caused by hardware are now very infrequent, except perhaps during the initial break-in period of a new system. All the other errors in some way relate to a person being responsible, but this is rarely acknowledged or clarified in media stories or even in explanations given by banks or other businesses.

And, as indicated above, there are possible solutions and alternatives to minimize these major sources of human error. Many people believe that because a computer cannot think or exercise common sense, computers are destined to continue making outrageous mistakes by not being able to detect the most bizarre errors. Examples are frequently given of paychecks processed for hundreds of thousands of dollars over the normal amount, or receiving 300 copies of the same bill. But computers can be given "common sense." By incorporating into the applications program the "norms" for quantities handled in the program and upon which decisions are made, the program can test for unusual amounts (usually caused by an input error) and notify a human so they can intervene and examine the situation more closely. When we realize how errors arise, we are in a better position to question stock replies such as, "It's the computer's fault." And, accordingly, the likelihood that these errors will be remedied is much greater when people understand how they come about.

Finally, the image of the computer as the "culprit" will slowly be eradicated, permitting a more realistic and meaningful partnership with the computer. To see if you can detect the likely source(s) of error in some actual cases, examples are presented from an article entitled "What Computers Cannot Do":

> *When one retail grocer ordered peaches, the computer informed him that none were in stock although peaches were literally stacked to the ceiling. Grocers who ordered twelve cases of soup received 240 cases. . . . Orders for napkins brought crates of toilet tissue. And computerized bills that should have been for $14 were sent out as $214. . . .A mere random survey shows that bank executives repeatedly find that computers credit deposits to wrong accounts and, in turn, cause computers to mistakenly return checks because of "insufficient funds;" a company which used computers to address 7,000 labels for sending a YMCA's registration catalog belatedly learned that some persons received sixty catalogs while others received none; companies selling lists of potential customers are being sued by dozens of direct mail houses because computers repeated thousands of names twenty or thirty times; and universities have discovered that computers infuriated seniors expecting to graduate by sending notices that they failed their courses (while simultaneously surprising other students with notifications of unexpectedly high grades).   (Surface, 1968)*

From the tone of these reports, which are not uncommon, one definitely has the impression that the computer is the perpetrator of these errors. However, using the information you have acquired from Table 4.1, try being a detective and explain how the errors may have been caused and how they could be avoided in the future.

A LOOK TOWARD THE FUTURE

Computers are continually developing in speed and capability, whereas people have the same information processing and decision-making skills that their ancestors possessed thousands of years ago. And, for many people, the fact that humans are not developing new capabilities leads them to believe/fear that computers will eventually replace or, at least, outperform humans in most, if not all, areas of endeavor. This type of thinking results from not clearly understanding the importance and uniqueness of humans as designers and users of computer systems. The fact that computers are evolving faster than humans only means that humans will be able to use computers to solve larger, more complex, and more meaningful problems—the types of problems and questions that will contribute to a deeper understanding of ourselves and our environment. As society's awareness of computers increases, we will see more imagination and creativity being used to tap the power of both humans and computers. In the remainder of this book we explore the numerous ways in which humans and computers are working together to improve the quality of our life.

However, a large majority of our population cannot participate or give any direction to the computer revolution—they remain mere spectators, often fearful of what may occur in the future. Those of you who were born after 1960 have grown up in the computer age and may not feel this alienation that is characteristic of many older people who have had little or no exposure to computers. Fortunately, this trend is now changing as the computer receives higher visibility in the mass media, throughout all stages of education, and in one's employment. This is bringing about greater computer "literacy," which is a necessary prerequisite if the computer is to be understood and used wisely. Also, the rapid growth of the personal computer market is allowing more people to have direct experience with "friendly" computers, rather than just through computerized bills and banking statements. Furthermore, privacy legislation, consumer ombudsman systems, and other protective and educational services are restoring confidence that individuals can exercise some control over the powerful computer. All these factors are contributing to a demystification of the computer, thus permitting the computer, for the first time, to be understood, appreciated, and seen as a powerful tool that can respond to public concern.

As we gain a better understanding of organizations, human decision-making processes, and how these interact with computer systems, we will have a better understanding of the impact computer systems have upon individuals. However, because people also have an impact upon computer systems, we need to have a better understanding of how the two interact.

The Role of Public Understanding

Clearly, we are already merged in an information-based society; however, we cannot rely on Congress alone to protect our rights and safeguard our future. We can only hope that education will play an important role in training individuals for the information age. For it is primarily through education that people can be prepared for the future. We are at a precarious time in our nation's development. As one author calls it, we are at "freedom's edge." If an active role is taken by individuals regarding the use of computers and technology, our freedom can be maximized. However, if people remain passive and unconcerned, our freedom may be jeopardized. Milton Wessel, in *Freedom's Edge,* states some very crucial guidelines for the future:

> *Government officials, professionals in and out of the computer industry, educators, and other leaders must study the impact of the computer on society, discuss and publish their efforts, and inform the public of their views.*

He also states some rules that indicate the mutual effort that must be made if we are to give direction to the computer revolution:

> *Public Understanding Rule 1. Laymen must not hesitate to ask questions of computer professionals because they consider the computer too complex or are reluctant to disclose their ignorance.*

> *Public Understanding Rule 2. Computer professionals must answer lay questions in terms that are understandable to laymen.* (Wessel, 1974)

Optimistically, education will open these important channels of communication and allow individuals to participate effectively in the creation and protection of their freedom. It was concerned and informed citizens outside of Congress and industry who campaigned for such reforms as environmental protection, auto safety, and close regulation of DNA research. These events seem to indicate that lay people can play an important part in questioning and giving direction to computer technology and its impact on society.

STUDY AND REVIEW

1. Briefly explain the relationship between information, how we perceive things, and how we behave. Use an example dealing with your perception of computers.

2. Using examples, briefly explain the difference between intentional and unintentional computer abuses.

3. Give some instances where you believe human-machine interface poses problems. Suggest some possible ways in which the problems could be remedied.

4. What are your views regarding automation and employment? What do you believe will be the impact of the computer within the next five years in the field you plan to work in?

5. Do you believe your privacy has ever been violated by the use of computer-stored information? If so, in what ways could this have been prevented?

6. Briefly describe five major sources of computer system errors. Give examples of each along with possible ways of preventing them.

7. What do you believe are the main reasons for computers being misunderstood and feared? What can be done to minimize these problems?

Part 2

APPLICATIONS

The bewildering volume of technical information about computers can do people little good, unless they also understand how that technology is applied in day-to-day life. Certainly computers can be an intimidating influence on most people's lives. Many use the apparent complexity of computers as an excuse for ignoring them. This attitude of course perpetuates many of the negative views society has about computers, and compounds many of the problems associated with them. Ignorance of computers may well be one of the most significant problems associated with them. Many writers have made mention of that in their works.

> *The dehumanizing effect of the computer is not the result of the computer, but of human ignorance that magnifies the computer into more than it is.* (Isaac Asimov, 1981)

> *Ignorance of computers will render people as functionally illiterate as ignorance of reading, writing, and arithmetic.* (James Michael, 1980)

Now that we have developed an understanding of basic computer concepts, the following portion of the book will help you develop a framework for understanding how computers are used, and what influences they are likely to have on our lives.

5

EDUCATION

PERSPECTIVE

Although computers have been used in education for almost 20 years, recently there has been great interest in this topic created by the microprocessor/personal computer revolution. Not only can you teach students how to use, operate, and program computers, computers can be used to teach subjects (both in school and on the job)—from basic spelling to advanced organic chemistry, from kindergarten level all the way through graduate school. Also, teaching people about computer uses and their impact on society (as in the course you are presently taking) helps to alleviate the fears and misunderstandings about computers and contributes to the computer "literacy" that is necessary in order to comprehend today's world. However, there is much apprehension by teachers, parents, and students regarding the impact computers will have on education. Part of this apprehension is expressed in the following quotation.

> *It appears that computers in education have a long, uphill struggle before they become well-established in the classroom. The computer will have to have a perceived relative advantage over older, more established teaching methods before it comes into widespread use.*   *(Martellaro, 1980)*

While some argue that computers will dehumanize learning, others claim computers will dramatically enhance learning and creativity. There is a need for much more investigation into the issues surrounding computers and education. Therefore, the material presented in this chapter will simply introduce some of the facts and issues so that you can begin to form your own opinion on this complex topic.

COMPUTERS IN EDUCATION

Most of the controversy about computers in education is centered around using computers to teach, but there are several other educational uses that are important and less controversial. The computer helps to accomplish the tasks of accounting, payroll, inventory control, purchasing, maintenance records, government reports, and other similar activities in the educational environment, just as it would in a business situation. However, there are some specific uses of the computer pertaining to education that are briefly examined before discussing how computers are used to teach.

Three Nonteaching Uses of the Computer

In terms of historical development, computers were first used in educational settings to provide support and assistance for administrative and business functions (such as those mentioned above). However, once computers were acquired by school systems for these services, other uses were quick to follow.

Educational Management   Much of the paper work in an educational institution is concerned with attendance records, grade reports, disbursing financial aids, scheduling students, courses, and classrooms, and other curriculum related tasks. Many of these tasks are repetitive, tedious, and time-consuming. Not only does a computer accomplish these tasks quicker and with greater accuracy, but it frees the employees to use their time delivering personal services rather than doing monotonous recordkeeping. Also, if a database management system is employed (Chapter 8), a great reduction in duplicated records results, because one file can be accessed by several different offices instead of each office using a separate, duplicate file. In addition to meeting existing administrative requirements, a computer can provide new services that are not possible with manual systems: for example producing detailed government reports, printing mailing lists and labels, word processing reports and letters, and the ability to offer short-term courses and other operations that involve flexible scheduling which are generally too costly and complex for manual systems. Finally, after information is entered into the computer it can be retrieved in several graphic forms, thus facilitating statistical surveys and other reports that can improve decision making and planning.

Counseling   Many high schools and colleges now use local, state, and national data banks to assist in educational and career guidance. Because the job market (with its intricate demographics) and college programs are continually changing, counselors find it almost impossible to keep informed of all the latest developments relevant to a particular student's goals. By accessing a central data bank that is updated frequently (at least monthly) and computer software that can sort through thousands of possibilities and retrieve the necessary information for making career choices, a counselor can provide timely information about the changing job market.

For instance, one program designed to assist students in locating a college that meets their individual needs allows the student to specify up to 20 criteria, such as the course of study, geographic area, size of the town/city nearby, total enrollment for the school, male-female ratio, public or private, tuition cost, athletic programs, accreditation, admission requirements, and so forth. After the relevant criteria have been specified, the computer will identify the colleges that meet the student's requirements. Another program used extensively by counselors provides career guidance regarding the current job market, salaries, geographic areas of high demand, and the education requirements to enter the field. In areas that are changing rapidly, such as computer science, it is almost necessary to have access to one of these large, up-to-date systems in order to make the best possible choice (see Fig. 5.1).

Computer-Managed Instruction   Perhaps one of the most valuable areas for instructors is the use of computers to assist in their bookkeeping. The generation of tests, correction of tests, item analysis, keeping track of scores and grades on individual students, and other housekeeping chores are ideally suited for the computer. Computer-managed instruction (CMI) accomplishes all of these tasks. It also provides timely, valuable feedback to the instructor regarding a student's progress, pinpoints specific areas or skills that need improvement, and evaluates the effectiveness of tests and determines in which areas students are having the most trouble.

Figure 5-1 In a large greenhouse at Smith College, a programmer uses a Honeywell visual display terminal linked to a computer to access a data base containing detailed information about Smith's botanical gardens. The college uses such terminals for scholastic, financial, and alumnae data, for accounting, ordering dormitory food, and even for matching compatible roommates. (Courtesy of Honeywell Information Systems, Inc.)

The information on student progress and test results allows the teacher to improve his or her own skills by showing the area where students have the most problems, thus allowing either the material to be explained differently or the testing questions to be rewritten or eliminated. Furthermore, CMI can provide information for the student, such as suggesting sections of the book that should be studied more or recommending other resources (books, magazines, films, and so forth) that would assist in clarifying or amplifying the topic. Not only is the detailed computerized information beneficial for improving instruction and learning, but the time usually spent doing this bookkeeping can be spent giving more individualized and personal attention to students. However, to fully optimize the benefits of CMI, it is best used in conjunction with computer-assisted instruction.

Computer-Assisted Instruction (CAI)

The computers provide an intensely visual, multisensory learning experience that can take a youngster in a matter of a few months to a level he might never reach without it, and certainly would not reach in less than many, many years of study by conventional methods.   *(Estrin, 1978)*

During the early 1960s, publishing companies and educators began experimenting with programmed-instruction texts—materials that permitted students to progress at their own pace by responding to questions and receiving immediate confirmation as to whether their response was correct or incorrect. These self-instructional texts were based on the learning theory developed by B. F. Skinner of Harvard University. Basically, the theory establishes that learning is facilitated if the student receives immediate feedback (reinforcement) after responding to questions on material that has just been presented. Ideally, the student will respond correctly and, thus, minimize the adverse effects of learning incorrect responses. If the student answers incorrectly, then the original material is repeated or presented in a slightly different fashion and followed by a question. When the answer is correct, the student advances to new material and new questions. The main limitation of such an approach is that it can progress only in a linear fashion; all material and questions are in a predetermined order. In addition to textbooks, mechanical learning/teaching machines were built, using the same strategy to present text material (often supplemented with pictures or diagrams) on a small projection screen. The student responded by pushing an answer key on a small keyboard. Then, with the advent of time-sharing and interactive programming languages in the late 1960s, some schools began using the computer to present similar material. This was the beginning of computer-assisted instruction (CAI)—using a computer to *assist* teachers in presenting instructional material.

Program Development Unfortunately, there were many false starts and many poorly written programs during the early stages of CAI. Because of these low-quality programs, many educators either rejected or ignored the possibility of effectively using a computer for instruction. Their disapproval was based on several important considerations. First, the equipment was very expensive and needed computer specialists to program the computer and maintain the equipment. Second, the early programs were primarily written by computer scientists who had little or no experience with teaching. Consequently, the programs tended to mimic the less expensive learning machines and programmed texts that were already available. Third, there were no standards or guidelines as to how to develop and construct CAI programs (often called *courseware*). This resulted in poorly written programs and programs that were difficult for both teachers and students to comprehend and use. Finally, all of the preceding difficulties led teachers and administrators to be very skeptical about CAI, sometimes fearing that this mechanization of the learning process would dehumanize and depersonalize education.

Fortunately, significant progress was made during the 1970s in the area of CAI program development and, essentially, most of the problems mentioned have been overcome. First, there have been dramatic cost reductions in both hardware and software. The equipment is also more reliable and easier to use. For example, a time-sharing system with 32 terminals that cost, say, $400,000 in 1970 probably cost less than $100,000 in 1980. Second, and perhaps most important, the quality of software has improved significantly along with the large reduction in cost. CAI programs that cost $10 per student hour to produce in the late 1960s are now produced for less than 50 cents per student hour. This major accomplishment is due to two factors: a vast library of high-quality public domain or commercial courseware and the capability of teachers to write their own CAI programs.

The first factor was achieved because of government and private grants to educational research centers so that high-quality software could be produced by experienced educators. For example, over a 15-year period the PLATO project at the University of Illinois developed low-cost, easy to use hardware and software that is now available through a nationwide network. Also, since much of the courseware was already in the public domain, it can be easily acquired for little or no cost by any educational system (assuming there is compatibility with hardware and software requirements).

The second factor responsible for the tremendous cost reductions in courseware was the development of easy to use interactive programming languages, such as BASIC or special Course Author Languages (CAL). Many teachers found they could write their own CAI programs because these languages were easy to use even if one had no previous experience with computers. The Course Author Languages, for example, allow a teacher to construct different types of CAI courseware (discussed in the next section) simply by supplying the material, questions, and answers—essentially no programming is required and the teacher can personalize the program by adding special comments and remarks to enhance the instruction and keep the students interested.

Even though there have been major advances during the last decade, some fear and apprehension still persist. This is due to educators who were exposed only to the early, low-quality products and who are not familiar with the more recent and far superior courseware and hardware. However, many teachers who are familiar with the new material still feel uncomfortable using CAI. Again, the question of dehumanization, or the fear of being replaced by a machine, still lingers and influences the majority of teachers. Most teachers have not been exposed to or educated by CAI, so it is difficult for them to be enthusiastic—especially when most support for CAI comes from administrators and manufacturers of CAI hardware and software. But, despite these reservations and resistance, CAI is definitely expanding and will doubtless be a part of most educational systems before the end of this decade. Also, CAI is not only being used in schools, but is finding wide acceptance in business and government as a means of training employees and providing valuable continuing education in professions such as medicine, law, and other occupations that are information intensive.

We now examine some of the different varieties of CAI in order to understand what it offers to students, teachers, and the educational process (see Fig. 5.2).

Types of Programs   Before discussing specific types of CAI programs, several important aspects of CAI should be emphasized. First, the most crucial element for the success of CAI is the skill with which the programs are written. CAI will play a significant role in education only if there are high caliber programs. Second, the real

Figure 5-2 A computer-aided instruction terminal (Courtesy of International Business Machines Corporation)

focus of computer-*assisted* instruction is on the fact that it primarily *assists* instruction; it does not replace human instruction. In most CAI environments, students usually spend only one to four hours per week actually working with the computer. Third, courseware should be designed so that the results of answers given can be automatically recorded; this will allow the program to be modified and improved according to actual responses.

Although CAI and CMI are independent, CAI works best when directly linked to CMI. Not only does this allow precise updating and revisions of the courseware, it also allows the program and the instructor to respond effectively to any difficulties the student may experience. Essentially, CMI, in conjunction with CAI, can construct a model of the student's learning pattern, pinpoint the student's deficiencies and strengths, inform the instructor, and actually modify the material and questions presented so as to insure student mastery of all the material. In this way the instructor can use class time and direct contact with the students to concentrate on each student's personal needs. Finally, CAI works best when the author of the program can actually talk with the students who use the program. Sometimes personal comments by the students provide valuable insights into CAI courseware that cannot always be captured in objective, quantifiable data. With these points in mind, we now briefly examine six types of computer-assisted instruction programs.

Drill and Practice In this mode the student is quizzed or tested on previously studied material, often with the help of diagrams, charts, or other types of computer graphics. As with most types of CAI programs, the material is usually presented on a cathode-ray tube (CRT) terminal or on a hard-copy typewriter. This is the simplest form of CAI and is well-suited for subjects such as spelling, vocabulary, arithmetic, foreign languages, and other similar subjects. Here is a sample from a Spanish program where the student must provide a Spanish translation (C: is the computer; S: is the student; letters that require an accent or tilde are underlined, and incorrect responses are indicated by hyphens).

C: I'M NOT GOING WITH MY MAMA THIS TIME.

S: NO VOY CON MI MAMA ESTA VEZ.

C: ¡BRAVISIMO!
   I GO TWO TIMES EVERY WEEK.

S: VOY DOS TIEMPOS CADA SEMANA.

C: VOY DOS ------- CADA SEMANA.

S: VOY DOS VECES CADA SEMANA.

C: ¡ESO ES!
   DO YOU ALWAYS ARRIVE ON TIME?

S: STOP

C: OK SUE. WE'LL STOP HERE FOR NOW.
   DO YOU WANT TO SEE YOUR SCORE?

```
S:  SI.

C:  LESSON                6
    TIME                  4
    PROBLEMS TRIED        12
    ANSWERED CORRECTLY    10
    PERCENTAGE            83
```

Tutorial With this type of program new material is usually presented (text, pictures, diagrams) and then the student is questioned. Often this mode incorporates techniques that allow the program to vary the order of the questions, skip material, or give easier or more difficult material, depending on previous answers. For example, if one student correctly answered the first three questions, the fourth question presented actually might be the eighth question in terms of difficulty. That is, the computer will continually adjust the difficulty of the questions and material to match the level of the student. In this way it is quite possible that no two students ever receive exactly the same set of questions during their tutorial sessions. And, most important, students should become neither bored nor frustrated because the material is too easy or too difficult.

Problem Solving This method allows the student to use the computer as a powerful "calculator" to assist in the solution of complex problems that could not be attempted otherwise. For instance, in chemistry or physics classes, data collected from a student's experiment can be entered into the computer and the computer will perform numerous calculations and inform the student whether or not the data submitted falls within the accepted norms for that particular experiment. Or, in accounting classes, the computer can perform all the necessary accounting procedures for a balance sheet as long as the student has supplied the correct debits and credits. The important feature of problem-solving CAI is that the student must understand the necessary formulas and supply the right input in order for the program to work. Sometimes, in solving very difficult problems, the student may be able to request hints or assistance in setting up the correct solution. Usually this means that points will be subtracted from the total score, depending on how much assistance is given. Although a newly designed problem-solving program may not be able to assist all types of difficulties, it should be able to keep track of requests that cannot be processed so that the author can revise the program to handle the most frequent requests that are not presently incorporated in the program. This feedback is extremely important for all types of CAI programs.

Simulation This is perhaps one of the greatest features of CAI: using the computer's ability to represent complex systems (see Chapter 12) to teach, often in the form of a game in which the student can participate. Physical systems, such as pollution, electronic circuitry, chemical interactions, and planetary movement—or social systems, like an economy, an election, or consumer buying patterns—can be simulated on a computer. CAI simulation programs allow the student to observe a system under varying conditions and to ask hypothetical questions of the form: "If this were to occur, how would the system be affected?" For example, in studying population growth, a student could ask what the effects would be if the ratio of males to females was 3 to 1, or if the life expectancy (of males/females) was increased by 10 years, or if the infant mortality rate was to increase/decrease by 10 percent, and other such questions. Simulation also allows students to work with systems that would be too expensive (gold) or too dangerous (radioactive material) to study in a classroom laboratory. Also, the system under investigation can be examined at different time or size scales to facilitate understanding of activities that would occur too fast/slow (such as a bullet penetrating a sheet of glass) or be too large/small (like a critical chemical reaction that takes place at the atomic level) (see Fig. 5.3).

Some of the most sophisticated CAI simulation programs are used in graduate schools to provide students with real-life decision-making situations of the type they will find in their area of specialization, such as in business, medicine, economics, law, and finance. Also, private firms and the military make extensive use of simulation to teach flying or the operation of other sophisticated types of equipment. Most colleges that offer business courses use some type of management simulation

Figure 5-3 A CalComp 4000 digitizer is used at Cornell University in its computer aided design instruction facility (Courtesy of California Computer Products, Inc.)

games, usually played by teams of students, to give students opportunities to manage businesses and observe the effects of their decisions on the production and profits of each organization being simulated. There is even a popular simulation game, called Hamurabi, that can be used by almost any age group to simulate the running of an ancient country. In this game you must make crucial decisions about land use, crop production, and food distribution. Some of the problems that are encountered are overpopulation, starvation, and impeachment (if too many people starve!). If you are not impeached, you run the country for a ten-year period and your results are compared with other leaders, such as Jefferson or Nero, depending on how well you did. The variety of CAI simulation courseware now in use is quite extensive; here are just a few examples: the theory of relativity, nuclear reactions, operation of the human heart, historical military battles, growing crops and forests, and managing an oil refinery.

Dialogue This is the most sophisticated form of CAI, in which the student can actually enter into a Socratic type of dialogue with the computer in order to ask questions, test ideas, obtain clarification, request additional data, and perform calculations before submitting a final answer. This form of CAI can actually incorporate all of the six different types of CAI. Since the computer must be capable of answering specific questions, the range of topics is usually limited to a very specific field, sometimes called a microworld. A microworld is a detailed database containing limited information about a particular topic or system, such as the human heart, the design of microelectronic circuits, or the economy of a particular city/state. Usually the dialogue program poses a problem (such as determining the best production schedule for a large business) and the student and computer "discuss" the problem, asking each other questions (with the computer supplying data about the business when requested). When the student believes enough information has been obtained, a solution is proposed. The computer tests the solution, showing the results of the student's decisions, and suggests other questions that should have been asked in order to improve the proposed solution. Although there are not many dialogue programs available (mainly because of the expense of development and the large amount of computer memory required), a great amount of knowledge about human decision making is gained through the development and use of these programs.

Large Database Learning in this mode enables the student to explore a large amount of information, much like browsing through a library. However, rather than using a card catalogue and looking through the shelves for the material, all searching can be done from a terminal. Usually this type of CAI would begin by the student requesting a directory (often called a "menu") of available subjects. From this menu a subject can be chosen and the topics available within this subject are then displayed. Because most data banks use online, random access storage, information is not stored sequentially or alphabetically. Consequently, it can be retrieved in different ways. If we had a database with articles on computers stored in it, we might wish to obtain a listing of articles on a specific topic. Rather than just an alphabetic index, many data banks use what is called a **key-word in context** (KWIC) indexing method. This means that when items are entered there are certain **keywords** or *descriptors* that are associated with the item that indicate important aspects of the material stored. For instance, author, date of publication, source of publication, and important topics or other individuals referred to in the article are typical keywords. So, if we want to obtain articles dealing with a specific topic, but we do not know any authors or titles, we might type in: COMPUTERS, EDUCATION, PRIVACY, 1978-1982. We would then receive a listing of the titles of articles to which all four of the above descriptors applied. If the keywords were too general, the computer might respond that there were over 200 entries and that we should perhaps add one or two more descriptors; or, if too specific, the computer might suggest that we drop two or three keywords if no items were found. A major factor in the success of any indexing system is the skill with which the original data is indexed and, equally important, the absence of errors (integrity) in the data itself.

In a fully developed large database CAI system, not only would bibliography information be retrieved, but the actual articles could be displayed on a screen or copied onto a paper printer. A real advantage of large database systems is that the information can be shared with many users over large geographic areas or networks, thus eliminating the high cost of duplicating this information in many different computer systems. This concept, sometimes called an electronic library, is discussed next.

Two Recent Approaches to CAI

The above discussion characterizes the growth of CAI during the last two decades. However, there are two fairly recent developments that will no doubt play a very important role in influencing the acceptance and direction of CAI during the next decade. Much progress has already been made in these two areas, so it is not premature to consider their impact on education.

Electronic Libraries and Networks   Many colleges and universities have already implemented electronic libraries that use the data bank and indexing techniques discussed above. These libraries are presently being used primarily for research and scholarly work, but already the public is gaining access to some of these networks via telephone lines and home/business terminals for personal use.

> *Future libraries will store many books, papers, and journal articles electronically. Users will browse by means of a screen and a telecommunications link. Many users could have access to the same book at the same time, and they could have pages printed if they wished. There will be no card catalog. Instead, the computer will maintain indexes that will permit rapid searching for items, using the terminal screens. Such libraries will contain any matter that today appears in print and much that does not.*   (Martin, 1978)

Though there are many legal and economic matters that will first have to be resolved before such techniques can be used, the United States government is already beginning to formulate policies that will be able to meet these new advances. In the meantime, there are numerous electronic libraries already in use and new ones being developed. Here are a few examples of those that are operational:

- Lockheed Corporation's "Dialog" containing technical, educational, psychological, business, and other bibliographic abstacts.

- *The New York Times* data bank, containing over 25 million articles.

- SDC Search Service, one of the largest bibliographic distributors, offering over 50 different data banks in: Agriculture, Business, Education, Energy, Engineering, Government, Industry, Science, Social Science, and numerous other fields.

- MEDLINE, a computerized medical and biological science data bank operated by the University of California, Irvine.

- The Dow Jones News/Retrieval data bank containing information on over 6,000 companies and financial news.

- A legal data bank with all of the statutes of the 50 states, the United States Code, and 14 volumes of United States Supreme Court decisions.

- SOLINET (SOutheastern LIbrary NETwork), an automated cataloging and bibliographic public library service.

- The city of Cambridge, Massachusetts, and the Massachusetts Institute of Technology (MIT) project that is being developed through a government grant to provide a community information service through libraries. The system would permit people to query the computer and obtain library information and also tutor people in basic reading and writing skills.

Also, Control Data Education Company, a subsidiary of the Control Data computer manufacturer, has made available through a nationwide network the PLATO computer-assisted instruction programs that were developed at the University of Illinois. These programs have had extensive testing in public school systems since 1960 and are now being distributed through private learning centers or in-the-home/in-the-office terminals. Some of the outstanding features of this system are its extensive use of graphics for presenting complex pictures to illustrate textual material. Also, much of this software is now available at nominal cost for personal computers.

Finally, some of the latest electronic libraries/networks have been designed specifically for the personal computer. The first two personal computing networks to enter this new field are The Source (operated by Telecomputing Corporation of America) and MicroNet (operated by CompuServe). These two networks provide services similar to the networks discussed above, and also allow users to send messages (electronic mail) to other users of the system. The advent of these networks also indicates the important role that personal computers will have in education.

Personal Computers The microcomputer or personal computer has already begun a new revolution in computing, and the effects are being felt both in homes and in schools. In fact, the personal computer and computer networks have made it economically feasible for low-cost CAI to take place either in school or in the home. Manufacturers of personal computer hardware and software have designed their products specifically to provide effective CAI capabilities. That is, in addition to CRT screens, many personal computers can easily handle sound, color graphics, and a wide variety of input/output devices—all of which significantly enhance the learning process. To give you an idea of how these systems might operate in the future, a brief description of a very sophisticated system follows.

> *Imagine having your own self-contained knowledge manipulator in a portable package the size and shape of an ordinary notebook. Suppose it had enough power to outrace your senses of sight and hearing, enough capacity to store for later retrieval thousands of page-equivalents of reference materials, poems, letters, recipes, records, drawings, animations, musical scores, waveforms, dynamic simulations, and anything else you would like to remember and change.*
>
> *(Kay and Goldberg, 1977)*

Science fiction? No. Except for the size, this capability exists right now. The Learning Research Group of the Xerox Palo Alto Research Center has been working since 1972 toward a notebook-sized computer called DYNABOOK, designed not only for educational use, but for anyone interested in exploring dynamic communications with a personal computer (see Fig. 5.4). Although early interim models were quite large and costly to build, in the 1980s DYNABOOK should have a cost low enough so that practically anyone may own one. In addition to the capabilities mentioned in the preceding quotation, DYNABOOK uses a high-resolution graphics screen that can be "mapped" into several sections or "windows," allowing multiple views of information. For example, while one window is displaying a story, another window could be presenting animated illustrations to accompany it, and in other windows the user/learner could be entering questions, drawings, or even viewing a foreign language translation—thus allowing many different simultaneous perspectives on a single activity. As new breakthroughs are made in microprocessor technology, the necessary hardware components for this "visionary" computer will soon be available. Already the software, called Smalltalk, allows anyone, from child to adult, from novice to expert, to communicate easily with the computer to accomplish interesting and exciting projects.

Impact on Education One of the main intentions of an educational tool like DYNABOOK, or some similar self-contained microcomputer, is that it be used as a **reactive system**. That is, the system should be highly responsive to the needs and requests of the user/learner and should make full use of its computing power by en-

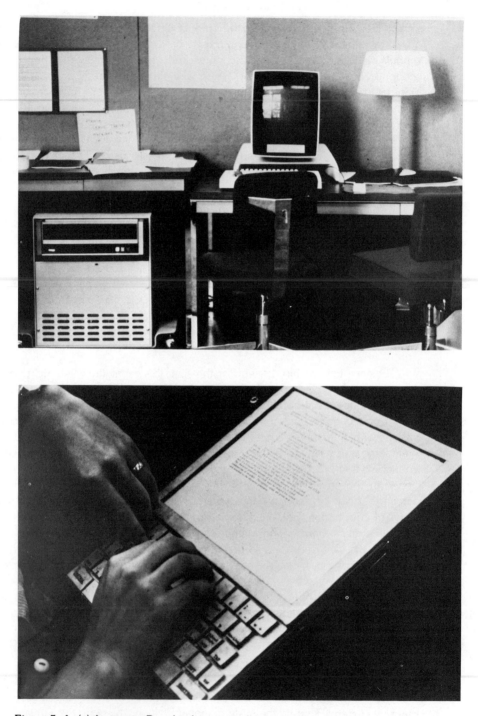

Figure 5-4 (a) An interim Dynabook system (b) A mock-up of a future Dynabook. (Courtesy of Xerox Corporation)

gaging in many activities simultaneously, all designed to supplement and complement the learning process. The possibility of expanding our mental capabilities by having access to such a resource is a very exciting prospect. However, there are some unanswered and difficult questions that should be investigated regarding the use of any computer in an educational environment. First, very little is known about the long-term (or even short-term) effects of learning from such sophisticated devices. Also, it could be that there would be significantly less social interaction among children, which could affect many aspects of their lives at a later date, if a large amount of time was spent with these devices. And there is the problem of cost; if only wealthy families have access to this technology, there could be educational disadvantages to children who could not afford to have these tools. Finally, what would be the "new" role of the presently little understood role of schools, educators, and parents if a large amount of education took place with computers? These are some of the challenging questions that must be explored further as we embark upon this remarkable journey.

SOCIAL IMPLICATIONS

The questions at the end of the section above pertain not only to personal computers, but to the use of any type of computer for education. In this section we consider some of the typical pro and con issues that surround CAI. The disparity of views regarding CAI is captured in this quotation:

> *Optimists see computers-on-chips making it possible through mass education for most students to achieve broad competence actively and in a developmentally appropriate manner. Inquiry, problem-solving skills, and representation will be integrated with concrete experiences via the computer.*

versus

> *Perhaps a unified information/education/communications network is merely the final step toward a nightmare world of thought control. At the very least, pessimists suggest, computers will do for thinking what the automobile did for walking and television did for reading.* (Banet, 1978)

Both of these views, from the same source, represent extremes, yet they do express the mixed reactions and attitudes toward computers in education.

Pro Arguments

One major reason why educators have supported CAI is that it is student-centered. Traditionally most classroom instruction is teacher-oriented, and is not directed at the speed/skill of individual students—but some students become bored and restless when instruction is too slow while others miss some points and feel frustrated if it is too fast. CAI proceeds at each student's own pace. Also, CAI is infinitely patient; the machine does not become upset or disappointed when students make mistakes. Unlike textbooks which are usually revised every three to five years, CAI programs can easily be updated regularly to incorporate the latest material and improve the method of presentation. For the handicapped, CAI allows several modes of presentation: audio for the blind, visual for the deaf, and special control feautres for other disabilities. And these multisensory features have been shown to improve learning for nonhandicapped students, too. Finally, principles of reinforcement, immediate feedback, and precise diagnosis of errors are easily implemented with CAI, but are difficult to accomplish in a class of 30 students using the traditional lecture method and only one instructor.

Con Arguments

Perhaps the most significant objection to CAI is that very little is known about the long-term effects of students learning from a computer. Although impressive results with reading, math, and spelling scores have been demonstrated in short-term studies, there are still many unanswered questions about performance and learning over a long period: Will students become lazy or unimaginative? Also, cost is still a limiting factor, especially for smaller school districts that do not already have adequate computer facilities. And when a system goes down, so does all CAI. (An advantage of using microcomputers for CAI is that, if one micro fails, other micros are not affected.) Furthermore, although there is an abundance of coursewave available, selection is very difficult and tailoring existing programs to meet specific needs can be expensive and time-consuming. Finally, because very few instructors have an adequate background in computers, there are still many myths and communication barriers when a school begins to consider installing CAI.

HARDWARE

The most dramatic impact on CAI, as in other areas of computer application, comes from the microprocessor. In fact, it is estimated that by 1983 or 1984 there will be a thousand times more personal computers in higher education that there are time-sharing terminals! However, it is not even necessary to have a personal computer in order to reap the educational benefits of the microprocessor. Already there are numerous electronic/intelligent games that perform some of the basic CAI functions. For example, there are inexpensive games (less than $30) that provide drill and practice in arithmetic and spelling, plus numerous recreational games that help develop a child's eye-hand coordination and problem-solving skills. Also, many of the video games use microprocessors that can present simple teaching programs on a TV screen.

A typical small educational system would consist of a microcomputer using a CRT screen for display and several manufacturer-supplied CAI programs along with programs developed by either the teacher or students. Some personal computers already have course-author-language software available (such as PILOT) so the instructor can easily create his or her own courseware. For a small additional cost, color graphics, audio output, and a printer could be added. (In fact, it is now possible even to integrate a video disk/tape capability for less than $1,000.) Such systems would probably cost from $1,000 to $3,000. And for an additional $4,000 to $20,000 it might be possible to have a microcomputer network that could support from eight to 64 (or more) microcomputers.

A medium-size system would use a large minicomputer or small to medium mainframe computer. There would be 12 to 48 time-sharing terminals, along with a high-speed line printer and a few hard-copy or graphics terminals, and maybe a plotter. This system would probably be dedicated to instructional use, although larger systems in this category could support both administrative and instructional requirements (see Fig. 5.5).

A large CAI system would use a large to maxi-size computer and would probably be capable of supplying its resources to several locations via a network. It would support 32 to more than 1,000 terminals and, in addition to the types of input/output equipment used in a medium system, it could utilize sophisticated devices such as microfiche, color slides, video tape, and laboratory data collection and analysis equipment. Systems this size would cost $100,000 to $4,000,000.

Figure 5-5 A typical medium-sized educational system (Courtesy of International Business Machines Corporation)

A LOOK TOWARD THE FUTURE

Although much enthusiasm is generated by low-cost personal computers delivering CAI, we detect a slower, more cautious growth of CAI in the future—particularly because there are now so many options and systems to choose from. More studies will probably be conducted on long-term effects of CAI; also, teachers will make more decisions regarding the adoption and use of CAI. Part of the growth will come from more users, the exchange of educational courseware, and a gradual acceptance of the computer as a valuable teaching resource if properly understood and used.

In terms of specific uses, we foresee more sophisticated administrative uses of the computer, especially for planning, records management, and word processing. Also, personal computers will most likely be used for specialized, dedicated tasks in CAI and the laboratory. Reactive systems, such as DYNABOOK, that are faster and more flexible will gradually replace slower, general-purpose systems. And on a larger scale, computers will play a crucial role in integrating all of a community's educational resources—schools, libraries, television, museums, and theaters can be interconnected and delivered not only to schools, but to businesses and homes. This type of integration and coordination will truly bring about life-long learning for all age groups in all environments.

Finally, there must be a gradual shift in the attitudes toward computers—from apprehension and fear toward understanding and acceptance—if CAI is to be widely used. One computer attitudes survey indicated that educators were less enthusiastic about the role of computers in society than were the general public. And administrators in education were far more enthusiastic about CAI than were teachers. Perhaps a more positive atittude toward computers in education will evolve as computer literacy becomes more common and more computer science curricula are developed to meet the needs of educators.

STUDY AND REVIEW

1. Describe three ways in which computers can be used in academic environments (other than for instruction).

2. Briefly explain four different types of computer-assisted instruction. What do you believe to be the strengths or weaknesses of each method?

3. What is DYNABOOK? What do you think would be the long term effects if a large amount of education were to be conducted via a DYNABOOK type of computer?

4. Briefly discuss three or four different types of electronic libraries and educational networks. Do you think that traditional books and libraries will ever become obsolete?

5. What are the major advantages and disadvantages of using computer-assisted instruction? What is your position regarding the use of computers in education?

6. Do you think personal computers will significantly change the ways in which children and adults learn? If so, in what ways?

6

ARTS, HUMANITIES, AND THE SOCIAL SCIENCES

PERSPECTIVE

The following quotation by artist Harold Cohen illustrates three very important points about the use of computers in the arts, humanities, and social sciences.

> *The computer is not only appropriate to the kind of investigations I want to do, it is also the first device capable of making a positive difference in the way people use their heads . . . The computer can demand that you function creatively—which is not to say that it gets used that way very often.*   *(Cohen, 1978)*

First, these disciplines are traditionally concerned with exploring the human mind, both artistically and scientifically. Second, creativity is a significant aspect of the human mind, but is little understood yet constantly pursued. Perhaps, as Cohen suggests, the computer will not only permit humans to use their minds more fully, but *demand* that they use it creatively. Finally, the quotation indicates that computers do not seem to be frequently used in ways that encourage users to be creative.

There are several reasons why computers have not been used extensively for creative purposes. Computer equipment was very expensive, and programming languages were complex and difficult to use. But, more important, there are indications that computers will be used more creatively in the future—mainly due to drastic reductions in hardware costs, easier programming languages, and the microprocessor. Also, with a larger, more diverse group of users in the social sciences, there will be more research into the crucial role of humans in computer systems and better understanding of the computer's impact on society. As computers become "friendlier" and more accessible, the social sciences will expand their research in the quantitative aspects of human problems and the humanities will, with the aid of computers, pursue questions about the qualitative dimensions of life.

We now examine some current uses of computers in each of these areas.

COMPUTERS IN THE ARTS

The main thrust of computers in the arts has occurred only during the last decade, though many pioneering efforts can be traced back to the late 1950s. There are now numerous fields within the arts that use the computer for both practical and creative purposes. For instance, several large museums in the United States use computers to assist researchers in locating particular pieces of art or other items that are held by other museums. By establishing a computer database for the thousands of articles museums hold, the exchange and retrieval of important information is greatly facilitated. To insure uniformity between different databases, national coordinating committees have been established in the United States, England, and Europe to assist in the development of museum data banks. After museums begin using computers for cataloging and inventory control, they can also use the computer for other purposes. For instance, the Lawrence Hall of Science in Berkeley, California, and the Children's Museum in Boston allow the public to use their computers so they can learn through direct experience what computers are capable of doing.

We now briefly look at how computers are being used in three areas of the arts.

The Visual Arts

The computer is now a close partner of the artist in both the applied and in the fine arts. In the applied arts, the computer is used extensively in architecture and structural design. It is estimated that about 99 percent of design time is spent making calculations and changes to original plans with only 1 percent of the time being spent creatively. With the aid of the computer this ratio can almost be reversed. By entering the original design into the computer, the computer can assist in every stage of development (from rough draft to the finished blueprints) by correcting lines that are not geometrically correct, presenting any perspective or size scale, and testing for structural strength and cost of materials. This use of the computer is called computer-assisted design (CAD) and is discussed further in Chapter 9. However, we now focus on a few of the applications of computers in the visual arts (see Fig. 6.1).

Pictures   Artists use the computer in several ways to produce graphic art. One way is to use special analog-to-digital (A/D) hardware that converts an ordinary picture or photograph into a computer-compatible digitized form that can be stored in the computer and later printed out on paper so it resembles the original (such as the

Figure 6-1 A 3250 graphics display system for CAD. (Courtesy of International Business Machines Corporation)

"computer pictures" sold at fairs and shopping centers). A more interesting version of this technique is when the stored picture is altered and modified by a computer program that was written by an artist, often producing very dramatic and creative effects. Another approach is to produce elaborate graphic representations of mathematical formulas, resulting in complex geometric forms and shapes that can be printed on a plotter or displayed on a graphics screen. By using a light pen on a special graphics screen or a special graphics sketch pad, an artist can draw pictures and put them into computer storage and later perform permutations, repetitions, and other variations upon the original drawing with the aid of the computer. Finally, one of the more sophisticated forms of computer art is when the artist attempts to express his or her ideas via a computer program. This approach is extremely challenging, for it requires that one's ideas be clearly stated and formulated in a rather limited programming language. In this mode the artist does not store pictures that are merely reproduced by a printer or plotter, but instructs the computer to produce art that conforms to the rules the artist has specified—rules that attempt to capture and express the human artist's style. One artist who has been quite successful in creating this type of art, insists that the audience see the pictures actually being drawn (by a small electronic "turtle" on a large canvas) so they will know it was not done by a human! As the artist commented after seeing one of his drawings being "created" in front of him:

> *I am fascinated. I can't carry on an intelligent conversation. I just look. When I watch the machine drawing, I recognize that it is exercising a very special kind of grip: both on me and on anyone else in the room . . . it seems to me that one of the things human beings find interesting about drawings in general is that they are made by other human beings, and here you are watching the image develop as if it is being developed by another human being.*   *(Cohen, 1978)*

Animation

Perhaps the most familiar forms of computer art are the computer-animated television commercials and computer-animated motion pictures, such as *Star Wars* and *Lord of the Rings.* This is the fastest growing area for the use of computers by artists. Although relatively sophisticated animation can be done on small microcomputers, in order to produce movie and television quality animation a larger, more expensive computer is required. Computers are ideally suited for animation because of the great amount of labor required to produce animated films. Conventional animation uses artists to handpaint each frame on plastic sheets called cels. One minute of film time requires about 1,440 cels. Although much skill and time are required to produce computer animation, after shapes, figures, and characters have been defined and stored in memory, they can be recalled, changed in size, color, perspective, and other forms of visual presentation with simple commands. Many animated films are being made on video tape; in fact, there are even some inexpensive home systems that permit personal computers to produce video tape material. However, one of the most sophisticated uses of computers in animation is by Dolphin Productions, which uses a large, interactive, real-time system that can produce either 35mm film or video tape. With full color and the capability of overlaying the graphics on other video channels (including live video broadcasts), Dolphin Productions and other companies that use similar equipment can produce incredible effects that are not possible with conventional methods— and at a lower price and shorter development time (sometime just two or three days for a television commercial)! Perhaps the most exciting fact about this type of animation is that it permits the artist to explore ideas and special effects that could never be done before. And some of the techniques that are unique to computer animation have already shown great promise in the area of visual communication, especially for educational purposes. The impact of computer animation has been so great that there are not enough studios with the necessary equipment to meet the demands for all the businesses that want their names and logos flashing and pulsating across TV screens. This is, no doubt, fast becoming one of the more popular art forms of the 1980s (see Fig. 6.2).

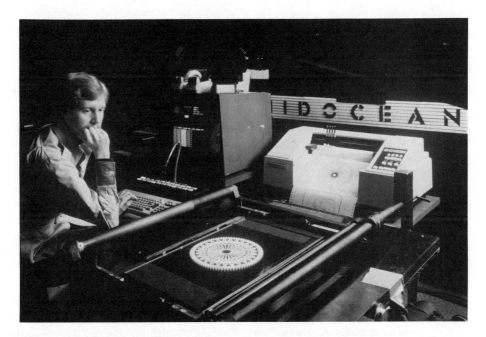

Figure 6-2 A CalComp 10/2 drum plotter is used at Mid-Ocean Motion Pictures to produce animation for television commercials (Courtesy of California Computer Products, Inc.)

Music

The two principal areas in which computers are involved with music are: the production/playing of music and the reproduction/recording of music.

Recording For several years computers and analog-to-digital devices have been used in recording studios to assist in the mixing and recording of sound. However, only recently have high-quality digital recorded disks been available in large quantities for the general public. Technically speaking, the current "digital" records are not truly digital. That is, although a sophisticated computer process is used to filter out noise and increase clarity and frequency range, the end product is still an analog record that can be played on conventional turntables. This is not to say that there is not a significant improvement over regular recordings, for these disks are extremely high in quality, and most audiophiles believe they are well worth the price (about double that of standard records). However, even more dramatic reproduction of sound will occur when completely digital systems are used for both recording and playback. When music is recorded directly on disks in a digital form and played over sophisticated digital/computer equipment, essentially all distortion, hiss, pops, and other background noise will be eliminated. This will be accomplished by the fact that no actual musical sound is recorded on the record, only a digital on/off code that would sound very much like morse code if it were played on a conventional record player. When this record is played through a microprocessor, however, the code is decoded (without any background noise since it is all "subtracted-out" during recording and the decoding playback) and then converted into a distortion-free analog output that goes directly into the speakers. Some of these systems are already operational, but the prices are too high to be commercially produced on a large scale.

Another feature of an all digital system is that it can also alter the original while it is temporarily stored in memory, and produce an infinite variety of different versions with minor or major changes in pitch, tone, tempo, and so forth. That is, the computer can essentially allow you to rewrite music by altering the ways in which the original music is stored and retrieved. This is very similar to the computer art discussed above in which the picture that is originally entered into the computer is modified in order to produce some creative and unusual effects. Not only will you be able to hear music reproduced exactly as it sounded in the studio or concert hall, but part of the computer's program will also allow you to modify the original to duplicate the acoustics of any of the famous concert halls around the world!

Producing Sound Electronic music synthesizers have been in use for over a decade, but it has been only in the last few years that microprocessor technology has been used to enhance these musical instruments. One of the most sophisticated synthesizers is the Synclavier, used by several European rock groups and a few American jazz artists. It is capable of reproducing a full orchestra along with a full range of special audio effects, such as reverberation, sustaining notes indefinitely, and repeating notes or melodies. Although professional versions of this system range in price from $6,000 to $15,000, the personal computer revolution has introduced special A/D hardware and software that can produce fairly elaborate sound for just a few hundred dollars more than the price of the microcomputer.

Basically, two types of systems are available: A hardware-driven system very similar to a synthesizer usually employs some sort of a keyboard for input, and uses the computer to control signals to oscillators, and filters which produce the sounds that are then amplified through a speaker (see Fig. 6.3).

Generally, the hardware synthesizer system is less expensive though less flexible than the software type, the reason being that the hardware system requires little storage capacity in order to control the sound-producing devices. The software synthesizer system makes extensive use of computer memory (both RAM—random access memory—and disk) which is relatively expensive. In order to produce one second of music from software input, the computer must calculate from 8,000 to 40,000 numbers to produce the waveform needed to make music. Since many microcomputers do not calculate this fast, the original numbers must first be obtained at a slow speed, stored on disk, and then played back from disk at real time. Despite the cost disadvantage, however, the software systems show greater promise for creativity and new music forms because under the control of a software program there are many more possibilities available to the musician to explore. Besides allowing new musical ideas to be developed, the software approach also

Figure 6-3 A music composition system for a microcomputer
(Courtesy of ALF Products, Denver, CO

allows music to be composed by using standard musical notation and then played back by computer. In this way, a composer can have immediate feedback on what a new composition will sound like when played by a single instrument or by an entire orchestra. This has been found to be a particular fruitful approach, especially for aspiring music students/composers who would not ordinarily hear their pieces played by a large group of musicians. Furthemore, time-consuming rearrangements can be added quickly and tested without requiring that the entire orchestra be present—all the "rough edges" can be removed before the first real rehearsal. Finally, just as a computer can be programmed to produce an artist's style, it can also be programmed to produce music (either randomly or with fixed rules). Some composers who have created computer-assisted compositions are John Cage, James Tenney, J. K. Randall, and Gerald Strang.

Theater

The entertainment field in general and theatre in particular is being increasingly impacted by the computer. The state of the art is rapidly approaching the point where a theatre professional can no longer say, "I cannot afford to get into the computer world," but instead must say, "I cannot afford not to."

(Sealey, 1980)

Computers have been used by theaters for many years to print tickets, book reservations, and to perform other front office functions. With the advent of the microprocessor, this limited role is rapidly changing. Now computers have entered into set design, lighting, sound engineering, and even choreography. By using microcomputers (or even pocket calculators), complicated scenes involving perspective, depth, and critical lighting can be calculated quickly and accurately, which results in greater realism at lower cost than trial-and-error methods. Again, because of the computer's great speed, new lighting and special sound effects can be accomplished. For example, by using short programs that control the stagelights or amplifiers, the lighting or sound coordinator can merely tap a few keys on a terminal and quickly execute a complex series of adjustments and special effects without further lifting a finger. This type of assistance is greatly appreciated by people involved with theater design and production because the complicated technical details no longer limit a director's imagination and creativity. Special effects, such as the same voice being projected from different parts of the stage with machinegun speed, or bolts of lightning alternating with brilliant rainbow colors, are now possible, but less expensive and more realistic than previous methods. Even if a theater does not have elaborate equipment, a small microcomputer can usually control all the necessary components for large-scale productions. And, although only a few theater companies are making extensive use of computers at present, almost all the new lighting and sound control systems make use of microprocessor technology for fast and convenient switching and level adjustments. With the computer being able to handle the time-consuming, repetitious, technical aspects of theater production, designers and directors can use their time more creatively to improve and expand artistic expression.

One of the unusual uses of the computer in the theater is for the design, testing, and writing of choreography. Because there is a special system of notation for dance, just as there is for music, computer programs have been designed to assist choreographers in the time-consuming task of writing dance compositions and sequences. Not only does the computer quickly convert the notation into a printed form, but it also can make corrections if there are errors of judgment or oversights that violate rules regarding timing, spacing, or visual appearance. Also, since the notation is stored in computer memory, it can quickly be recalled, altered, and tested without actual rehearsals every time a modification is made. This approach is affording the same freedom to dance composition as to music composition discussed above. It seems as though the prediction made in the quotation at the beginning of this subsection is fast becoming a reality.

COMPUTERS IN THE HUMANITIES

As mentioned in Chapter 5, computers are being used to teach subjects such as English, foreign languages, spelling, and reading—all of which are in the area of the humanities. Writers in the humanities are finding that the ease, flexibility, and low cost of word processors/text editors make such personal computers welcome assets at all stages of manuscript development. By freeing the writer of technical concerns about editing, spacing, error correction, hyphenation and other time-consuming tasks, the writer can use the available time more creatively and more productively.

In archeology, computers are becoming valuable tools for conducting research into ancient civilizations. Archeologists use the computer to store detailed information about their findings in the field and, through the use of statistics and sophisticated simulation programs, can reconstruct buildings, street plans, or smaller artifacts based on predictions from incomplete data. This archeological information can also be useful to museum data banks (discussed earlier in this chapter) and researchers in the social sciences, such as anthroplogists and sociologists. These examples indicate the diverse use of computers in the humanities.

We now look at three applications that focus on language, the cornerstone of the humanities (see Figure 6-4).

Figure 6-4   A typical word processing system (Courtesy of International Business Machines Corporation)

Literary Analysis

There are two major ways in which computers can assist researchers in this area: By assisting in the identification of authorship, and by the evaluation of writing style. Both methods employ a technique called stylistics—the tabulation and statistical summary of features such as vowel and consonant frequency, commonly used phrases, length of sentences and paragraphs, and similar measures of a writer's style. Although this technique has been used for centuries, the computer allows this to be done with much greater speed, a larger amount of data, and with more accuracy than with manual methods. In the case of identifying the author of a particular piece of writing, a stylistic profile is made of possible authors and then the unidentified work is analyzed to determine if one of the known authors could have written it. This method has been successful in identifying likely writers of certain parts of the Old and New Testaments, the authors of some of the *Federalist Papers* that were published anonymously, and numerous other highly contested manuscripts.

Not only can stylistics assist in resolving disputes about authorship, it can provide a very powerful tool for analyzing a writer's style. This can be useful in at least two ways: First, by having a very accurate profile of a particular writer, computer analysis can help determine when a particular piece of writing, or even part of a work, was written. For example, this method indicated with a very high degree of probability that Ernest Hemmingway's *The Old Man and the Sea* was written in about 1936, not in the early 1950s when it was published. Besides helping to determine the chronological order of an author's writing, the analysis of style can help improve a writer's style by giving an accurate summary of word length, average number of syllables per word, and other important indicators that most writers are unaware of. This method has been of great use to authors in tailoring their writing to special audiences, such as technical/scientific, lay people, government reports, and so forth. By being able to monitor your own writing style with precision, improvements and changes that enhance readability and understanding can be implemented and tested for effectiveness.

Concordances

Another valuable research tool for those engaged in literary analysis are concordances—detailed alphabetical listings of important terms and concepts with page references to where the terms are used in a particular writing or group of writings. Concordances have been compiled manually for centuries; now, the computer permits larger, more complete concordances to be prepared at lower cost and in less time. Currently several concordance-generating programs have been designed to make this tedious task a little more manageable, but even with the assistance of a computer for indexing, cross-referencing, and other bookkeeping chores much human effort still remains. One method of reducing some of the manual labor required to enter all such data is to use optical scanning methods to input the material together with special programs to extract the key terms once data are in computer-usable form. Even this technique presents many challenges, because such programs and equipment must be specially designed, tested, and debugged. And, more than likely, the material to be searched must be retyped, using special type fonts that can be read by optical scanners.

Despite these obstacles, numerous concordances have been prepared with computers. Some of the major existing concordances are: Classical Latin and Greek prepared at Dartmouth, 17th and 18th century English developed at Cleveland State University, plus numerous others for classical, biblical, and modern literature. In fact, an elaborate concordance was prepared from the Watergate tapes and transcripts by a researcher at Cornell University. Concordance preparation remains the major use of computers in literary research and, besides producing valuable indexes, it also provides a large database from which further, more detailed research can be made.

Linguistics

Scholars in the humanities have been fascinated and perplexed by language since the time of the early Greek philosophers 2,500 years ago. This curiosity has never been eliminated or even reduced. And now, with the aid of the computer, explorations into language, thought, and mind have opened even more questions for further investigation. Is language rule-governed or mainly intuitive? Are there rules for semantics (the meanings of words) just as there are rules for syntax (the grammar of sentences)? How do people understand language? Will computers ever be able to converse in a natural language, such as English? These are but a few of the questions currently being probed by researchers. Properly speaking, many of these questions go beyond the field of linguistics and involve other disciplines such as psycholody, philosophy, anthropology, computer science, and mathematics. Although we will examine the topic of computers understanding natural language in Chapter 14 (Artificial Intelligence), we now briefly look at some of the subjects of interest to researchers in the area of linguistics.

In order to better understand syntax and semantics, and their relation to each other, linguists use computers to model and test their ideas about how language operates. After the rules of a particular language have been stated in a formal manner, such as in a computer program, comparisons with other formal approaches or comparisons with the rules of another language can be more easily and quickly carried out. Although significant progress has been made in the area of syntax, there are still many problems with capturing the subtleties of semantics. One way in which linguistic theories are tested is by attempting to translate one phrase into another language. Early attempts at computer language translation, particularly English-Russian translations, seemed promising. However, further studies indicated severe limitations of such techniques, especially in dealing with ambiguous words and phrases, such as "the book is hard" or "vegetarians don't know how good meat tastes." Despite some difficulties, several language-translation programs do produce excellent translations—especially from English to Spanish. And, as long as the vocabulary is limited, the context defined clearly, and ambiguous terms eliminated or provided with alternate meanings (as with scientific or technical language), computer translations can be extremely fast and accurate.

Not only have there been attempts to interpret language with the computer, but there have been many attempts to produce both prose and poetry. Although no computer prose has won any awards (nor does it seem likely to do so in the near future), several computer-generated poems have received recognition and, in a few cases, have actually been accepted as human creations! The important aspect of these computer excursions into language is not an attempt to replace humans, but merely one new technique for trying to understand and more deeply appreciate the human mind and its remarkable abilities to communicate.

COMPUTERS IN THE SOCIAL SCIENCES

The use of the computer in the social sciences is another "nontraditional" area where computers are quickly gaining acceptance through many diverse applications. Although we focus primarily on its use in economics, history, and psychology, there are several other areas that we will first briefly mention. The field of geography makes use of the computer to evaluate land use and the distribution of our resources. By simulating previous policies and their effects, predictions can be made about the likely results of new policies and legislation. Closely connected to geography is the production of maps in the discipline called cartography. Conventional map-making techniques are extremely expensive and relatively slow. However, by using computer-stored information gathered from satellite photographs, aerial photography, and other sophisticated techniques, maps can be produced quickly, in varying sizes and scales, and with a variety of specialized information. In fact, it is now possible to generate a tailor-made map with specialized data, such as oil and mineral deposits, underground water supplies, and other such information, for only a small fraction of the cost of conventional methods. Anthropology researchers find the computer an excellent tool for doing detailed cross-cultural studies since it permits the storage of such large quantities of data and relatively fast and complex ways of comparing them. And, in the area of political science, one of the ways the computer is being used is to simulate complex political theories and how they affect international relations and domestic policy. These few diverse applications indicate the great benefit that can be obtained by using the computer to investigate social phenomena. We will now look at three areas in a little more depth.

Economics

Because a large portion of business decision making involves econonics, economists are responsible for the research that develops the sophisticated computer programs that are eventually used by business. By using large databases of specialized information in conjunction with computer simulation techniques, economists develop econometric models for decision making and forecasting. Some of the topics that are researched in this area are: how managers use information; market trends; the effects of automation; employment trends; the effects of different marketing techniques; and the effects of economic sanctions and incentives. Many of the economic models rely heavily on demographic information (population, incomes, employment levels, etc.); however, it would be too costly for each economist or group of economists to collect such data. Consequently, some universities, private research firms, and the state and federal governments collect data and then distribute them (usually on computer-readable magnetic tapes) for use by different organizations. For example, the Bureau of the Census supplies its data; Lockheed Corporation's network, called Dialog, offers online retrieval of population and economic data; and Control Data Corporation's Cybernet division, in conjunction with Economic Information Systems, Inc., provides online data about what part of the market a particular firm has in any of the major industrial, geographic, or business areas in the United States. With such a wealth of information the real challenge is to use it wisely—and this can be accomplished only by using computers.

Economic models are excellent to demonstrate basic behavior patterns within a certain market or part of the economy. They can show the likely effects of price increases/decreases, new advertising methods, labor shortages, and new taxation policies. However, their real drawback is that they are extremely vulnerable to unpredictable changes, such as stock market crashes, foreign and domestic embargoes, political upheavals, and natural disasters. But these are not insurmountable barriers; they just indicate the caution that must be exercised in using models for decision making. Their strengths lie in the ability to integrate vast quantities of information, weight the different variables in a variety of ways, and simulate hundreds or thousands of alternatives in search of the optimum solution.

History

Before reading any further, pause for a minute and write down some ways you believe computers are used by historians. Now you can compare your ideas with the examples that follow. One way in which historians use computers is to enter large amounts of pertinent data about important military battles and then simulate the effects of different strategies or resources upon the outcome of the battle. This type of historical game has become so popular that smaller commercial versions are already available for personal computers so you can play the role of Napoleon at Waterloo or the captain of the Bismarck during World War II.

Another use of computers by historians is to collect large amounts of background information (usually gleaned from public records, personal correspondence, and other documents) in order to investigate a particular question. Some studies conducted in this fashion included an extensive examination of the individuals who engineered the American Revolution (they were largely inexperienced businessmen with little legal background who simply didn't like the British directing their lives); a detailed project showing the social mobility of different ethnic and religious groups over long periods of time; and a comprehensive study that showed it was not young single men, but mainly young families who settled the West.

Psychology

> *The major goal of education is to develop the student's mind. As long as we do not know how the mind works, the process of education will be rather haphazard. Teaching methods are now developed on an experimental trial-and-error basis, rather than according to any formal principles. If we understand the mind better, we might be able to use that understanding to devise dramatically better educational techniques. Instead of studying animals in the hope that strong analogies to human mental behavior can be discovered, or studying humans with awkward experiments that can gather only indirect evidence about mental processes, some psychologists are studying computer models of human mental behavior.*
> (Raphael, 1976)

The area of psychology that studies mental processes such as perception, memory, language, and problem solving is called cognitive psychology. As indicated in the above quotation, it is difficult to study these cognitive processes. However, through the use of complex computer models and the simulation of mental processes, it is now possible to investigate these topics.

During the last two decades many psychologists have begun using concepts borrowed from computer science such as input, output, processing, storage, retrieval, and the like, along with computer simulation to describe, test, and evaluate hypotheses in cognitive psychology. This has resulted in a view called the information-processing theory that basically claims there are some very important similarities between the way people and computers process information. Although only a few researchers claim there are important similarities between computer hardware and human physiology, they are saying there are important similarities in the ways in which humans and computers solve problems, use strategies, and search large amounts of data. Even some of the initial criticisms of these comparisons—primarily those about computers being unemotional—have been overcome by developing programs that exhibit emotional behaviors such as paranoia, impatience, and discouragement. Still, there remain the same problems as in studies with animals; namely, just as there are important dissimilarities between humans and other species, so there are important dissimilarities between humans and computers. However, despite the differences, many significant experiments have been accomplished on the computer that could not have been done with people or animals. Perhaps even greater achievements will be made in psychology with the aid of the computer as a powerful analytic and experimental tool.

SOCIAL IMPLICATIONS

Although the use of the computer in the arts, humanities, and social sciences does not have as extensive an impact on our lives as does, say, the use of computers in banking or government, there are important aspects of such use that should be examined. Computers affect individuals and society in numerous ways, and it is primarily the work of researchers in the humanities and social sciences that reports this impact. And, just as society is affected by computers, so are the people who conduct this research. A major question these researchers are concerned with is: In what ways does the use of computers alter an individual's concept of self? That is, are computers enhancing or diminishing the value, creativity, and uniqueness of humans?

Pro Arguments

One important advantage of using computers in the arts, humanities, and social sciences is that researchers can better understand the computer's impact by using computers to collect, store, exchange, and analyze their data. There is no doubt that computers permit better, more sophisticated, and timely research. They also greatly facilitate the exchange of ideas and information among researchers. Social scientists are particularly pleased with the large data banks of pertinent economic and demographic information that provide a valuable resource for understanding our complex society and developing and testing new social policies. In the arts, the computer is now becoming an art form itself for the creation of art and music. In addition to assisting the artist and musician in expressing their ideas, the computer is also raising provocative questions about creativity. For example: Can computers be creative? Is computer-generated art, music, or poetry truly art? Some researchers, through the use of and exposure to computers, are thought to be developing a deeper understanding and appreciation of humans and that, contrary to one con argument, this understanding may lead to improvements in the quality of life.

Con Arguments

One of the more extreme views against the use of computers, particularly in the arts and humanities, is that computers are dehumanizing and contribute to human alienation. Another, more specific, complaint is that there is a basic psychological conflict between humans and technology, especially when the technology is as advanced and sophisticated as are computers. Many people in the arts and humanities have not been trained in science or computers and find computers puzzling, overwhelming, maybe even threatening. Also, it is claimed that computers contribute to a decline in human communication and communication skills because it is possible to conduct all or most of one's work on a computer with little or no human contact. Furthermore, by placing emphasis on statistics and other quantifiable aspects of life, there seems to be less concern with the qualitative dimensions of our existence. Closely related to this quantitative limitation is the argument that many people accept the computer printout as "gospel" because the computer is usually considered always correct or, at least, impossible to challenge. Finally, a technical, but very important, question has been raised regarding the effects (such as eye strain and radiation) of using CRT terminals. Because many people in the humanities, particularly writers and newspaper journalists, use this equipment to earn their living, they hope that this question will be resolved. Early indications are that people who use CRTs on a regular basis have a higher incidence of eye disorders and job related stress and boredom. In summary, there is a general mood that humans are becoming too dependent on computers and are not fully developing their own uniquely human skills.

HARDWARE

Although business, government, and other large users of computers did not have to wait for the microprocessor revolution in order to make extensive use of computers, the arts, humanities, and social sciences are definitely more receptive to computers now that there have been such drastic price reductions. Now, with even an inexpensive personal computer, artists and musicians can use the computer as a creative tool, and do not have to depend on expensive computer systems that were once available only at a few universities. For only a few thousand dollars (or less) a microcomputer system with floppy disk storage, an analog to digital (A/D) conversion board for music, or a graphics tablet and small printer or plotter for art, can accomplish what could be done only with a hundred-thousand-dollar system a few years ago. Drastic cost reductions in hardware have been accompanied by comparable advances in software so even amateurs can start creating without any previous programming experience. And for the writer, there already are several outstanding text editors to assist in the production of manuscripts. Unfortunately, letter quality printers presently cost just as much as a microcomputer with a floppy disk, but these prices should drop as the demand increases (see Fig. 6.5).

A medium-size system would include a littler larger CPU along with a hard disk or disks for storage, and a wider variety of input/output equipment, such as a color graphics terminal and a color plotter or synthesizer for music. A medium-size system would probably cost $20,000 to $100,000 and would be capable of producing color animation or the composition and playing of symphonic music, or conducting fairly sophisticated social science research. The exact configuration of equipment would depend on whether the use was for the arts, humanities, or social sciences. Generally speaking, the arts would emphasize A/D equipment for graphics and music, while the humanities and social sciences would be more interested in data storage, retrieval, and high-speed analysis of information.

A large system would probably involve computer networks, requiring telecommunications equipment, large amounts of disk storage, high-speed printers, and

Figure 6-5 A typical small- to medium-sized system, (Courtesy of Honeywell Information Systems, Inc.)

other sophisticated input and output equipment, depending on whether the application was in the arts, humanities, or social sciences.

A LOOK TOWARD THE FUTURE

Computer art and music, much like photography when it first began, will probably be slow in gaining acceptance and popularity. However, with the microcomputer, high costs no longer prevent many artists and musicians from using the computer. Already the film industry recognizes the crucial role of computers in the production of elaborate and otherwise too costly scenes and animation. Within a few years there will be numerous home-made computer-animated films or video tapes that will be appearing in film festivals and other types of art shows.

The use of computers in the humanities will probably witness the slowest growth, but humanists will become more involved in weighing and assessing the impact of the computer upon our lives. Eventually researchers in the humanities will be using computer networks to exchange ideas and data on a worldwide basis, not just for technical applications but as a new mode of communication.

Computers will also permit researchers in the humanities and the social sciences to work closer in their attempts to understand society. Perhaps a "soft" science will emerge, interdisciplinary in nature and combining the skills of many

121

diverse disciplines in an attempt to better understand our social conditions. By using the computer as a powerful analytic tool, better social planning should be possible. Through the exchange of information via worldwide networks, experts from many different areas will be able to combine their resources in a concerted effort to understand and solve problems such as crime, violence, and other difficulties that plague us. We are optimistic that computers, once viewed as the culprit by many people in these areas, will play a crucial role in fostering our understanding of humanity, in exploring our ideas and values, and in giving a positive and meaningful direction to the ways in which computers are used.

STUDY AND REVIEW

1. What are some of the ways computers are being used in television, film, and animation? Do you think these techniques are actually a new art form?

2. Rapid developments are occurring in the field of computer music. What are some ways in which computers are affecting the recording and playback of music?

3. Explain briefly how computers can assist composers in creating their music.

4. What do you believe to be the main reasons why computers were not readily accepted in the humanities and arts? Why is this no longer so?

5. Describe how computers are used in literary analysis and in the preparation of concordances. See if you can find two or three concordances that were prepared by a computer.

6. Discuss how computers are used in economics and history. What are the advantages and disadvantages of these uses?

7. How do psychologists use computers, especially in the fields of cognitive and experimental psychology?

8. What do you think are some likely ways that people in the humanities and social sciences will be using computers in the near future? Do you think microcomputers will play a significant role in these uses?

7

MONEY

PERSPECTIVE

There are, perhaps, no better examples of the information explosion than the areas of banking and finance. With billions of dollars being exchanged daily over national and international computer networks, we are truly becoming an information dependent society. The volume of our daily money transactions has become so great that it is no longer possible to perform the necessary paperwork without computers. In fact, it has been suggested that if the computers that support our financial institutions were to be sabotaged our entire economy would come to an abrupt halt. As the following quotation suggests, the institution of banking is rapidly changing.

> *When banking goes totally electronic, bankers hypothesize, the consumer's perception of what a bank is will change. Instead of viewing banks as marble monuments, consumers will choose a bank based on the quality of its electronic services. When this happens, the bank's image to its depositors becomes a reflection of the plastic it issues to its customers—that is, the debit cards that tap into ATMs, point-of-sale terminals, and, perhaps, even home banking devices.*
> (Business Week, *1982)*

In order to grasp how much our money system depends upon computers, we examine banking, the stock market, and financial management in this chapter. You may be surprised to discover the magnitude of the social impact that electronic banking already has on your life and, no doubt, will continue to have in the future.

Before reading any further, stop and reflect for a moment and try to imagine the ways in which computers affect the way in which you carry out your money transactions. If you think things will continue as they have in the past, please read further!

COMPUTERS IN BANKING AND FINANCE

A significant portion of the information explosion discussed in Chapter 1 can be attributed to the "paper explosion" in banking. From 1940 to 1970, the number of checks written increased 1,100 percent. Because 90 percent of all money transactions in the United States are completed by check, it has been estimated that more than 50 percent of our workforce would be needed to process checks if they had to be handled manually. In 1980, more than 40 billion checks were written (approximately 20 checks per month/per person), and this volume has been increased at a rate of about 6 to 7 percent each year. Fortunately, in the early 1960s, this huge volume of checks began to be processed automatically by *magnetic ink character recognition* (MICR) input devices that can read, 10,000 times faster than humans, the information coded at the bottom of a check. Not only have checks been computerized, but many other business documents used in banking are capable of being read directly into a computer through *optical character recognition* (OCR) input devices. For example, Bank of America has an optical page-scanning system that can read six standard type fonts at the rate of 14,000 characters per second. The scanner can complete in 10 seconds work once performed by a keypunch operator in one day. This page reader can process transaction documents from over 950 branch banks via telecommunications (see Fig. 7.1).

Although for many years charge cards have been issued by retail chains for use within their own stores, it has been only with the advent of bank charge cards, such as VISA and MasterCard, that charges began to represent a significant portion of the money transactions in the United States (about 10 billion charges in 1980). Since the early 1970s there has been a movement to merge features borrowed from both checking and charge cards into one system. In fact, as early as 1965, Thomas J. Watson, Jr., then president of IBM, envisioned a system that only recently is becoming a reality:

> In our lifetime we may see electronic transactions virtually eliminate the need for cash. Giant computers in banks, with massive memories, will contain individual customer accounts. To draw from or add to this balance, the customer in a store, office, or filling station will do two things: insert an identification into the terminal located there; punch out the transaction figures on the terminal's keyboard. Instantaneously, the amount he punches out will move out of his account and enter another.

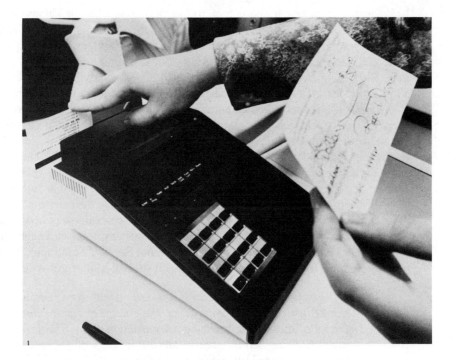

Figure 7-1 A financial services terminal for banking transactons (Courtesy of International Business Machines Corporation)

> *Consider this same process repeated thousands, hundreds*
> *of thousands, millions of times each day; billions upon bil-*
> *lions of dollars changing hands without the use of one pen,*
> *one piece of paper, one check, or one green dollar bill. Fi-*
> *nally, consider the extension of such a network of terminals*
> *and memories—an extension across city and state lines,*
> *spanning our whole country.* (Watson, 1965)

The Evolution of Electronic Funds Transfer

What the president of IBM was speculating about is called **Electronic Funds Transfer** (EFT)—the computerized handling of money transactions. Although such a system is operational in only a few geographic areas, the components of a nationwide system have slowly been evolving during the last 15 years.

Credit Verification For banks and credit card companies to protect themselves and their customers (both stores and individuals) from improper use of accounts (forgery, overdrafts, stolen cards, insufficient credit, and so forth), methods had to

125

be devised so that check and charge transactions could be quickly and easily verified. One way was to develop large credit information bureaus, such as TRW-Credit Data Corporation, that provided stores with telephone and terminal verification systems tied into the TRW computer system that kept up-to-date records on individuals. Also, large charge card companies such as American Express, Diner's Club, VISA, and MasterCard provided their own telephone or terminal verification system to businesses that accepted their cards. But because many of these systems require telephone calls that are often time consuming—especially during seasonal high-volume periods—many businesses have turned to terminal input devices that read the account identification off a magnetic strip on the back of the card while the salesperson types in the amount of the purchase. The computer then responds, without any human intervention, indicating whether or not there is sufficient credit to cover the present transaction. The reader can even lock the card into the terminal if the card has been reported lost or stolen. However, an example of how both check and credit card verification can be built into one system, thus eliminating the need for separate services, was given by City National Bank of Columbus, Ohio. This progressive bank installed two terminals in each store of a large grocery chain:

> *By inserting either a bank-supplied debit card or a BankAmericard into the terminal, the customer obtains approval of a check or credit-card transaction form. The terminal is connected to what is called a negative file—a continuously updated bank record of bad risks.* (S. Rose, 1977)

Debit Cards   Not only did this technique save time and money, it also afforded the opportunity to introduce two new concepts in banking: the capability of using credit cards to buy groceries, plus the use of a debit card. Debit cards are issued by banks to individuals and can be used only in stores that possess the necessary terminals to deduct money from the user's account. At the same time money is deducted, it is credited to the store's account; therefore, both the user and the store must have their accounts with the same bank. Although this type of system does not have the flexibility of national credit cards, it is a step toward all-electronic banking.

Automated Teller Machines   Closely associated with debit cards are **Automated Teller Machines** (ATMs). These input devices are sophisticated terminals that allow the user to enter a special account code that is known only to the bank and the user. After entering the code the user can request a withdrawal, make a deposit, transfer funds from savings to checking, or vice versa. Usually the ATMs are conveniently located in supermarkets, shopping centers, or outside the banks so customers can make their transactions anytime of day or night. Presently there are more than 10,000 ATMs in operation and, as the cost decreases from the current price of $30,000 (about $3,000 for the terminal and $27,000 for the enclosure and security!), there will no doubt be more (see Fig. 7.2).

Point of Sale Terminals   Often similar in appearance to cash registers, **Point of Sale** (POS) terminals not only record a sale, but also can update inventory, keep

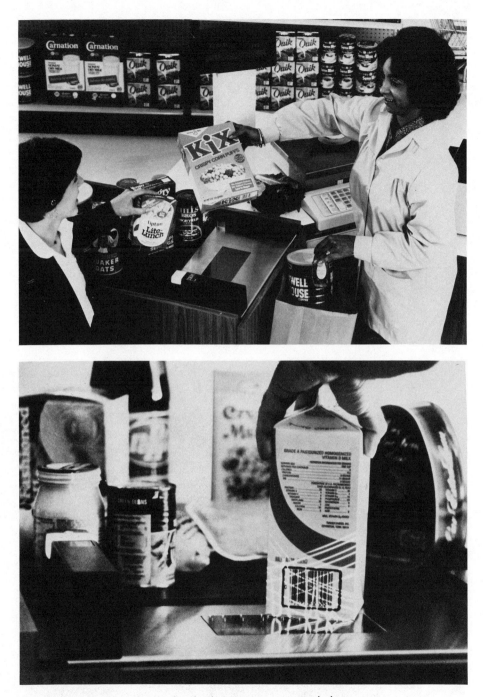

Figure 7-2 (a) A point-of-sale checkout scanner using holography ,(b) When a product bearing a Universal Product Code mark nears the holographic scanning window, a laser beam wraps around the product. (Courtesy of International Business Machines Corporation)

track of sales commissions and—if it is a charge customer—directly debit the account. The POS terminal can be used in conjunction with debit card services to provide all-electronic banking on a small scale.

Universal Products Code   Some POS terminals now in grocery stores use a scanning device that automatically reads the **Universal Products Code** (UPC) as items are passed over a small window in the checkout counter (see Fig. 7.3). The method of operation is very similar to the magnetic codes used in retail stores.

> *The code is represented by a rectangle of light and dark bars printed on the product by the manufacturer. An automated check stand scans the UPC symbol and transmits the data to a computer that looks up the price, possibly updates inventory and sales records, and forwards price and description information back to the check stand. Grocery retailing organizations expect that the new check-out equipment and the use of the UPC will increase supermarket efficiency and provide customers with faster and more accurate service.*
> *(Sanders, 1977)*

Although the equipment is very fast and efficient, greatly reduces waiting time for customers, and eliminates mistakes by the cashier, there are a few problems.

Figure 7-3 A typical point-of-sale terminal for a retail store. (Courtesy of International Business Machines Corporation)

One of the major economic incentives for stores to adopt this equipment was the time and labor saved in not marking prices on items, since the computer stored the price and printed it out on the itemized receipt. This advantage was soon lost, however when consumers protested the absence of prices, resulting, in some states, in laws being passed making it mandatory that prices also be stamped on the items. Another problem is the high cost of these terminals; only large chain stores have installed them so far. However, since over 80 percent of all grocery purchases are paid by check, the possibility of using the POS terminal for check verification purposes may well provide the extra incentive for small businesses to purchase POS terminals, thereby increasing the demand and lowering the price.

All of these electronic input techniques are having a social impact on the consumer. By gradually exposing the public to computer devices, the foundation is being laid for the eventual transition to a checkless and less-cash EFT economy. Most people are already accustomed to the POS terminal—but are they prepared to accept a completely electronic and checkless money system?

The Checkless Society: Electronic Fund Transfer (EFT)

> *Major businesses have for a long time not needed cash to deal with each other, and the wide use of checks and credit cards means that we have almost changed from monetary exchanges to exchanges of information. In the age of the computer-communication utility, cash will completely disappear. When homes, stores, offices, and banks are linked through computers, one need only enter a transaction through the nearest console, and two bank accounts will be automatically credited or debited.* (Kemeny, 1967)

Since the technological ingredients for an EFT system already exist, it is not very difficult to imagine the following situation soon taking place. The EFT cycle begins when a customer's paycheck is automatically deposited into his or her bank account by the employer's bank each payday. From the account, automatic deductions of authorized, regular, recurring bills (house payments, car payments, insurance premiums, and so forth) will be made by an already operational *Automated Clearing House* (**ACH**) system. (Hundreds of thousands of employees already participate in this aspect of EFT.) When the customer goes into a food market, retail store, service station, or any other business firm, the purchase-payment transaction can be handled at a POS terminal. When the purchase data are entered, the terminal inquires into the customer's account to see if there are sufficient funds; if so, the customer's account is debited, and the store's bank account is credited—even if customer and business use different banks.

> *It is as if each bank account had its own telephone, and the shop's terminal set up a conference call between itself and*

> *the customer's account (its "phone number" is on the credit card) and the shop's account (its "phone number" is permanently stored inside the terminal). This analogy makes clear that the EFT network must indeed be a utility—a network used by many different shops and banks with free access to all—rather than the property of a single bank.*
>
> *(Arbib, 1977)*

Advantages of EFT   As previously mentioned, the transaction would also update inventory accounts, credit commissions, issue an order for more items, and so forth. The main advantages of an EFT system are economic. For the retailer, the inventory is updated automatically, accounting and inventory control are largely automated, and because all transactions are electronically credited to the store's account, there is no worry about bad checks or robbery. For banks it means less paper work, which in turn reduces the cost of processing account debits and credits. It would enable the consumer to withdraw or deposit money at any POS terminal and earn interest if the transactions can be deducted from a savings account. Other consumer advantages include not having to carry cash and spending less time waiting in lines for service. The Federal Reserve System would not have to subsidize as large amounts (more than $20 billion daily) of "float," the interest-free money that banks and consumers take advantage of while checks are in transit. There seem to be compelling incentives for many segments of business to adopt EFT—particularly for large economic organizations like the Retail Stores Association, the American Banking Association, and the Federal Reserve.

Disadvantages of EFT   Nevertheless, there is an increasing awareness by consumers and lawmakers that these economic bonuses may well be outweighed by serious social problems that would affect everyone. Of primary concern is the threat to individual privacy. For EFT to be profitable, a large percentage of all money transactions would have to be handled electronically, because it is not cost effective to have a system in which cash, checks, and charges must be processed along with electronic transfers.

But EFT transactions record far far more information than do check or charge-card transactions. With EFT, the date, time, place, and type of merchandise is recorded. This could be used by the retailer, marketing firm, government, or law enforcement agencies to monitor all of an individual's activities. It would be quite possible to enter a person's name into the system's computer and within seconds find out where and when that person last made a purchase, what hotels were visited, the type of books, clothes, food, entertainment, and so forth, that person has purchased—in essence, all of an individual's money activities could be put under surveillance. And, because large amounts of cash would be a hindrance to this system (bank pick-ups and deliveries, possible robberies, balancing receipts each day), it might happen that many stores would not accept cash because of the expense and risk of handling and storing it; cash transactions would take longer to process. Already several car rental agencies will not accept cash for rentals, even though you might have enough cash to buy the car you wish to rent! Although a cashless society is not necessarily the intent of EFT proponents, it certainly could be a by-product.

Another serious disadvantage of EFT is possible error; for example, if the EFT system erroneously indicated that your credit was inadequate, you would be denied the ability to purchase because most systems would use the same records for check authorization. Obviously, a traveling person who is not carrying cash (if cash was still accepted!) would be incapacitated in an EFT system. Finally, the implications of a real-time, no-float financial system are incredibly large overall; it would place strict restraints upon all of our lives and produce a degree of governmental control that we would normally associate with a significant loss of personal privacy and freedom.

Possible Safeguards   Fortunately, many of the potential problems were anticipated in the United States Privacy Protection Study Commission Report of 1977. It recommended:

> *That individually identifiable account information generated in the provision of EFT services be retained only in the account records of the financial institutions and other parties to a transaction, except that it may be retained by the EFT service provider to the extent, and for the limited period of time, that such information is essential to fulfill the operational requirements of the service provider.*

> *That procedures be established so that an individual can promptly correct inaccuracies in transactions or account records generated by an EFT service.*

> *That no government entity be allowed to own, operate, or otherwise manage any part of an electronic payments mechanism that involves transactions among private parties.*

Although the National Commission on Electronic Funds Transfer (NCEFT) agreed with these first two recommendations and other protective measures (which were incorporated into the 1978 Financial Institutions Regulatory Act, the Fair Funds Transfer Act, and the Right of Financial Privacy Act), it dissented on the last suggestion. The NCEFT also stated that the government should encourage development of EFT systems that allow POS terminals to interconnect with different banks so that the problem of a banking monopoly could be averted (see Fig. 7.4).

Further Considerations   Although robberies for cash may decrease with EFT, the probability of more computer crime will increase. Computer-aided crimes (manipulating funds, stealing information, and the like—see Chapter 16) usually involve much larger sums of money and are harder to detect and prevent than conventional

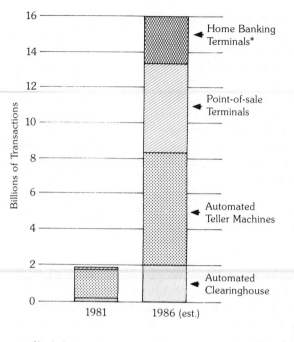

Data: American Bankers Assn.,

Figure 7-4 The growth of electronic fund transfer payments via credit and bank cards.

crimes. Closely associated with computerized embezzlement would be the vulnerability of EFT systems to sabotage and destruction. If an EFT, or worse yet, *the* EFT system were crippled, most money transactions would cease and our economy would be paralyzed.

There are also many legal problems that have not yet been resolved, such as: How would people be given or denied access to the system? How would large banking or telecommunications organizations be prevented from monopolizing the system? How should EFT be regulated? And how can fair prices be established for these services? Milton Wessel, an attorney with extensive experience in the area of legal and quasilegal computer problems, believes measures should be taken to establish rules governing EFT networks. For example, three of his rules or "commandments" that are particularly relevant to EFT are:

> *A computer utility credit card shall not unreasonably be withheld from any individual.*

> *Public and quasipublic-sponsored computer services must be supplied on terms and conditions which result in their fair and equitable distribution to the public.*

> *The supplier of computer services to the public must afford*
> *the ultimate consumer reasonable human response and*
> *interaction, or be liable absolutely for error and harm done.*
> *(Wessel, 1974)*

Before any EFT system becomes a reality, all of the problems and questions raised in the above discussions should be closely examined and resolved to the public's satisfaction.

The Stock Market

Computers have been used during the last few decades to assist in printing and distributing stock certificates, to do accounting, and to provide statistical services for the New York Stock Exchange (NYSE), the American Stock Exchange (AMEX), and several other regional exchanges. Only in the last few years have these exchanges actually used computers to buy and sell stock on a very limited basis. As the "Big Board" (NYSE) volume gradually moves upward toward 100-million-share days, brokers, the Securities and Exchange Commission (SEC), and financial consultants ponder the question: "Can the present method of on-the-floor trading survive such trading levels?" In an attempt to avert large-volume disaster that has plagued the NYSE in the past, studies are being conducted to determine the best way to handle increased trading activity.

Two Approaches to Stock Trading In 1975 Congress mandated that a national market system be developed that would be highly computerized and would consolidate the several existing exchanges. Movement in this direction has been slow however, and to date, only two experimental systems for computerized trading are seriously being utilized.

Intermarket Trading System The larger system, called Intermarket Trading System (ITS), interconnects the NYSE, AMEX, and four other regional exchanges. In this system a customer places an order with a local broker, who sends the order to the firm's member at the NYSE. There the member goes to the post where that stock is traded, views a computer display of the buy and sell prices on the five other stock exchanges, and compares them with the NYSE price. If a lower price is available at another exchange, a buy order is placed and transmitted by wire to that exchange where it is displayed. Within less than two minutes (sometimes in only 5 seconds) the transaction is completed and relayed back to New York. The ITS system can cover only about two-thirds of the major traded stocks on the Big Board, and currently has a daily volume of about 500,000 shares. Although there is not much resistance to this system, many brokers find it difficult to work with and tend to ignore tha other markets provided by this service. Supporters of ITS claim it makes it much easier to get better prices for their clients.

The Cincinnati Stock Exchange The other system, at the Cincinnati Stock Exchange, is smaller in scope but much more controversial in its impact. In this experiment, all trading takes place by computer and floor traders are essentially eliminated—transactions can occur in fractions of a second. Because of much criticism, mainly from traders who see their jobs being eliminated and from smaller brokerage firms who argue that this type of system permits large firms to buy and sell from their own inventories, the Cincinnati experiment does not seem likely to succeed. However, advocates of this system claim that cost savings, speed, and accuracy of trading benefit their investors and result in lower trading fees. The only issue that is clear at this point is that computers will be needed to carry out some volume of the trading in the very near future. And, as an acceptable system is used that provides critical support on large volume days, it will eventually play a larger and more important role.

Monitoring the Stock Market In addition to recording all the daily stock transactions for accounting purposes, trading activity must be continually examined to detect any unusual buying or selling patterns. The SEC is responsible for monitoring all trading, analyzing corporate news releases, and detecting activities that violate federal law. However, with increasing volume and new financial instruments, such as money market funds and stock options, the market is becoming too complex for the SEC to monitor effectively. For these reasons, a watchdog computerized monitoring system has been proposed by the SEC. The system, called Market Oversight Surveillance System (MOSS), will be able to scrutinize and integrate information from all of the nation's stock and options exchanges. MOSS should be able to detect any irregular trading and greatly facilitate the inspection and regulation of the exchanges. As with most surveillance systems, however, there is much concern in Congress about its economic and social impact. Opponents claim it will be too expensive to implement fully, duplicates existing systems, and increases cost for the investor. Proponents argue that it is the only way for the SEC to fulfill its duties, that the system is very simple in design, and that most resistance is due to misunderstandings about how the system will operate. Whether MOSS is accepted or rejected is perhaps not as important as the awareness, by members of Congress and the financial community, that better monitoring of exchange activity is necessary.

Money Management

> With the double-digit interest rates, nobody can afford idle cash balances. With modern techniques, nobody need have them.
> (Saltzman, 1979)

A most challenging task for large corporations and financial institutions is to utilize their cash surplus for investment effectively. At the beginning of each working day decisions are made as to how to invest this money for maximum profit. Since national and international money markets change second-by-second, timely and accurate information can mean the difference between earning $1,000 or $20,000 with one day's surplus. In an attempt to penetrate the complexities of this rapid trading, elaborate computer programs and telecommunications equipment are necessities. This approach to cash management is fairly recent, going back to 1976 when several large New York banks developed a network interconnecting banks with large corporations. Called ChemLink, this network provides detailed information on more than 400 banks. Companies, such as Equitable Life Assurance Society, use this network (there are more than 40 similar networks to choose from) to perform transactions that transfer millions of dollars daily. For example, securities can be traded, "repurchase agreements" bought, and commercial notes sold—all in a matter of seconds in several different markets, including international ones. If a large amount of money is received after east coast banks have closed, it can be invested quickly on the west coast. Although only very large corporations can participate in such high-speed finance, this type of cash management is fast becoming the standard that provides the crucial hedge on inflation, high interest rates, and a volatile international money market.

Fortunately you do not have to be a multinational conglomerate to partake in the computer revolution in finance. Several small, medium, and even large-size investment firms are using microcomputers to make portfolio evaluations and other types of sophisticated financial analysis. Besides being able to perform these procedures, print to charts and graphs (even in color!), and to produce reports, these personal microcomputers can retrieve data from the data banks, such as the Dow Jones database, United Press International, the New York and American stock exchanges, historical data on more than 4,300 companies from Media General Financial Services, plus Standard and Poor's investment information. It is now possible to compete with large investment firms, from the privacy of your own home, with an initial investment of less than $4,000 for all the necessary computer and telecommunications equipment. This is just one example of how the microcomputer can revolutionize our lives by democratizing big business (see Fig. 7.5 on page 136.)

SOCIAL IMPLICATIONS

Most of the major issues pertaining to EFT and related technologies have already been mentioned in previous sections. For example, we introduced many of the advantages and disadvantages of electronic banking in our initial discussion to emphasize how closely the issues are intertwined with EFT developments. The cautious optimism of the final report by the National Commission on EFT clearly expresses the awareness that the apparent irreversible trend toward EFT is necessarily accompanied by far-reaching personal, social, and economic issues; and that these issues must be resolved if EFT is to be completely feasible. Therefore, in the pro-and-con discussions that follow, we will only briefly state some of the major points surrounding EFT and emphasize issues that apply to banking and finance in general.

Figure 7-5 At the *Los Angeles Times,* programmers use PLAN-CODE software to build one of several financial planning models run by the newspaper's business office. (Courtesy of International Business Machines Corporation)

Pro Arguments

The major advantages of computers in banking and finance are: the elimination of unnecessary paper documentation, the reduction of "float," and a tighter control of our money supply. These factors constitute a significant reduction in operating costs, better money management, and perhaps savings that will be passed on to the consumer. In addition to these economic benefits, there are three important by-products from the computerization of money and stock transactions. First, because of the speed with which these activities take place and the timely information that accompanies them, better decision making and planning is possible. Second, there is a greater variety of financial services available to the consumer (like paying bills by phone or banking at an automated teller)—all of which are quicker and more flexible than with previous systems. Finally, in an age where the conservation of our resources is important, computers permit a significant savings in the amount of paper and energy needed to provide these necessary services.

Con Arguments

Because all of our money transactions could be documented, one major drawback of EFT is the lack of adequate safeguards to protect individual privacy regarding the access and use of EFT information. There could also be economic disadvantages for those earning low and moderate incomes, who would perhaps have to pay more for goods and services, if they were not permitted to enter the EFT credit system. Another critical problem that affects all financial institutions is that, as greater reliance is placed on computer technology, the systems become increasingly vulnerable to security violations, fraud, sabotage, and other types of computer crime. Because there would be less paper documentation accompanying financial transactions, there would also be a tendency for the consumer to have less control over his or her finances, which usually results in the spending of more money. Furthermore, it is almost impossible to foresee the long-term effects of a "float-free" banking system on our economic, social, and political institutions. Finally, it is not yet clear, but it is possible that extensive use of computers in all areas of banking and finance could significantly reduce the number of people employed in this large sector of our economy. The ultimate questions deal with whether or not such systems are cost-effective in human terms.

HARDWARE

For the last three decades banking and finance have been dominated by large mass-storage computer systems. However, the microcomputer has been making significant inroads into this area. In fact, you can actually enter the world of banking with just a Touch-Tone telephone if you participate in one of the many pay-by-phone banking systems. Some banks are already allowing customers to carry out all of their banking via their own personal computers at home. On a more advanced level, sophisticated software has been developed to allow the personal computer to participate in activities such as stock, portfolio, and other types of financial analysis and forecasting. Some banks and investment firms are already using in-house microcomputer networks in conjunction with their own databases. There are also financial information networks, like the Dow Jones and Company News/Retrieval Service, that are available to the personal computer user via telephone dial-up. Also, with just a small keyboard device that can be attached to a telephone, retail stores can access large credit and check verification systems. So, with less than a $1,000 investment, many users can now have access to information and computing power that was available only to large financial institutions just a few years ago (see Fig. 7.6).

A typical medium-size system, of the type you might find in a small local bank

Figure 7-6 A typical medium-sized banking system (Courtesy of International Business Machines Corporation)

or brokerage firm, would consist of a large minicomputer or medium-size mainframe with a large amount of on-line and/or off-line storage. There would be a variety of input devices, such as card readers, key-to-tape or key-to-disk, plus optical scanners and, in banking environments, some MICR equipment. Because of the large volume of output, there would probably be a few high-speed line printers, and maybe even a plotter for financial analysis graphs. Although the system could "stand alone" and be dedicated to just one location, it is likely that there would be some remote job entry terminals or other input devices in other branch offices using leased lines for data communication.

A large system would consist of from one to several maxi-size mainframes, such as the type of configuration used in a national or international financial network. This would involve massive on-line storage and, perhaps, the capability to exchange information with several different types of computers via telecommunications using microwave, fiber optics, and satellite technology. There would be an extensive amount of input/output equipment, including the capacity to handle hundreds or thousands of terminals, numerous high-speed printers (including extremely high-speed laser printers), and even computer output microfilm/microfiche. In fact, there would probably be several subsystems within such a network that would be specifically dedicated to just one task, such as handling communications, performing only output operations, or only coordinating input activity. To develop such a system would require an investment of $5 million to $100 million dollars!

Finally, in both medium and large-scale systems, there will be great emphasis upon security. As will be discussed in Chapter 16, when systems are large and complex, they are vulnerable to attack—especially if they handle hundreds of millions of dollars in daily transactions. To provide adequate security for financial systems may cost up to one third of the total price of the system.

A LOOK TOWARD THE FUTURE

The computerization of banking and finance will continue to grow, and there will be a definite trend toward less paper and checks. Initially the most rapid growth will be in commercial banking and large financial institutions, mainly spurred on by the dramatic advances in telecommunications, networks, and satellite technology. However, before the end of the decade a significant number of consumer transactions will take place electronically. Computer terminals or microcomputers in the home will allow individuals to pay bills, transfer funds, buy or sell stock, purchase tickets, make travel reservations, and buy items from electronic catalogs. All of these services are in operation now and, in one particular case, are standard features built into new condominiums in New York City. In order for these types of activities to occur nation-wide, however, there must be better security and better laws than are presently available.

On the other hand, even if costs drop dramatically and security improves significantly, there may still be some hesitancy in moving toward a checkless and cashless society. Business leaders remain divided on the issue of a cashless or less-cash society; some foresee a decline in EFT and a return to more traditional approaches; others claim the all-electronic banking system is only a few years away.

The conflict is a real one. Whichever prediction is most correct, one can be assured the public will eventually pay the price of either alternative. The question that remains is: "Which system do you want?" Perhaps the deciding factor will not be big business or government, but the intangible force of an informed public—maybe even a public that wants to resist machines, no matter what.

There is a lesson in this for all business as the world goes rushing into the electronic age. For 10,000 years, and perhaps more, people have been learning to deal with people. They have developed elaborate behavior patterns—persuasion, anger, flattery, indignation, distress—to evoke responses from other human beings. They are not equipped emotionally to deal with machines, which respond to nothing except the buttons on the keyboard.

The frustrating thing about a machine is that it assumes no responsibility and cannot be held accountable for failure. Man can be ashamed of himself. A machine cannot. . . .

The public's wariness may be unjustified. It may add to costs and cut efficiency in the long run. But for the present, the best strategy seems to be to keep the machines in the backshop and put people out front.

(Business Week, *April 18, 1977)*

STUDY AND REVIEW

1. Do you think the banking industry could survive without computers? Why or why not?

2. What do you think will be the impact of microcomputers on banking and finance?

3. Briefly describe an EFT system. What are the major arguments for and against EFT systems? What is your position?

4. How are computers presently being used in the stock market? What are some likely uses in the near future?

5. Describe what money management is and how computers (both mainframes and microcomputers) assist in money management.

6. What do you think would be the advantages and disadvantages if we had a completely "floatless" economy?

8

BUSINESS

PERSPECTIVE

While the first computers were created in the laboratory, and used primarily for scientific applications, the first commercial use of computers was in business. As time passed, a wide variety of areas other than business have benefited from advances in computer technology. Yet some of the most sophisticated advances in computer technology have had the most dramatic effect on how modern organizations conduct business. Today any businessman who is not familiar with computer technology is at a distinct competitive disadvantage. The following quotation by a management expert points out the position a modern business executive is in with respect to computer technology.

> There are still a good many businessmen around who have little use for, and less interest in, the computer. There are also still quite a few who believe that the computer somehow, someday will replace man or become his master.
>
> Others, however, realize by now that the computer, while powerful, is only a tool and is neither going to replace man nor control him. Being a tool, it has limitations as well as capabilities. The trick lies in knowing both what it can do and what it cannot do. Without such knowledge, the modern executive can find himself in real trouble in the computer age.
> (Drucker, 1966)

The first computer applications in business were in the area of repetitive clerical operations. These had previously been accomplished by punched card accounting machines that were descendants of the equipment Herman Hollerith devised for the 1890 census. Now, most large firms, a large number of medium-size firms, and an increasing number of small firms depend to some degree on a computer to handle their clerical operations. With increasingly sophisticated management techniques, advancing comptuer technology, and the increased amount of information handled by today's organizations, the use of a computer and related electronics technologies can no longer be confined to the processing of routine clerical operations. Today, highly refined management techniques, combined with computer technology, are reshaping the organization and operation of even the smallest business enterprises.

In this chapter we trace the major developments in computer technology and management science that are influencing modern organizational structure. We also explore the wide variety of new electronic products that have been developed from computer technology and are changing the traditional ways people perform work in any organization.

COMPUTERS IN BUSINESS

The applications best suited to the computer in business are those that require little in the way of computational power and logic, but require that the same simple set of operations be performed on large sets of similar data. A good example of this type of application in business is the use of a computer to process payroll. Although the computations that a computer is required to perform for each employee are simple, they must be performed many times (see Fig. 8.1). While relieving an organization of considerable manual labor, such applications do not take full advantage of the computer's capabilities. Surveys have found that, although a computer will increase productivity and efficiency by automating clerical activities, a complete analysis of total information needs, coupled with completely new systems to meet those needs, will increase organizational efficiency well beyond levels attained by simple payroll automation or similar activities.

When an organization has completely assessed its information needs and designed a computer-based system to meet those needs, it will probably expect to save money. However, that is often not the case. Rooms full of clerical help may be replaced by electronic machines, but along with the machines will come an army of expensive support personnel. Although an organization might hope to save money by installing a sophisticated electronic computer, more than likely it is moving in the direction of computers because its business systems have become too big and complex for manual data processing activities to handle, and because the computer system can do things that a manual system cannot (see Cart. 8.1).

Figure 8-1 Large batch computers have long been well-suited to the needs of business data processing. (Courtesy of International Business Machines Corporation)

I'm sorry to announce that, as of July 1, this entire department
will be replaced by a tiny silicon chip.

Information Systems

Few concepts of data processing for business are discussed more than are information systems, or what has come to be known as management information systems
(MIS). Information systems, or management information systems, use computers to
provide personnel within an organization with information they need for making decisions regarding the organization's activities.

More formally, management information systems are systems integrating
machines, computers, people, and communications equipment to provide information pertinent to an organization's activities.

Information systems improve management's ability to make effective operational decisions. Computer-based information systems enable most aspects of decision-making processes to be reduced to quantitative terms and be stored inside the computer. With this computerized quantitative information, less time is required to make effective management decisions and, in some cases, the quality of decisions improves. An effective computerized information system provides information to management that in most cases is more current than could be provided by old-fashioned paper information systems. These current data enable management to react to changing business conditions as they occur, and in some instances before they occur.

Elements of an Information System

Basically, an information system consists of a database or data bank. A database is all of an organization's information resources stored inside a computer. Although typical databases are centralized, distributed processing techniques enable an organization to maintain its database in one computer, with access provided by local and remote terminals, or in several separate but connected computers.

The single most important function of a database is to centralize the data resources of an organization to eliminate duplication, increase accuracy and standardization, and facilitate the exchange of information between functional units of an organization (see Fig. 8.2).

In a database computer system, files are usually stored in online auxiliary storage devices. Users of a database system can instruct the computer to access information in the database and to prepare reports from it. Or users at terminals, either local or remote, can query the computer, requesting that it locate specific information and output it on the terminal.

Database Management Systems

Data are an obvious resource of an organization, and one of the most effective means of managing this important resource is by the creation of a database system in a computer. While the first step in creating an effective database system is to physically store the data in the computer, probably the most important step is to create an adequate system of management for the database. This management system must encompass procedures within the computer for building and maintaining the database, as well as external procedures for using it effectively.

Structuring a Database Because computers already have auxiliary storage capacity, structuring a database becomes a problem of developing the operating systems and applications software necessary to build, maintain, and utilize the database. This software, sometimes offered as a package by a variety of manufacturers, must provide seven functions. It should

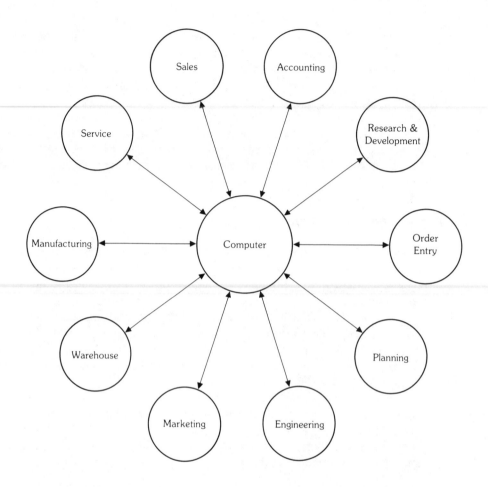

Figure 8-2 Computers can facilitate communications between functional units of an organization.

1. Define what data are to be contained in the database, and the interrelationships of data.

2. Establish procedures for querying the database and for output formats.

3. Establish the physical structure of the files in the database.

4. Allow for the inputting of data to create the database.

5. Allow users access to the database.

6. Provide for continuous updating of files within the database.

7. Allow users to manipulate data—Query language (see Fig. 8.3).

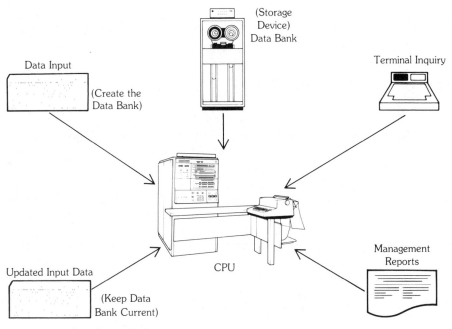

Figure 8-3 Data base management system

Impact on Organizations

So far in this chapter we have followed the evolution of the computer's role in organizations. We have seen that computers were used originally to perform routine clerical tasks, and later became part of sophisticated "information systems." While these information systems have made organizations more efficient, they have also changed the structure of many organizations and redefined the manner in which certain activities within organizations are performed. These changes have occurred primarily in the administrative activities of planning, organizing, and controlling. These are important operations in any organization, because the successful achievement of organizational goals depends on how well they are performed.

We have also noted that new types of information systems have been implemented in organizations. However, we have not explored the fact that the implementation of these sophisticated information systems has often led to significant organizational changes. Probably the most significant change that has been brought about by computers is the degree to which an organization concentrates or centralizes its authority. When a computer is used, a greater degree of centralized control can be supported in an organization because top administrators can be furnished with information from distant operations in time to decide on appropriate action. Without computers, such action must often be determined by lower-level managers because of time, distance, and familiarity factors. While greater centralized control can be supported with a computer, it is not necessarily a requirement. The degrees of centralized authority and control that should exist in the new computerized system are determined as well by managerial philosophy and judgment, and not by computer usage alone.

Business Computer System Applications

Business uses of computers vary widely. One reason for this variance is that the needs of managers differ. In general, the higher the level of management, the more summarized information tends to be. At each level of management, consolidations, averages, and so forth are passed up to the next level. At the top, the information is the consolidation of consolidations.

Another reason why computer use varies is that managers need different types of service. Sometimes business computer systems produce status information. The information may be historical, like accounting systems that produce year-end reports; it may be current, like inventory systems that maintain item counts; or it may be future, like market forecasting systems that predict the size of a market next year.

Not all managers use the computer to obtain status information. Some use the computer for the production of information-bearing documents. A payroll system produces checks that inform banks to move money.

Finally, some managers delegate control to business computer systems. For example, an inventory system is designed to compare stock levels to projected sales and automatically generate reorders when appropriate. At every level of management and in every business specialty there are computer-based information systems. One way that such systems might be organized is by business areas. So in this section we examine business systems in accounting, finance, sales and marketing, and manufacturing.

Accounting and Finance Computer accounting systems have proved the most successful at satisfying business needs and have won the greatest acceptance. Basically, the purpose of a computer accounting system is to maintain data that accurately represent the financial state of a company. Major applications of computer technology in accounting operations include payroll, billing, accounts receivable and payable, general ledger, and inventory control.

Finance is the specialty of managing money. People who work in a finance department assess the company's need for money, determine ways to raise capital when needed, and evaluate proposals to spend it when appropriate. Finance personnel use the computer for three reasons. First, the calculation of interest rates, rates of return, or investments and other such financial measures is crucial to managing money. Second, much financial work is repetitive. Third, in finance the alternatives to be evaluated often have complex interactions that can be processed better by computer than by humans. Financial planning involves answering many "what if" questions. These kinds of questions can be answered easily by computer systems; the analyst needs to change only one or two input values and submit a request for another computer run to obtain the required answer.

Examples of financial computer systems uses include capital expenditure analysis, financial planning, cash planning, merger analysis, and credit analysis.

Sales and Marketing   Sales and marketing are two closely related disciplines involved with the selling of goods and services. Some sales and marketing systems are used in direct support of business operations, like order entry or the production of form letters. Other systems analyze sales and marketing data. The most common sales and marketing computer systems include order entry, mail order processing, order status, advertising assistance, marketing analysis, and sales agent effectiveness.

Computers in Small Businesses

Computers have usually been considered as tools of large organizations. Originally, they were so large and so expensive that only wealthy organizations could afford them. Small businesses that wanted to use computers often found the cost factor prohibitive. The first break for small businesses came when computer service bureaus were formed, offering either time on their computer or a data processing service for a fee. This has not always proved satisfactory for small businesses because it usually requires a small business to change many of its administrative practices to the way the service bureau provides its data processing services. More recently, electronics technology has evolved to the point where computer manufacturers can produce computer systems that, price-wise, are well within the reach of virtually any business, large or small.

These new small, inexpensive computer systems bring advantages to small businesses that previously have had to rely solely on manual data processing activities. For an investment of several thousand dollars on up, the small business organization can now receive the benefits of computerization that were previously available only to big businesses. The computer systems now available for small businesses have the computing power of the larger and more expensive computers of 10 years ago (see Fig. 8.4).

The typical small business computer available today does not require an extensive technical background on the part of the operator. An average system might consist of a keyboard unit and TV monitor for input and output, a central processing unit, floppy disk drives for storage, and a printer for hard-copy output. Frequently, the purchaser of such a system knows absolutely nothing about computers. So, because a computer requires programs to make it run, the purchaser will buy with the computer prewritten software packages that are designed to be used with a particular type of computer and in a particular type of business. In effect, this enables small business owners to purchase a complete computer package (sometimes referred to as a turn-key system), take it to their places of business, plug it in, and almost immediately begin integrating the computer into the routines of the organization. Most of the activities that large organizations perform on computers can now be implemented on microcomputer systems for small organizations.

Figure 8-4 Microcomputer systems like this offer small business firms computing power that was too expensive ten years ago. (Courtesy Tandy/Radio Shack

Office Technology

The term **office automation,** sometimes used to describe extraordinary advances made in office technology, first appeared in a special report printed in *Business Week* in 1975. The article predicted that great strides would be made by 1980 in introducing these technologies into business offices. However, by 1980 this revolution had not occurred. Offices were slow to accept new technologies, and the motivation to exploit these new technologies came primarily from lower echelon office technology specialists rather than from general management.

It seems now that this situation is changing because senior management is becoming increasingly aware that the cost of office operations is rising faster than the costs in any other segment of business. Current statistics indicate that office costs are rising 12 to 15 percent per year. Virtually no business can tolerate a situation in which office costs double every six years. Furthermore, statistics indicate that while blue-collar productivity in a recent 10-year period increased by more than 2 percent, white collar productivity has grown on the average only 0.4 percent. Manufacturing industries invest about $25,000 in equipment and new technology per production worker, but white collar businesses—which account for half of the nation's employees—invested $2,000 to $6,000 per office worker. Thus, the movement toward a truely automated office is gaining momentum. The target of the movement is to boost white collar productivity and effectiveness by systematically applying the appropriate technology to a restructuring of the office environment.

Word Processing Word processing was a term first used by IBM as a marketing description for its broad line of office products. Today there are many definitions of the term, but the one that seems to make the most sense is: **word processing** is the manipulation of words, sentences, and paragraphs by advanced hardware, while **data processing** is the manipulation of numbers. Word processing equipment is considered to be the cornerstone of the automated office. Word processing is gaining momentum because businesses can no longer afford the custom approach to doing office work. Paperwork is growing explosively, and the traditional "one-on-one" office arrangement—the secretary-boss combination—cannot keep up with the increased volume.

Word processing began quietly in 1964 when IBM introduced its MT/ST (magnetic tape, Selectric typewriter). This was an automatic letter-writing machine whose main feature was the repetitive typing of form letters. The automatic typing was done by recording keystrokers in electronic form, and storing them on magnetic tape for fast, precise replay. Revising or correcting was done by typing over the word or sentence to be changed, while the machine rerecorded the tape at that spot. There were no sophisticated "text editing" capabilities that enabled a typist to rearrange the text by adding, deleting, moving or revising whole lines or paragraphs of what had previously been recorded.

The second generation of word processing equipment now on the market has a TV screen that displays a page of text. The keyboard is separate from the printer so that a page can be typed automatically while the typist or operator works on the next page (see Fig. 8.5). What the operator types shows directly on the screen rather

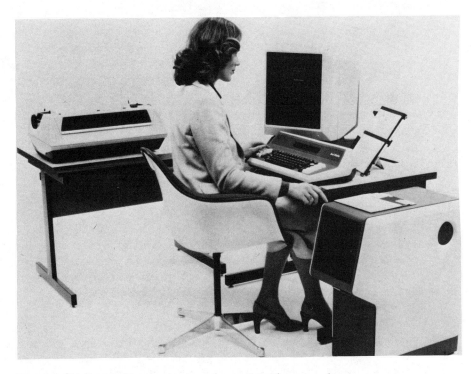

Figure 8-5 A complete word processing unit, with screen for document preparation, floppy disk drive for storage, and high-speed printer to produce finished copy. (Courtesy of Dictaphone Corporation, Rye, NY)

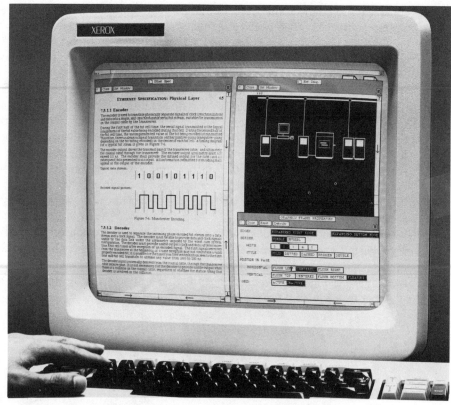

(a)

Figure 8-6 A Xerox Star word processing system enables users to create documents that include graphic symbols as well as type-written text. This system is designed to connect to communications lines such as ETHERNET and to send and receive information to other workstations, both local and remote. (Courtesy of Xerox Corporation)

than on a piece of paper. When the document on the screen is correct, the operator pushes a button to store the document in a tape or disk memory and/or to print it out on the typewriter. While the typist is entering the text, or at some time in the future, the text already input to the processor can be manipulated in sophisticated ways, according to the desires of the operator.

The basic components of a word processing system consist of a central processing unit (CPU), a workstation (cathode-ray tube display or some form of CRT), some form of storage, and a printer. The CPU, which need not be very powerful, provides the capabilities for inputting and manipulating the text. The CRT enables the operator to input the text, display it on a screen, or recall a document from memory and display that on a screen. The most common type of storage

(b)

device is a floppy disk drive that is capable of storing up to 100 pages of text on a single disk. The final component is a printer, which enables the prepared documents to be printed out as "hard" copy on paper (see Fig. 8.6).

Before text can be edited on a word processing system, it must be originated, and still the best way to do it is by using dictating machines. Although fewer than 40 percent of those in offices who should use dictating equipment actually do so, this is one key to success in the automated office of the future.

Some offices have established electronic dictation centers where employees can phone in correspondence and other paper work, have it recorded electronically, and processed later by a central secretarial staff on word processing equipment. This method may improve efficiency, but it is not very popular in many offices because it eliminates the boss-secretary arrangement that has had status implications in most offices. The operators of word processing equipment, the secretaries of the automated office, are also not all that happy with the new technology. The machines may increase productivity, but they reduce personal contact within large offices and tend to lead to the establishment of high production levels. This leaves the operators feeling as if they are merely part of the machinery.

Many technological breakthroughs are being made in the area of speech-activated machinery. Voice recognition systems, which are currently under development, will enable operators to activate various functions of machinery with spoken command. It is entirely possible—in fact probable—that word processing systems in the future may be activated entirely by voice, eliminating the need for any keystroking of text. This, of course, would have a dramatic effect on secretarial requirements within organizations that used such systems.

Micrographics Another part of the automated office is information storage and retrieval. An alternative to traditional paper-based file storage systems can possibly be found in the field of micrographics. Although it may be more desirable to store information on magnetic storage media, or in a computer, the most cost effective method for the storage of the large volumes of information being generated in offices today may be found in the use of film. Business documents routinely flowing through a modern office can be easily photographed and placed on a film strip or a small photographic card called **microfiche** which can contain hundreds of documents. Special viewing devices are used to enlarge and display a selected microfiche document on a large screen; the viewer can be connected to a paper printer should an actual copy of the document be desired (see Fig. 8.7).

More sophisticated microfiche viewers can be used in conjunction with a terminal connected to a computer. The operator can request a document through the terminal. The computer then can activate a retrieval mechanism within the viewer, and the document can be automatically displayed for the operator.

Many reports produced by computers are routinely generated as microfiche rather than in paper form, to save space and money. The process of generating microfiche from a computer is called Computer Output Microfilm (COM).

Communications

Fast efficient communications are essential in today's modern organizations. Traditional forms of communications within organizations have become too cumbersome and expensive under the crush of information that daily flows through them. The goal of the automated office movement is not only to improve the methods by which letters, reports, and other routine documents are prepared and stored, but to streamline the communications process and reduce costs also. These goals are being accomplished by changing the ways organizations handle interoffice and intra-office communications, as well as the way an organization communicates with the outside world. In the automated offices that are now emerging, paper is being eliminated as much as possible (see Cart. 8.2). Paper-based filing systems are disappearing and in their place are computerized database systems. As we have seen, a database is simply all of an organization's information resources stored inside a computer. Work stations throughout an organization can be equipped with terminals connected to the central computer. Xerox offers an office information network known as ETHERNET which enables various pieces of office equipment to com-

Figure 8-7 Microprocessor-controlled devices can retrieve microfilmed documents quickly. When the documents are first microfilmed, a bar code is printed at the bottom which enables the documents to be retrieved. (Courtesy of Eastman Kodak)

Ms Johnson, I'd like to know just what this piece of paper is
doing on my desk?

municate with each other as well as with a central computer. As demand for information arises, a worker can access the information through the terminal. By using
special query languages implemented on the computer, an employee can perform
sophisticated operations on information within the computer without a knowledge
of computer programming. With such computerized information systems, vast
amounts of paper can be eliminated while the information available to employees for
decision making purposes is increased.

Centralized computer systems within organizations can also be used as
message switching systems. Rather than generating a traditional memorandom,
communications could be entered into a terminal at one work station, and the computer can be used to route the message to the terminal of the intended receiver (see
Fig. 8.8). Where companies maintain branch offices in geographically separate locations, computer systems within each office can be tied together into a computer network by existing communications technology, and be used to handle interoffice
communications electronically. Such systems, already in use, have been effective in
streamlining the communications process, and have been able to do so at a significantly lower case than prevailing postage rates.

Another category of communication devices currently in use is facsimile transmission equipment. When there is a need to move paper documents from one place
to another with minimum delay, facsimile devices can be used to transmit an image

Figure 8-8 Systems like this enable employees to use normal phones, with little or no special equipment, to communicate with other work stations or a central computer

of a paper document over telephone lines. The document is placed in a transmitting device at one one of the connection and is electronically carried over normal telephone lines to a receiving device at the other end, which decodes the electrical impulses and produces paper copy of the original document (see Fig. 8.9).

Although telephones are considered by many executives to be time wasters, the phone is an essential part of any office. Electronics technology is revolutionizing the use of telephones in modern offices, and with deregulation of the sales of tele-

Figure 8-9 Facsimile transmission devices enable paper documents to be transmitted electronically over normal telephone lines. (Courtesy of QWIP Systems, Division of EXXON)

phone equipment, a variety of independent companies are offering sophisticated office phone systems. These new phone systems could serve as the hub of the automated office, handling phone calls and terminal based inquiries, as well as electronic mail, document distribution, and a host of other communications functions. A more detailed description of computerized communications systems is presented in Chapter 11 on Communications.

Integrated Office Systems

What has been discussed previously as related but separate pieces of equipment used in offices may soon be integrated into systems that have the characteristics of all of the equipment we have mentioned up to this point. It is entirely conceivable that many of the "workstations" in large offices will be centered around a single piece of equipment that will provide for word processing, data retrieval from a central computer, electronic mail, and even facsimile transmission. Furthermore, with advancements in electronic technology, such workstations may not even have to be located in a central office. Some employees may be able to perform work duties at home, at a workstation that is tied to the office by telephone lines. The implications of such a scenario are of course, wide ranging. Not only would such a workstation change the relationship between an employee and his/her job, but many societal impacts would emerge as well. More employees performing work at home, or telecommuting, might lessen the demand for energy, reduce congestion on highways, relieve the demand for inner city services, and of course have a positive influence on the environment. A possible implication that we cannot even begin to visualize or predict, centers around inter-personal relationships. How will people relate to one another in the future when more and more personal and business related activities can be performed without leaving the comfort of home?

The Office in a Briefcase

Portable terminals that are capable of communicating with distant computers through telephone connections are vastly increasing the efficiency and productivity of business personnel who must travel. A portable terminal the size of a small briefcase can allow a traveler to connect to a computer in the home office and receive messages from a secretary and other personnel in the firm, direct messages back to personnel in the office, retrieve information from the firm's computer, transmit correspondence through a word processing system at the portable terminal, and enter orders for products received as a result of the day's sales activities. Many organizations claim that, by using portable terminals on the road, both the Post Office and manual information-handling systems can be bypassed, and correct information can get to the right place at the right time. And now, with briefcase-sized and handheld microcomputers, traveling personnel can perform sophisticated data processing tasks without the necessity of even being connected to a central office computer (see Fig. 8.10).

Figure 8-10 A new generation of microcomputers is appearing which offer powerful computing capabilities in units barely larger than a briefcase. This Osborne[1] unit has two 5¼ floppy disk drives and can be operated on power supplied by an internal battery pack. (Courtesy of Osborne Computer Corp.)

Computers in Retailing

Modern retail businesses have found that the best way to handle the increased transactions, meet the needs of increased accountability, and still provide customers with price, selection, and service, is to turn to computer technology. New computer systems in use in the retail industry are designed to speed up the actual store-level transactions—providing customers with more efficient service—and use a computer system to assimilate all of the transactions in order to prepare detailed accounting records.

A new generation of machines has replaced the old-fashioned cash register. The new electronic generation of cash register is called a Point Of Sale or POS terminal. These sophisticated new "cash registers" can, at a simple level, automatically compute sales tax and add it into the sales price and, at the more complex level, act as actual data entry stations to a central computer. If the POS terminal is to be used to enter data directly into a computer, however, there is some concern over the accuracy of the data being entered into the POS terminal at the time a transaction is taking place. Various coding methods are used on actual merchandise to make the process of entering data into the POS terminal more efficient and accurate. One of the most common coding systems used is the bar code. Products are encoded with tags on which are printed a series of bars that are unique to each product. A special light pen attached to the POS terminal is passed over the bar code, and it "reads" the bar-coded product identification number into the POS terminal. If the POS terminal is a stand-alone unit (not connected to a computer), then the clerk enters a sales price, and the transaction is stored in the memory of the

159

terminal for use later. If the POS terminal is connected to a computer system, the terminal transmits the product ID number to the computer, the computer looks up the price of the product in its memory, and communicates it back to the POS terminal. When the transaction is complete, the computer system automatically updates the appropriate accounting records, and also generates reorders for merchandise that is low in stock.

The grocery industry is the biggest user of full-scale POS systems. With the large number and wide variety of products offered for sale in grocery stores, the best way to manage a large store effectively is to use computers. As mentioned earlier, major advantages of POS systems are: faster checkout, better inventory control, better accounting records, and the elimination of unit pricing. In this last area, unit pricing, there is public resistance to the use of full POS for UPC systems. Store managers claim that because the prices of products are stored inside of the computer and are accessed by the POS terminal at the check-out stand, there is no need to mark the prices on every product; the shelf price should be sufficient. Consumers say the shelf prices are often wrong and they are then buying products blindly, with no guarantee that the prices in the computer are what they believe them to be. Further advancements in this field may be limited not by technology, but by public resistance to what is viewed as the human disadvantages of computer systems in retailing.

SOCIAL IMPLICATIONS

Pro Arguments

As indicated in the main body of this chapter, productivity in modern business has not increased significantly in the last 10 years, whereas the cost of performing tasks within organizations (labor costs) have increased dramatically. Computers offer organizations the opportunity to increase productivity without the increased costs associated with human labor. Although machinery is expensive originally, once in place and in operation, the cost per unit of work performed is much lower than with strictly manual labor.

The computer and related technologies, however, are not entirely replacing people in organizations; some jobs may be lost as a result of the applications of new technology, but remaining employees will be better able to perform their duties when aided by a computer. More powerful computer equipment will also enable employees to perform more tasks without being overworked. Information management systems coupled with computerized workstations will provide employees with more information to make decisions that affect the organization. In addition, with the wealth of information that will be available at one's finger-tips, organizations can be more responsive to both internal and external demands for information.

From a management perspective, the increased use of computers and related equipment offers the organization better overall control and utilization of its resources. These resources can include materials inventories, personnel suppliers, customers, and accounting reports. By better controlling resources, management can exert tighter control over costs in the organization, and make better use of whatever financial resources are available.

Con Arguments

A computer enables an organization to centralize information resources for better management utilization, but it increases the potential harm that may be done to an organization if some disaster destroys part or all of the information management system. Another possible negative side effect of the centralization of information is the potential damage that could be caused by an intentional misuse of information stored inside a computer. A criminal who breaks the security system of a computer might have access to much more information than may have been available in old-fashioned nonautomated information systems. Furthermore, with the widespread use of communications technology in modern computers, it is conceivable that someone might break the security of a computer system from thousands of miles away, and steal information without being detected.

There is no doubt that computer technology is becoming more complex; in fact, it is already more complex than the average individual can understand. As organizations become more dependant on high technology, fewer individuals within the organization are able to understand the technology. When problems or massive equipment failures occur, the effects on the administrative organization are likely to be monumental. It is conceivable that the administrative function of an organization could come to a screeching half should large parts of the technology fail. Employees whose jobs depended entirely on the computer would be unable to perform their duties, and would probably be unable to continue any work without the computer.

Machines are altering the ways in which people perform work. Organizations must cope with training problems as new machines are introduced. Most computer equipment cannot do anything without some human involvement. Organizations must also cope with the problems of retraining workers who may be displaced, or even unemployed, because of the introduction of new technology. In addition to the training problem, machines have a psychological impact on people. Machines induce fear, can severely curtail or eliminate human ingenuity, and have a tendency to decrease job flexibility. In other words, people are more often expected to adapt to computers, rather than adapting computers to people. One final note: computers are expected to increase productivity. However, often this focus on productivity results in a reduction of concern for the human dynamics involved in any organization. While the computer increases organizational control, personal accountability is increased and people begin to get the nagging feeling that "someone's watching."

HARDWARE

Not all organizations will be able to afford the best that technology has to offer. What may be possible in large organizations may be cost prohibitive in smaller organizations. But all organizations, regardless of size, can benefit to some degree from advancements in computer technology.

Small organizations may be limited to the use of microcomputer systems to assist in the process of maintaining accounting records. Although these small systems may also offer information management and word processing capabilities, they cannot begin to offer the features available on larger, more expensive systems. Medium-size firms that have the volume of transactions to support a larger system might have a minicomputer located in each branch office that is tied into a computer network. These computer systems can share information resources and operational capabilities, and allow for the type of electronic mail system described in this chapter. Secretarial tasks are likely to be carried out on stand-alone word processing systems that have access to facsimile transmission devices. Although many of the workstations within the organization are likely to have terminals connected to the local minicomputer, all the equipment would probably not be integrated into one massive company-wide communications system.

Large organizations, with both enough volume of transactions to require expensive computers and money enough to buy them, are likely to have full-blown computer systems, utilizing the latest in communications technology. Large central computer systems will be connected with smaller computer systems located in branch offices. The smaller computers will meet local data processing needs and communicate summarized activity data to the large central computer. Furthermore, a significant number of workstations within the organization will have the computerized equipment mentioned in this chapter. These stations will be connected into large communications networks that will permit point-to-point communications anywhere within the organization.

It is, of course, difficult to predict exactly how each individual organization will utilize the technology available to it. What we have attempted to do here is to make broad generalizations as to how technology will be applied in the future. Within the fast-paced field of computers, it is even possible that new equipment may at any time make everything currently in use obsolete. What is certain is that we can project the direction technology will take, but by no means can we accurately predict how far.

A LOOK TOWARD THE FUTURE

Many new pieces of equipment will be developed for business use in the future, but probably the most significant developments in technology will take place in the field of communications. In this chapter we have discussed some current developments in communications technology that have impacted modern organizations. While these developments are considered to be sophisticated, they represent only the beginning. In the future, machines and, therefore, people are going to be more interactive. More information will be gathered from wide-ranging sources and used to control an organization. The computerized workstations mentioned in this chapter will be tied together into complex communications networks that enable employees to share information more readily with one another and with outside organizations.

As already mentioned, it may even be possible for employees to execute job responsibilities at workstations at home, connected to the office by communications links. Teleconferencing, electronic mail, computerized workstations, and more machines will characterize the organizations of the future.

The computer in these organizations will also relieve employees of routine tasks, freeing them to perform more activities that require human creativity and ingenuity. Many routine decision-making processes will be delegated to the computer, and as a result work responsibilities may be redistributed throughout an organization. The role of human labor in organizations will probably be completely redefined. Humans also may not be required to work as many hours in order to perform a given volume of work. As a result, work hours, length of work, and place of work may all be in for changes in the future.

STUDY AND REVIEW

1. What is the basic purpose of an accounting business computer system?

2. What are the three major reasons why business use of computers varies widely?

3. What is a management information system? What are its component parts?

4. What are the four major types of business computer system applications? Describe two systems or applications within each of these areas.

5. How do you see the role of the computer evolving in large and small organizations over the next 10 years?

6. What is the "automated office"? Is it here yet? Are we likely to see it in the near future? Why or why not?

7. What effect do you believe an increased use of computers in business will have on the people commercial organizations serve?

8. What is word processing? What effects, positive and negative, does word processing have on organizations that implement word processing systems, and people who operate them?

9. What is a data base management system? How is a DBMS used in an organization?

10. What are the organizational implications of computer systems?

11. Summarize the positive implications of computer systems on modern commercial organizations.

12. Summarize the negative implications of business computer systems.

13. Can you foresee any other types of business applications of computers/electronic systems other than those mentioned here?

14. In what ways do you think business management can minimize the negative implications of computer technology on people?

9

INDUSTRY

PERSPECTIVE

For years, U.S. industry has pointed with pride to superior production records and at the volume of mass-produced goods coming out of its factories. It was taken for granted that the pace could and would continue, and that U.S. industry would always be the leader. However, according to Department of Labor statistics, U.S. manufacturing productivity growth during a recent 10-year period ranks at the bottom when compared to major free-world economies in Europe, Canada, the United Kingdom, and Japan. At the top is Japan with a productivity growth rate four times greater than that of the United States. To help solve this problem, caused by inflationary pressures on labor costs, interest rates, and the need to increase productivity to stay competitive in world markets, we are seeing a revolution in computer usage in manufacturing. In fact, as the following quotation suggests, computers may be the only answer industry has to raising productivity and remaining competitive in world markets.

> *The answer to lagging productivity and to the problems of labor costs in industrial plants could be computers, as the managers of industry learn to use them on the production floor.* (Lusa, 1979)

In this chapter we examine the ways in which modern industry, large and small, is beginning to introduce the use of computers to the factory floor. The areas in the production end of a business, where the computer is expected to have the most dramatic effect, include computer-aided design, computer-aided manufacturing, materials requirement planning, and the exciting, fast-moving field of robotics.

COMPUTERS IN INDUSTRY

The computerization of the factory is increasing. Industry has always been a big user of computers, but the use by many has been limited to accounting and bookkeeping functions. Now computers are beginning to be seen on the factory floor and the systems that control the factory floor. The first big users of the computers in factories were the processing industries—petro-chemical, food, and metals—where continuous processes could be electronically monitored and controlled. Other big users of computers are the aerospace and automotive industries. Both are deeply involved in computer-aided design (CAD) and computer-aided manufacturing (CAM). However, in spite of the gains in computer usage in these industries, the big steps are yet to come. Today, less than 25 percent of the U.S. industrial output is the result of mass production. The rest is produced by batch manufacturing, a system plagued by long lead times, high parts inventories, low machine utilization, and very little automation.

As the productivity problems indicate, there is room for improvement and part of the problem will be solved by the computer (see Fig. 9.1). That, however, is easier said than done. A speaker at a conference on computer-aided manufacturing, spon-

Figure 9-1 This is the interior of the largest indoor assembly plant in the world —the 747 jet assembly line at Boeing in Seattle. Computers are essential in coordinating the entire assembly process (Courtesy of the Boeing Company)

sored by the National Research Council, pointed out that " . . . the deeper you get into what's coming in manufacturing technology, the less sure you are about anything except the fact that what's coming is rapid change and a vast range of new capabilities."

As indicated earlier, some industries are already well along in the use of computer technology to increase the efficiency of manufacturing activities. At one of its plants Digital Equipment Corporation, a manufacturer of minicomputers, is using bar-coded labels, like those now found on most grocery items, to track all phases of assembly and testing of printed circuit boards. The labels are read with hand-held light pens and are located at the various stages of assembly and testing. Because each circuit board is tracked individually, the computer can "watch" each assembly step.

The steel industry is using computers in a unique program. Through the Systems Communications Committee of the American Iron & Steel Institute, a Steel Customer Communications System has been developed. The SCCS is intended to improve the speed, accuracy, and cost efficiency of ordering and shipping steel and managing inventories. The system is for use of the steel companies' customers. Large steel buyers can obtain shipping status information to manage large inventories. The SCCS information exchange system enables customers to make inquiries of the steel companies' computers to obtain instantaneous updates on the status of their orders. Some customers have been able to reduce inventories by a matter of days and schedule production with more certainty.

Thus far we have discussed the use of computers in manufacturing environments in very general terms. We have mentioned process control, computer-aided design, and computer-aided manufacturing. Each will be dealt with further in separate sections of this chapter; but before doing so, we should mention two of the most significant applications of computer technology that promise to have possibly the biggest impact on manufacturing, namely, Materials Requirement Planning (MRP) and robotics.

Materials requirement planning is one element, and a growing one, of an overall computerized manufacturing control system. It includes activities such as shop scheduling, vendor scheduling, material yields, and predicted shortage lists. Its purpose is to enable a shop to react on a daily basis to changes in the master manufacturing schedule, bill of materials for each manufacturing activity, and general parts inventory (see Fig. 9.2).

Robots, considered by some to be the ultimate machine worker, are beginning to find their way into the factory. These devices, representing the ultimate extension of the computer, will perform dreary, dirty, dangerous tasks without complaint. They don't take long coffee breaks, they don't take vacations, and most of the time they don't get sick. There are about 4,000 robots in use in the U.S., another 1,500 in Western Europe, and an estimated 35,000 in Japan, according to the Robot Institute of America. The big auto makers seem to be leading the way with computer-controlled robots, but other industries are rapidly joining them. Westinghouse Electric Corporation has developed a program aimed at replacing people with robots in

Figure 9-2 Many industries utilize computer systems to maximize the yield from materials which must be cut from some raw material. This system helps companies determine how to place patterns on pieces of fabric to minimize wastes from cutting. This particular system can be adapted for use in the clothing and shoe industries. (Courtesy of CAMSCO, Richardson, Tx.)

assembly line jobs. The program is intended to increase productivity in low-volume or batch manufacturing which, according to Westinghouse, accounts for 75 percent of all U.S. manufacturing and 30 percent of the gross national product. The system consists of computer-controlled workstations with robot arms and grippers, programmable conveyors, and television cameras used as a visual sensory system.

Computer-Aided Design

Economists claim that the productivity of workers depends on three important factors: the attitude, training, and health of the individual; the availability of natural resources; and the amount of sophisticated technological equipment available to assist the individual in performing tasks. Computers, as we have seen many times already earlier in this book, are tools that can increase productivity in some given situations, and result in definite economic gain for the individual worker and the business organization. Computers have been used to help control manufacturing processes, but now they are being incorporated into the design process to improve productivity even further (see Fig. 9.3).

The development of a wide range of products, from electronic circuits to buildings, requires a number of very specific steps, which include:

1. preliminary design
2. advanced design
3. model development
4. model testing
5. final design
6. production and construction.

Figure 9-3 Engineers can perform many special tests on parts designs, using computers with graphics capabilities. The capability for doing such testing increases product quality and performance while reducing development costs. (Courtesy of the Boeing Company)

All six of these steps can be made more efficient through the use of computers.

Prior to the use of computers, engineers made preliminary sketches, design drawings, and engineering drawings by traditional hand drafting. As the product moved through the design phase, component parts were evaluated and changes in design were made where necessary. As these changes were made, all of the design drawings had to be altered or completely redrawn to reflect new modifications. Thus, the preparation of drawings could occupy a substantial portion of the designer's time, and the time spent drafting meant that time could not be spent working on the product and perfecting better designs.

Computer technology now allows engineers to use a light pen and enter drawings directly into the computer through a CRT. Changes in the basic design can then be made instantaneously. After the design is entered into the computer, programs can then be implemented to analyze the design and report on certain characteristics (see Fig. 9.4). As the results of testing in the computer are reported, the engineer can change the characteristics of the design quickly and easily and have the test per-

Figure 9-4 Computer graphics systems enable engineers to test specific designs extensively before construction takes place. Should tests reveal flaws, the design can be altered easily and tested again. (Courtesy of General Motors Corporation)

formed again. When the design has been completed, the computer can be instructed to prepare detailed engineering drawings from the design, and even used to direct other machines to produce component parts of new products according to the designs stored within the computer. It is becoming increasingly common for an engineer to interact with a computer from the time an idea is conceived until the final production steps are completed (see Fig. 9.5).

Computer-Aided Manufacturing

In manufacturing companies, the scheduling of production and control of the inventory are very important. Production scheduling computations are typically of such a volume that the task is difficult to perform manually. Furthermore, since more than one production schedule may be possible, the computer can be helpful in carrying out the complex calculations that are necessary to discover the best schedule for reducing cost and more efficiently utilizing production resources. Computer scheduling is also more dynamic because it allows for rapid response to changes in the availability of or demand for materials and facilities after production has started.

In production planning it is necessary to determine in complete detail the number and skill of the workers needed, machine requirements, and all of the raw material and parts that are required for the manufacture of every item. After the volume of production is determined, a series of calculations for materials requirements are made. Assemblies are broken down into subassemblies, subassemblies into parts, and so on, resulting in a complete list of every item required. This list is compared with existing inventories, and if raw materials, parts, or subassemblies must be bought, purchase requisitions and orders are issued. Most of this can now be accomplished by computer and, as indicated earlier in this chapter, is referred to as Materials Requirement Planning (MRP).

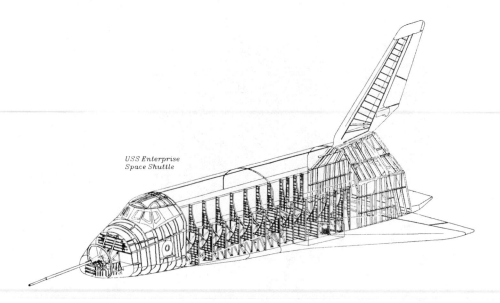

USS Enterprise
Space Shuttle

Figure 9-5 New printer/plotters are capable of producing high quality architectural and engineering drawings. This picture of the main structural members of the space shuttle, was produced on a graphics printer

Production control requires the careful coordination of people, machines, and materials (see Fig. 9.6). Computers are used to control overall production. They also have the capacity to cater to each individual order. In the automobile industry, for example, many cars are built to fill specific orders from customers who can choose from among thousands of combinations of colors, accessories, and optional equipment. After orders are entered into the computer, it controls the movement of parts along the feeder lines that run through a plant, assuring that the correct part gets to the right worker at the right time.

Industrial Automation

Automation involves the use of various technological devices and methods in performing manufacturing operations, or any other processes, without the direct intervention of a human being. In a broader and more technical definition, automation has been described as "the substitution of mechanical, hydraulic, pneumatic, electrical, and electronic devices for human organs of observation, decision, and effort, so as to increase productivity, control quality, and reduce costs.

The ability of machines to regulate themselves—is a fundamental aspect of automation—is made possible by the technology of feedback. Feedback is accomplished by routing part of the result of a process back to the device that regulates the input of the process through various sensing devices.

Among the sensing techniques used are photoelectric cells, infrared cells, high-

Figure 9-6 Data capture terminals such as these, enable a computer to monitor and direct an entire manufacturing process. A worker can insert a specially coded card into a terminal and receive special handling instructions from the computer. (Courtesy of Hewlett-Packard Company)

frequency devices, and x-ray components. The sensing unit, usually located near the output end of an automated system, observes the operations or finished products continuously. Information about what is being accomplished is transmitted to the measuring unit (computer) that compares the information it receives with the per-

Figure 9-7 Robots can be used to load and remove parts from heavy machinery, deliver machined parts to a laser controlled gauging station, and to stack finished items in a storage bin. (Courtesy of Cincinnati Milacron)

formance requirements stored in its memory. Any differences between the two are determined, and this information is relayed to the control unit. The control unit automatically activates forces that make the necessary adjustments to correct the error.

This cycle of continuous operations is called a "closed loop" because it is performed entirely by units built directly into the automated system. Therefore, an automated system with a self-controlling closed-loop feedback has no need for a human operator to make corrections or adjustments in its performance. This is contrasted with an open-loop system where a human operator is responsible for making any necessary adjustments.

Numerical Control of Machine Tools   One of the more important aspects of computer-aided manufacturing is numerical control. This is a means of automatically controlling the positioning and operation of machine tools. These tools are used to cut, drill, grind, press, turn, punch, mill, and otherwise alter the shape of metal pieces. Conventional methods require a skilled machine operator. The metal-working industry, however, is installing more numerical control systems to produce metal parts automatically.

Figure 9-8 Many modern industrial processes could not be controlled without computers. This picture shows the main control center for a computer controlled blast furnace in a steel mill. (Courtesy of Inland Steel Company)

Specifically, a numerical control system is one in which actions of a machine are controlled by the use of numerical data. The numerical control system reads numbers, translates them into instructions, directs the machine tool to perform the instructions, and compares machine performance with the instructions (see Fig. 9.7).

Numerical control is not restricted to machining alone. The fundamentals of control by numbers are being applied to many other fields. For example, metal-forming equipment such as punch presses, tube benders, and metal fabricators have been equipped with controllers and are being operated under numerical control.

Process Control   In contrast with numerical control, which provides automation of discrete operations, process control provides automation of continuous operations. The process industries were the first to use computer control on a large scale. These are industries in which ingredients flow continuously through all stages of a process as they are converted from raw materials to an end product or group of products (see Fig. 9.8). Included in this category are petroleum refining, steel processing, electric power generation, and the manufacture of paper, chemicals, steel, cement, and food products.

Computer process control is being used increasingly in such industries to automate the manufacturing process and to control a large number of variables that are impossible for a person to control simultaneously. Factors occurring in production processes of this type, including variables such as time, weight, pressure, temperature, size, volume, and revolutions per minute, are monitored at critical places in the factory. By means of an analog-to-digital converter, these continuous physical measurements are changed into discrete numbers. These data are instantly relayed to the computer for comparison with standards or planned results programmed into the computer beforehand. If there is a difference between the two, the computer decides what adjustments are necessary and sends an appropriate command to the control mechanism in order to bring operations back to standard (see Fig. 9.9).

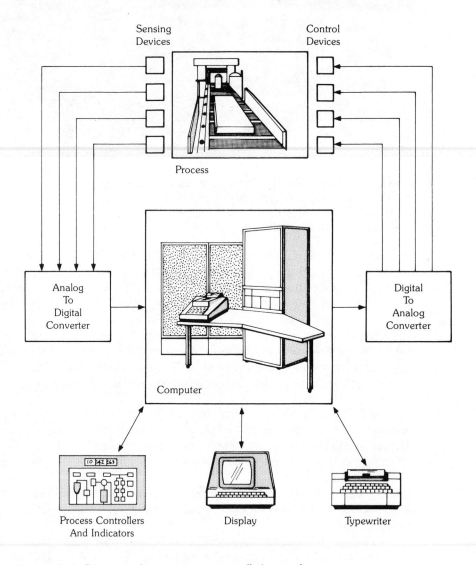

Figure 9-9 Diagram of a computer controlled manufacturing process.

Integration of Business and Process Control Systems

In general, there is a close interaction between the information required for control of the manufacturing process and that required for overall management of the business. For example, information about various factors of production, raw materials, process yields, and the status of work in process is of common significance. All of the data available to the process control system through measurements of the physical process can be made available to management by having a human operator record and report instrument readings periodically. Reports printed out by the control computer may also be transmitted for management use. As a result of technological advancements, however, it is now possible to capture data at its source automatically and communicate it immediately rather than at some later time. In other words, computers are capable of both analyzing operating data for control of the physical process and reporting data for control of the business. Modern data communication techniques also make it possible to transmit to remote locations the data required for management functions. The result is an integrated system that both controls manufacturing processes and provides information to carry out engineering, financial, marketing, and other management functions.

Industrial Robots

The first industrial revolution took place at a time when people were able to transfer physical skills to machines. We are now, as many observers claim, in the infancy of a second industrial revolution, but this time the revolution centers around computers and involves the transfer of intelligence from humans to machines. This transfer of intelligence from humans to machines is only just beginning, and it is highly improbable that we will be able to create machines that can perform like humans in almost every situation. Evidence also exists that we may yet be able to create "intelligent" machines that can perform tasks better than humans in some specific circumstances. Where this is most evident is in the field of industrial robots. Industrial robots are already in use, but none currently is sophisticated enough to handle intricate, tricky assembly operations.

Webster's definition of a robot begins by describing it as a "machine in the form of a human being that performs the mechanical functions of a human being." Today's robot manufacturers, however, are not attempting to create anything that looks or acts human. While it is entirely possible to design a robot that walks on artifical legs or speaks a human language, it is much cheaper and more efficient to keep the robot standing in one place and to speak to it by using sophisticated computer programming languages.

A robot's basic function is not to look or behave like a human being, but to do a human's work. For such work it needs a guiding brain (a computer) and an arm with claws for fingers (known as a "gripper"). The computer can be plugged into an electrical outlet; cables run from the computer along the robot's arm and transmit instructions in the form of electric impulses to the gripper. The gripper can also be activated by movements of pulses of air, or for heavy work, hydraulic pressure. The Robot Institute of America, an industrial trade group, offers a more contemporary definition of a robot than Webster's: "A reprogrammable multifunctional manipulator designed to move material, parts, tools, or specialized devices through variable programmed motions for the performance of a variety of tasks."

This is a rather cumbersome definition, but it does include some key terms that focus on the advantages of the new robots. Reprogrammable and multifunctional are the key words. Factories have long used automatic machines to mass produce goods, but these devices could perform only one task at a time. New work routines required new machinery or extensive retooling. The new industrial robots, or "steel collar" workers, now being installed have control and memory systems, often in the form of minicomputers. These enable the robots to be programmed to carry out a number of work routines and, when necessary, to be programmed to carry out even more (see Fig. 9.10).

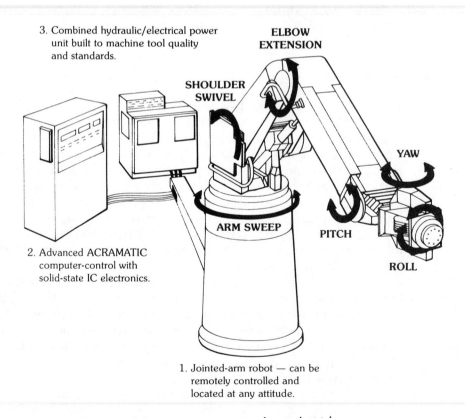

3. Combined hydraulic/electrical power unit built to machine tool quality and standards.

ELBOW EXTENSION

SHOULDER SWIVEL

YAW

ARM SWEEP

PITCH

ROLL

2. Advanced ACRAMATIC computer-control with solid-state IC electronics.

1. Jointed-arm robot — can be remotely controlled and located at any attitude.

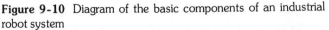

Figure 9-10 Diagram of the basic components of an industrial robot system

The fact that the robot's instructions can be changed is critically important to its industrial use. A standard assembly line must produce a large amount to operate economically, and it takes months to alter or renovate its component machines. A robot can be reprogrammed for a new task in a few minutes. Furthermore, at least 60 percent of U.S. manufacturing is done on batches too small for assembly lines. Robots can do many of those jobs, and it is estimated that they can reduce costs in small-lot manufacturing by 80 to 90 percent.

The simplest of robots now being used in industry are referred to as "pick and place" machines that are capable of only the simplest of assembly operations. These machines can be guided through their operations by programs provided on pegboards full of wires. These are reminiscent of early punch card data processing equipment. To make these robots more versatile, the mechanical pegboard programming method can be replaced with an electronic memory. A human operator can then program the robot by using a hand-held control to guide the robot through its motions, and then have the electronic memory store the desired activities to be repeated again and again in the future without a human operator. By adding a computer, as mentioned earlier, the robot can be directed to perform a certain movement, and have the computer work out the actual movements of the joints in order to perform the desired activity. The integration of a computer into a robot may also one day provide the robot with the capability to use feedback from its surroundings to adjust its movements. If a particular piece that a robot is supposed to pick up is not in the exact position it should be, then a robot with feedback capabilities would be able to determine or sense the exact position and adjust its movements to pick it up. In another instance, if some parts that the robot is trying to assemble do not go together easily, the robot would be able to move them around until they fit.

This last example is not yet feasible with current technology; however, it does not appear to be very long before robots can be given a practical feedback capability through the use of TV cameras for "sight," and sophisticated electronics for "touch" or tactile capabilities.

For the present, limited sensory feedback can be added to robots through the use of a laser. A laser beam can be focused on an approaching part, and the brightness of the reflected light can be used to gauge its distance. When parts are more than several feet away, a technique similar to radar can be used. A pulse of laser light can be directed toward an oncoming part, and the time required for the reflected beam to come back to a sensing eye can be measured and used to judge distance. Sonar, a mechanism now also used to focus cameras, can be used to assist robots in locating parts. Such rough techniques may allow robots to locate objects, but they do not provide the fine positioning movements needed to fit parts together.

One solution to the problem of fine positioning is to have the robot put parts together by feel. Sensors on a robot's hand could measure the amount of force exerted on a particular item during a particular movement, and use this information to adjust the motions of the robot's hand to complete the positioning of that particular part. It is also possible that robots of the future will be able to assemble a variety of parts into a finished product by using the same tools a person would use.

The Who's Who of Robots

The industrial robots of today and the near future will look nothing like the robots popularized in the movie "Star Wars." What they lack in appearance, however, may be offset by the fact that they have become increasingly smarter and more versatile in recent years. What follows is a framework for describing the types of robots that exist now, and those that are likely to be developed in the future.

Industrial robots—These will have armlike projections and grippers that perform factory work customarily done by humans. The term is usually reserved for machines with some form of built-in control and capable of stand-alone operations.

Pick and place robots—These are the simplest versions, accounting for about one-third of all U.S. installations. The name comes from its usual application in materials handling: picking something from one spot and placing it at another. Freedom of movement is usually limited to two or three directions—in and out, left and right, and up and down. The control system is electromechanical.

Servo robots—These are the most common industrial robots because to some degree, this group includes all the robots listed below. The name stems from one or more servomechanisms that enable the arm and gripper to alter direction in mid-air without having to trip a mechanical switch. Five to seven directional movements are common, depending on the number of joints or articulations in the robot's arm.

Programmable robot—This is a servo robot directed by a programmable controller that memorizes a sequence of arm and gripper movements. This routine can then be repeated perpetually. The robot is reprogrammed by leading its gripper through a new task.

Computerized robot—This category contains robots that are servo robots run by a computer. The computer controller does not have to be taught by leading the arm-gripper through a routine; new instructions can be transmitted electronically. The programming for such "smart" robots may include the ability to optimize or improve its work routine instructions.

Sensory robot—This is a computerized robot with one or more artificial senses, usually sight or touch.

Robots' Influence on the Labor Force

The new technology of robotics is making it possible to replace more skilled workers. The latest computer-controlled robots are considerably more versatile than their simple-minded predecessors of a few years ago—a new generation of robots that "see," "feel," and even "think" is emerging from the laboratories. Some automation experts say that such smart robots could displace 65 to 75 percent or more of today's factory workers. Others say that we are in the very bottom of a market explosion, and the future growth is going to resemble what happened with transistors and pocket calculators in past years.

The potential roadblock in the U.S. will be, of course, opposition by organized labor. Thus far the unions have been relatively quiet about the subject of robotics, mainly because they recognize that technological progress is essential, and economic growth has offset any job losses. Moreover, robot applications to date have relieved people of work that is hazardous, dirty, or monotonous, such as loading stamping presses, spraying paint in confined areas, and making the same spot welds day in and day out (see Fig. 9.11). A United Auto Workers' official noted that when you take into account the need that robots have to be maintained and fed parts to work on, they are not so great a threat to working people. But the new generation of smart robots and totally automated factories could quickly harden labor's somewhat lax attitude.

Some claim that robotics will not eliminate jobs, but will create jobs. However, the new jobs that will be created will not be the same kinds of jobs that will be eliminated. There is a parallel that can be drawn between the impending robotic revolution and the agricultural revolution earlier in this century. Robots will uproot people from the factory just as machines took over farming, and society could derive

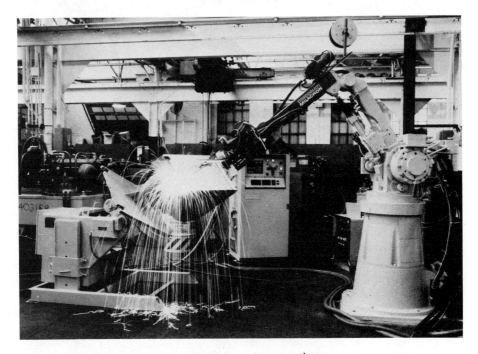

Figure 9-11 Robots can work efficiently and accurately in environments which could be hazardous to humans. Pictured here is a Cincinnati Milacron T³ industrial robot suitable for welding operations. (Courtesy of Cincinnati Milacron)

Hi! I'm here to fix your computer . . .

a net benefit. Some displaced workers will move to perhaps more satisfying jobs, such as programming and building the robots.

SOCIAL IMPLICATIONS

Pro Arguments

Productivity is the biggest problem in American industry today. The computer offers promise of solutions to some of the productivity problems. Although computers are just being introduced onto the factory floor, their impact will be widespread in a short time. Such use of computers in factories will also lead to numerous advantages other than a simple increase in productivity. Due to continuous monitoring of manufacturing processes by computers, the items manufactured should be of higher quality, and the general defect level, usually associated with mass production techniques, should be reduced. In addition, the speed and accuracy of the mass production process should increase through the use of computers. Computers will also enable more customizing of products in mass production facilities, which have long been characterized by repetitiously similar items.

Computer-aided design is revolutionizing the methods by which products are traditionally designed, tested, and put into production. Computers offer the opportunity for engineers to design products on the CRT screen of a graphics terminal connected to the computer. Computers can then run various tests on the design and quickly report findings back to an engineer. With very little time delay, the engineer can then change certain aspects of the design and run the tests again. CAD improves the efficiency of the design process, while dramatically reducing the costs associated with it. When engineers have completed the design process, computers can be instrumental in preparing engineering documents and programs that may be used in the computers that are to control the manufacturing process.

Materials Requirement Planning (MRP) will allow large organizations better control of material resources. MRP can help insure that too many materials are not on hand, increasing inventory costs, or make sure that enough materials are available so as not to slow down the production process. The computer can also be used to track production of items through the factory. It can specify what materials are required at what stations, monitor whether the materials arrive, keep track of how long a certain operation is taking, and report at what stage of the production process a particular product is at any time.

Robotics offer industry the ultimate automation tool. Robots can be programmed to perform intricate tasks, and be expected to perform them continuously with very little interruption. Although it is feared that robots will take away some human jobs, they can perform many jobs that humans consider dirty, dangerous, and tedious. Robots also offer tremendous cost advantages over humans. Currently, the average hourly total compensation for a manufacturing worker is about $20 per hour. When in place, the hourly cost of a robot can be less than $6 per hour.

Con Arguments

The biggest fear about the increased use of computers in industry, of course, is automation. The use of numerical control on machine tools, replacing workers, and the use of industrial robots capable also of replacing humans in the assembly process, have many people predicting a completely unmanned factory in the future. Although proponents of computers and robotics claim that increased use of these tools will actually increase the availability of jobs, this remains unproven. At the very least, as jobs are eliminated through the use of computer technology, the displaced employees will have to be retrained to fill other positions. As is often the case, the jobs created by computers will require a higher skill level than those they may have eliminated. Age and other physical and mental characteristics can affect any displaced worker's ability to be retrained.

Many experts in the use of computers in industry say that the computerized factory of the future will not be an unmanned one. However, as computers and computer-controlled machines become more commonplace, those workers who remain may find that they have little to do with the actual process of building products. Job satisfaction may well be low, and if people become just monitors of computers, mass boredom may still be commonplace. Though technological innovation is moving rapidly, one of the controlling influences on how fast computers take over in industry is likely to be labor unions. Labor unions, already fighting mass layoffs and changing working conditions, will hopefully still have some influence on retaining the human factor in factories of the future.

The economics of the fully automated factories are not clear. Initial expenditures for equipment are high, and reliability is uncertain. As factories move more toward the increased use of computers, an increasing dependence on high technology will naturally follow, requiring highly skilled technicians and well-trained repair personnel. Fewer and fewer people will be able to understand and, therefore, control the entire manufacturing process. Although computers will generally increase the precision of the manufacturing process, increased demand for human precision may cause some additional problems. Many MRP programs instituted in industry are not as fully effective as had been expected, because such systems require extremely high degrees of accuracy of records, which humans are not used to producing.

HARDWARE

Different sized manufacturing organizations will always use computer technology differently, depending mainly on the cost of the equipment. Small organizations are likely to use individual pieces of advanced technology equipment to improve manufacturing efficiency, while large organizations are more likely to use integrated manufacturing systems to improve productivity.

Small manufacturing organizations that develop their own products will most certainly use computer-aided design during development. Administrative computer systems will probably be used for production planning and scheduling, but not for actual manufacturing management. The administrative computer is likely to be a large batch-oriented computer, while actual production management will probably be performed by one or a number of minicomputers placed in the factory, and possibly hooked together into a network. Some robotics will be used, but smaller firms may find the cost of expensive intelligent robots prohibitive, and therefore limit their use of robots to the less sophisticated "pick and place" variety. Computers will be used to keep track of inventories of raw materials, goods in process, and finished goods, but again the cost factor will probably prohibit the use of full-scale computerized production tracking systems.

Large manufacturing organizations have the volume of production and the money to take advantage of fully integrated manufacturing systems. One or many computers within a large organization will be used expressly to control the manufacturing process. Such systems may report to administrative computer systems, but they will be separate. These integrated computer systems will enable engineers to design and test products. After products are designed, the computer can produce the actual working drawings needed to plan for production, analyze materials requirements for production, and manage the inventory of these materials during production. In addition, the computer can produce programs that will be used to control machines that are actually involved in the assembly or manufacturing process. Furthermore, such industrial computers will be able to monitor performance at various stages of the manufacturing process and make any necessary changes. They will also be able to track the production of goods through the entire manufacturing process. All in all, industrial computer systems will increase the productivity and efficiency of industrial organizations while helping to produce a wider variety of higher quality products. This may be accomplished without the loss of many human jobs.

A LOOK TOWARD THE FUTURE

Although it is not yet clear what exact impact new industrial technology will have on humans, computerized factories are one possible solution to our national problem of sagging productivity. We can expect computers to be used increasingly in the design phase of product development, even reaching the stage some day where design computers will be given general product specifications and the computer will design products for us and direct robots to manufacture them. Robots will become more and more intelligent as they are given the capabilities for sight, touch, and logic. As they become more intelligent they will become capable of performing more complex operations, possibly replacing humans in difficult jobs. The sophistication of computers and robots may bring the advantage to the consumer of a wider variety of products that can be customized to a degree never before possible. These products should be of a higher quality than products made with older manufacturing techniques, and be available at a lower cost.

Firms will continue to use computers not only to design products and control the actual manufacturing process, but to control the use of materials and resources to a greater degree. Such systems in use now are not providing organizations with the degree of control they desire. This is mainly due to the fact that people have not yet learned enough about how to utilize technology and work with it. Although it can be only theorized at this point, our hope is that the use of computers in industry will result in better products in the future, but not at the expense of fewer jobs.

STUDY AND REVIEW

1. What is MRP? Why is it important to a large manufacturing organization?

2. What are the principal advantages of robotics in manufacturing environments?

3. Discuss the two sides of the robotics issue.

4. What is the difference between CAD and CAM?

5. What is the biggest single negative implication of industrial automation? How is that fear usually countered?

6. What is the difference between process control and numerical control?

7. Why do business and process control systems need to be integrated?

8. What are the problems with productivity in the U.S.? How does industry propose to solve them?

9. Summarize the positive social implications of computer technology in manufacturing organizations.

10. Summarize the negative social implications of computer technology in manufacturing.

11. Can you foresee any other types of manufacturing applications of computer systems other than those mentioned here?

12. In what ways do you think manufacturing organizations can minimize the negative implications of computer technology on people?

10

TRANSPORTATION

PERSPECTIVE

Getting people from one place to another in our society is an important task. We are a mobile society, much of whose freedom lies in the ability to move about with relative ease. Of equal importance with the transportation of people is the transportation of goods and materials across country and around the world. Much of our standard of living is dependent on how efficiently our transportation systems function. In the past decade tremendous population and economic growth have placed a large burden on our transportation systems. Airlines have experienced tremendous growth; passenger traffic has increased many times, freight traffic is up, and mail volume has grown. Vehicular traffic is an increasing problem in all of our major cities. Rail and ocean shipping facilities are experiencing an increase in the request for their services. Energy availability, environmental effects, and government regulations are causing increasing concern about the role of the automobile and mass transit systems in our society. It is little wonder that various transportation systems are turning to electronic computers for solutions to the growing problems associated with the transportation of people and products. It is even possible that new communications/computer technologies may replace some forms of physical travel. Such a view is held by the noted author Alvin Toffler, in his book *The Third Wave.*

> *Today's plummeting cost of communications suggests the substitution of communications for many transport functions. It may be far cheaper, more energy conserving, and more appropriate in the long run to lay in an advanced communications network than a ramified structure of costly roads and streets. Clearly, road transport is needed. But to*

185

> *the degree that production is decentralized, rather than cen-*
> *tralized, transportation costs can be minimized without*
> *isolating villages from one another, from the urban areas, or*
> *from the world at large.*   *(Toffler, 1980)*

In this chapter we explore the applications of computer technology in the field of transportation. As you read, note that the discussions of computer technology as applied to transportation systems are divided into two distinctly separate but related areas: (1) the application of electronics and computer technology within the transportation form itself (engine control systems in automobiles, flight control systems for airplanes, etc.); and (2) the use of computer technology to schedule, direct, and control entire transportation systems (air traffic control, rail switching, travel reservation systems, etc.).

COMPUTERS IN TRANSPORTATION

Aircraft Computer Systems

Airlines are experiencing a rapid growth in the demand for their services. Coupled with this increased demand is an increase in the number, variety, and speed of aircraft, and in the complexity of the control systems. Today, aircraft computers are used for: (1) systems monitoring; (2) plane and passenger scheduling; (3) guidance and navigation; (4) flight data display; (5) communications; and (6) collision avoidance. Though it was navigation that first brought computers into aircraft, now virtually no area of airline activity remains untouched by computer technology.

Computer control with human supervision in aircraft is the trend in commercial aviation. In today's large sophisticated planes, seldom do pilots fly with their hands on the control wheels—they have become button pushers or, in the jargon of the industry, "flight managers" or supervisors. The newest commercial aircraft have computer-generated displays that can include, among other things, a complete picture of all neighboring aircraft. The pilot now has a wide variety of control options. The aircraft can be asked to attain a certain altitude, heading, or speed and hold its position. By pushing some buttons, the pilot can command a gyroscopic system to fly the aircraft to within a half-mile of any latitude and longitude. More and more aircraft regularly use a computer "autoland" system that lands the aircraft without the pilot touching the controls. The passengers cannot distinguish the computer's landing from the pilots'. The autoland system can function when ceiling and visibility are very poor, though in the U.S. such "zero-zero" landings are not yet authorized by the Federal Aviation Administration.

Aircraft themselves have become so complex that it is virtually impossible for a human being, or even several humans who make up a flight crew, to monitor the condition of all aspects of the aircraft's operation while in flight. Special-purpose computers, unlike the data processing computers discussed in other chapters, are used to help the flight crew maintain control over an aircraft. Computers can monitor all of the important functions within an aircraft and display their conditions to the flight crew. These electronic controls can also make adjustments in various flight control mechanisms without human direction, relying on preprogrammed instruction (see Fig. 10.1).

In many instances, aircraft control mechanisms are becoming too complex for single computer systems, located on the flight deck, to handle. Usually, aircraft utilize several special-purpose computer systems to monitor and control distinct areas of operation. With the advent of microelectronics, microprocessor-based control systems can be tied together to form a sort of computer network that controls flight, reports status to a central flightdeck computer system, and tests for correct operation of aircraft systems.

Air Traffic Control   Computer control of all air traffic is essential to enable airspace utilization to keep pace with the sophistication of new aircraft. The Federal Aviation Administration has developed a computer controlled air traffic system for use at major airports, and is planning a more sophisticated system for the future. The cur-

Figure 10-1 An interior view of the flight deck of a Boeing 747 (Courtesy of Boeing Company)

rent system is capable of controlling take-offs, enroute flight, and landings to relieve conjestion at airports. It also provides accurate control of planes in flight to reduce the possibility of collision.

The computer controlled air traffic system uses high-precision radar to locate aircraft. The radar generates a beacon signal that can communicate with transponder units located in flying aircraft. The device automatically transmits a return signal that contains information such as the identity of the aircraft, its altitude, and speed. When received by the air traffic control computer system, data about each plane within a certain geographical area is displayed on a CRT screen operated by a human air traffic controller (see Fig. 10.2). The positions of planes within sectors are displayed as spots of light on the screen of the controllers' consoles. Each of these spots of light is accompanied by a data block that gives the plane's identification, altitude, and speed, and other information. From this display, the traffic controller can maintain safe distances between many aircraft flying in the same airspace, and direct them to land without mishap.

The FAA is developing a new computerized control system called Automated EnRoute Air traffic control system (AERA). It is part of a new $2.8 billion computer system the FAA hopes to install in its 23 regional air traffic control centers by the early 1990s.

Figure 10-2 A view of the console and radar screen in a typical Federal Aviation Administration air traffice control center. (Courtesy of Dept. of Transportation, FAA)

Under the current system, commercial airline pilots must wait until a controller approves their flight plans to make sure they keep a safe distance from other jets. While a pilot uses a computer to provide information on other planes in his air space, it's the controller who actually surveys the situation and gives the pilot clearance. AERA computers, using FAA radar, would automatically survey the skies along the plane's route and signal the pilot when it was safe for him to proceed without ever talking to the controller. They could also automatically warn both pilots and controllers of an impending crash and, unless the controller intervenes, transmit instructions to the pilot on how to avoid it.

Flight Simulation Systems   Computers are used extensively for flight simulation systems. Economic and safety considerations are primary reasons for using flight simulators. Computer flight simulation systems can be used to train and upgrade pilots in the operation of aircraft realistically without ever leaving the ground. They may also be used for experimentation purposes to test instrumentation and pilot reaction to the design characteristics of an aircraft before it is actually built.

Through electronic and hydraulic systems interlinked as well as controlled by computers, the pilot senses the forces he or she would experience in actual flight. The instruments are real flight equipment with information generated from a digital computer. Even the inflight sounds are artifically generated. The cockpit is installed in a cab mounted on hydraulically operated gimbals to give the pilot a more realistic sense of flight. For example, the cab actually travels forward, dives, climbs, and rolls, simulating the motions of a real plane. These aircraft dynamics are represented by complex mathematical equations in the computer.

To further enhance the impression of flight, a visual scene is shown to the pilot through color television monitors in the windsheild of the cab. Runways, airport buildings, helicopters, trees, highways, mountains, towns, and even a ship rolling on ocean waves pass beneath the plane at appropriate speed and altitude (see Fig. 10.3). This visual scene is actually produced either by mounting a TV camera over a small-scale mockup of actual terrain, and controlling the movement of the camera

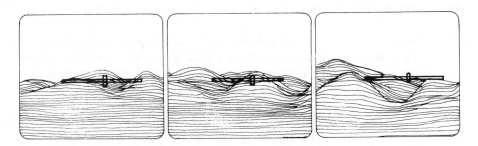

Figure 10-3 Pilots could guide aircraft in low visibility situations by observing electronic pictures such as these projected on the windshield of the cockpit by graphics-producing computer systems. Such systems can be used for flight similators also.

through the computer, or by using extensive computer graphics systems that can simulate terrain without TV cameras and mockups.

Scheduling   in addition to using computers to control aircraft, computers can be and are used to maximize the efficiency of aircraft. Airlines utilize computers to schedule the use of their fleet of aircraft, as well as to maintain accurate maintenance schedules. Outside of the actual control of aircraft, however, the biggest use of computers in the airline industry is for ticketing. With the computer, airlines can make maximum use of every seat up to the moment of a plane's departure. Computer-controlled reservation systems provide airline clerks and travel agents with almost immediate access to up-to-the-minute information on space availability for all flights. When the reservation agent enters the proper numbers on a keyboard, he or she can instantly get a picture of the availability of all seats near the departure time requested. The information is either presented on a CRT screen, or printed on the ticket agent's terminal. As the reservations are entered into the system, the transactions are edited by the computer to insure that all necessary information has been included. Then the computer can issue tickets and update seat availability information to reflect the sale of a certain number of tickets.

If space is not available to a traveler on a specific flight, the agent can advise the computer to put him on one or more waiting lists. When cancellations are received, the computer will automatically check these lists and notify the proper agent of the passenger entitled to the available space.

With the congestion in and around major airports, computer systems are being devloped to streamline the ticketing process at an airport itself. Some airlines are installing computerized ticket vendors that can be operated by the passenger. Passengers may insert a magnetically encoded credit card into the machine, and purchase tickets without the aid of airline personnel. These Automatic Ticket Vendors (ATV) are connected with the airlines reservations computer in order to provide the passenger with accurate seat availability information.

Aerospace Transportation

Although aerospace transportation systems transport only a few people, many things learned by flying in space are applicable to more conventional modes of transportation. Hundreds of computers are used in NASA aerospace systems, and many technological advances in the computer field are direct spinoffs from these applications.

The mission of a space vehicle with astronauts is complex and hazardous. Reliable guidance and control systems are a necessity. Computers represent probably the only method of providing accurate, reliable guidance and control systems for space flight. The computer on a spacecraft supervises the guidance of the craft, as well as coordinates the flight. The astronauts let the computer control most of the flight while they check its progress and provide input information (see Fig. 10.4).

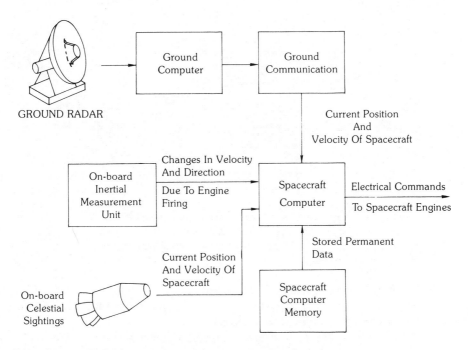

Figure 10-4 Typical computerized guidance system for space craft, utilizing ground-based and on-board computers.

The guidance and control system stores information about the spacecraft's position and speed, automatically projects the craft's future course, calculates any needed course corrections, and automatically controls the firing of engines to move the craft back on course. A mechanism called the inertial measurement unit provides the computer with a fixed reference by which to gauge the spacecraft's altitude, and to sense and relay to the computer any changes in speed and altitude that result from engine firings. Another source of information is the network of radar tracking stations on Earth. In both Earth orbital missions and deep space missions, these stations are the computers' main source of data. The radar tracks the spacecraft and, using a computer, calculates the spacecraft's velocity and position. The calculations are then radioed to the spacecraft's computer. The third source of input data is information from the star and landmark sightings made by the astronauts themselves. A space mission would be impossible without computers for communication and control of the mass of data necessary for a successful mission.

What has been described here so far is manned space flight. Many space explorations in the future will be initially too hazardous for humans (see Fig. 10.5). Control of spacecraft will have to be accomplished completely by computer. Some spacecraft will travel such great distances from Earth that communications will become a problem. In the example of the Viking Lander mission to the surface of Mars, the distance between Earth and Mars was so great that the time dealy for communications between Earth and Mars was about 20 minutes. This meant that

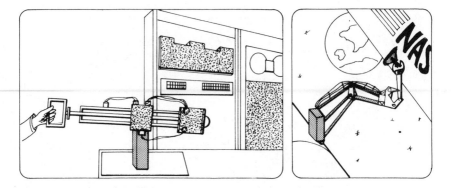

Figure 10-5 Scientists on earth may be able to move objects in space, repair space vehicles, or conduct experiments by remote control. A joy stick is moved by earthbound scientists to control a robot and arm in space.

the direct control of the craft from Earth was not practical. The Viking Lander was required to act under its own control much of the time. Because no human being was on board, a computer was necessary.

In addition to controlling the flight of a spacecraft such as the Viking Lander, experiments can be conducted by on-board computers without human control, and the data transmitted back to Earth for analysis. The data received from a space mission can keep teams of scientists busy for years after the space mission is completed. And even then, without a computer scientists would not be able to analyze the data effectively.

The National Aeronautics and Space Administration's space shuttle program, which began regular operation in the early 1980s, makes extensive use of computers. Before actually flying into space, computers are used to help design, build, and test the spacecraft that will be used in the program. After a shuttle is built, computers are used to provide astronauts with flight simulation for training and systems testing to locate problems before the space vehicle is actually flown. The space shuttle vehicle itself contains five on-board computers that are part of the guidance system. In addition, other computers on board will monitor the physical conditions of the crew, the operation of important systems, and conduct a wide variety of scientific experiments.

These five on-board computer systems received considerable public attention in 1981 during the first flight of the space shuttle. A problem developed which prohibited the four main control computers from communicating with the fifth backup system. As a result, the mission was delayed several days (see Fig. 10.6).

The four main control computers are identical, using the same hardware and software. The fifth computer, the backup, is a different computer, but it was programmed to perform the same control functions as the four main systems. This fifth system, to perform the same functions, was programmed by a different team of programmers, using different methods. The hope was that any oversights or unex-

Figure 10-6 An interior view of the flight deck of the space shuttle orbiter, showing the vast array of dials and controls of the space craft's primary flight control station. The commander's station is at left; the pilot's station is at right. (Courtesy of NASA)

pected occurrences not foreseen by the first team of programmers might be accounted for by the second team and incorporated into the design of the software for the back-up system, thus giving the overall control of the shuttle craft a much higher degree of accuracy and flexibility.

The same guidance data were fed into all five computers. Theoretically, all computers, including the backup, should digest the input and produce the same output to be used for control of the spacecraft. Should one of the computers produce a result that differed from the others, then majority rule would prevail and that computer would be ignored. Should two of the main computers produce a result that differed from that of the other two, then the fifth—the back-up system—would provide the tie-breaking "vote" that would determine the control maneuver to be performed.

Almost all of the actual "flying" of the craft is performed by computers. In those instances where the astronauts actually fly the spacecraft, they are flying the computer rather than the spacecraft itself. A human cannot possibly exert control over all of the mechanisms necessary to fly the spacecraft. An astronaut will relay control information to a computer through a stick or wheel. The computer will then compute the necessary actions and direct the various mechanisms to perform the maneuvers desired by the astronaut.

The landing systems for the shuttle's return to Earth consist of four independent systems, each capable of landing the shuttle without human assistance. The astronauts can select which system to use during re-entry. On the first shuttle flight, the craft landed within two feet of what was considered a "perfect" landing.

Shipboard Computers

For many years computers have been used aboard naval vessels to help in their own defense and track hostile aircraft, ships, and submarines. Until recently, however, the use of computers aboard merchant and passenger ships has been limited. Maritime disasters, many causing environmentally damaging oil spills, have focused attention on navigation safety both on the open ocean and in confined waterways. These and economic factors, along with increases in both vessel size and numbers, have in many instances alerted owners to use computers to help control the operation of their ships.

Merchant ships can make use of computers to control their engines, aid navigation, keep track of nearby ships, warn of potential collision situations, and monitor cargo, fuel, and electrical equipment. They also perform ship accounting functions such as payroll accounting, stores inventory, management reports, and cargo manifests.

Late in the 1950s and the early 1960s, the U.S. Navy developed a satellite system called Transit. The system, which uses four satellites in polar orbits, was initially conceived as a navigational aid for submarines to provide a worldwide, accurate, all-weather, passive system. Today, Transit provides satellite navigation to ships throughout the world.

Satellite navigation is completely passive, requiring receiving but no transmitting equipment. The satellite beams a precise timing mark and a navigational message that describes the satellite's position at that mark. The computer on a ship at sea uses this information to determine the vessel's precise position. (see Fig. 10.7).

The spectacular passenger liner Queen Elizabeth II was built with the aid of computers, and sails with the help of two on-board computers. One of these can select the proper course for the ship, taking into account the water flow of the various currents, the weather reports from Earth satellites, and other details. It does not usurp the captain's position, however. When necessary, it provides three choices, and he selects the one he wants. In facing a storm, for instance, the com-

Satellite
Orbit

Shore-Based
Station Sends Orbit
And Time Data To
Satellite

Ship
Receives
Data

Figure 10-7 A satellite in a fixed orbit over the earth enables
ships to determine their positions at sea accurately.

puter will find one route around it, another straight through it, and a third based
solely on economic considerations.

As mentioned earlier, ships are becoming larger, more complex, and more
numerous. As this happens, control of a vessel becomes more critical. Many of the
same techniques for simulation in aircraft pilot training are also used for the training
of ships' captains. A simulated control room or bridge utilizes sophisticated computer graphics systems to display scenes that duplicate those which may be seen by
a captain in real-life situations. Commands given to the simulator by the trainee are
fed into a computer, and the computer changes the scene according to the change in
the position of the vessel.

Computer-Directed Railroads

Computers are being used more by the nation's railroads in an attempt to improve the efficiency of the industry and increase profits. Many railroads are using a computer system that has been developed to improve the control of the nearly two million freight cars being used to haul shipments across the U.S. and Canada. The system is called Automated Car Identification (ACI). It uses trackside scanners to detect color-coded identification panels on the sides of passing cars. The trackside scanners are connected to computers, that can then provide status and location information for loaded cars (see Fig. 10.8). One of the biggest difficulties in operating a railroad is knowing the location of the rolling equipment at all times, and making the most efficient use of it. Management must not only know where each car is, but also what condition it is in, and whether it is empty, loaded, or at a customer's siding being loaded. Computer management systems for both empty and loaded cars can improve railroad car utilization significantly.

Figure 10-8 A railroad worker uses a status board and a terminal to track rail shipments and route empty cars to specific destinations for loading. (Courtesy of Missouri-Pacific Railroad)

Another efficiency drain in railroad systems is in the classification yard where cars are assembled into trains. The industry estimates that currently, for each working day of a typical freight car, there are three idle days where the car sits at a customer's siding, or in a classification yard. The bottleneck in the classification yard is being solved through the use of computers. The computer stores in its memory a list of what cars to route to what parts of the yard, and controls switches in the yard to direct cars to the proper trains (see Fig. 10.9).

Mass Transit Systems

Increasingly computers are being utilized to control sophisticated mass transit systems. Most such systems are actually railroads and make use of the computer for scheduling, routing, and train control. Through the use of figures that indicate patronage, or actual numbers of people who use a particular transit system during

Figure 10-9 A train dispatcher sits at the control panel of a computer-controlled switching system. The display board in front of him shows a large train system track layout. Lights on the board indicate the position of various trains. (Courtesy of Missouri-Pacific Railroad)

different hours, the computer can schedule how many trains need to be on the system at different times to meet passenger demand. Once on the system, a central computer can, with sensing devices located along the railway, determine the position of each train in order to maintain maximum speed while keeping a safe distance between trains (see Fig. 10.10). Such control systems are also utilized to control the length of time a train will stop in a station, and even the opening and closing of access doors. While many of the newer mass transit systems, such as the Bay Area Rapid Transit (San Francisco) or the Washington Metro (Washington, D.C.), are controlled entirely by computer, human operators are still utilized on the trains, if for no other reason than to ensure passengers that computers have not taken over everything. Operators on board computer-controlled trains can monitor various train systems and, in the event of an emergency or computer failure, can override computer control and operate the train at minimum speed.

Urban Transportation

Congestion in and around our nation's cities is growing worse each year. Traditional solutions to transportation problems in urban areas, namely, building more roadways, are no longer practical either economically or environmentally. The principal

197

Figure 10-10 Main train control center for the Bay Area Rapid
Transit system in San Francisco, California (Courtesy of BART)

problems are caused by the large number of automobiles utilized by the public, and
the reluctance to switch to more efficient modes of transportation. Most people hesitate to change from using the automobile for transportation because of convenience—no other form of transportation offers the freedom of mobility that the
automobile does. Transportation engineers and urban planners are increasingly
turning to computer technology to make automobile transportation more efficient,
and to develop systems for making alternative mass transportation modes more
reliable, more effective, and more convenient.

Urban Planning and Traffic Control

With the current knowledge possessed by urban planners, new cities can be laid out
so as to provide the best possible traffic flow. Computers can be used to project
population trends into the future, and traffic models (mathematical models) can be
implemented to analyze projected traffic flow, enabling planners to develop roadway
systems that will provide for efficient automobile usage, with a minimum impact on
the environment or general quality of life.

While this may be good for new urban areas, established cities cannot replan
and redevelop their entire roadway systems to meet existing and future demands.
Computers can be used in this instance to help planners analyze traffic flow patterns
through a city, determine major transportation corridors and principal destinations,
and help to focus attention on the rebuilding of a portion of an urban area's roadway
system to increase traffic flow and carrying capacity (see Fig. 10.11).

It is impossible to plan and develop a new transportation system, or rebuild an
old one, that centers entirely around the construction of freeways. Much traffic must
still flow through regular city streets. Traffic flow on regular city streets is regulated

STREET NETWORK

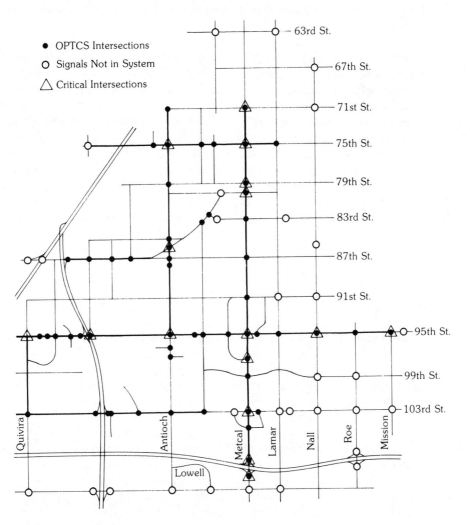

Figure 10-11 After an extensive traffic study in Overland Park, Kansas, using roadside monitors connected to a central computer, this street network map was generated, showing major streets with heaviest traffic, and intersections which would best benefit from a centrally controlled, computerized traffic light control system.

by stop signals, and these stop signals can be controlled by computer systems to regulate traffic through certain areas. The computer can be connected to a sensor embedded within the street to detect the flow of traffic past that certain point, and regulate a stop signal to optimize traffic flow past that point. To provide the most effective signal-traffic control systems, however, monitoring devices on the street link together an entire area and communicate with a single computer system that will regulate signal lights to favor streets that are carrying the heaviest traffic at a particular moment (see Fig. 10.12).

Scheduling   As mentioned earlier, people are reluctant to give up their automobiles entirely and switch to alternative modes of transportation. The principal inconvenience of mass transportation is that you must travel when the bus, plane, or train is ready, and not necessarily when you are. Computerized scheduling can help alleviate many of these problems. On a large scale, computers can be used to analyze transportation demands and coordinate the scheduling of several different transportation systems to provide efficient transfer capabilities. On a smaller scale, computers can help form car pools, matching people, areas, and destinations. Computers are also being utilized in specialized "dial-a-ride" bus systems. People wanting transportation can call a bus dispatcher who will use a computer to work that person's location into the bus route and tell him or her when they will be picked up. After the bus driver picks up a passenger he is notified by radio where to go next. The bus route is not fixed, but takes shape in the computer as passengers call in for service.

Automotive Electronics

While computers have become increasingly responsible for many aspects of the design, planning, and production of automobiles, only recently has the use of computer equipment in cars unveiled a new age of automotive electronics. Over the last 30 years, 17 automotive electronic systems have been introduced, excluding communications and entertainment equipment. Sixteen of these original electronic applications in automobiles still remain in use.

The size and complexity of an automobile electrical system makes it a prime candidate for the application of advanced electronics technology. In addition to the 16 electronic systems previously mentioned, an automobile can have over 400 feet of electrical cable, 80 switches, 15 electric motors, 70 lamps, 30 sensors, as well as fuses and breakers to protect circuits. All of these are tied together with as many as 100 or more connectors. Most of these can be replaced with solid state devices.

Emissions and Fuel Economy   Two government regulations regarding emissions and fuel economy will have a significant impact on the continuing applications of electronics to the automobile. The first of these regulations, put forth by the Environmental Protection Agency (EPA), requires that automobiles be so designed as not to exceed certain emissions standards. The second deals with fuel economy. While the exact mileage figures are subject to change, laws require that auto manufacturers improve fuel economy and meet average fleet fuel economy levels in the future (Corporate Average Fuel Economy—CAFE)

Fuel economy improvements are being achieved, first by making vehicles smaller and lighter, and second by improving engine and power train efficiency and

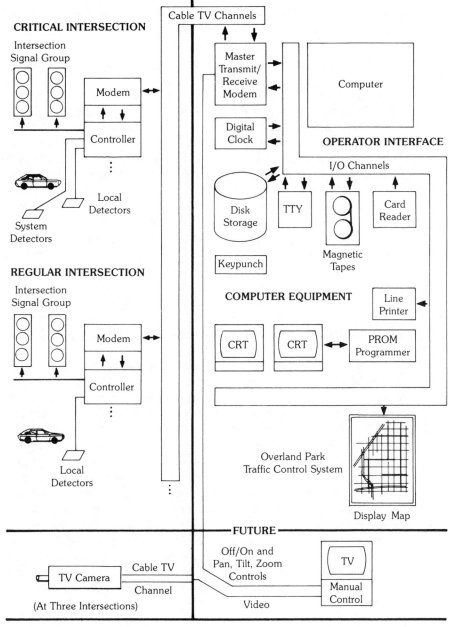

Figure 10-12 This diagram shows the Overland Park traffic control system. Sensors embedded in the street communicate with roadside controllers built around microprocessors. The controllers communicate with a central computer, which analyzes the information from all of the controllers and directs them to change signals to regulate traffic flow in each particular area.

performance. It is in this second area that electronics is expected to be applied most heavily. While various manufacturers are developing their own specialized electronic engine control systems, we can describe two general types of electronic systems: electronic engine control systems and multidisplacement engine systems.

Electronic Engine Control Systems   These types of electronic systems are probably the most comprehensive of the two types that we will examine. Such electronic emissions systems incorporate features for controlling air/fuel ratio in the carburetor, spark timing in the distributor, and shifting points in automatic transmission. They also continuously monitor the condition of the emissions control devices on the engine. Such engine control takes place through the use of sensors placed at certain critical locations in the engine and connected to a microprocessor controlled unit. This electronic unit can then communicate with various mechanisms in the carburetor, distributor, and transmission to alter the performance of the engine to meet the demands being put on the engine while maintaining maximum fuel economy and minimum harmful exhaust emissions. Such a system, introduced on 1981 General Motors automobiles, is shown in Fig. 10.13. In addition to controlling engine performance, the General Motors system, called "Computer Command Control," can detect faults in the engine control system, store these faults in its memory, and communicate these faults to a service technician with special electronic diagnostic equipment at the time the car is brought to a dealer for repair (see Fig. 10.14).

Multidisplacement Engines   One method of improving fuel economy in automobiles is to reduce the size of the engine. Although reducing the size of the engine lowers dangerous emissions and decreases fuel consumption, the performance of the vehicle suffers. Several systems have been developed to allow vehicles to retain large displacement engines, but, through electronic and mechanical controls, the number of cylinders of the engine in use at any one time is regulated by the demands placed on the engine. For example, an automobile may have a large displacement 8-cylinder engine, but electronic controls can regulate how many cylinders are in operation at a given time. Under hard acceleration all 8 cylinders operate. As power demands on the engine decrease, the electronic control deactivates the valve assembly and cuts off the fuel supply to certain cylinders. The engine then cuts down to 6 cylinders, and at cruising speeds the engine cuts back to 4 cylinders. Because the electronic control device continuously monitors engine power demand and adjusts performance, when the automobile is cruising on 4 cylinders hard acceleration causes the electronic control unit to reactivate 2 or 4 deactivated cylinders to provide more power when needed.

For the Driver   The engine is not the only component of an automobile that provides the potential for the application of advanced electronics. The driver, as well as other operating systems within the automobile, can benefit from electronics. Electronic systems under development can control the suspension system to provide the best ride and handling characteristics under a wide variety of situations. Anti-skid

Figure 10-13 (a) The "brain" of the General Motors Computer command control system (Courtesy of General Motors Corporation) (b) A schematic diagram of the electronic systems which may be found in cars of the future.

THE COMPUTER-CONTROLLED AUTOMOBILE — TODAY AND TOMORROW.

1. Engine Control Module
2. Diagnostic Module
3. Brake Module
4. Electronic Ignition Module
5. Navigation Module

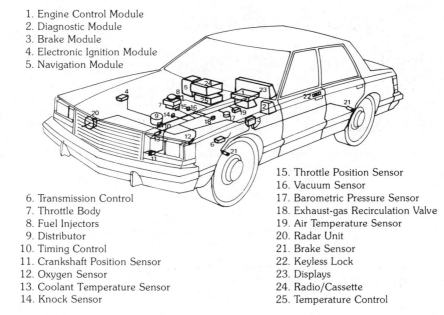

6. Transmission Control
7. Throttle Body
8. Fuel Injectors
9. Distributor
10. Timing Control
11. Crankshaft Position Sensor
12. Oxygen Sensor
13. Coolant Temperature Sensor
14. Knock Sensor

15. Throttle Position Sensor
16. Vacuum Sensor
17. Barometric Pressure Sensor
18. Exhaust-gas Recirculation Valve
19. Air Temperature Sensor
20. Radar Unit
21. Brake Sensor
22. Keyless Lock
23. Displays
24. Radio/Cassette
25. Temperature Control

Figure 10-14 An electronic diagnostic computer can be connected to the electronic control module in a General Motors engine to check vital engine functions and diagnose problems or failures. (Courtesy of General Motors Corporation)

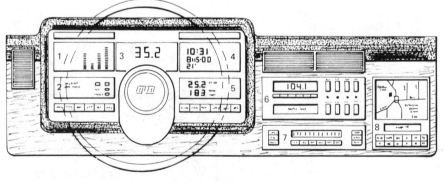

DASHBOARD DISPLAY

1. Fuel Gauge
2. Diagnostics
3. Speed
4. Time, Temperature

5. Trip Computer
6. Radio/Cassette
7. Temperature Control
8. Navigation Module/Map Display

Figure 10-15 The "control center" of an electronic car of the future.

TABLE 10.1 MODERN AUTOMOTIVE ELECTRONIC SYSTEMS

Headlight control	Wheel-lock control
Alternator rectifier	Clock
Voltage regulator	Intrusion alarm
Tachometer	Air-cushion control
Cruise control	Electronic fuel injection
Electronic ignition	Lamp timing control
Climate control	Spark timing control
Windshield wiper control	Electronic digital displays

braking systems, connected to actual radar warning systems, could help prevent accidents in the future. And, in conjunction with roadside traffic monitoring computers, systems within automobiles may help a driver determine the best route to take to arrive at a specific destination across town.

The instrumentation within the automobile is becoming considerably more precise and informative as the result of electronics. Sophisticated instrument panels, actually information centers, check brakes, lights, fluid levels, and engine functions, and give time, date, speed, fuel level, and other sorts of trip information. Some systems can actually communicate with the driver by using audible tones and even a limited vocabulary of spoken words. Buttons, dials, switches, and levers are being replaced with digital displays, with functions activated by touch-sensitive controls. Electronic climate control, memory seats that automatically adjust position for different drivers, keyless car entry systems, theft deterrent systems, and traffic control systems are all electronic marvels that are beginning to appear on cars. With the rapid advance of electronics technology, these applications will soon become commonplace in a new generation of automotive wizardry (see Fig. 10.15) and (Table 10.1).

SOCIAL IMPLICATIONS

Pro Arguments

We have discussed many diverse areas of transportation in this chapter. Although it is difficult to make specific statements that may apply to all modes of transportation, we can make some general statements about the positive social implications of an increased use of computers and advanced electronics, and some specific comments about particular types of transportation.

When people are as mobile as we are today, transportation systems must be able to meet our demands. Transportation systems that serve us today cannot operate efficiently without being coordinated. Urban planners are using computers in various distinct activities to help design roadway systems, mass transit systems, and bus systems that will serve large populations. Planners are also coordinating transportation systems with one another by using computers, in order to provide people with efficient, convenient connections between transportation systems. As our natural resources become scarcer, more people may be forced to give up or limit travel by personal automobile. Instead, they will turn to various mass transit systems that will be scheduled and controlled by computer to provide a level of service that approaches the convenience offered by the automobile, at a similar or, possibly, reduced cost.

The machines of our various modes of transportation—automobiles, planes, spacecraft, trains, and ships—are becoming so complex that it is almost impossible for people to maintain control without the use of computer technology. Monitoring systems built around computers or other electronics technologies allow human operators to focus on the control of a particular type of vehicle rather than on the various operational systems within it.

In many instances, such as in airplanes and spacecraft, computers can actually monitor operational systems and control the operation of the vehicle more effectively than humans. By reducing the margin for human error, computers can make various transportation systems more economical, more efficient, and safer, while providing a higher level of service to humans.

Computer technology is now applied to the design and operation of automobiles and will continue to exert a positive influence for some time to come. Automobiles are being made more economical, more efficient, and safer, as a result of computer-aided design techniques, as well as by the application of computer technology to the controlling of their various operational systems. Traditional mechanical controls in automobiles cannot meet the stringent emissions and fuel consumption standards mandated for today's vehicles. Only the application of electronic control systems in automobiles can provide performance that will meet current and future performance requirements.

Con Arguments

There is no doubt that technological advances in the computer field have increased at a greater rate than the average human's ability to understand them. The result is that an increasing number of machine devices and vehicles are controlled by mechanisms that are beyond the comprehension of most people. While such advanced devices may provide more efficient operation and control of certain types of vehicles, they also require an elite crew of technicians to support their operation and maintenance. When systems become so complex and interrelated, it takes several narrow-focus specialists to understand and repair them. Gone are the days when a single person has enough knowledge to be able to understand all aspects of the operational systems that control various types of vehicles. The implications of this are, of course, that personnel involved in the maintenance and control of electronic systems must have a much higher degree of specialized training. Furthermore, since electronic equipment is so specialized in certain types of systems, a narrow-focus technician may not be able to work on more than one type of system. In other words, a mechanic trained to diagnose electronic control systems in General Motors automobiles may not be able to work on a Ford engine that has a different electronic control system. Prior to electronic control systems, mechanical systems were basically similar to the extent that a good mechanic could service a car without concern for brand or type of control system.

As computers replace human control in transportation systems, single electronic devices can monitor and control more activities than a human being can. Although this is considered an advantage, it also has a negative implication. For example, in a large mass transportation system that may rely on human control rather than on electronic control, many humans will be employed to perform a variety of tasks. Should one human within the system fail to perform a specific task, or make an error, the effects on the entire system may be minimal. However, if one computer system is utilized to control an entire transportation system, and the computer fails or malfunctions, the effects are much greater than a mistake made by one human being. In other words, we have become so dependant on computers for control that when there are problems with a system, they often mean chaos.

In a final analysis, transportation systems have become so complex, and we as a society have become so dependent on them for efficient service, that we can no longer trust ourselves or other uncontrolled humans to operate them. This leads us, however, to depend on systems that most of us cannot even begin to understand.

HARDWARE

Certainly the advent of microelectronics is having the most dramatic effect in the development of transportation vehicles. Various small monitoring functions of systems within planes, trains, ships, and cars can be monitored by microprocessor controlled devices, and status information relayed to the human operator for action. Some systems can be operated automatically by electronics and only report to the operator should a malfunction occur. In automobiles, electronics can control various engine functions, while still leaving control of the vehicle to a human operator. In airplanes and spacecraft, however, small computer systems (microprocessors) can monitor and control various minor functions and report to an onboard master computer system that completely controls the operation of the craft, merely reporting conditions and progress to human operators. In other transportation systems such as trains, ships, and buses, microprocessors can again control minor functions within the vehicle, and the vehicles can communicate with a computer that, though located in a distant facility, performs routing and tracking functions for the entire system.

Computer technology is such today that mass transportation can be entirely controlled by computers. Again, vehicles actually utilized in a mass transit system can have various onboard functions monitored and controlled by microprocessor devices. Communications gear in the vehicle can be used to report vehicle location to a central computer. This can be accomplished either by having a human operator actually report physical location, or by having sensing devices that are located along different routes report location information automatically to a central computer. The central computer can then give the operator of the vehicle routing information as in the case of bus systems, or actually control the routing and speed of the vehicle as in high speed train mass transit systems.

A LOOK TOWARD THE FUTURE

As in all areas of computer applications, it is difficult to accurately predict the future. Technological breakthroughs seem to happen at such an amazing rate that even the most well-researched and conservative predictions cannot be relied on. It should be easy to see, however, that within the transportation field electronics and computer technologies are going to continue to have a dramatic effect. First, vehicles that are utilized in the various transportation systems are going to be designed entirely by computer in order to make maximum use of available resources and provide a vehicle that optimizes performance for the demands placed on it. We will continue to see more electronics control mechanisms built into various vehicles. These mechanisms will provide for better overall control of the vehicle, as well as for better fuel consumption. It is hoped that such mechanisms will also provide various vehicles with a higher degree of reliability than is available today.

Although many computer-related devices will continue to be built into transportation vehicles, probably the most significant applications of the new technologies will be in the area of computers that monitor and control the operations of entire transportation systems. This includes airline systems that can schedule plane utilization and also maintain complete reservations systems that enable a traveler to make all travel arrangements for a trip through one reservation agent. It also includes what are likely to emerge as "urban transportation control" systems that can monitor traffic flows on roadways, regulate speed limits to provide maximum traffic flow, and ultimately be able to provide routing information to vehicles traveling on roadways within the system.

As we have seen, electronics are rapidly taking over control systems within automobiles. This trend will continue, and probably accelerate. Anti-skid braking systems are under development, as are radar-controlled collision avoidance systems. Perhaps in the future automobiles will be able to communicate with central "urban transportation control" computers and receive routing information that will allow the vehicle to travel to its destination with minimum delay, avoiding congested areas. Some people are even speculating that some day an operator will be able to enter a vehicle and key a destination into an on-board computer system that will communicate with a central traffic control computer. Then the traffic control computer will take over operation of the vehicle and direct it to its destination without human control.

STUDY AND REVIEW

1. In general, what advantages can computer technology bring to transportation systems?

2. Beyond the fact that computers integrated into cars and airplanes can control components better than humans, why are they needed?

3. What role can computers play in urban planning?

4. What is the advantage of computer-controlled flight simulation systems?

5. How are computers used in aerospace transportation systems?

6. What is the role computers/electronics have in the operation of automobiles?

7. Briefly summarize the positive implications of the use of computers in transportation systems.

8. Briefly summarize the negative implications of the use of computers in transportation systems.

9. Do you see any other applications for computers in the transportation field which have not been mentioned in this chapter?

11

COMMUNICATIONS

PERSPECTIVE

Our advanced civilization has been made possible to a large degree through various forms of communications, and that ability to communicate is what distinguishes us from other animals as life forms. Communications media have already done much to alter the nature of society. As the following quotation points out, the technology of communications is in a revolutionary stage. Improving society's communications facilities will most likely result in further significant changes.

> Today we are beginning to build networks with multiple paths like spiderwebs which interconnect computers and computer users. These communications networks are spreading worldwide, and will become accessible from the home, possibly via a color television set, with a keyboard added. While the networks are spreading, computers and information storage are dropping in cost at a phenomenal rate, and will continue to do so until powerful computers connected by communications networks become as common as telephone sets. *(Martin, 1979)*

The communications technologies described in this chapter will change the way people work, are educated, spend leisure time, receive health care, buy and sell merchandise, and conduct other financial activities. Advanced communications could also improve the fundamental workings of our democracy, the processes of government, and the news media.

Telecommunications facilities in the future will act as a substitute for travel, with people able to see each other and operate machines at a great distance (see Fig. 11.1).

The demand for communications services from both commercial organizations and private individuals is growing daily, and the technology that provides those services is changing and improving at a very fast pace. Communications are depending more heavily on computer technology and, as computer users demand more diverse communicating capabilities, the two are starting to overlap—a merger that could be termed "compunications".

At the heart of these changes are digital transmission techniques and microprocessor-based communications hardware that make it possible to transmit information in massive quantities and in formats that would have been unthinkable a generation ago. Voice and video signals can be converted into bits of data that can be stored in a computer, retrieved, and transmitted to distant locations by satellites, by fiber-optic cables made of glass, or simply by ordinary telephone lines. And with the cost of small computers plummeting and recent advances in switching technology, computer data itself can also be stored, manipulated, transmitted, and distributed in ways that are changing the operations of many businesses.

The explosion in the communications field is just beginning to be felt. As an editorial in a major national newspaper stated:

Figure 11-1 Satellites are helping to expand human communication capabilities by providing long-range, high-speed communications capabilities. (Courtesy TRW, Inc.)

> *Mankind now has a tool for the instantaneous and simultaneous exchange of information and ideas on an almost limitless basis. That ability will be harnessed for the betterment of mankind in ways yet to be suggested or adopted.*
> (San Francisco Chronicle, *1981*)

It is difficult to predict accurately just where it will lead; however, several major areas of development point the way toward the future. These areas, namely, electronic mail and information networks along with several other smaller topics, are the focus of the remainder of this chapter.

COMPUTERS IN COMMUNICATIONS

Information Networks

Various automated methods for filing and indexing human knowledge have been developed in recent years, and have become essential to keep pace with the rapid growth in the amount of information being generated by our society. As the amount of information grows, the problems associated with search and information retrieval also grow. Computerizing much of this information may someday enable people to search, with computer assistance, through information that might be available in a vast, worldwide computer network (see Fig. 11.2). Telecommunications links would enable users to access such information networks through ordinary telephones, microcomputer, or cable television hookups while at home, in an office, library, or virtually anywhere.

Much of the information available today is research that is not of equal value to all people. Another type, probably more useful to more people, is personal, business, or convenience information. This category includes stock market quotations, weather reports, theater listings, housing information, various buying guides, transportation system schedules, and so forth. Although much of this information is now available in a variety of video, audio, and printed formats, there is such an abundance in other formats that a single human being cannot effectively manage it and utilize it.

Computerized information systems, utilizing advanced communications technology, are attempting to consolidate the many varied convenience information sources into one easy-to-use, all inclusive system that can be accessed by people through telephone or cable television in their own homes. Basically, such systems will merely communicate information in one direction, from the source to the user. Ultimately, however, they will be interactive, enabling users not only to request and display certain information, but to communicate back through the communications link and perform certain activities with a central computer. These activities could include checking bank account balances, paying bills, ordering merchandise, making airline reservations, buying tickets, and responding to special surveys.

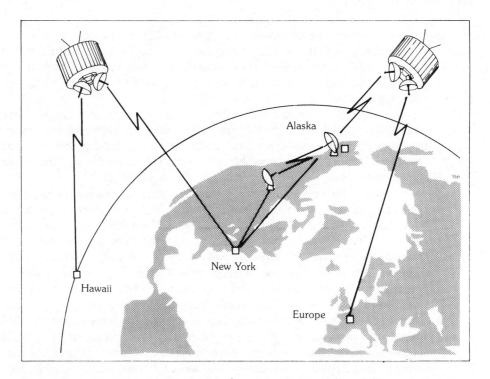

Figure 11-2 Satellite networks can provide world wide communications capabilities.

For purposes of this book, the major types of information networks are: (1) telephone systems, (2) microcomputer-telephone systems, and (3) cable television systems. Competitive factors and governmental regulations will mainly determine which of these systems will become the more widely used.

In the following sections we describe each of these types of systems, the services offered by each, and how they could be utilized in the future. The potential that such systems have for the future should be evident to the reader.

Telephone-Based Systems   The telephone is probably the most common piece of communications equipment in existence today. We tend to take this seemingly simple piece of equipment for granted, yet the complex lines and switching mechanisms that back it up are what will make much of the sophisticated communications modes of the future possible. The telephone is the one device that goes into almost every building where there are people. The spiderweb-like lines that fan out across the land have long provided society with almost instantaneous point-to-point communication. Now these lines are beginning to carry considerably more than voice communications.

Although not yet very successful, Picturephone service that allows you to see what is going on at the other end of a phone line will become more commonplace. A primary objection to Picturephone at this point is its cost, which future technology should reduce. Another system, being developed by RCA and called Videovoice, transmits a still rather than a moving picture, and needs about one-three hundredth of the Picturephone's transmission capacity requirements; it could easily be used with existing phone lines.

A third system, being developed by Bell Laboratories, uses normal telephone lines with a special phone device that enables users to transmit handwriting over phone lines between phone sets. The sender will write a message or draw a diagram on a special screen with a special light pen at one end of the line, and that image will appear on a screen in the phone unit at the other end of the line.

Although the developments in communications technology just described are significant, they are not as important and will probably not have as much impact on our society as the use of normal phone systems to establish elaborate information communication networks. Normal phone lines have been used for some time to communicate digitized information back and forth between computer systems. However, this is not the type of information that most people are interested in having access to; it also requires you to connect a computer to your phone in order to receive it. A. T. & T. is now marketing a computer-based phone information system that allows subscribers to hookup to a central computer system by utilizing a special keyboard and video display unit connected to a phone (see Fig. 11.3). By activating the push-buttons on the phone, the user can retrieve information from the computer and display it on a screen. This service, known as Electronic Information Service (EIS), allows subscribers to access the white and yellow pages of the telephone directory, as well as time, weather, sports, general consumer news, and various classified, display, catalog, supermarket, and department store advertising. Such a system is still in an evolutionary stage, but A. T. & T. is contemplating enhancements for uses such as electronic mail, teleshopping, and even remote computing.

Microcomputer-Based Systems   The A. T. & T. phone information network is not the only type of information network available. A second type, providing the same services, but with more information, is a system that enables a subscriber to use a microcomputer connected to an information network through a telephone to retrieve

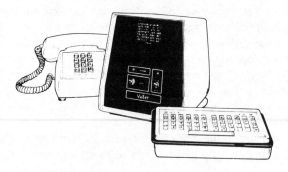

Figure 11-3 A small video display, coupled with a compact keyboard connected to a telephone, can provide access to an information system such as A.T. & T's.

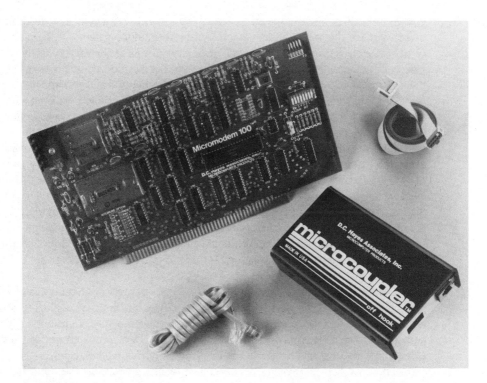

Figure 11-4 Electronic circuit boards, such as the micromodem and microcoupler pictured here, enable microcomputers to be plugged directly into a home telephone jack for connection to information systems such as The Source. (Courtesy of Hayes Microcomputer Products, Inc.)

various types of information (see Fig. 11.4). One such network now in existence is The Source. Though geared primarily to small businesses, this network and others like it, that are sure to appear in the future, can be used by anyone with a microcomputer and the proper software. For an hourly fee, ranging from $15 to $25, a subscriber can retrieve information from regional news publications, international news services, and magazines. In addition, users can access everything from up-to-the-minute stock market reports to the latest sports scores. And with a growing body of relatively inexpensive software, designed for these information networks, a small business can incorporate massive amounts of previously unavailable data, such as economic forecasts, into its daily computations of operating information. Nonbusiness users can play computer games and send messages to other subscribers via the networks "electronic mail" system.

Television-Based Systems Both television sets and telephones exist in large numbers in homes today. The two previous types of information networks require that a subscriber have a special piece of equipment connected to a telephone in order to utilize the information service. With information systems based on the use of a television receiver, a subscriber need not purchase an additional, expensive piece of electronic equipment such as a terminal or microcomputer system. Rather, the subscriber can connect a television set to a telephone, dial the telephone number of the information service, and use a control panel in conjunction with the television set to access information available through the network. This new service that integrates telephone and television technology is called teletex. With a local telephone call the owner of a television set with a teletex addition can also gain access to computer systems that store information and programs. Millions of pages of data will become available, each designed to be displayed in color on the screen of a television set. The home user can look at news reports, movie listings, theater guides, real estate listings, buying guides, weather forecasts, stock market figures, racing results, and so on. Business people can look through files of financial reports, or receive instruction on various aspects of managing a business. Both will interact with their television sets that will enable them to browse through the vast data files maintained in a central computer (see Fig. 11.5).

Computer programs as well as data will be stored in the centralized teletex files. These programs could be used for preparing tax returns, analyzing stocks, learning languages or mathematics with computer-assisted instruction, playing games, and an infinite number of other purposes. Teletex customers will also be able to keep their own files, and leave messages for other teletex users.

The data and programs contained in a teletex system can be contributed by

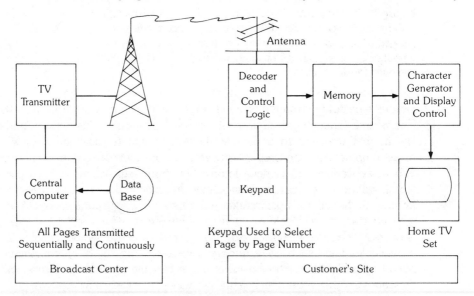

Figure 11-5 (a) One type of videotex system, the "broadcast videotext" provides one-way access to fixed, continuously broadcast files of information.

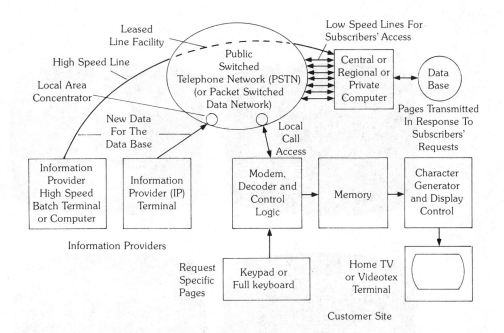

Figure 11-5 (b) The second type uses standard coaxial cable, such as that which currently goes into many homes, to provide interactive access to a wealth of available information.

anyone. Individuals can put data or programs into the files and, when any subscribers access it, the originators will be paid a small royalty. Similarly, advertising organizations, department stores, government agencies, or big corporations can make their data or programs available. It might be considered a new form of publishing.

Some of the data contained in the central files will be constantly updated, such as news, weather, and stock market data. Some, like encyclopedias, will remain unchanged for years. Society produces vast quantities of data that would be useful to people, but the problem until now has been gaining easy access to it when it is needed. The teletex system could possibly provide this at a reasonable price.

Teletex is actually the generic name used to describe an interactive information system for home or office utilizing a telephone and a television set. Different firms operating within different countries will most likely develop individual trade names for their teletex systems. A survey of emerging system names already includes: Videotext, Antilope, Ceefax, Telematique, Inteltext, Prestel, Oracle, Telidon, and Cabletext. Cabletext is a system currently in operation in the U.S., based in Atlanta, Georgia (see Fig. 11.6).

How It Works The television sets needed to receive the view data service are not yet in mass production, and are not likely to be until the late 1980s. An adapted television set, capable of accessing a teletex system, consists of a box of electronic

217

Figure 11-6 Typical screen displays offered by the British Teletext system called PRESTEL (Courtesy of PRESTEL)

circuitry, a modem, and a plug-in or attached keypad. Controlled by one or more microprocessors, this box of large-scale integrated circuitry features an auto-dialer, an identification number, a character generator, a page store, and an interface board. The auto-dialer stores the telephone numbers of the computers it is likely to access, and dials them at the press of a button. An identification number lets the central computer know which terminal to bill for information access. The modem enables the set to be connected to telephone lines.

To obtain teletex information with a television set, the subscriber turns on the set, plugs in the keypad-control unit, and switches on the unit. During this process, the auto-dialer makes a local telephone call to a teletex computer center. Then the computer scans the identification number built into the subscriber's set. If the user is accepted and a welcome message is displayed, the user can then access a specific page of information, or request that a series of indexes be displayed enabling the user to select an information category for viewing.

Electronic Mail

The cost of delivering mail in the United States is high. Americans are the most communicative people on Earth. They not only make more phone calls than anybody else in the world, they send and receive more mail than anyone else. The U.S. Postal Service is the world's largest nonmilitary employer, and it spends more than $15 billion per year to deliver the mails. The service is heavily subsidized by taxpayers because it does not pay for itself. Currently, studies indicate that a large percentage of manually delivered mail could be delivered electronically, at a fraction of the cost.

The term electronic mail, as used in this book, can be defined as moving communications normally considered mail by electrical signal through a particular medium or device. This definition includes any electronic message system. As with the previous section of this chapter on information networks, there are several different systems in operation or under development to provide electronic mail services. Specifically, these systems are: (1) private electronic mail systems, (2) subscription mail systems, and (3) public electronic mail systems. All of these systems will use essentially the same technology; however, they will provide different levels of service for users.

Private Electronic Mail Systems Like the first computer systems that were large and expensive, the first electronic mail systems were installed by large companies that could afford them. These same companies gained tremendous savings as well as convenience and speed from having an internal electronic message system. The advent of the microprocessor has helped lower the cost of electronic mail systems, and has helped to enhance their capabilities to the point where smaller businesses whose organizations operate in multiple locations can now afford an electronic mail system.

At the heart of a private electronic mail system is a well-established distributed processing network that enables a large organization with many different operational centers, or branch offices, to maintain control over data processing activities while meeting diverse, decentralized needs. Recall that a distributed network is one in which computers in different geographical locations can communicate with one another through communications links (see Fig. 11.7). While such a system provides for local needs, it also allows a free flow of information between systems in the network.

At its simplest level, an electronic mail system utilizes a central computer system to which are connected terminals that are located at different workstations throughout the organization. These terminals can utilize the traditional capabilities of the computer, as well as invoke special system software for electronic mail. A user can enter a message into the central computer through the terminal, along with special commands and routing instructions, and the central computer will route that message to the terminal at the workstation of the intended receiver. The central computer, or distribution center, in an electronic mail system performs the ad-

Figure 11-7 An increasing number of computer systems are being designed specifically for distributed processing or networks. The Hewlett-Packard systems pictured here are compatible with a number of communications technologies, which allows them to work together although located miles apart. (Courtesy of Hewlett-Packard)

ministrative functions of authorization, transmission, reception, forwarding, dissemination, dispatching, and confirmation.

With increasingly sophisticated equipment the capabilities of an electronic mail system grow. The simple terminals already described could be replaced with intelligent terminals that are equipped with microprocessors and a memory that can perform data entry, word processing, accounting, and reporting, as well as just electronic mail. Such computerized workstations could also have a facsimile transmission device that would be able to communicate paper documents through an electronic mail system.

The major advantages of an electronic mail system to an organization come not from communicating between workstations in the same location, but from communicating between workstations at separate locations. This can be accomplished by having remote terminals connected to a central switching computer or, better, through a network of computers. In such a system, workstations would communicate with and exchange messages with other computers in the network. There can be many variations on these systems, depending on the organization and the equipment available. Workstations could be equipped with a memory for receiving and storing messages, and a printer for producing messages as printed output; or the messages could be received by the office computer, prepared on printers, and distributed through the office by traditional methods (see Fig. 11.8). A study conducted by Hewlett-Packard Company, the large minicomputer manufacturer who uses a network for all communications between company branches, found that the communication efficiency within the organization has increased, while the cost has significantly decreased. They found that they were paying a transmission cost (the equivalent of postage by traditional means) of 7/1000 of a cent per average letter. First class mail can never approach that cost, or provide the speed of delivery offered by such electronic mail systems.

Subscription Electronic Mail Systems   Not all organizations are large enough to support the type of distributed processing network described in the last section. Furthermore, organizations may find that some type of electronic mail system that allows for communications between organizations would be desirable. In both instances, organizations might benefit from electronic mail services that could be provided by an independent firm. Several firms, such as IBM with SBS-1, and Xerox with ETHERNET, are providing electronic mail services to organizations for a fee, and other firms are likely to do so in the future. Because the service is offered by an independent organization, both the sender and the receiver have to be subscribers. This, of course, limits the extent to which an electronic mail system can be used, since communications may only be transmitted between subscribers, but it increases the speed and efficiency of communications between organizations at lower costs.

Many different types of services are available, but the three general categories of subscription services are: (1) systems based on facsimile transmission, (2) sys-

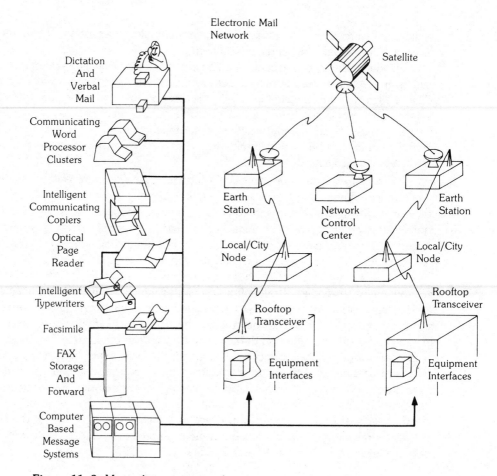

Figure 11-8 Many diverse pieces of equipment can be incorporated into an electronic mail system.

tems based on the use of an independent computer, (3) and systems based on the use of a private communications satellite (see Fig. 11.9).

Public Electronic Mail Systems The two previous categories of electronic mail systems include services that allow large organizations to send and receive communications electronically. However, such systems are not suited to the needs of the average private citizen who does not have the money or the volume of communications necessary to utilize the other systems. On the other hand, when considered as a large block, private citizens do generate enough communications to warrant the use of an electronic mail system. As mentioned earlier in this chapter, our traditional form of mail delivery is very expensive and often inefficient. It also represents a tremendous drain on natural resources—trees for paper, petroleum to

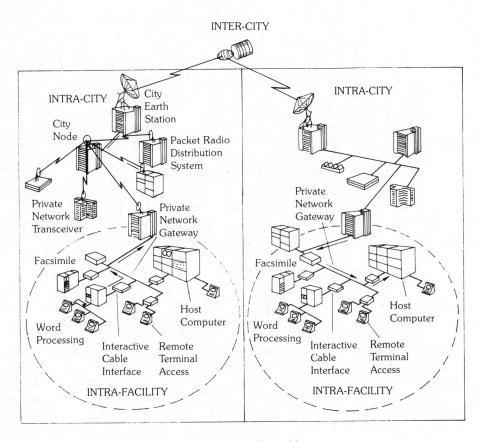

INTER-CITY

INTRA-CITY

City
Earth
Station

City
Node

Private
Network
Transceiver

Packet Radio
Distribution
System

Private
Network
Gateway

Facsimile

Word
Processing

Interactive
Cable
Interface

Remote
Terminal
Access

Host
Computer

INTRA-FACILITY

INTRA-CITY

Private
Network
Gateway

Facsimile

Word
Processing

Interactive
Cable
Interface

Remote
Terminal
Access

Host
Computer

INTRA-FACILITY

Figure 11-9 Private and public satellite networks enable users to
share information both inter- and intra-city.

make gasoline for transportation, and so on. Although much mail consists of important, legitimate communication, some is "junk" mail that is largely unread by the receiver and thrown away. What a waste! Electronic mail systems of the future, which are likely to be maintained by national postal services, could reduce the cost of mail service, and increase the efficiency of the service.

In a public electronic mail system, users would be connected through traditional telephone lines or possibly through coaxial cable. These would connect a television set to a local message switching computer system that would be part of a national and, eventually, international message switching network. The receiving unit in each location could be a microcomputer system or, more likely, an electronic module that is connected to a television set. While we are traditionally used to receiving mail at a designated time each day, electronic or instant mail could be sent or received at any time. A message received by the electronic box would activate a light which would signal that a message was waiting. The receiver could then ac-

223

tivate the television set and use a control panel attached to the television to display the message. A printer could be attached to the set and activated should the receiver desire a printed copy of the message.

To send a message the transmitter would key the message into the electronic box through a keyboard connected to the television set. The message would include certain routing information that would allow the switching computer to direct the message to the proper location. Once we can have messages delivered in this manner, almost instantaneously, the way we utilize them may change completely— two people may be able to talk back and forth via their television sets. Although this form of communication may not be as convenient as the telephone, it may be less costly than long distance telephone charges.

As communications technology advances, many of the services offered through the various technologies will begin to overlap. Thus, initially, an individual will have many choices of similar services. Ultimately, economics and competitive factors will narrow the choices, and those services that are offered will complement one another. For example, with electronic mail systems, a bank, department store, or other credit card company computer could prepare your monthly bill and send it to you. It would be received by the electronic box on top of your television, and you could display it on the screen. You could then call your bank's computer and, by using the buttons on your Touch-Tone phone, instruct the computer to deduct money from your account and electronically deposit it in the account of your creditor. At the end of the month your bank could prepare a summary of the bill-paying activity in your account, and send it to you electronically. All of this could take place instantaneously, not relying on traditional mail service, using any paper resources, or generating any bills or checks that would have to be manually processed by the credit card company and the banks involved. Furthermore, electronic mail systems could use facsimile transmission when it is absolutely necessary to transmit a paper document.

Not all forms of mail will necessarily be adapted to electronic transmission. Routine correspondance, personal messages, and business mail could all be delivered electronically. However, advertising letters and promotional materials may not be considered as potential for electronic delivery because they may contain glossy or high quality reproductions. Newspapers and magazines may also be excluded, although there have been many discussions of customized news being delivered to homes. The communications that are not delivered electronically would still be delivered by traditional services, but postal service volume would probably be reduced.

Electronic News Media

Newspapers, magazines, and other periodicals could be delivered electronically, but the receiver would be limited to viewing the material on the television set. Most people, however, prefer their reading material to be more "portable."

Nevertheless, the potential exists to dramatically alter the manner in which news or information can be presented to people. Some newspapers are now experimenting with the electronic delivery of newspapers to the home. One such system electronically collects newspapers in a central computer, and a subscriber can dial the computer through a normal telephone, connect the phone to a microcomputer, and receive one or several of the newspapers electronically. The user can then browse through the paper electronically, displaying it on the screen of the microcomputer.

If papers and magazines were delivered electronically, much more information could be contained in them than is now physically or economically feasible. Pictures might be displayed in the normal still format, or film clips could be included in the electronic paper. And, instead of written quotations from newsmakers, audio recordings could be incorporated into the electronic paper and played back as the paper is "viewed" through a television set.

After a newspaper or magazine has been delivered electronically, to a box connected to a television set or to a microcomputer, the viewer may be able to exercise considerable control over how the information may be displayed. By using a remote control connected to the television, the viewer could sit back and page through the paper in normal sequence. Or the television could be programmed to display sections of the paper in a specific sequence, and even search through the paper electronically and display only the articles that are about specific topics of interest to the viewer. Many news sources or news organizations will also maintain large central database systems that will contain a wealth of current and historical news information. Such databases can be accessed through microcomputer-telephone hookups, or through a teletex system. The New York Times Consumer DataBase is one such system currently in operation, and the Associated Press network or "Newsline" is another.

Communications Technology

In the first sections of this chapter we discussed the two major areas that are affected by evolving communications technology. A variety of other important but somewhat less significant developments in communications technology are a result of the computer electronics revolution that we examine in this section.

Satellite Communications Communications satellites also hold tremendous potential for the future. One satellite of reasonable size in orbit today could have enough transmission capacity to provide every man, woman, and child in North America with a computer terminal. Four appropriately designed satellites could handle all the long-distance telephone and data traffic of the United States.

A communications satellite is, in essence, a mirror in the sky: radio signals are sent to it, and it sends them back. It is placed in a special orbit 22,000 miles above the equator. Satellites, originally developed to communicate with remote areas, are becoming cheaper. As they become cheaper and more powerful they are being used to carry voice, video, and computer data. Satellites can broadcast signals down to Earth over a wide area, and many users can receive the transmission if they are equipped with a receiving dish. The cost of these dishes or receiving stations is also dropping rapidly, and private citizens may soon be able to afford one on the roof at home.

Voice Mail A service that could be integrated with electronic mail in the future is voice mail. It involves the storage of voice messages in digital form for convenient delivery at a later time, either as reconstituted speech or, conceivably, as hard-copy text output. Voice mail will not replace normal telephone communications because many calls require a dialog. However, it should minimize the disruption caused by trivial calls and eliminate the time-wasting practice of "telephone tag," where two people return calls to each other repeatedly without making direct contact. Voice mail also offers a number of convenient features, such as delivering a voice message to groups of people, or sending it to a distant office overnight when rates are cheaper.

Some large firms are installing voice mail systems internally, and many will follow suit in the future. On such internal systems, a user dials a special number to get on the voice mail system and dictates his or her message immediately; but if the recipient is unavailable, the system files it in its memory. Later, when the recipient dials his voice "mailbox," the system reconstitutes the digital data back into the sender's voice and delivers the message.

Users can instruct the system to redial at regular intervals for urgent messages, or set specific delivery time or dates. Users can also dial their own extensions and dictate memos to themselves as reminders of future meetings or actions to be taken. In addition, voice mail systems can be installed at several locations and interconnected by leased lines, or by the dial-up telephone network, to provide organization-wide voice mail capability.

Fiber Optics Another exciting technology within communications is a new form of transmission: fiber optics. Fiber optics is the use of glass wires no thicker than a human hair to transmit information by using light pulses generated by lasers instead of electrical signals (see Fig. 11.10). Fiber optic cables are capable of transmitting thousands of times more information than copper cables. They are seen as a likely means of transmitting the massive volumes of digital data that will be required for voice, video, and data communications in future telecommunications networks.

Telephone Systems

Implemented with the latest digital technology and augmented with computer power, the telephone switchboard is integrating many an organization's voice and data communications. In addition, it promises to be the pivotal device in future

Figure 11-10 The laser (Light Activated by the Stimulated Emission of Radiation) pictured here, is what would be used to transmit communications through optical fibers. (Courtesy of Pacific Gas & Electric Co.)

automated offices, switching communications traffic among such diverse devices as word processors, telephones, data terminals, facsimile transceivers, and intelligent copiers (see Fig. 11.11).

Early automated telephone switchboard units or PBXs (private branch exchange) used mechanical switches to make telephone connections under the control of dial pulses. Subsequently, the electromechanical switches were replaced by electronic devices, with the switching put under the control of a microprocessor.

The most recent developments convert analog voice signals to digital form before switching. This is the device that could serve as the hub of the automated office, handling phone calls and terminal-based computer inquiries as well as electronic mail, document distribution, and a host of other communications functions. These digital switching systems can handle more information than the older analog devices, and are cheaper to manufacture and easier to maintain.

Figure 11-11 An example of the new generation of computerized telephone systems. (Courtesy of ROLM Corp.)

Voice-Video Teleconferencing

While voice communication can be effective and efficient, nothing is quite the same as "being there." New technologies will enable those in remote geographic areas to participate in the same conference or conversation at the same time. Equipment now allows many individuals to be linked together for a voice teleconference. Some private corporations have established special facilities equipped with video equipment that will enable groups of people in different locations to participate in a conference, and be seen as well as heard.

Electronic Libraries

As mentioned earlier in this chapter, the volume of published documents in our society continues to grow at an astronomical rate. Computers are being used to manage this volume and, coupled with communications technology, are providing new ways of accessing information from libraries. Old-fashioned card catalogs are being replaced with computer database systems that provide more convenient searching and allow fast, thorough cross-referencing. Book summaries, and sometimes even entire books, are being stored in computers and retrieved by researchers through terminals. With the types of communications networks that may be available someday, people will be able to sit in their homes and browse through the books in great libraries around the world, generating copies of material they desire on printers attached to television sets.

SOCIAL IMPLICATIONS

Pro Arguments

Humans have been developing communications skills for centuries, but nothing in history, with the possible exception of the invention of the printing press, has done as much to facilitate communication between people as computers and other related electronic technologies. The communications technologies that are evolving now will tie all areas of Earth in a "global village," so that information originating in one area will be instantaneously available to people throughout the rest of the world. People will also be able to keep closer contact with one another at less expense. Organizations will be able to exert better control over distant operations, thus expanding business activities and, ultimately, increasing profits.

Computers have long been able to store large amounts of information, and through communications technologies these vast information resources throughout the world will be at the finger tips of anybody with a telephone, television, or microcomputer. Research work on any topic can be more comprehensive, more efficient, and less expensive through worldwide computer networks. Such networks will incorporate a vast quantity of different peoples' knowledge and skill. In short, computers will act as a storage battery for the human intellect and provide the means of distributing the resource.

Emerging computer, television, and communications technologies are also revolutionizing the manner in which people receive information at home. Not only will more entertainment be brought into the home, but television will become more of a window on the world. More public affairs information—news, political activity, etc.—will develop a better informed populace. With two-way public response communications systems, a more responsive political system also may be developed. With more information channels, television should be able to offer more educational programming to meet the needs of a wider segment of society.

Finally, communications technologies will develop spiderweb-like networks, connecting vast geographical areas; this may indirectly solve some of our pressing societal issues. People will be able to perform many work-related activities at home through the use of workstations tied to a central office by communications links. This will mean fewer automobile trips, lower energy consumption, less pollution, and less need for urban centers. People will be able to live and work in larger geographical areas while still performing the same volume of work as in crowded centralized "work centers."

Con Arguments

The future is not all bright with advanced communications technologies. There are many potential roadblocks to much of the communications technology presented here. Jurisdictional disputes, legislative battles, and many competitive factors lay in the path of providing society with the communications systems that technology can provide, and citizens will accept.

It is said that information is power, and that those who control information can ultimately control those whom the information is about. New communications technologies will make vast quantities of information easily available to all people. There are those who will not only seek to control the information people will receive, but will also use technology to gain access to information that can be used to influence peoples' behavior. What may not be developing at the same rate as the technology are the security mechanisms, procedures, and laws that will prevent, or at least lessen, the harm that can be done with the new technology.

People are overloaded already with technology that they cannot understand. New modes of communications will bring about more complicated machines that fewer and fewer people will understand. People may begin to feel less and less significant in society, and may suffer psychologically as the world around them becomes more complex, and still more difficult to understand. As work becomes easier to perform, it will require shorter time commitments. This, however, will create more problems with how to spend leisure time. Will we become pampered pets of technology or use our leisure creatively to maximum advantage?

From its inception, television has always had great potential to provide valuable information to viewers. However, its potential as an educational medium has not yet been fully realized. One need only look at today's offerings to realize that television is far short of what it could be. Now advanced technology makes television a more powerful medium. Will the mistakes of the past be recognized, corrected, and used to shape the future of television, or are we bound to continue in the same direction, only on a grander scale?

Finally, a significant problem in the advancement of computer/communications technology is one that has been around for some time but is taking on an increased significance today: interface standards. With all of the electronic systems in existence today, little consideration has been given to standardizing the manner in which equipment is connected together, and how this equipment will communicate with other equipment. Before the technology discussed in this chapter can go much farther, interface standards will have to be developed to make connecting equipment together easier, but not allow only a few giant companies to dominate the marketplace.

HARDWARE

With the diversity of computer technology applications within the communications field, it is difficult to describe all of the different types of hardware that will be used for communications purposes. In this section we describe two different scenarios, one for private individuals and the other for commercial organizations. These two situations represent a survey of the types of equipment that is and will be available. The reader should then be able to project the applications described here into many different areas.

Communications technology will continue to have a dramatic effect on the way organizations will conduct business. The company computer will be used now for communications management as well as for data processing activities. The CPBX (computerized switchboard) will act as a switching point for the variety of voice and data communications equipment in use within the organization. More employees will have direct access to a terminal that will not only provide data processing capabilities, but act as an entry point for both an in-house and public electronic mail system. Many workstations will consist of a number of different pieces of equipment integrated into one unit, providing the employee with word processing, electronic mail services, facsimile transmission, and information retrieval capabilities. Such computerized workstations will enable employees to perform work away from a central office.

With the advent of voice mail, the regular telephone will become a more efficient communications tool. Organizations will use long distance communications facilities provided by public carriers over normal telephone systems, as well as communications satellites that are beginning to offer organizations efficient, economical communications capabilities.

The other major area where new communications technology will have a dramatic effect is in the home. An increasing number of homes will have their own microcomputer systems. Used in conjunction with a telephone, the microcomputer will provide access to a wealth of information as well as computing power through a large national-international telecommunications network. The traditional telephone may be replaced by a picture or video phone, and through the Touch-Tone keyboard the user will be able to communicate with distant computers. Television sets will provide expanded services, enabling users to access many information resources, receive electronic mail, and communicate back through the set to the originators of certain information. Satellite technology is decreasing in cost to the point where it will be inexpensive enough for anyone to install a receiving dish on a roof and receive a wealth of communications from orbiting satellites.

A LOOK TOWARD THE FUTURE

One of the most significant future influences of today's communications technologies is that there will be considerably less need for physical travel than in the past. Banking will be done at home through EFT systems accessed through the telephone. Also, much shopping from a variety of stores will be accomplished at home, using a combination of telephone and television. Working at home will be encouraged and made easy by using videophones that transmit pictures and documents as well as speech. Some homes will have machines that can receive transmitted documents. With such machines the user will be able to obtain business paperwork, news items, financial and stock market reports, mail bank statements, airline schedules, and so on.

Cash will be virtually eliminated. Restaurants and stores will accept bank cards that will be read by machines that can transfer funds between bank accounts by telecommunication. To a large extent businesses will be run by machine. Paperwork will be avoided by having computers send orders directly to other computers, and by making most payments, including salary payments, by EFT systems.

Home communications equipment will be used to provide a wide variety of sophisticated entertainment options. Many educational opportunities, including degrees and computer-aided instruction, will be available through computer-television technologies. The communications channels in homes also will be used to provide medical care, enabling a doctor in a remote location to provide help to patients over a wide area without having to visit them.

Probably the most significant influence that communications technology will have on the future is that people, who once moved to big cities in order to have jobs and participate in many activities, will no longer have to do so. Telecommunications will provide these opportunities without moving. In fact, more people will probably migrate out of cities when they realize that they can take advantage of the opportunities offered by cities, but live in rural areas.

STUDY AND REVIEW

1. What major effects on society do you foresee as a result of some of the sophisticated communications systems described in this chapter?

2. Compare and contrast the three types of information networks described in this chapter.

3. How do you think the evolving communications technologies will affect interpersonal relationships?

4. How can businesses and other large organizations expect to benefit from new communications technologies?

5. What is electronic mail? Compare and contrast the basic types of electronic mail systems.

6. What are the negative implications of electronic mail systems for the general public?

7. How can voice mail be used?

8. What effect are television-based information systems likely to have on normal day-to-day human activities?

9. How are telephone systems evolving?

10. In your opinion, is all this complex communications technology really necessary? Why or why not?

11. Assuming that television-based information systems will become commonplace in

homes in the near future, what in your opinion can be done to make sure that such systems do not make the same mistakes that commercial television has made during its evolution?

12. Briefly summarize the positive implications of the evolving communications technologies described in this chapter.

13. Briefly summarize the negative implications of the evolving communications technologies described in this chapter.

14. Can you see any other implications that were not mentioned in this chapter?

12

SCIENCE, ENGINEERING, AND ENERGY

PERSPECTIVE

The computer itself is a product of scientific research and development. In its earliest developmental stages, the computer was not of much actual benefit to the scientific community; it was almost more trouble to use than it was worth. However, scientists could easily foresee the tremendous potential that the computer held for the future. The computer quickly graduated from being a hybrid, temperamental, laboratory project, to an indispensable scientific tool.

The principal activity of science is research. As we can conclude from reading the following quote, scientists depend on computers to assist them with the research process. Discoveries made during research endeavors lead to processes and products for the future benefit of human beings. It might be said then that scientific research enables humans to "engineer the future."

> The effectiveness of the research process depends critically on scientific and technical communication, a process that is deeply and increasingly intertwined with the continuing electronic revolution. *(Baker et al. 1977)*

The word research does not help very much in conjuring up mental pictures of computer use in the sciences. We will have to elaborate in order to understand more clearly what is meant when we say that the computer is an important scientific research tool.

COMPUTERS IN SCIENCE, ENGINEERING, AND ENERGY

Research and Development

The advancement of human knowledge is made possible to a large extent through scientific research. We may typically envision research as taking place in a secret laboratory, with a white-frocked mad scientist pouring foaming chemicals from one beaker to another. Although it may seem as though many scientific discoveries are the result of chance occurrences, stumbling across the solution to a problem while engaged in advanced research/experimentation, most are the result of careful planning and hard work.

An actual scientific research project begins with a very clearly stated hypothesis. This hypothesis is a statement of the expected results of the research effort. After the hypothesis has been formulated, experiments are constructed to either prove or disprove the original hypothesis. Usually the general research process involves five phases: (1) hypothesis formulation, (2) planning, (3) experimental design, (4) experimentation, and (5) analysis of results. All of these steps require that detailed, lengthy mathematical computations be performed on vast amounts of raw data.

Many different types of research are being conducted today. In general, however, there are two broad categories of research: pure or "blue sky" research, and applied or developmental research. Pure research engages in activities that are not aimed at developing specific products or results with economic value, but on increasing the sum total of human knowledge. Applied or developmental research is concerned with implementing concepts in a practical way, or taking what is already known and using it more effectively. This research often results in actual products, from which some economic benefit may be derived.

As already mentioned, most research involves a considerable amount of mathematical computation. This is where the computer comes in, because it is extremely good at performing complicated, lengthy, mathematical computations. Many of the significant scientific achievements of past generations involved almost a lifetime of calculations, performed largely by hand. The computer has radically altered the nature of modern research. Computation is now no longer a major stumbling block in research. More extensive experimentation can be performed, thanks to the speed of the computer.

In addition to being fast, computers are extremely accurate. This is important in scientific research. There is nothing more embarrassing or potentially dangerous than a decision based on invalid experimental conclusions arising from computational error. As a result of computational speed, and almost unbelievable accuracy, the computer has become the most important modern research tool. In the following sections we explore the general use of computers and related electronics technologies in scientific research, and then describe a number of actual applications.

Monitoring and Measurement

Most types of scientific research involve some form of physical experimentation in which processes must be monitored, measured, and controlled (see Fig. 12.1). Scientific experimentation before computers involved the use of a wide variety of independent measurement devices, most of which were mechanically operated. These devices were not totally accurate and required frequent recalibration to assure some reliable degree of accuracy. The devices were only for measurement purposes and relied on human observation for monitoring and recording results. Practically speaking, then, if experiments took place over a long period of time, the monitoring and recording process could be only periodic—a human could not watch and record results continuously for a long time.

Computers and other electronic test equipment based on computer technology are ideal devices for scientific experimentation. Actual measurement is performed and displayed by highly accurate electronics. Mechanical instruments required that humans interpret the relative positions of various indicators on scales. This could lead to inaccurate readings. Electronic equipment uses an analog device that simulates a physical occurrence, such as a thermostat, which converts the measurement to electrical impulses that can be decoded by electronic circuitry and displayed digitally (as a numerical light display) (see Fig. 12.2).

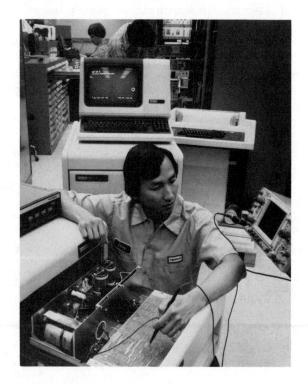

Figure 12-1 Much of today's sophisticated electronic equipment requires other sophisticated equipment to maintain it. (Courtesy of COMSAT Corp.)

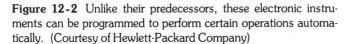

Figure 12-2 Unlike their predecessors, these electronic instruments can be programmed to perform certain operations automatically. (Courtesy of Hewlett-Packard Company)

Some experiments may require more than the measurement and recording of an on-going process. The experiment may require some physical alteration of various components as time passes. Again, a human may not be timely or accurate enough in performing adjustments. A computer, however, can be programmed to control precisely various components of an experiment and still provide a measurement and recording function. Computers can do this by using principles of process control, which were described in Chapter 9, Computers in Industry.

Experimenting and Testing

While some forms of experimenting may be for monitoring an on-going process, others involve the monitoring and control of experiments that seek to determine how long something will work, when something will fail, or how something will function under harsh or destructive conditions. Computers and other electronic equip-

Figure 12-3 The plastic model of an automobile body is being vibrated and stressed, with measurements being monitored and analyzed by computer controlled equipment. (Courtesy of General Motors Corporation)

ment can control and monitor such experiments, providing researchers a degree of insight never before possible (see Fig. 12.3).

Destructive Testing Before producing products, manufacturers often seek to determine the life of a product under both normal and abnormal conditions. How long will a light bulb last? What is the life of a tire? What is the combustion point of different fabrics? How will certain components of an automobile perform in a crash? All of these involve the destruction of a product to determine how it will perform in actual use. With some objects, such as a light bulb, tests conducted on a small number of samples can be statistically analyzed by a computer and the results used to describe the characteristics of all of that type of object.

In intentional destruction of an object, such as crashing an automobile, the event might take place so fast that a human could not possibly observe and record all significant occurrences. Sensors and other electronic devices can be used to monitor and record minute details about a process that would be missed were scientists to rely only on visual observation. In circumstances where observers might want to determine the effects of a crash on the occupants of a vehicle, humans cannot be used. Instead, dummies equipped with various electronic sensors can be used to provide accurate information.

Fatigue Testing Some types of materials or products may have their deterioration and failure accelerated by stress. To determine how long an object will last under stress, the object can be continuously stressed until it fails. This may take thousands of hours or years of stress before something breaks. It is often not possible or practical to test something for that length of time. By using electronic sensors and computers, objects can be monitored under stress conditions and observations that would be impossible without computers can be made. The data gathered from such observations can also be mathematically analyzed by the computer to determine the actual point of failure. In addition to monitoring the stress factors, a computer can be used to control environmental factors such as temperature and humidity, which might have an effect on the object being observed (see Fig. 12.4).

Dangerous Experimentation Many times science needs the answer to the question: What would happen if . . . ? However, the circumstances being proposed are often

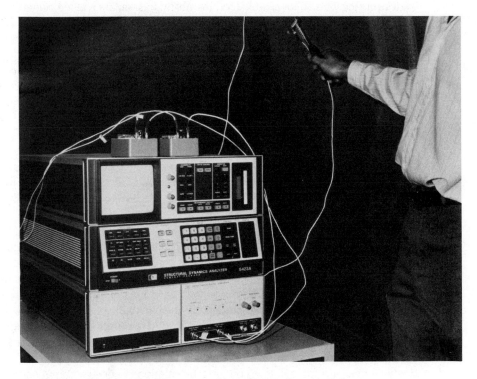

Figure 12-4 A structural dynamics analyzer. Pieces of equipment pictured here can record observations and display status information, as well as record the information for transmission to a larger computer. (Courtesy of Hewlett-Packard Company)

dangerous or hazardous and should not actually take place. For example, science may wonder what would happen in a nuclear reactor in event of some accident or disaster. We cannot risk the danger by actually experimenting on a nuclear reactor. If the medical community develops a new drug, it is unsafe to test it directly on humans. In both instances, and in many more, important questions must be answered before a product can be certified as safe for public use or human consumption. To accomplish such testing, scientists use the mathematical capabilities of the computer to construct a model of the process or event, and then they manipulate the model. By using the model, predictions can be made as to how things will perform in actual use. Initially the model can simulate conditions that can be tested in real life. This can be done to test the validity of the model, and increase the confidence that the results obtained when simulating dangerous conditions will be accurate. Modeling and simulating are discussed in detail in the next section.

Modeling and Simulating

The capabilities of a computer to analyze complex mathematical expressions provides science with an invaluable tool: the ability to simulate real-life occurrences in a computer without the danger, expense, or the logistics of conducting a full-scale real-life experiment.

Computer Models   Sometimes computer models are called mathematical or formal models. They differ from physical models because their mathematical or formal representations are stored within a computer as sets of mathematical formulas and programming language statements. Unlike mental models that are limited assumptions and beliefs about something, computer models must be constructed out of very precisely stated facts and formulas. We can define a **computer model** as a numerical representation of a system for demonstrating behavior of the system. Because of the large storage capacity and high-speed calculating power of the computer, systems can be described with greater precision and more detail than with mental models.

Computer Simulation   Up to this point it may not be clear as to why computer models are so important. It may seem that these formal models are merely extensive lists of formulas and statements that are stored in a computer and remain static and unchanging. Actually, computer models are very dynamic and are continually being updated and revised. Computer models are the backbone of an extremely significant computer capability called computer simulation. **Computer simulation** is the use of computer models to develop and evaluate ideas concerning real or hypothetical situations. Just as we base our predictions about the future behavior of another person, the weather, or a football team on past information, so does a computer model via simulation. But unlike the vague and incomplete data we usually base our mental models on, computer simulation takes advantage of its high speed and vast quantities of data to make much more accurate and detailed predictions.

Note, however, that not all systems or problems have been modeled completely or successfully. Frequently, problems or systems are ill-defined, data are incomplete or inaccurate, logical and causal relationships cannot be determined, or the final program predictions never match the actual data closely enough. Nevertheless, even an unsuccessful computer model has great value—the deeper understanding and appreciation of the problem under consideration.

Simulation In Science   In physics, chemistry, engineering, medicine, and related fields, computer modeling has had monumental impact. Because of the extensive number of factors that can be examined at low cost under a wide variety of experimental conditions, simulation has played a vital role in many important discoveries. Particularly in medical research—where timely experimentation involving enormous amounts of minute details can mean the difference between life and death—the computer has allowed lengthy studies to be reduced in time and cost. Some of the most remarkable breakthroughs in cancer research are a result of the use of simulation to understand better the advantages and disadvantages of different treatments by modeling what is occurring at the molecular level in terms of such factors as blood cells, drug/radiation absorption, side effects, and the like. Even in the relatively complex area of diagnosis, computer simulation is making it possible to share the insight and knowledge of one of the nation's leading diagnosticians. Dr. Jack Meyers of the University of Pittsburgh has been working with computer programmers to develop a program that uses a large database of medical information so that doctors anywhere in the network may access a program that will help diagnose and suggest a list of treatments for their patients. The program does not replace the doctor, but aids in the diagnosis by making available the most sophisticated methods of analysis plus relevant current information. Unlike a human clinician, however, this program is available 24 hours a day, never tires or forgets available information, and does not hesitate to ask for assistance when information is incomplete.

Another area that has presented problems for prediction is weather forecasting. Because the factors that influence weather patterns are numerous and globally distributed, it has been extremely difficult to obtain accurate long-range predictions. Now that information is available from weather satellites and world-wide weather stations, an accurate computer model of climatic change is possible. This means that when the relationships between large-scale global systems are distilled from the extensive data, accurate predictions should be possible. Such predictions would be of great benefit to agriculture, construction, and the world economy in general by permitting better planning. Meanwhile, for the first time, meteorologists are becoming able to assess the human impact upon weather. For example, they are determining the effects of the atmosphere's increasing carbon dioxide content (from the burning of fossil fuels) on global climate.

Data Analysis

Any significant scientific research or experiment generates a massive amount of data. The more complicated the project, the more voluminous the amount of data produced. This data must be analyzed by scientists or observers in order to draw valid conclusions from the experiment. In the past, without computers, scientists had to expend considerable effort to organize, classify, and actually process results in order to put the data in a form that could be analyzed and used to produce conclusions. Much of this activity involved routine clerical types of tasks that were not considered adequate use of highly skilled scientific talent. Often, in fact, more energy would be expended compiling results of an experiment than in the actual analysis of results (see Fig. 12.5).

Computers now provide the opportunity for scientists to focus their energies on the significance and application of results derived from research and experimentation, rather than on the tedious task of compiling and analyzing results. The results may then be taken from an instrument and manually entered into a computer, or test equipment may be connected directly to a computer and results directly communicated for storage and compilation. The computer's computational power allows scientists to compile and analyze data faster than in the past. Furthermore, the computer can manipulate, compare, and correlate data in many ways that were virtually impossible before. Thus, the computer may discover some significant result or relationship between results that could have gone unnoticed had it not been for

Figure 12-5 Desktop computers, such as Hewlett-Packard's H-P 85, can be connected to measurement equipment and used to analyze and display results. (Courtesy of Hewlett-Packard Company)

the computer's ability to perform all sorts of manipulations on massive amounts of data in a relatively short time.

Data Storage and Retrieval

While scientists are trying to expand human horizons and search for new knowledge, they must also be aware of, and be able to use, existing knowledge. As we stated earlier, the amount of information that could have a bearing on any new research is formidable. Therefore, before conducting any significant new research or experimentation, scientists must determine the extent of what has already been done in any area. Then, after conducting research or experimentation, results must be compared with other research efforts in order to determine if any significant new discoveries have been made, or new light shed on old discoveries. Finally, after research has been completed, results must be made available to the scientific community at large. All these steps would be almost impossible if today only manual methods were used.

Because of the computer's massive storage capabilities and almost instantaneous data retrieval, the collective wisdom of any number of scientists can be stored and made available to anyone in the future (see Cart. 12.1). Through the communications technology described in an earlier chapter, computers at different research

Uh, what do you mean, you forget?

centers and technical libraries can be connected together into a network that makes available this wealth of scientific information. One such major network is AR-PANET (Advanced Research Projects Agency Network), which connects 50 scientific research centers worldwide to share their information resources.

Scientists are also using computer terminals that connect to a large research network so that they have access to large amounts of data, can exchange messages quickly and conveniently, and share in the development and use of an evolving store of programs and data. A research effort, however, cannot have maximum impact until its results are formally documented, published, abstracted, indexed, and used.

When written information exists, scientists depend heavily on libraries to help them find it, and libraries are using computers in a growing number of ways to become more efficient and effective. For example, the Bell Laboratories Library Network consists of 25 libraries, serving more than 10,000 technical and managerial employees in nine states. To help these libraries work together as a single entity, the BELLREL system maintains an on-line file of the entire book and journal collection. A complete catalog is published annually in book form with monthly cumulative supplements, and copies are available to provide ready access for all employees.

Also at Bell Labs, the library's MERCURY system uses a computer to route, on the basis of subject matter and other criteria, internal technical reports to interested employees. The library also publishes a dozen current awareness bulletins, prepared in whole or in part by computer from external magnetic tapes or locally entered data, or both. For information retrieval, the library provides literature searching of commercial databases, and often publishes the results as specialized bibliographies.

Applications

In the following sections we briefly describe a number of different applications of computer technology in science, engineering, and energy. While the applications vary and may not use all of the same computer capabilities, they incorporate features of computer technology that have been discussed here and in other chapters.

Outer Space Studies   Initially, computers are used to help conduct the necessary research and experimentation that leads to the design of spacecraft. When built, computers control the operation of the spacecraft and monitor its performance. As a spacecraft reaches its destination, whether it be in orbit around Earth, on the moon, or some distant planet, computers continue to monitor and control it as well as direct experiments, collect data, and report to control stations on Earth.

In cases where a space mission is to a distant planet, human control is impossible because distances make instant communications infeasible. Thus, computers must control all aspects of such a space mission, according to extremely detailed programs worked out on Earth under simulated conditions before the mission. In the explorations on Mars, for example, distances were so great that communications between Mars and Earth took 20 minutes, making human control of the spacecraft impossible. All control, experiments, data collection, and transmission, therefore, were under the control of computers. After the data recorded in space is transmitted back to Earth, it is stored in computers. Computers then help scientists analyze the information, allowing them to discover important facts about space, and hopefully apply that knowledge to further understanding the universe in which we live.

Astronomy Earthbound scientists also make extensive use of computer technology to help them explore the very distant reaches of space. Modern research telescopes, such as the 200-inch wide Mt. Palomar instrument in southern California, are actually just large variations of a telescope design invented more than 300 years ago. This design uses a single lens to concentrate the light it gathers to a focused image; the larger the mirror the better. This design, though, seems to have reached its largest practical size. Astronomers concluded that a 1,000-inch wide telescope could be built, but it would cost $2 billion and require 50 years to shape. To avoid such cost and delay, several thousand small mirrors, all moving in unison, were mounted on servo motors that are activated by a central computer to maintain precise alignment. The alignment is constantly checked and reported to the control computer by laser-based sensing devices. One such telescope now exists in Arizona and similar systems are planned for the Universities of Arizona, California, and Texas.

With the limited power of telescopes for observing heavenly bodies, and with the increasing number of space vehicles and satellites in orbit, it has become difficult for astronomers to keep track of the movement of objects in space. So computers are now assisting them. A system developed by TRW Inc. connects computers to telescopes and monitors the movements of objects in space. In effect, this system provides a continuously changing map of the heavens. It is so powerful that it can track the movement of an object the size of a soccer ball 22,000 miles from earth (see Fig. 12.6).

Weather Electronic equipment has been used for years to help predict the weather. However, never before has weather forecasting relied so heavily on scientific techniques and sophisticated electronics technology. In weather forecasting and research involving Earth's atmosphere, weather data supplied by a worldwide network of space satellites, airplanes, and ground stations are fed into computers. Computers utilize complex models that have been developed to simulate the variables involved in weather forecasting (see Fig. 12.7). Although computers are fast and powerful, they cannot evaluate all the variables to the degree necessary in a short enough time to produce completely accurate timely weather forecasts. But with increasingly faster and more powerful computers, forecasts will become more detailed and accurate.

Farming With the increasing world population, the production of adequate food supplies is essential. Science is continuously searching for ways to make farming

Figure 12-6 Telescope used in conjunction with the TRW system described in the text. (Courtesy of TRW Inc.)

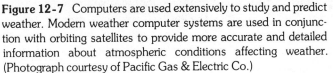

Figure 12-7 Computers are used extensively to study and predict weather. Modern weather computer systems are used in conjunction with orbiting satellites to provide more accurate and detailed information about atmospheric conditions affecting weather. (Photograph courtesy of Pacific Gas & Electric Co.)

more productive. In addition to using computers to manage the business end of a farm, farmers use computers to plan crop rotation, analyze soil conditions, determine fertilizer requirements, mix feed according to the nutritional requirements of livestock, keep track of breeding records, and plan land utilization so as to maximize crop yield and profit to the farmer.

Research is being conducted in laboratories with the aid of computers to develop plant strains that are healthier, resistant to disease, faster growing, and have higher yield. Satellites in orbit above Earth are using infrared and heat-sensitive photography to help scientists explore factors that contribute to the productivity of crops planted in certain areas. Such research will enable science to help farmers plan what, where, when, and how to plant so as to maximize crop yield.

Engineering and Construction   Engineering and architecture can make extensive use of computers to model and simulate, and display complex graphics. Many factors in product or structural design require testing in order to determine each operational characteristic that will have a bearing on the final design. Computers also enable engineers to test theories without having to physically build actual models. They can manipulate the model, and even push it to destruction, to see what will happen without fear of any physical damage. Graphics systems can enable engineers to see their models in three-dimensional form, enabling them to visualize their designs and make changes that are necessitated by weaknesses discovered by the computer, or by esthetic considerations. The use of computers in this capacity is known as Computer-Aided-Design (CAD) which is described in considerable detail in Chapter 9, Computers in Industry. Computers also assist engineers and architects with the complex calculations necessary to design modern products and structures.

Energy

Energy is an increasingly important subject in today's society, considering its rising use and decreasing supply. Computers are being used in many areas to help discover new sources of energy, make the utilization of existing sources more efficient, manage existing resources, and help conservation efforts. In this section we briefly explore each of these areas.

Exploration and Development   Computer technology is helping scientists search for new sources of energy. These may be new supplies of energy-producing substances that are already in use, such as petroleum, natural gas, coal, or geothermal wells. However, most of the sources of energy that we use today, or are likely to use in the future, are buried deep within the earth. Computers, coupled with ultrasonic transmitters and receivers, radar-like devices, and heat-sensing devices enable scientists to map large subterranean areas in their search for possible additional energy sources.

After energy sources are discovered, computers help scientists and engineers determine efficient methods for extracting the energy-producing material. Computers also help to process or convert raw materials into useful energy sources, such as converting coal into natural gas or petroleum. Furthermore, computers can run a manufacturing process that produces energy from raw materials. Such is the case with modern oil refineries.

Production, Distribution, and Utilization   After an energy source is discovered and developed, the source must be managed and efficiently distributed. Some sources, such as neclear energy, are so complex and potentially dangerous that computers are relied on completely to monitor and control the production of energy (see Fig. 12.8). However, whether nuclear, electric, or petroleum energy, it must be transported from its source to where it is needed. The distribution lines, whether high voltage electrical transmission lines or petroleum or natural gas pipelines, require close monitoring and control for efficient operation. In a large number of energy distribution systems, the computer is taking on this responsibility (see Fig. 12.9).

Even when energy reaches the consumption point, the computers' role in the energy field is not finished. Many of the products that use energy are not very effi-

Figure 12-8 The control room of a nuclear power plant. (Photograph courtesy of Pacific Gas & Electric Co.)

Figure 12-9 Power distribution grids for large utilities are computer controlled to ensure uninterrupted service to customers. (Photograph courtesy of Pacific Gas & Electric Co.)

cient; they waste considerable energy. Scientists and engineers utilize computer technology to help design automobile engines that use less fuel, home appliances that use less electricity, and many other devices that decrease our dependence on vital diminishing natural resources.

Conservation   One sure way to solve many of our energy utilization problems is to use less and less, or find ways of conserving energy while still engaging in our same day-to-day activities. Pacific Gas & Electric Co., in northern California, in 1981 offered subscribers a new service. A representative will visit a home and conduct an "energy survey" (insulation, weatherstripping, etc.). The information is then entered into a computer via a portable terminal and telephone. The computer analyzes the information, and responds with suggested conservation measures, anticipated costs, and expected energy savings.

Another application of computers in energy conservation is in the area of environmental control. Computers can be connected to a variety of sensors (temperature, pressure, humidity) both inside and outside buildings. Then, with a program in the computers, they activate and deactivate heating and air conditioning, and automatically open and close windows for ventilation. This can be accomplished in large buildings by a sizable environmental control computer, or on a small scale in a home where systems are controlled by a microcomputer.

SOCIAL IMPLICATIONS

Pro Arguments

This chapter has dealt with a wide variety of applications, but the general advantages offered by computers can apply equally to all of these diverse areas. Computer technology is enabling scientists and engineers to perform much more thorough research than at any time in history. The availability of research information through computers reduces the chances that research efforts will be duplicated, and increases the opportunity for scientists to develop projects that are based on current, timely, valid research completed recently. The results of research projects may be stored in computers so that other researchers can use results in their personal projects, or existing research can be used to develop new projects or processes for consumer use.

Electronic test equipment enables scientists and engineers to obtain a degree of accuracy in measurement never before possible. Furthermore, electronics can monitor experiments or processes in such detail that occurrences that may have gone undetected before the new types of equipment were in use can now be measured and recorded for important, detailed analysis.

Now that experiments can be monitored and controlled by computers, they can also be much more extensive and complex than at any time previously. Some physical experiments, especially dangerous ones, need not even be performed.

Simulation and modeling can be used to provide scientists with invaluable experimental tools.

The use of computers in the energy field can result only in positive influences. Computers will help us do more thorough geographic research to locate energy supplies, develop methods to efficiently refine and distribute energy, and ultimately help us produce products that use energy more efficiently yet allow us to maintain our standard of living.

Con Arguments

As stated earlier, scientific research produces a large quantity of information. Some of the information may be created in the public domain and, therefore, available to anyone. However, much private research produces proprietary information, or trade secrets that cannot and should not be shared. Furthermore, some research must be top secret, such as nuclear weapons research. Thus, while computers make it easier for the scientific community to share information, proprietary and top secret research data must be protected.

Modeling and simulation offer great potential to the scientific community. However, there are several disadvantages to these techniques. First, simulation works well in situations where the system being monitored is well understood. Where the system is not well understood, a model that works can be constructed, but may not be accurate. Therefore, if the system being simulated is not well understood in the first place, then researchers may not realize that the results produced by the model are inaccurate. Second, the model may be confused with the system it is to simulate. Scientists may become so involved with the performance of the computer model that they may neglect real-life experiences or the workings of a prototype model. Finally, it is difficult to factor human dynamics or social impact into a model. These must be taken into account when evaluating the performance of a computer model before assuming that things will work the same way in real life.

HARDWARE

Two different categories of equipment were described in this chapter, namely, electronic test equipment and full-scale computer systems. Electronic test equipment utilizes the latest in solid state technology. Most advanced devices have their primary functions controlled by one or more microprocessor chips. The device will include some ROM memory chips that will contain the predefined operating instructions for the device. Some pieces of equipment will also contain some RAM memory that will allow the user to program the device with a desired set of instructions. Additional memory will be available to store test results for display later, or for communication to a computer through interface capabilities that are built into the machine. Equipment will allow a variety of analog measuring devices to be connected to supply data. Additional features of such equipment will be continuous self-diagnostics and calibration.

Computers that will be used in many of the types of applications mentioned in this chapter are likely to be large, time-share systems with large auxiliary storage units for information storage and retrieval. Typical computers will also have communications capabilities that will enable them to function as part of a communications network to send and receive information. A wide variety of input devices will be used in conjunction with scientific computers. Standard terminals will be used for routine input and output, and the computer will have the capability of interfacing with various pieces of electronic test and measurement equipment.

A LOOK TOWARD THE FUTURE

Certainly, with the costs of physical research and the complexity of experimentation growing, the scientific community will use the power of the computer to model and simulate more extensively. As scientists become more familiar with the computational powers of the computer, they will be able to construct more intricate models that simulate forces that exist in real life. As scientists also refine their abilities to use this tool, they will be able to perform research and experimentation well beyond what is being done now.

In circumstances where physical experimentation is essential, advanced equipment with more powerful features than available today will monitor experiments, record data, provide control of the experiment, analyze results, and within certain limits even draw conclusions.

Scientific information computer networks will enable institutions to coordinate research efforts on a global basis. Scientists working on opposite sides of Earth on similar projects will be able to instantaneously draw on each other's experiences. Such sharing will eliminate duplication of efforts and lead to more precise, productive research.

While it is true that computers help us locate new supplies of energy, a much more important function of computers is to help us develop energy sources that are renewable, such as solar, wind, and nuclear. Computers will increasingly be used for this purpose.

STUDY AND REVIEW

1. What are the types of uses of computer technology that support scientific research?

2. What are the phases of the research process? How can the computer help in each of these phases?

3. Describe the two broad categories of research. What is the distinction between the two?

4. What are the drawbacks of human observation in the monitoring and measurement of scientific experimentation that can be eliminated by the computer?

5. What are the types of experimentation that seek to determine when something will fail, how long something will work, or how something will perform under harsh or danger-ous conditions? What is the computer's role in each?

6. What are modeling and simulation? Are they different? How? How is each used? Of what use is the computer in each?

7. How can database management systems (DBMS) and computer networks serve scientists during research?

8. Some people question whether we can continue to advance human knowledge at the same pace as we have in the past. Others believe that with the role of the computer in scientific development we are just opening the door on a new era of explosive growth in human knowledge. What is your view on this subject?

9. Describe the use of computers in engineering.

10. Describe the role of computers in the energy field.

11. Summarize the negative implications of computer technology on science, engineering, and energy.

12. Summarize the positive implications of computer technology in science, engineering, and energy.

13. Do you recognize any applications of computer technology in science, engineering, and energy other than those mentioned in this chapter?

13

MEDICINE

PERSPECTIVE

Health care is heavily dependent on large amounts of data and information in order to provide the best possible diagnosis and treatment. However, without computers it would be almost impossible to collect, analyze, store, and retrieve the necessary information for health services. As the following quotation indicates, the computer is truly revolutionizing all aspects of the field of medicine.

> Hospitals and private practitioners alike are beginning to use computers to perform a myriad of behind-the-scenes tasks that ultimately mean shorter and better treatment for patients. Laboratory tests are being performed more quickly, and with a lower incidence of error. Nursing care is becoming more efficient and personalized. Medical education is being tailored to the specific needs of the student. Patient awareness and education are increasing. Sophisticated diagnostic tools and research facilities are becoming available to small institutions with limited funds and to private practitioners.
> (Grosswirth, 1980)

But adapting computers to the medical profession is not an easy task. Medical decisions often rely on ambiguous and difficult to classify complex information, whereas computers work best with clearly defined, logically organized data. The resulting tension between ambiguity and logic have given birth to a new discipline: medical information science. This new science is a blend of medicine and computer science and has been primarily responsible for adapting the speed and accuracy of advanced computer technology to the growing needs of the medical sciences. Health care costs have been rising faster than the national rate of inflation. Fortunately, there is great promise that there will be containment and eventually a reduction of these costs by improving the efficiency of health care delivery through the use of computers. Significant progress has been made, and the remainder of this chapter examines how it has been accomplished.

COMPUTERS IN MEDICINE

There are five major areas in which computers are used in medicine: health care services, laboratories, medical information systems, education and research, and advanced technological applications. The five divisions, although somewhat artificial, are employed to assist in organizing the large amount of information pertaining to medicine. However, all five areas are closely interconnected through their emphasis on sophisticated use of the computer to improve the quality of medical care.

Health Care Services

There are three major ways in which health services are delivered to the patient: Hospitals, physicians' offices/clinics, and preventive medicine facilities. Although each of these methods emphasizes different aspects of medicine, they share similar uses of the computer for bookkeeping, scheduling appointments, and other business functions. But since these business uses of the computer have already been discussed in Chapter 8, we will focus on those applications that are unique to each area.

Hospitals Because of their size, financial resources, and the fact that many of the cases handled are emergency life-or-death situations, hospitals are finding it almost impossible to operate without computers. Three areas in which computers are now being used are: administration, patient care, and emergency services.

Administration From admission to discharge, hospitals are required to maintain complex, up-to-date records on every patient. To deal with this glut of information, several database information retrieval systems—sometimes called Hospital Informations Systems (HIS)—have been designed to meet this challenge. Although some of these systems can provide information to assist physicians and nurses in their duties, most systems are used for record keeping, such as billing, preparing insurance forms, doing payroll, scheduling rooms and equipment, keeping track of inventory, and documenting all patient expenses. The main idea is to consolidate all this information, allow it to be accessed and updated easily (usually from one of many terminals), thereby reducing costs, eliminating duplication, and providing better information for decision making and planning. Computers are also a necessity in order to meet the government reporting requirements for Medicare and other documentation such as that required for Professional Standards Review Organizations (PSROs), which are local peer evaluations of activities relating to patient care and service (see Fig. 13.1).

Patient Care Sometimes the accuracy of patient records and the speed with which they can be accessed can determine whether a patient lives or dies. To meet this challenge several patient record systems have been developed to facilitate the integration and dissemination of information. One system, developed by Duke University and called Patient Care System (PCS), coordinates communications among physicians, nurses, testing laboratories, dieticians, pharmacists, radiologists, and all other departments that are involved in treating the patient. Not only does this system keep track of all pertinent information and allow easy access and updating by authorized personnel, it also provides security measures to protect the information from unauthorized use. By efficiently organizing patient information from admission to discharge, several hospitals claim they can save more than $1 million per year (not to mention a number of lives) through more effective use of resources, reduced laboratory test time, and less time spent in the hospital.

Another system, called Problem-Oriented Medical Information System (PROMIS), is very sophisticated in that it integrates four separate functions: (1) a very large database of current literature on more than 36,000 medical problems; (2) the initial complaint, medical history/inventory of the patient and the physician's formulation of the problem; (3) the initial plans for treatment; and (4) progress notes. After the patient information is entered, it can be retrieved in many different ways: By patient, date, problem, medication, treatment, abnormal findings, and so forth. This integrative approach not only assists physicians and other staff members by having both reference literature and patient data so they do not have to rely on memory so much (especially in critical or stressful situations), but it also provides a very powerful research and treatment tool by summarizing and displaying information in just about any way imaginable. Finally, a special programming language called MUMPS (**M**assachusetts **G**eneral **H**ospital **U**tility **M**ulti-**P**rogramming **S**ystem) has been designed to handle the special problems of ambiguity and complexity found in medical environments that cannot be addressed by traditional languages such as FORTRAN or COBOL.

Emergency Services Perhaps one of the most remarkable computer accomplishments, in terms of its ability to save lives, is Direct Patient Monitoring (DPM) that is often used in intensive care units and post-operation rooms. Very similar to the process control techniques used in industry (see Chapter 9), DPM uses very small sensing devices to record a patient's vital signs, such as blood pressure, pulse, temperature, venous pressure, blood chemistry, and urine. The permissible range of values for each patient is entered into the computer program that is monitoring the sensing devices, and these values can easily be changed as the patient's condition changes. Whenever any of the values *start* to indicate a trend that would go outside the acceptable range, a warning (a buzzer or flashing light) is initialized on a control panel that is being monitored by a human who can take the appropriate action. The important point is that the measurements are made so frequently, and with much

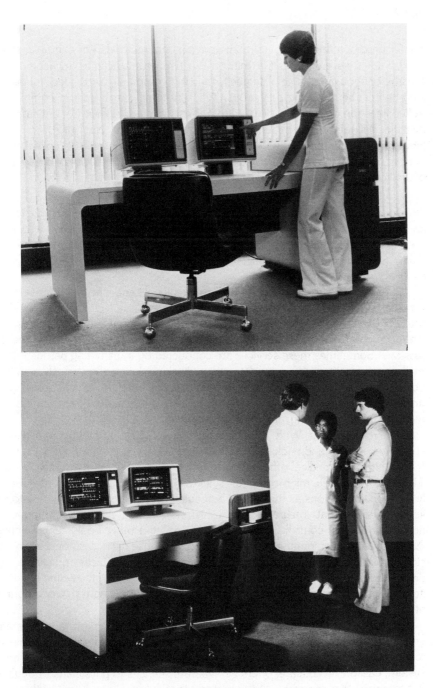

Figure 13-1 A patient information center with its compact and efficient design, displays sharp ECG waveforms and alpha-numeric data together so that the staff can see more information at a glance. (Courtesy of Hewlett-Packard Company)

greater precision and sensitivity than conventional methods (for example, samples can be taken several times per minute and temperature can be measured in hundredths or thousandths of a degree!), that the computer can detect crucial trends long before they become dangerous. Also, in some cases, special computer-controlled injection devices can be used to administer small dosages of critical fluids or medicine to stabilize the patient until the physician arrives. Not only does this technique provide tireless, accurate monitoring, it also can be used to collect very important research information on patient recovery, the effectiveness of different types of medications, and the success of various types of treatment.

Offices and Clinics Computers are finding their way into even small private offices and medical clinics. No longer do you have to be a large organization with vast resources in order to benefit from computer technology. Three major ways the computers are affecting medical offices include service bureaus, microcomputers, and medical networks.

Service Bureaus A number of local, regional, and national service bureaus provide bookkeeping and patient record services for the medical professions. Often these services are operated by members of a profession, such as dentists, physicians, optometrists, and others who are familiar with the special needs of these professions. Sometimes these services are conducted by transmitting pertinent data by mail, by courier service, or by data entry terminals located in the office. Although bookkeeping is the primary function of such service bureaus, larger bureaus provide time-sharing terminals so that detailed patient records can be kept on line for immediate access, updating, and billing information.

Microcomputers With low cost, increased disk storage capabilities, and specially designed and packaged software, microcomputers are now being used effectively in small medical offices. For an initial low cost of approximately $3,000 to $10,000, a complete microcomputer system can be purchased to provide essentially the same operations as the service bureaus. Many doctors are beginning to establish databases that integrate patient histories, billing procedures, appointment notices, inventory control, payroll, tax records, and other bookkeeping activities. Also, new microcomputer-operated devices, like those used in optometry to test vision and select the correct lenses, are being used in small offices and clinics. Sometimes the initial installation of this type of equipment, which saves time and is more accurate, serves as a catalyst for a doctor to consider using a microcomputer for other office tasks (see Fig. 13.2).

Medical Networks Although we will examine medical information systems in greater depth later in this chapter, it is interesting to note that some systems are already delivering their services to individual practitioners in their offices. One such system, called Preventicare, offers 21 separate services to physicians through in-office terminals that connect with the system via telephone lines. Some of the services available are: collection of medical histories, preparation of special diets, health hazard appraisal, medical education courses, disease diagnosis, and the analysis and delivery of laboratory results. With advanced networks like this, it will not be

Figure 13-2 (a) A microcomputer-based eye examination system (b) A microcomputer-based lens analyzer (Photos courtesy of the Humphrey Optical Instruments)

long before even the smallest office in the most rural part of the country will be able to benefit from, and have immediate access to, the latest medical information and life-saving techniques—all at a very reasonable cost!

Preventive Medicine   For several years great emphasis has been placed on preventive health care, which involves identifying and removing factors such as pollution, chemical contaminants, excessive noise, and environmental conditions that are known to produce injury or disease. Closely related to these public health measures are some relatively new approaches by the medical profession to detect health problems at an early stage and, if possible, prevent them from developing.

   Automated Medical Histories   Medical researchers have found that an accurate and detailed medical history is a very important diagnostic tool for detecting and preventing disease. However, taking a detailed history is time consuming, and just one oversight or neglected question can produce incorrect results. For these reasons the computer has become an excellent method for collecting and analyzing medical histories in hospitals, clinics, and private offices. Elaborate programs have been developed to take histories (usually from a computer terminal) that actually are more accurate than those taken by humans. This greater accuracy is due to several factors: The program never forgets to ask all the relevant questions; humans seem more comfortable divulging sensitive information to a computer than to another human; the program skips irrelevant questions or asks more detailed questions, depending on the answers given; and if a person does not understand a question, it can be explained in simpler terms or with the assistance of a diagram. Also, because the program collects much more information, it can often make several suggestions to the physician concerning problem areas or unusual responses, and provide an excellent resource for medical research. Finally, since patients do not have to take valuable time away from the physician to collect the history, the doctor can spend more time with the patient discussing and attending to more important matters.

Computer-Assisted Physical Examinations Another approach toward preventive medicine are the multiphasic health centers (presently over 300 in the United States) that compile medical histories and perform all the detailed laboratory work of a physical exam, integrate and analyze these data, and send computer printouts of the results to the individual's physician. Besides providing these detailed reports, the real advantage of these centers is that they keep a cumulative computer file on each individual so that future examinations include a comparison of major tests (vision, heart, lungs, blood chemistry, and so forth) with the results from previous years. In this way the patient is not compared with national norms (which can be misleading), but rather with his or her own results from earlier tests so that any significant changes are easy to detect. For example, an individual's blood pressure or EKG could be within normal ranges over a two-year period in terms of group statistics, but could have been at the bottom of the range one year and the top of the range the next year—indicating a very significant change for that person. Not only does the computer provide these benefits, but it does it at a much lower cost than with conventional methods. Both automated medical histories (which sometimes are a part of the multiphasic examination) and multiphasic examinations often include health hazard appraisal or risk factor analysis. These aspects of the medical history attempt to identify factors that are known to cause illness, such as smoking, drinking, stressful working or living conditions, exposure to dangerous chemicals, and other relevant conditions. By determining how many of these "risk" or "hazard" factors are present, estimates can be made as to how many years can be subtracted from a "normal" life expectancy. This quantification of risks along with suggestions about proper diet, exercise, sleep, and other factors that can improve health, seems to be a very important part of preventive health care. Not only are there these additional benefits from automated medical histories and multiphasic examinations, but these benefits are provided at a lower cost than with conventional, noncomputer techniques (see Fig. 13.3)

Figure 13-3 A terminal for entering laboratory results directly into medical histories. (Courtesy Honeywell Information Systems, Inc.)

Medical Laboratories

Perhaps the most important resource for the diagnosis and treatment of disease are the reports from the medical laboratories that collect and analyze data for physicians. In a typical large hospital lab, over 500 different tests are performed, producing over 3,000 reports per day with one to 20 results per report. With this extraordinary amount of data, the possibility of error (particularly under emergency conditions) is very great—yet the accuracy of the tests can be a life-or-death matter.

We now look at two ways in which computers are being used in conjunction with laboratory tests.

Data Collection   One of the major ways in which errors are introduced in the collection and analysis of medical data is through transcription—the recording of initial values, intermediate results, and final reports. Through the use of computerized laboratory equipment, most of the transcription activities can be done by computer. Another source of error is the equipment itself: it may not be properly calibrated or just difficult to read the results. Again, through the use of computerized (usually microprocessor controlled) laboratory instruments that can test and calibrate themselves and print out or digitally display results, this source of error can essentially be eliminated (see Fig. 13.4).

In a typical medical lab all the testing equipment would be connected to a central computer that would classify (by patient, date, test, physician, and so on), store all results, and print out the necessary reports for the physician, billing, inventory, and other statistical summaries. In addition to performing these functions,

(a)

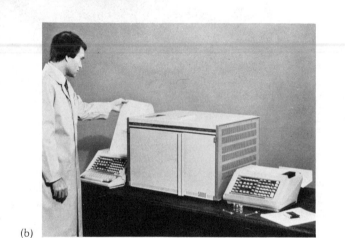

(b)

(c)

Figure 13-4 (a) A direct insertion probe, (b) A gas chromatograph. These are typical computer-based laboratory devices. (c) A computer-controlled ultraviolet visible-light spectrophotometer (Photos courtesy of Hewlett-Packard Company)

there are many benefits that were not possible with manual methods. For example, results are immediately available via computer terminal in the patient's room or even in the operating room. The computer can detect and alert the staff to any unusual data that seem implausible, results are more precise and have fewer errors, and the overall costs for laboratory work are lower. It has been estimated that several hours per day (thousands of dollars per month) are saved just by the clerical time that is eliminated in looking up results and giving verbal reports over the phone. Most important, however, is the great reduction in time for these vital tests. This permits more tests to be performed in a given amount of time, so rather than just one cycle of tests per day there can be almost two cycles, which means a shorter patient stay in the hospital and lower costs. For instance, one of the common tests, the blood count, used to take approximately 4.5 hours but takes only 1.5 hours in the computerized laboratory.

Database Studies   Besides the above mentioned benefits of the automated laboratory, the data that are stored in the computer can also be used for important medical research. The laboratory information provides a valuable database that can be used for studies regarding the effectiveness of different tests. By performing statistical analyses upon these data, which would be impossible if it were stored in manila folders, important relationships and significant results are easily detected. The results of these database studies have already proven successful in uncovering unfruitful diagnostic procedures and in improving management control of laboratory procedures. These studies not only improve the quality of medical care, but at the same time help to contain or reduce health care costs.

Medical Information Systems

> *The rapid growth of biomedical information has created an available body of knowledge (facts, concepts, and their inter-relationships) far greater than any individual can assimilate. Even the most industrious and astute physician uses less than the total amount of potentially available relevant information and knowledge in making decisions. Computers, with their massive information-handling capabilities, are looked to as potential expanders of the physician's information and knowledge resources.*
> *(Schoolman and Bernstein, 1978)*

With more than 5,000 medical and health science journals published each month, it is not surprising that most physicians can use only a small fraction of the relevant information available. And, as the above quotation suggests, even if all of this information was conveniently located in the physician's office, just locating the pertinent articles and remembering the important details would be beyond human capability. Fortunately, the computer affords several ways in which to organize and disseminate this information in a timely and inexpensive manner. However, merely entering all of the journal articles into the computer is not the solution. As mentioned in the beginning of this chapter, a special discipline (medical information science) has evolved just to meet the challenge of organizing, integrating, cross-indexing, and distributing this knowledge. Although these problems are faced any time a large database is developed, they often become crucial, considering the complexity of medical information and the urgency of obtaining the correct information in emergency situations.

However, these difficulties become even more severe when, in an attempt to reduce costs by sharing information among different databases, the problem of different coding techniques is encountered. Several coding schemes have been designed to facilitate the classifying and cross-referencing of data; SNOMED, ICDO, and SNOP are the names of three of these systems. But since there is not just one system of classification, it is sometimes difficult to exchange or cross-index information that is stored in different databases. To overcome this problem, computer-stored translation tables and concordances are used so different systems can communicate with each other. Even within a single database, locating information can be difficult and time-consuming, especially if a word is misspelled. To combat this problem large, computerized dictionaries are used to detect misspelled technical words and substitute the correct spelling. And to deal with nontechnical words, such as patient names, a system called SOUNDEX is used to identify and list words that sound similar to the word entered. For example, if a patient's file was not located under the spelling "Taylor," SOUNDEX would also suggest and locate alternate spellings like "Tayler" or "Tailor."

We now look at three different types of medical information systems, all of which are essentially large electronic libraries that distribute their information through network communications to hospitals, clinics, research centers, and private medical offices (see Fig. 13.5)

Reference   The most comprehensive electronic medical library is Medical Literature Analysis and Retrieval System, (MEDLARS), developed by the National Library of Medicine (NLM) in Washington, D.C. It contains references to more than 1,000,000 articles, indexes about 20,000 articles per month from approximately 3,000 journals, and distributes this information to more than 40 countries throughout the world via satellite networks to on-line terminals. The information can be retrieved in many different ways, such as by title, author, topic, research location, and so forth; and, because of the very large audience (more than 1,000,000 searches per year), the costs are fairly reasonable.

Another reference system widely used by physicians and pharmacists, especially in hospital environments, is a drug interaction database. By entering all prescriptions a patient is presently taking, the program can detect potentially harmful combinations of drugs, taking into consideration the dosage, patient's age, and other relevant factors. The program responds in different ways, depending on the

Figure 13-5 A medical information system retrieval terminal (Courtesy of International Business Machines Corporation)

severity of the interaction; in some cases it will merely caution or warn the physician about possible side effects or, in critical situations, not even allow the prescription label to be printed. Because so few physicians are expert in the field of pharmacology, especially when more than one drug is being taken, it is estimated that this type of reference information saves hundreds of lives each year—it can even detect improper dosages! One unique reference or educational system is called HIBABY. Developed in Ohio for use in maternity wards, HIBABY provides child-care training and information to new mothers via terminals placed at their bedsides. As questions arise, a mother (or anyone who might be visiting a mother) can make inquiries into the system via a menu (an index displayed on the terminal screen) of several different categories of child-care information. By providing instantaneous feedback on important questions at the time questions occur, learning and child care is greatly facilitated.

Diagnosis In an attempt to bring the vast resources of computer databases and networks closer to the decision-making process of physicians, several information systems have been designed to assist in medical diagnosis. Besides having access to large amounts of recent information, these programs also simulate the heuristic strategies or protocols that a physician employs during diagnosis. Perhaps the most sophisticated program of this type is called CADUCEUS (formerly called INTERNIST), named after the emblem of the medical profession and developed at the University of Pittsburgh by Jack Meyers, M.D., and Dr. Harry Pople, computer

265

specialist. A physician enters some initial data (symptoms and lab results), and the program proceeds to ask relevant questions about the patient in an effort to narrow the range of possibile diseases. The program can pursue many different possibilities simultaneously and suggest questions and further tests that the doctor may conduct (while also considering the cost, discomfort, and importance of the tests being recommended). The great advantage of CADUCEUS is that it is based on the strategies of a world-famous diagnostician, and it never forgets relevant factors that a doctor might overlook due to fatique, the "fading" of memories, or mental saturation. Currently CADUCEUS contains complete information on about 500 diseases, along with more than 3,000 disease manifestations. In relation to most physicians, CADUCEUS is extremely accurate; however, it does have difficulty when unrelated ailments are present and the order in which events occur must be evaluated. In the future programs like this will probably be developed and updated by larger groups of doctors so as to benefit from a consensus of more experience and knowledge.

Another program, called MYCIN, has been developed at Stanford University to diagnose bacterial blood infections and suggest treatment. Normally, it would take a week or longer to grow a culture in a laboratory in order to identify certain bacteria. However, with MYCIN this process can be done in hours. The program works in a dialog fashion, with the medical professional answering a series of questions posed by MYCIN that are designed to narrow the field to a few likely candidates. At this point the program presents the most probable organisms that could have produced the symptoms and the other laboratory results already obtained. It then indicates the appropriate dosages of antibiotics that would destroy the likely bacteria. If the doctor wants to review the chain of reasonings that led to MYCIN's conclusions, they can be recalled and listed.

Both diagnostic medical information systems demonstrate the power of the computer to assimilate large amounts of data and to turn data into timely information (perhaps even knowledge) that can assist the medical profession in providing the best possible care for its patients. It has already been demonstrated in studies of diagnostic systems that physicians (whether they be interns, first-year residents, or second-year residents) are able to detect twice as many medical problems/events with the aid of the computer than without it. However, it is not expected that computers will ever replace doctors, but it is very likely that computers will contribute to better treatment for more people at lower costs (see Fig. 13.6).

Emergency Information Numerous medical information systems have been designed to provide timely information over large geographic areas for critical emergency situations. A large number of these databases provide services for organ donors and transplants. Time is an extremely important factor in organ transplants; often the recipient must be matched with the donor within 24 hours or less. Because of the complex information involved in these transplants, such as blood and tissue compatibility, how long the recipient has been on the waiting list, geographic locations of the donor and recipient, and so on, the computer essentially makes it possible for the transaction to take place by locating candidates in just a few seconds.

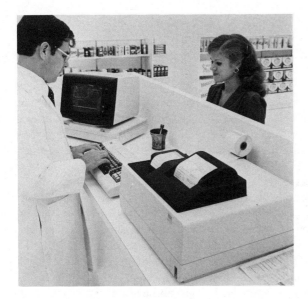

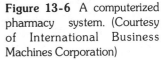

Figure 13-6 A computerized pharmacy system. (Courtesy of International Business Machines Corporation)

There are separate data banks for eye, kidney, heart, and other specific organs. However, there has been a recent trend to create regional and national networks of these data banks in order to share computer resources and data. For example, in the southeastern United States 132 organ-transplant centers have been linked together so physiological data on prospective recipients can be quickly matched with available organs. It has been estimated that this network increases the chances of a successful transplant by about 50 percent.

Poison information centers are another type of emergency systems that provide timely, life saving information. By storing large amounts of data on everything from common household materials to exotic laboratory chemicals, these systems can quickly retrieve the most appropriate type of treatment, depending on whether a physician, chemist, or lay person requests the information. They can also take into consideration the resources the person has available with which to treat the victim. Some of these systems are interconnected with other emergency services, such as hospitals, ambulances, and fire or police departments, so assistance can be immediately dispatched. Most of these systems can be accessed either by phone (for the general public) or by computer terminal for hospitals and other emergency services that use this information frequently.

Education and Research

Many of the applications we have already discussed have demonstrated the numerous benefits and by-products of using computers to collect, store, and distribute medical information. After the data is entered, whether it be for a patient's record, the results of laboratory tests, or technical reference material, it can be retrieved, summarized, and analyzed in many different ways. This capability not

267

only assists in the statistical analyses of researchers, but allows a similar flexibility in presenting information for medical education.

We now look at some of the computer techniques that are used in the areas of medical education and research.

Education   In Chapter 5 we discussed several different types of computer-assisted instruction (CAI). Although several different methods of CAI are used in medical education, simulation seems to be the most widely used. In many medical schools, 40 to 50 percent of the first- and second-year students receive instruction in the basic sciences via CAI. Although methods such as drill and practice, tutorial, problem-solving, and large database are used, we will focus on the use of simulation since it allows the students to explore their knowledge in the greatest depth.

Simulation   One application, developed under the MUMPS system mentioned earlier, uses physiological simulation to test the treatment medical students recommend when they are presented with hypothetical emergency situations. The student is presented with a typical emergency ward case and is provided with only a minimum amount of information about the patient. The student can request additional information or tests, administer drugs, and take other courses of action. If the student makes a mistake, does not act quickly enough, or overlooks something, the patient will either return later with a more serious development or, perhaps even die!

The advantages of this approach are that the student can be exposed to a wide variety of critical situations, accurately simulated by the computer, and see the results and errors of their suggested treatment in a very short time. All of this takes place without a real patient ever dying! In this way a student is exposed to many more cases than would normally be encountered during the intern period, has the opportunity to develop quick decision-making skills, and obtains immediate feedback on the treatment being used so inaccurate strategies can be replaced or modified before he or she actually begins practicing medicine.

Another system, called Computer-Aided Simulation of the clinical Encounter (CASE), presents three typical patients who must be evaluated and treated by an internist. This program simulates the internist's procedures in order to assess the knowledge, skills, and clinical judgments employed. This procedure is used by the American Board of Internal Medicine for evaluating the competence of Board-certified internists who are already practicing medicine.

Finally, one of the most fascinating uses of physiological simulation is Sim One. Used primarily for training medical students in anesthesiology, Sim One is a life-size mannequin that simulates heart beat, blood pressure, eye dilation, jaw movement, and even muscular twitches—all under computer control. If a mistake is made during the administration of anesthetics, either a warning is given or the "patient" dies. After the simulated operation is over, a complete critique of the student's techniques is printed out by the computer.

Research   Closely related to medical education is medical research. Research often takes place in academic environments, and both medical research and medical education make extensive use of computer simulation. Because computers can make exhaustive searches of large quantities of data, perform sophisticated statistical analyses, produce charts and graphs, and accomplish other useful consolidating and summarizing techniques, they are ideally suited for research.

Simulation Because the computer can accurately model physiological systems, from the level of molecular structure in DNA studies to particular body organs such as the heart or lungs, all the way to complete systems such as the respiratory or circulatory systems, it is not surprising that new applications are being developed almost monthly. After an accurate model of a system is developed, the effects of different variables such as drugs or surgical techniques can be tested quickly and their results measured. Significant advances have been made in cancer research by using a computer to simulate the molecular interactions of drugs with cancer cells. The drug structure is modified on the computer until it is effective, then researchers attempt to synthesize the drug in the laboratory. It has been estimated that one day of computer simulation can be more useful than a year or two in the lab.

Another area where the computer is extremely effective is in helping to perfect surgical techniques. When operating on delicate organs (like the inner ear) or in reconstructive surgery (such as correcting speech impediments), it is often difficult to predict the exact results of surgery; one minor mistake can completely nullify the operation. By using simulation, the surgical procedure can be practiced many times, and the effects—say, upon hearing or speech—can be estimated before the operation is actually performed.

Database Studies   Throughout this chapter we have discussed many ways in which computers are used to collect and store medical information. We have also indicated that after data is stored in a computer it becomes a very valuable resource for statistical analyses by medical researchers. What follows is a brief list of typical studies conducted in this fashion:

- analyzing medical histories to determine the most effective treatment for different diseases or injuries

- analyzing physiological records obtained through direct patient monitoring to find optimum methods for treating shock and other problems that often occur in intensive care units, and to determine exactly what takes place when a patient goes into shock

- reducing a large amount of experimental data into a useful form so it can easily be understood and compared with other data

- finding correlations between dietary and environmental factors and disease by examining large numbers of medical records

- finding the best method of treating drug addicts, based on hundreds of different techniques and hundreds of thousands of addicts and their treatment histories

- determining the most reliable laboratory tests for diagnosing specific diseases

Sports Medicine   One of the newest areas of medical research that is making use of the computer is sports medicine. With the growing interest in competitive sports, the

Olympic Games, and physical fitness, the computer was soon recognized as a valuable tool in this area. The Soviet Union and other Eastern European countries have been using applied physics in their study of the human body in sports for many years. However, it is the United States that is the pioneer in using computer technology, especially computer graphics, to perform biomechanical analyses to quantify and improve human performance in sports (see Fig. 13.7).

The primary method used is high-speed (slow motion) movie films to study the movements involved in a particular skill or activity. The developed film is then digitized into a computer-usable form that allows stick figure forms to be created and studied in great detail, displaying and quantifying factors such as body motion, velocities, forces, and center of gravity. Some of the events that have been studied thus far are long-distance and sprint running, hammer throwing, figure skating, shot putting, golf, and tennis. Several important breakthroughs in how these events have traditionally been understood have been made. For example, it was found that each runner has an optimum stride (which is *not* the longest possible stride), and that using the computer to calculate this improved the runner's performance by about 20 percent. Also, by studying films of gold medal winners such as Olympic diving champions, it is possible to discover exactly why their performances are so outstanding, and then incorporate this information into the training programs. There is no doubt that the computer and sports will have a long and successful partnership!

Advanced Technology

Most of the applications discussed previously utilize current computer technology. In addition to the rapidly advancing automated laboratory instrumentation, however, there are several other medical applications that employ fairly sophisticated advanced-computer technology. Although it is not possible to examine all the uses

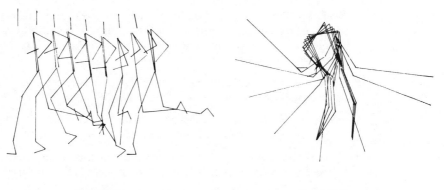

RUNNING   GOLF

Figure 13-7   Two examples of computer biomechanical analysis of sports activities.

of this advanced technology, we discuss three areas in which significant contributions to medicine are being made.

X-ray Technology Traditionally, x-rays have provided the best method of observing internal organs and their physiological processes. However, besides the dangers of excessive exposure to radiation, there are other problems and limitations: pictures are not sharply focused, other tissues or organs can obscure the target area, and often painful and unpleasant procedures, such as ingesting special fluids, must accompany x-rays. Sometimes these problems require that exploratory surgery be conducted when inadequate information is obtained. Fortunately, the computer has provided some better and safer alternatives.

Computed Tomography This technique, abbreviated CT, permits more accurate pictures (with less radiation) to be made by rotating an x-ray emitter and detector around the patient, thus allowing a 360-degree cross-section of a human body to display particular organs. The rays that pass through the body are sensed by the detector, resulting in thousands of data items pertaining to absorption rates. From this large amount of data a computer is used to reconstruct an accurate, color presentation of the particular organ being studied. However, the resulting tomogram presents only a slice of the organ, not a complete picture. In order to overcome this limitation, a more powerful method has been developed (see Fig. 13.8).

Dynamic Spatial Reconstruction This method, abbreviated DSR, uses procedures similar to CT but differs from it in several ways: it pictures a volume rather

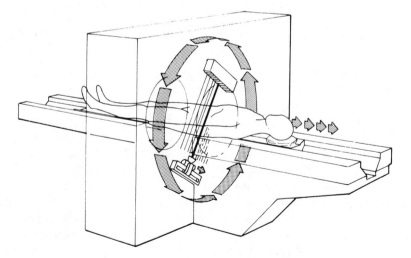

Figure 13-8 A CAT scanner. The patient lies on a table while a source and its detector rotate together (indicated by the arrows), taking X-rays of the patient from all angles. Each rotation produces a slice of the target, and the patient is moved (in the direction of the arrows) as the process is repeated to produce a complete image.

than a slice; it can stop action to eliminate blurring; and it can take up to 60 pictures per second so that movements, such as heart valves, can be studied easily. Although it has these advantages, the DSR method requires greater computational power because it collects data at a rate 10,000 times greater than CT and it cannot image large areas such as a whole chest. Nevertheless, the DSR method shows great promise in the experimental stages and will probably become one of the most powerful tools for studying heart functions.

Two other computerized diagnostic techniques that supplement or replace x-ray and use computers for analyzing and displaying data are ultrasonic imaging and digital blood flow analysis. Ultrasonic imaging devices use radio waves instead of x-rays to measure and represent constrictions and blockages in arteries which often precede strokes. Cerebral blood flow analysis enables researchers to locate and study different functions of the brain by displaying digital images of the brain with different colors that represent different levels of activity. Both methods permit medical researchers to view internal functions of the body with greater accuracy, and with much less danger to the patient than previous techniques.

Biomedical Implantable Microelectronics

> For many humans the quality of life is greatly diminished by loss of some natural function. Heart block, paralysis, chronic pain, loss of a limb, deafness, and blindness are afflictions suffered by many. The powerful and compact sensory, computational, and display capabilities of microelectronics make possible exciting new avenues for prostheses to remedy these functional deficiencies.   (Meindl, 1980)

Because of their small size and weight, low cost, low energy consumption, high reliability, and biological compatibility, microelectronic technology is allowing otherwise impossible accomplishments in the areas of diagnostic, therapeutic, prosthetic, and research medicine. They are ideally suited because they present only a minimum amount of interference and infection risk, can provide constant monitoring and stimulation, and last a relatively long time. There are so many incredible achievements in this area that we discuss only a few of the major applications.

Prostheses Since microelectronic sensing devices that are compatible with neural signals have been developed, it is now possible for small (about one-inch square by one-eighth inch thick) implanted devices to assist in the processing of sensory information. Some of the applications are: cardiac pacemakers (over 100,000 of these are installed each year just in the United States!), microelectrode arrays (which convert sound or light into signals that can be used to stimulate the appropriate part of the brain and bypass damaged parts) for the profoundly deaf or the blind, microoptical sensors and tactile stimulators for optical-to-tactile reading aid for the blind, voice-actuated wheelchair control, and voice- or nerve-impulse-activated artificial limbs.

Therapeutic Uses In this area implants are used to provide chemical, electrical, and mechanical stimulation to control or assist certain bodily functions. A few examples of current applications are: small electric currents to accelerate bone healing, neural stimulation of the spinal cord for relief of chronic pain, muscle stimulators for paraplegics, nerve stimulation for alleviation of hypertension, sensors for controlling hyperthermia, and electrical stimulation for bladder dysfunction.

Monitoring As stated in an earlier section of this chapter, direct patient monitoring (DPM) has greatly improved the quality of care in intensive care and post operation units. In fact, DPM is now being extended to paramedics through portable units that can be carried in ambulances and used to send critical information to the hospital while the patient is enroute. Now, with the reduced size and cost of biomedical implants, it is possible to monitor patients outside the hospital without the need of exploratory surgery or prolonged hospital stays. The primary monitoring technique is through telemetry where a miniature sensing device and transmitter (which can be surgically implanted or, in some cases, swallowed in a capsule) is used to send data to a receiving and recording device external to the patient. Some of these uses are diagnostic, such as implantable telemetry for coronary bypass monitoring, or ingestible capsules for pH monitoring. Other applications are for collecting data that normally could only be monitored in a hospital. For example, cerebral pressure telemetry, and electroencephalograph (ECG) telemetry. Not only do these techniques reduce hospital visits, they reduce the number of surgeries because the implant can be made once and then used to collect data over long periods of time. However, there are several areas of concern that are being investigated, such as possible tissue damage from toxic material being generated at electrode sites, stress from the presence of the device, and problems of heat being generated by the implant. Despite these side-effects, the long-term benefits seem to indicate that the microelectronic chip will have an important role in medicine, making life more tolerable for large numbers of patients.

SOCIAL IMPLICATIONS

Perhaps you have already thought of some of the advantages and disadvantages of using computers in medicine. Before reading the pro and con arguments, it would be interesting for you to list briefly some of your ideas about the social implications of computers in medicine.

Pro Arguments

Because we have already mentioned several of the benefits of computers in medicine, we mainly summarize now. With the ability to collect, store, and analyze large amounts of data, it is very likely that better medical diagnosis and treatment will result from access to this information via computer networks. The diagnostic systems should also be of great assistance to physicians, freeing them from information overload so they can attend to the more subtle aspects of diagnosis. Detailed analysis of laboratory and medical history data should provide a better understanding of medical problems and trends, leading to improved preventive medicine. Automated laboratory instrumentation permits higher quality control of lab tests while decreasing the time required for diagnosis and treatment. In the administrative area, hospital information systems speed paperwork, provide better control of resources and inventory, allow statistical analyses for effectiveness, resulting in better decision making. Biomedical implants are enabling the handicapped and impaired patients to lead more normal lives with a minimum amount of interference and side effects. All of these advantages will free physicians and staff from tedious tasks and allow them more time to spend with the patient. Finally, it is very likely that these uses will help to reduce or stabilize soaring medical costs and permit the delivery of better health care to a larger number of people.

Con Arguments

It may seem that the above advantages preclude or offset any possible disadvantages. However, individuals both in and outside the medical profession have raised several important questions regarding the use of computers in medicine. Many feel that the extensive use of computers will lead to a depersonalization of health care and less reliance on common sense and human sensitivity. In fact, studies have clearly demonstrated that the doctor's "bedside manner" is a crucial factor in patient recovery. Perhaps even more serious are the problems (or disaster) that could result from computer system failures, particulary in life-support and monitoring systems. What happens when these computers "crash"? Also, there are very technical legal problems surrounding the question of who is liable for the resulting damage when a computer system fails or does not operate properly. For example, if a death results, is the hospital, physician, computer manufacturer, or the programmer responsible? Similar legal and moral questions arise in relation to the collection, storage, and dissemination of sensitive medical information in computer data banks. What is the patient's right to privacy in respect to this information? Who is liable for inaccuracies or improper use of the information? How does the storage of data affect the doctor-patient relationship, especially when the information is distributed to insurance companies? Because of these uncertainties, many physicians and hospitals are hesitant to purchase new computer systems. Although computers may lead to reduced costs in the long run, most systems are fairly expensive and have not yet been fully tested or proven. Finally, with all the sophisticated technology, there is the possibility of information overload and "computer shock" that could lead to a degradation in the quality of health care.

HARDWARE

A few years ago (with the exception of some digital laboratory equipment) a fairly large investment (perhaps $50,000 or more) had to be made in order to use computers in medicine. However, with the advent of the microcomputer, this situation

changed dramatically. It is not unusual now to find a small microcomputer, with a terminal, single or dual floppy disks, and a printer, being used in a small private office for billing, patient records, and a small database of medical histories. A small microcomputer equipped with a few A/D cards can also be used to monitor or control laboratory equipment. The biomedical implants that use microtransducers, microsensors, and other microelectronic devices for telemetry and prosthetics are relatively inexpensive; however, the surgical procedures to implant the devices may cost more than $100,000 (see Fig. 13.9).

Medium-sized systems in the $20,000 to $100,000 range would be used in small hospitals, medical clinics, or specialized laboratories. Systems oriented toward record keeping would probably use a medium mainframe, disk or tape storage, a printer, and perhaps several terminals. In a laboratory situation, most of the money would be allocated for instrumentation and analysis equipment supported by a mainframe, disk or tape storage, one or two terminals, and a small printer. Or, in an intensive care unit, a medium-size system could be used for DPM, supported by sophisticated sensors, A/D conversion circuitry, and a few display terminals.

Large systems would cost about $100,000 to several million dollars. These systems would be used in large hospitals, research centers, sophisticated laboratories, and for medical information networks. They would consist of a large mainframe, several disk storage devices, perhaps a few printers (maybe even COM in large hospitals), many terminals, and telecommunications equipment. Specialized diagnostic installations, such as computer tomography or life-support systems, do not require large-size computers because they do not need to store great amounts of information; however, they do require fast calculating speed and are usually supported by specially designed computers that are dedicated to one special task.

A LOOK TOWARD THE FUTURE

However remarkable these systems are, the future promises even more. The costs of computers continue to plummet as their sophistication increases. As they become cheaper, they will show up not only in the hospital or doctor's office but on the patient. *(Meredith, 1978)*

The future suggested by this quotation of just a few years ago is already here. Biomedical implants are making it possible for the handicapped and physically impaired to live more normal lives, and the future will see the improvement and extension of these devices to cover even more dysfunctions, such as brain disorders. As medical information and diagnosis databases grow and telecommunications equipment becomes less expensive, this knowledge will be quickly and inexpensively distributed to even the most rural parts of our country and the world. This should result in a better distribution of higher quality health care to a larger number of people. In fact, medical information may become a very valuable resource to deliver to undeveloped countries via worldwide networks. Because data collection, both from individuals via implants and from research centers from all over the world, will be greatly impoved along with the analytic programs to evaluate the data, we should witness more timely and better medical decision making in all areas of medicine. There should be significant advances in preventive medicine and many services, such as diagnosis or sophisticated lab tests, that could be offered only at hospitals will be available through medical networks right in your physician's office. Yes, the future looks very bright for computers and medicine. However, if the problems and questions raised in the pro and con arguments are ignored, serious difficulties may result. To achieve all of the possible future benefits requires that we look closely at questions and not neglect the social implications of technological advances. We are confident that concerned and informed individuals, such as yourselves, can play a significant role in shaping the partnership between computers and medicine. Let your views be heard.

STUDY AND REVIEW

1. What are three different ways in which computers are being used in hospitals? What are some of the advantages and disadvantages of these uses?

2. Briefly describe how microcomputers and networks are used in medical offices and clinics. Do any physicians' offices in your area make use of these technologies?

3. Discuss two different ways in which computers are being used in preventive medicine. What are some of the advantages and disadvantages of these uses?

4. Explain how computers can be used to assist in diagnosis. Do you think that computers could ever replace the physician in diagnosing disease?

5. How is computer simulation used in medical research and education? What are some of the major advantages and disadvantages of these uses?

6. Briefly describe how computers are used to improve x-ray and related technologies. What are the advantages of these methods as opposed to x-rays?

7. What do you think are the two most important uses of microelectronics in the area of biomedics?

14

ARTIFICIAL INTELLIGENCE

PERSPECTIVE

Artificial intelligence essentially has two goals: One is to understand the basic processes that make intelligence possible, and the other is to develop computer systems that are more useful. However, discussing the research field of artificial intelligence (commonly referred to as AI) is quite difficult for several reasons. First, as the quotation below suggests, there is much controversey regarding what constitutes intelligence and whether or not computers can possess it.

> *Artificial Intelligence is the study of ideas which enable computers to do the things that make people seem intelligent. But then, what is human intelligence?*   *(Winston, 1977)*

Second, many people view AI as frivolous because of the very abstract nature of its projects. This complaint is not due to a lack of useful accomplishments in AI, but rather to the fact that as soon as practical systems are designed and developed they become absorbed by the field that uses them. Although there are relatively few researchers in AI, their impact is profound and widespread, especially in areas such as business, engineering, linguistics, and psychology, to mention a few. For example, systems like intelligent robots, medical diagnosis devices, automatic pilots, and others are no longer associated with AI after they have been proven and have become commercially available. Finally, the cumulative effect of the previous two difficulties combines with the emotional element brought about when people envision computers becoming as intelligent as, or perhaps even more intelligent than, humans. Because of this conceptual and emotional confusion surrounding AI, we present material, questions, and ideas so that you can make your own decision about the value of this research. And, in the process, you may even come to a better understanding of what intelligence might be.

COMPUTERS IN ARTIFICIAL INTELLIGENCE

Will humans ever be able to understand the nature of intelligence as we have come to understand the nature of flight? Will scientists be able to construct thinking machines as they are able to construct flying machines? At one time, not very long ago, only birds could fly and it was thought frivolous for humans to contemplate machines flying. Granted, airplanes do not fly in the same manner as birds do, yet we do not hesitate to say planes "fly." Are there insurmountable barriers preventing the imitation or simulation of intelligent processes in computers? We do not have answers for these questions, but we hope that you will at least gain an understanding of the type of research that goes on in AI so you can develop your own viewpoint and, perhaps, your own answers.

The Thinking of Humans and Machines

Can people think? This may appear to be an absurd question, one not worthy of investigation or even a reply. However, the purpose of the question is not to challenge or doubt that humans can think, but to indicate the difficulties involved when we try to decide what constitutes thinking—whether done by a human, animal, plant, or even a computer. When we make simple errors in arithmetic, forget appointments, nervously scratch our heads, put ice cream in a cupboard instead of in the freezer, or make numerous other similar mistakes—are we really thinking? When we reply without error to the question "What is 2 + 2?"—does our answer really require thinking? Is all thinking intelligent?

The question "Can machines think?" faces similar problems as our question regarding humans. The difficulty with both questions is not in knowing what humans or machines can or cannot do, but in establishing an adequate definition of thinking or intelligence. Frequently, different and more demanding criteria than would be used for humans are used to demonstrate that machines cannot think. For example, it has been claimed that computers cannot think because they cannot beat a Bobby Fischer at chess or understand complex sentences. On these grounds, many humans would have to be judged incapable of thought! In order to overcome this built-in bias, a British mathematician-philosopher named A. M. Turing proposed a test in 1950 for answering the question "Can a machine think?" Simply stated, it would involve a human communicating via a teletype terminal with two different entities (one a human, the other a computer). If, at the end of a 30-minute period, the human could not correctly determine which entity was the computer, then the computer would be said to have been thinking. If a computer were to pass this Turing test, would you be willing to say it was thinking? Probably the greatest barrier to approaching the question rationally is the fear that accompanies the idea of thinking machines—fear that humans may someday be replaced or conquered by tireless machines, fear of no longer being the most intelligent species on this planet, fear that activities once attributed only to a human soul can now be done by a machine of electronic circuitry.

In the twentieth century we have come to accept the reality of television, atomic bombs, and space travel to other planets. Just as these inventions were unimaginable in the eighteenth century, the advance of science and technology is now making it possible to do with machines that which was once done only by humans. We must examine carefully how we decide if something can think or be intelligent. Are humans, just because they are humans, guaranteed to be thinking in everything they do? Are machines, by virtue of being machines, automatically excluded from the realm of thinking? Either of these positions is dogmatic. As the late philosopher Ludwig Wittgenstein proclaimed whenever confronted with similar types of questions, "Look and see." If we approach the topic open-mindedly we can learn more about both computers and humans—and reach our own conclusions as to whether or not machines can be intelligent.

Early Research

The nature of thinking has been investigated for thousands of years, beginning with early philosophers and scientists such as Plato and Aristotle. Now the computer allows us to explore both human and machine abilities in much greater depth and detail than ever before. Artificial intelligence—the use of computers to produce behavior similar to intelligent human behavior—is a controversial subject. Most current experimentation in AI is done under government contract or private grants at prestigious research centers such as Massachusetts Institute of Technology (MIT), Carnegie-Mellon University, Stanford University, Bell Laboratories, and Stanford Research Institute (SRI) International.

Background   Since the advent of our species, we have developed many different tools to extend our physical capabilities: the club, axe, plow, cotton gin, steam engine, radio, and television. Fascination with the possibility of automatons or robots was exhibited in the thirteenth century. Mechanical automatons became popular during the seventeenth and eighteenth centuries when miniature dolls that danced or performed acrobatics were attached to music boxes and clockworks. With the industrial revolution of the nineteenth century and the automated factories of the early twentieth century, the fear arose that machines would replace the human work force. A recurring theme in early science fiction was the takeover of the world by robots or androids. Not until the electronic computer of the 1950s did the duplication or imitation of human mental capabilities actually become possible. These machines add and subtract and perform human-like activities such as sorting, classifying, comparing, and altering the course of their own operations based on previous results.

John von Neumann Early computers were bulky, unreliable, and costly, and it was commonly thought that any attempt to reproduce human mental processes would be doomed to failure. Nevertheless significant contributions were made to the early theory of automata. One of the most far reaching ideas was developed by John von Neumann, a brilliant mathematician who was instrumental in the design of the EDVAC computer. Von Neumann, who died in 1957, made remarkable insights into the ways in which humans and computers process information. Although men and machines have radically different appearances and are made of completely different materials, von Neumann saw that there were important similarities between the human nervous system and the electronic circuitry of a computer. Just as our nervous system transmits its messages—for example, from the eye to the brain through the firing or nonfiring of neurons (called nerve impulses)—a computer transmits information in a similar binary code of 0s and 1s. The internal computer "1" is an "on" state, like the firing of a neuron; a computer "Zero" is an "off" state similar to when a neuron does not fire. Whether we are seeing, hearing, or touching, our information is communicated in a two-state code very similar to the computer's binary code.

Norbert Wiener Another pioneer in AI is Norbert Wiener, who coined the term **cybernetics** in the 1940s to describe the study of control and communication in both machines and living organisms. Wiener used the concept of a *negative feedback* system to explain how information about our environment is communicated so we can use it to control our actions. A familiar example of a negative feedback system is a heater thermostat. Without negative feedback—some way of sensing the real temperature and comparing it with the desired temperature set on the thermostat, the thermostat could not control the heater. In similar fashion, we could not pick up an object unless we received negative feedback that informed us whether we were too far to the left or right of the object. That is, in both machines and organisms (whether they be amoebas or humans) there are receptors or sensors for receiving information and processes for using this information for control of on-going activities, such as movement or even thought. It is this negative feedback system that permits organisms to adapt to their environment, learn from experience, and survive.

Our sensations and memory allow us to survive and adapt to our environment through communication and control, resulting in the effective organization and use of information. These same activities can be carried out by a computer. A significant aspect of Weiner's work was his view on information that stresses that machines can be made to organize and disseminate information with less distortion than humans. Theoretically computers should be able to control their environment and communicate with the world with less error and confusion than humans.

The Impact of von Neumann and Wiener The significance of both von Neumann's and Wiener's ideas for AI was not clear until long after their original contributions—and may not yet be fully realized. Although von Neumann indicated the similarities between computer codes and the binary nature of the nerve impulse, this did not affect computer development because so little was known about the human code for storing and transmitting information. Then, as the nerve impulse became better understood, it was learned that although the impulse is binary, (on-off) the conditions that determine whether or not it fires are not electrical/binary but rather chemical/analog.

In the early years of computers, there were no corresponding analog components to imitate the partly understood codes. Besides, early development was concerned with making computers to solve mathematical and business-oriented problems—not imitate thought. At present there are many miniature analog/digital components and *perhaps* (if the codes were better understood) a computer modeled after the architecture of the human brain could be built. But if one could be constructed, there would be no guarantee that its performance would approximate the intelligence of a human or, for that matter, even that of a rat! Theoretically von Neumann's ideas can now be explored and tested, providing a completely different approach to AI.

Wiener's contribution was more immediate and is still evolving. As early as the late 1940s and early 1950s his ideas led to the automation of factory processes and later to industrial robots and the space exploring "intelligent" robots. Now, in the sophisticated biological implants and prostheses that interact with human systems to control pain, stimulate the heart, and move artificial limbs, we see the merger of both Wiener's and von Neumann's ideas. Where these ideas will eventually lead is a source of interest and great debate.

Now that you have been introduced to some of the early background of AI, we next look at developments within four major research areas of AI: heuristics, the representation of knowledge, natural language, and reasoning.

Heuristics

Some of the earliest experimentation in AI involved games—primarily checkers and chess. Games were not chosen for their recreational value, but for their similarities to real-life situations—particularly problem solving. In game playing, alternative choices must be evaluated and decided upon; short- and long-term planning is necessary. There are usually both defensive and offensive strategies; there are rules that must be obeyed. Winning a game involves either achievement of a specific goal or, if there can be more than one winner, the minimizing of losses and maximizing of gains. All aspects of game playing are present in our complex, everyday choices in life: choices that usualy require the exercise of intelligence. We are not always fortunate enough, however, to have the liberty or the time to experiment with our daily decisions as we can with computer decisions. Thus, a computer provides an excellent tool for studying human problem-solving techniques.

Computers can compare thousands of possibilities in just seconds. In the game of checkers, there are 10^{40} possible moves—and in chess there are 10^{120} possible moves (10 and 120 0's after it or approximately the same quantity as the number of atoms in the universe!). To deal effectively with so many choices, a method of selecting the "best" move from all logical possibilities must be devised; this method is called a **heuristic**.

The development of heuristics or heurisitic searches is one of the crucial areas within AI and can be compared with finding the "rules of thumb" that permit a computer to make a choice and then evaluate its choice depending on the results—a form of trial and error or negative feedback. This process usually involves generating alternative paths toward solutions, setting up intermediate goals or subproblems, managing the search resources and evaluating the alternatives. The heuristics employed help to reduce drastically the number of searches/alternative solutions that would have to be examined. In checkers or chess for example, if a particular opening move leads to a high percentage of winning games, that move would be given a higher value or priority than opening moves that led to losing games. Through the progression of the game, as pieces are moved and lost, strategy changes continually and the heuristics become more complicated. Checker playing programs were first developed in the early 1950s. In 1967, Dr. Arthur Samuel of IBM wrote a program that eventually beat state champions, though it lost to the World Champion.

Chess   Computer chess did not progress as rapidly as checkers because the heuristics were so much more complicated. There are several reasons, according to International Chess Master David Levy, why computers have not yet attained the highest levels of chess: very few humans understand the problems of master-level chess; programs do not have an "intuitive" feel for positions; very few grand masters work with programmers pursuing this problem; and it is difficult to describe clearly the thought processes of master chess players. Another factor is that very little money is used by AI researchers in this area; most chess programs have been developed during the spare time of volunteer workers. Nonetheless, a program (Chess 4.4) developed at Northwestern University by David Slate and Larry Adkin played Mr. Levy in 1975 at the Sixth United States Chess Championship. Chess 4.4 played at a rate of 20 moves an hour, losing ten games, drawing three, and winning none. At the time it was estimated that less than 2,000 people in the world could beat this program.

Revisions of the Chess 4.4 program reigned as world computer chess champion until Chess 4.9 (entered by Slate) was defeated in 1980. In this championship the final playoff was between a program called *Chaos* from the University of Michigan and a program called *Belle* designed by Ken Thompson of Bell Laboratories. *Chaos* employed a selective search strategy that used more sophisticated knowledge of chess in order to narrow the number of moves that must be evaluated. *Belle* used a "brute force" strategy that used specially designed hardware to increase its ability to search a large number of moves—it could examine approximately 30 million positions in the three-minute time period allowed for each move! It is estimated that programs such as Thompson's can beat about 99.5 percent of human players (see Fig. 14.1).

This progress has been made without any direct support from federal agencies

that support most AI research. There are prizes offered for accomplishments in the field of computer chess, however. For example, MIT professor and inventor Edward Fredkin has established The Fredkin Prize of $100,000 to be given to the author of the first program to win the world chess championship (for humans); Volmac, a Dutch computer software firm, has offered $50,000 to the author of a program that can defeat international grand master Max Euwe of the Netherlands by January 1, 1984. It has long been argued that computer chess is an important part of AI research, but many researchers are beginning to feel that the "brute force" systems are really not relevant to the goals of AI. The main criticism is that such systems do not incorporate enough knowledge of the game, but rely merely on computational speed; their programs do not enhance the development or understanding of heuristics that can be applied to areas other than chess, nor do they contribute to making computers more useful. And understanding intelligence and making computers more useful are the two primary goals of AI, as you recall. One current proposal is to encourage the development of more useful heuristics by offering prize money for the solution to specific problems that are agreed upon as significant and important for the advancement of AI. However, many researchers are of the opinion that heuristics alone will not produce intelligent machines. They see the crucial problem as one of how to represent knowledge so computers can use it in conjunction with heuristics.

Representation of Knowledge

To write pseudo-intelligent programs, we need only use our knowledge. To write intelligent programs, we must make our knowledge explicit. The volume of knowledge needed for useful problem solving and the inaccessibility of much of it

> *pose a serious problem. Failure to grasp this problem has caused much of the excessive optimism with which the field of AI has been afflicted. It has also impaired the effectiveness of AI research.*   *(Whaland, 1981)*

This quotation points out both the necessity and the difficulty of incorporating knowledge into computer programs. To answer even the simplest questions concerning our everyday experiences requires an extraordinary amount of knowledge, a great deal of which we are not aware. For example, if someone were to say, "I like to eat large green apples," we must involve a great deal of our knowledge about the world in order to understand what is meant. We must know about objects (apples) and their properties (green), relationships (liking, large), and processes (eating). In addition to this explicit conceptual knowledge, there is an extensive amount of implicit cultural and personal knowledge that is extremely difficult, if not impossible, to represent. That is, our preferences, habits, expectations, fears, moral values, and other similar aspects of our life, which to a large extent make us unique, are not easily specified but are an integral part of our understanding of the world.

Microworlds   One approach within AI intended to overcome these problems is to deal with very limited, specific domains called microworlds. The justification for this method is that if you can get computers to behave intelligently regarding very specific tasks, such as proving mathematical theorems, developing hypotheses in organic chemistry, or discussing a world of building blocks, then you could expand and apply the technique to larger domains. Within these microworlds, there has been a great amount of success. However, the assumption that procedures within the microworlds can be applied to larger domains is under serious scrutiny and doubt. Some critics claim that there is no connection between these limited domains and real-life situations, that the principles used are irrelevant to intelligent behavior. For instance, most programs cannot adapt to minor modifications in the microworld; they are not flexible enough nor do they have the capacity to learn and adapt as humans do. Also, it is often argued that the amount of knowledge required just to display common sense about our everyday world goes far beyond the capacities of even the largest computers. However, even if knowledge about the world could be incorporated into a computer, there would still be the problem of how the computer would communicate this knowledge and interact with the outside world. Most researchers agree that a natural language such as English would have to be used and that the computer would have to understand and convey its responses in a natural language—knowledge and heuristics alone are not adequate for developing an intelligent machine (see Fig. 14.2).

Robotics   As discussed in Chapter 9, there are two main categories of robots: industrial and intelligent. Researchers in AI work with both types, but primary emphasis is on intelligent robots. Rather than concentrating on routine, repetitious operations, researchers in this field concentrate on investigating questions about

(a)

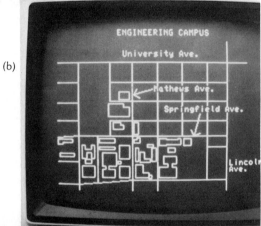

(b)

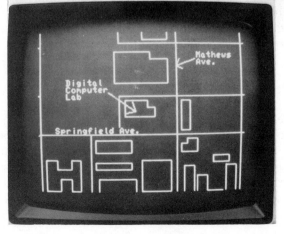

(c)

Figure 14-2 Three different views of a "microworld" university campus. (a) the entire campus, (b) the engineering campus, (c) the computer laboratory. (Courtesy of SubLogic Communications Corp.)

285

sensory perception, learning, and how such knowledge can be represented in computer systems. Through this research a great amount of new knowledge has been gained concerning how humans perform these tasks—something we have long taken for granted and do not fully understand. One benefit resulting from this new knowledge has been the development of computer-assisted vision, hearing, movement of limbs, and other prosthetic devices that use microprocessor technology. In fact, one noted scientist believes a miniature computer that would fit under the scalp could be designed to be compatible with our natural brain processes and could either extend our mental capabilities or carry out functions destroyed by brain damage. Although such a device might not be possible for 50 years or more, the consequences would be far reaching—perhaps fulfilling the predictions of von Neumann and Wiener.

On the more practical side, intelligent robots are being designed to probe the oceans below and the heavens above. Because it is difficult and extremely dangerous for humans to work in these environments, intelligent robots are being developed to perform exploratory work without human intervention. Human-controlled robots are no longer feasible for probing outer space because of the distance involved. For instance, the distance between Earth and Mars is so great that it would take more than six minutes for a command to reach the robot, more than enough time for it to go over a cliff or become damaged in some way. Consequently, robots presently used by NASA are fairly independent, capable of picking up rocks, collecting soil specimens, and performing other exploratory investigations—all without human direction. Stanford Research Institute International is currently working on a general purpose intelligent robot that can assemble equipment much like a human. Present cost of this device is around $100,000, but it is hoped that the cost will be less than $10,000 when it is finally marketed. However, before a truly intelligent autonomous robot can be made, researchers must first learn more about the processes that control and direct human behavior.

Slowly, through the combined efforts of neurologists, physiologists, psychologists, and computer scientists, we have acquired a much deeper understanding and appreciation of vision, hearing, touch, and the methods by which we move our limbs. However, one of the remaining and most difficult frontiers yet to be crossed is one that is perhaps most important—language.

Understanding Natural Language

The development of computer languages that are easier for humans to use has been one of the major accomplishments of computer science. It seemed it would be only a short step further to develop software that would permit humans to communicate with computers in a natural language, such as English. But this apparently minor difficulty has presented perhaps one of the most challenging and, according to some, insurmountable barriers for AI. With the early success of English-Russian computer translations in the 1960s, researchers thought the language problem would soon be conquered. Although a certain amount of progress has been made, the complexities and subtleties of language are not yet fully understood; hence, they cannot be programmed into a computer. For example, one application of computers and language resulted in rather inadequate machine paraphrasings. The expression,"The spirit is willing, but the flesh is weak" was paraphrased, "The liquor is prepared, though the meat is not tough." The expression, "Out of sight, out of mind" was paraphrased, "Invisible idiot."

Syntax and Semantics Natural-language computer translators, even in the early stages of research, demonstrated fairly high expertise in their ability to comprehend and produce grammatically correct sentences. However, this achievement in the area of syntax has never been matched (with the exception of a few microworld programs) in the ability to grasp the meaning (semantics) of sentences. It is now understood that this significant gap between syntax and semantics is due to the fact that a large amount of what we understand is obtained from context and from our knowledge of the world. That is, as mentioned previously, the tacit personal, social, and cultural aspects of our life exercise a great influence on the meaning we attach to sentences. Attempting to quantify and make objective this dimension of human understanding and communication is no doubt one of the most challenging aspects of AI research. In order to better comprehend the difficulties and limitations of such projects, we now look briefly at two programs that are capable of communicating in natural language.

ELIZA Perhaps one of the most interesting language programs was developed by Joseph Weizenbaum of MIT. Technically speaking, the program does not really translate but follows a script and syntactically rearranges sentences. ELIZA imitates a method of psychological interview in which the therapist reflects the thoughts of the patient. For example, if one of the keywords in the interview script of the program is encountered, such as "mother," "father," or "sister" in the patient's conversation, ELIZA responds with something like, "Tell me more about your family." The syntactic part of the program transforms patient statements like, "I have been very unhappy recently" into computer responses like, "I am sorry to hear you are unhappy." And when words or expressions are encountered that are not part of the program, ELIZA replies with statements like "Go on," "Please continue," or "I understand." However, if a factual question is asked, such as "Can rabbits talk?" ELIZA can respond only by saying "Please return to the subject," or "Don't change the topic."

The following is an excerpt from a conversation between ELIZA and a young woman (taken from Joseph Weizenbaum's book referenced below). ELIZA'S remarks are all in capital letters.

Men are all alike.

IN WHAT WAY

They're always bugging us about something or other.

CAN YOU THINK OF A SPECIFIC EXAMPLE

Well, my boyfriend made me come here.

YOUR BOYFRIEND MADE YOU COME HERE

He says I'm depressed much of the time.

I AM SORRY TO HEAR YOU ARE DEPRESSED

It's true. I am unhappy.

DO YOU THINK COMING HERE WILL HELP YOU NOT TO BE
UNHAPPY

I need some help, that much seems certain.

WHAT WOULD IT MEAN TO YOU IF YOU GOT SOME HELP

Perhaps I could learn to get along with my mother.

TELL ME MORE ABOUT YOUR FAMILY

Surprisingly, this simple program has caused a great controversy because so
many people, including those in psychotherapy and AI research, wanted to use this
program in clinical situations for therapy. The author of the program was quite dis-
mayed by the reaction to his creation, particularly by the intimate conversations and
the attachment that people developed for ELIZA. In fact, he wrote a book (*Computer Power and Human Reason*) in which he tried to put his work and other work in
AI in perspective. As he stated in 1976:

> *What I had not realized is that extremely short exposures to
> a relatively simple computer program could induce powerful
> delusional thinking in quite normal people. This insight led
> me to attach new importance to questions of the relationship
> between the individual and the computer, and hence to re-
> solve to think about them.*

PARRY Another natural language program, which employs very different
methods for understanding language, was developed by Kenneth Colby of Stanford
University. Unlike ELIZA, this program (called PARRY) does understand language;
however, its understanding is limited to the microworld of a paranoid patient!
PARRY uses several stages of translation in which it gradually transforms the input
text and produces a response. Briefly, the program performs five processes: looks
up all the main words in a dictionary; remaining words not identified are looked up in
a dictionary of commonly misspelled words; if a word is still not located, it can look
up possible words by just examining the last few letters or by looking at a dictionary
of contractions; and if a word is still not found, it is treated as a mistyped word and
the computer performs numerous operations on the word until it is identified; finally,
PARRY determines how the translated word relates to its paranoid world. For ex-

ample, if a person (H) interviewing PARRY (P) were to enter into a dialogue, it might go something like this:

> H: What's yljr nime?
>
> P: Why do you want to know my name?
>
> H: When did you come to the emergency room?
>
> P: I was taken to the hospital yesterday.
>
> H: How long have you been disturbed?
>
> P: I'm not crazy. . .buzz off!

These few lines indicate PARRY'S ability to handle a wide range of questions and, as in the first line, even typing errors. Although this program deals with a very special and limited world, it does exhibit a great deal of what would normally be called understanding. In fact, in an experiment where trained psychiatrists saw transcripts of PARRY'S conversations with doctors, a majority of the psychiatrists did not identify PARRY as being a computer—essentially PARRY passed the Turing test mentioned earlier in this chapter! However, even with an accurate representation of a limited world, a restricted context of meanings, and a sophisticated translation scheme, programs such as PARRY still have limitations—namely, the ability to perform reasoning and to make inferences that go beyond the information given. We consider this area of research next.

Reasoning

Researchers in AI have been concerned with investigating two types of human reasoning: formal and informal. Formal reasoning is the type we use in solving mathematical and logical problems; it is mainly deductive (going from general rules to specific cases), such as the reasoning used in problems like "all humans are mortal; Janet is a human; therefore, Janet is mortal" or "A is greater than B; B is greater than C; therefore, A is greater than C." By studying this type of reasoning, sophisticated programs in AI have been developed, enabling computers to prove complex theorems and formulas in logic and math. Informal reasoning is more general, the type we use in solving our everyday problems about how to repair a bicycle, fix a flat tire, plan a menu, and other such situations.

Here are some of the major areas that are studied within the topic of reasoning.

1. *Puzzle solving:* One of the first areas to develop within AI; mainly focuses on the solution of more complicated problems involving special knowledge and facts about the world.

2. *Question answering:* deals with how to answer questions and make inferences based on stored knowledge; these systems tend to be specialized in a relatively small area (microworlds) and cannot solve common-sense problems.

3. *Common-sense reasoning:* the ability to answer questions and to ask questions to supplement the initial knowledge—similar to human learning and problem solving.

Rather than discuss these areas in great detail, we now briefly look at some of the approaches that have made significant contributions to understanding human reasoning.

General Problem Solver   Alan Newell and Herbert A. Simon of Carnegie-Mellon University were among the pioneering investigators in the area of human problem solving. Their initial method of obtaining information with which to develop problem-solving programs was to ask humans to think out loud when solving problems so they could make explicit the procedures or protocols they were employing. A great amount of their data was gathered from analysis of the protocols used to solve cryptarithmetic problems—puzzles in which numbers are substituted for letters to obtain the solution. A simple problem and its solution would be:

$$\begin{array}{r} AA \\ +BB \\ \hline CAC \end{array} \qquad \begin{array}{r} 22 \\ +99 \\ \hline 121 \end{array}$$

After conducting numerous experiments with such problems, programs could be written that incorporated the human protocols that permitted the computer to solve quickly crytarithmetic problems such as "DONALD + GERALD = ROBERT" (*HINT*: D = 5). From this technique the General Problem Solver (GPS) program was developed, which could solve a variety of problems by analyzing their component parts, finding the subgoals, and attaining the subgoals until the ultimate solution is reached. This approach essentially employs a means-end analysis and closely approximates how humans solve problems. By describing the initial state, the goal state, and the operations that can be performed along with the differences that can occur between states, GPS can solve problems like moving four objects (a man, goose, fox, and corn) across a river in a boat that can hold only two objects, without leaving the fox and goose alone, or the goose and the corn alone. Although GPS is rather rigid in its pursuit of subgoals, often ignoring the quicker solutions that humans might detect, it has greatly clarified the problem-solving technique that humans frequently use. However, a major question that remains from this type of analysis is how humans retain information so they can apply their knowledge in a wide range of similar situations.

Schemas and Scripts   One approach to the question of how humans reason about the world is to provide the computer with a context so it can make inferences and apply its knowledge to similar situations. Researchers in the field of cognitive psychology have provided insight into this by investigations into human information processing knowledge structures—the ways in which humans store, associate, and retrieve information. One type of knowledge structure is called a **schema**, a group of related concepts that permit us to make inferences about the world. For example, if someone were to say, "I was disappointed that there was no salt in the basket" we can make many inferences about this situation: maybe it was a picnic basket, there were probably eggs in the basket, and so forth. We have schemas not only about the association of words, we have causal schemas also from which we draw conclusions about what types of things or events cause certain situations to occur. For instance, if someone said, "I kicked the dog and had to get a rabies vaccination" a listener would probably infer that the dog bit the person, although that was not stated explicitly.

Similarly, **scripts** are knowledge structures that deal with interrelationships and the sequence of events. A most interesting computer application of scripts has been given by Roger Shank and Robert Abelson of Yale University. In their now famous restaurant script, there are several perspectives from which the following sequence of events can be interpreted: the customer's, cook's, waiter's or cashier's. For example, one part of this script deals with the customer's point of view: the customer enters the restaurant, is seated and given the menu, orders fish, stays for a while, eats, and leaves. By entering this information, the program can answer questions about information that was not stated explicitly, such as, "What did the customer eat?" or "Did the customer leave before paying?" based on the typical sequence of events that are stored in its script. The important aspect of schemas and scripts is that they do not specify in detail every possible combination of concepts or events, but rather the relationships that normally exist and which can be applied to a large number of situations. This seems to approximate, very closely, the type of informal, common-sense reasoning that we use in everyday life. It also brings AI researchers closer to producing intelligent computer systems.

Although the above areas use very complex and sophisticated programming techniques, they are providing insights into human problem solving and a deep appreciation for human capabilities. One surprising fact that has come from attempting to simulate common-sense reasoning is the extraordinary amount of information necessary to answer relatively simple questions about our everyday world. And equally surprising is the amount of secondary knowledge or "metaknowledge" that is required in order to instruct the computer about how to use its knowledge of the world. We hope that all of this research in AI will result in some very significant breakthroughs, such as the type suggested by the following quotation:

> *Just as psychological knowledge about human information processing can help make computers intelligent, theories derived purely with computers in mind often suggest possibilities for how to educate people better. Said another way, the methodology involved in making smart computer programs may transfer to making smart people.*   (Winston, 1977)

SOCIAL IMPLICATIONS

The use of computers in artificial intelligence research raises many far-reaching questions. Unfortunately, many arguments, both pro and con, suffer from a lack of clarity and agreed upon definitions. It could well be that if an adequate definition could be accepted as to what constitutes intelligent behavior, many of the problems and frustrations could be eliminated. However, this does not seem very likely to occur in the near future, and so we will try to present some of the major arguments that deal with general issues rather than focus on specific applications.

Pro Arguments

One of the primary by-products of AI research has been a better understanding and a deeper appreciation of human abilities (both mental and physical). Researchers are often astonished by the amount of knowledge that is required to perform the simplest tasks. As more knowledge is gained about human problem-solving techniques, computers can provide more assistance, both in complicated tasks (predicting weather, crime, economic trends) and in tedious, clerical tasks (routine bookkeeping, file management, and other repetitious jobs). In the industrial environment, AI research has developed industrial and intelligent robots to perform both monotonous, dangerous, and difficult tasks. The general thrust of these applications of AI is that it frees humans to use their time more efficiently for uniquely human activities, such as creative work, design, and interpersonal communication. Finally, in the area of medicine and other highly technical fields in science, the advances of AI are producing solutions to problems that could not be solved without computers. But, as mentioned in the opening of this chapter, after these "useful" aspects of AI reach the marketplace, they are no longer associated with their birthplace (AI) and only the controversial investigations of the research laboratory are discussed and criticized as being either frivolous or threatening to the status of humans.

Con Arguments

A major criticism of AI is that it fosters a mechanistic, materialistic view of human nature—that it ignores the religious, spiritual, and qualitative dimension of humanity. As the argument goes, this leads to a degradation and depreciation of humans, and fosters a view that humans are things, not persons. This type of thinking radically changes the self-image that people have of themselves; people feel they are worth less, are less important because machines seem to be replacing both their physical and mental abilities. Besides replacing humans, it is leading to a situation where humans are highly dependent on computers and, if this trend continues, we may become controlled by decision-making computers. This theme has been presented for years via science fiction and it now seems to be coming true as more and more sophisticated tasks (diagnosing illness, flying spacecraft, composing music, and so forth) are introduced. Finally, a different type of criticsm does not rely on the fear that is characteristic of the earlier arguments, but rather attacks AI research as wasteful of taxpayer's money and as pursuing unachievable goals. Hence, AI should be abandoned.

HARDWARE

Because AI is such a specialized field of research, it uses very little commercially available equipment; its needs are very sophisticated and advanced. Therefore, this section is rather brief because many of the applications of AI already have been discussed in their specific areas, such as industry, medicine and science.

Little work in AI can be done with the small, microcomputer systems because so many of the research projects require very large databases and extremely fast computations. However, some work in the area of software is extending special AI languages, such as LISP and SMALLTALK, to the microcomputer. Low cost analog-to-digital equipment is also becoming available so some of the activities normally associated with AI, like voice synthesis and voice recognition, can be done relatively inexpensively on personal computers.

In order to actually engage in AI research a medium-size system would usually be the minimum requirement. A typical laboratory would use a medium-size mainframe, a few terminals, and a large amount of high-speed disk storage. However, this would permit only programming-type tasks and would not include the wide variety of input and output devices necessary if research was being done in the area of, say, vision, hearing, or robotics.

A large system with multiple high speed disk storage devices (perhaps of the fixed head type), and highly specialized input and output equipment would be required for most AI research. Some of the typical pieces of equipment used in many of the AI labs would be analog-to-digital television cameras for vision and robotics experiments, special voice synthesizers for speech recognition and speech production, elaborate mechanical arms and other assembly equipment for industrial robot design, and specially designed hardware such as multiprocessors and serial processing for high-speed calculations and heuristic searches. Again, the exact configuration of equipment would depend on the type of research being conducted.

A LOOK TOWARD THE FUTURE

The progress and difficulties mentioned in this chapter will largely determine what we can expect in the future. Further reduction in size and cost of computers will not play as significant a factor as in other areas of computer applications. The main limitation is software, not hardware. Whether or not the language barrier is ever broken, or when it is broken, will undoubtedly be the deciding factor for AI in the future. As we saw, to get a computer to understand natural language and to behave intelligently requires that all four of the major research areas (heuristics, knowledge representation, natural language, and reasoning) be incorporated into one system. However, in the meantime, AI research will continue to have major impacts upon many disciplines. Advances that are most likely to occur in the next 20 years include:

- voice-controlled typewriters
- computer-controlled artificial organs
- robot tutors for almost any subject
- insightful weather analysis system
- robot chauffeur
- insightful economic and governmental decision-making systems
- an animal-machine interface

Although progress in AI may not be very impressive to laymen, some very serious questions must be considered. As AI makes more advances, there will be even more criticism, particularly from those who do not believe that human knowledge and thought can be mechanized. We hope this criticism will bring about a closer examination and scrutiny of the nature and possible impact of such research. If society does not assess these advances accurately, it could be possible for AI to bring about significant changes in our lives—changes we may not consider if AI is viewed as being impossible. We feel there should be some type of lay advisory boards, similar to environmental impact agencies, that can carefully examine and evaluate the impact of AI reserach. In the absence of such scrutiny, we will not be able to obtain the benefits that are possible from this research. If progress is made with the advice and consent of the public, we feel the future can be one in which the computer and humans can work together as partners rather than as antagonists or enemies. For real progress to be made, it must be cooperative, with humans gaining a deeper understanding of themselves, their role in the world, and how they can use the abilities of the computer effectively to create a better world. Perhaps, with the aid of the computer, humans will be able to understand better the causes of disease, crime, and violence, and be able to solve problems that have remained insoluble for ages.

STUDY AND REVIEW

1. What contributions did Von Neumann and Wiener make to early AI research?
2. Describe briefly what artificial intelligence research is and why heuristic techniques are important in this area.
3. What is the relationship between microworlds and the computer's ability to reason?

4. What is the difference between the way ELIZA and PARRY process natural language? Do you believe computers will ever be able to understand natural language?

5. What is the difference between scripts and schemas? How do they contribute to a computer's ability to solve problems?

6. Do you believe computers will ever be able to think (give both pro and con arguments)?

15

HOME

PERSPECTIVE

The microelectronic revolution has had its impact on virtually every area of human technology. Definite signs indicate that the greatest impact is yet to come. The key element here is the microprocessor chip, which has made data processing equipment more sophisticated, and has enabled a large portion of the equipment we use in society to be brought under the control of a computer. Such computer control allows manufacturers to build many new products with capabilities far beyond those of their predecessors. Further, as the quotation that follows indicates, these new products will be friendlier to humans.

> *Advances in integrated circuit technology, computer operating systems, and programming techniques will make interaction between a person and a microcomputer natural and understandable.* *(Whitney, 1980)*

Until recently, advanced electronic technologies were most evident in large computers and complex scientific equipment. The cost factor involved with electronics was such that the average citizen had very little contact with such equipment. Television sets, radios, and stereos were made more reliable with new electronic technologies, but electronics were too expensive to be used to build many consumer products that would be used in the home. Now it is different. Not only are the televisions, radios, and stereos offering more features, but every other electrical appliance we use at home is being affected by new electronic technologies. Further-

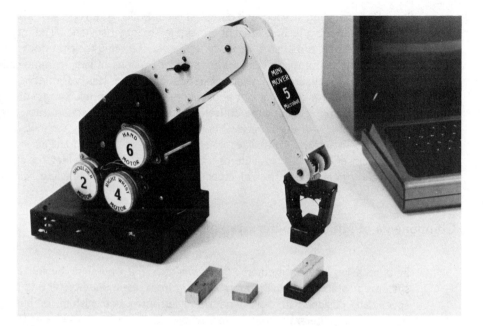

Figure 15-1 Robot arms have been manufactured that can be controlled by the type of microcomputer which would be found at home. Is this the forerunner of an automated housekeeper? (Courtesy of Microdot)

more, a whole wave of new products is beginning to be introduced into the home (see Fig. 15.1). These products range from programmable microwave ovens, dishwashers, washing machines, children's games, and environmental control systems to complicated entertainment equipment. Perhaps the one new product that is likely to have the most dramatic effect on household routines is the microcomputer system. Microcomputer systems, which initially were perceived as sophisticated, expensive toys, will most definitely do more than simply allow members of the household to play games in the future.

COMPUTERS IN THE HOME

Microcomputers—What Are They?

The easiest way to begin describing a microcomputer is by comparing it to normal-sized, commercial computer systems. A microcomputer is much the same as its larger counterpart. It has the same basic components of large computers: input, central processing unit, storage, and output. It is controlled by an operator who uses the same programming techniques that are applied to larger systems. The major differences, of course, are in size, capacity, and cost. To bring the cost down, many of the components for micro systems are smaller versions of large commercial equipment. Thus, they are slower in operation and offer less information handling capacity. However, the types of applications generated in microcomputing or personal computing are less time critical, and usually involve considerably less data than applications in a commercial environment. Furthermore, technology is constantly improving the capabilities of microcomputers to the point where they are coming closer and closer to features found in larger systems. In fact, the capabilities are already greater than those of larger computer systems of just a few years ago.

Components of Microcomputer Systems

In purchasing microcomputers, the buyer has the option of buying a package system, in which all of the components are from one manufacturer and have been specifically designed to work together as an integrated system, or buying components from different manufacturers whose equipment may offer a wider range of capabilities and costs. In a package system the buyer has more assurances that the equipment is compatible, and that one manufacturer is responsible for service on the entire system. With a separate component system the buyer can "fine tune" his microcomputer system by selecting components that offer features best suited to the buyer's needs and budget. Service is sometimes a problem, however, because with equipment from different manufacturers, responsibility for a problem may not be determined easily or quickly. Furthermore, because there are different interface standards in the microcomputer field, not all components are "plug compatible" or hook together easily. Many require special, sometimes expensive interface devices that enable them to be connected and work together.

The simplest microcomputers consist of very few individual pieces because most of the components are built into a single unit (see Fig. 15.2). This single unit could include the central processing unit, a keyboard for entering data, programs and commands, a television screen for displaying input and output, and a modified cassette recorder for auxiliary storage. Many options are available for use with microcomputer systems, to expand the basic capabilities and result in a more powerful system. The most common options are floppy disk drives that use a magnetic-coated mylar plastic disk to store information in place of a cassette recorder (disk drives offer more storage capacity than cassettes, and operate faster) (see Fig. 15.3), and printers that enable the user to obtain output on paper instead of in the temporary form of light images on a television screen. Other options include modems (for connecting a computer to a telephone), speech synthesizers (for voice input and output), minimechanical robot arms, and a number of interface devices that enable the microcomputer to be connected to other electronic equipment for control purposes.

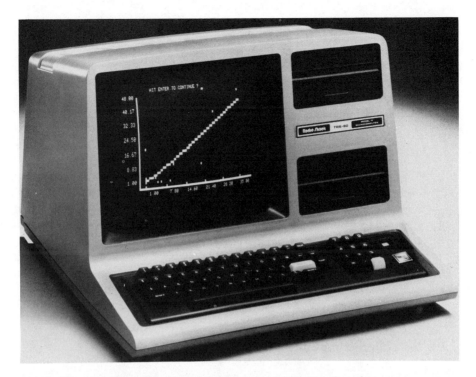

Figure 15-2 The Radio Shack Model III is a popular "package" system, with a wide range of add-on devices available. (Courtesy of Tandy/Radio Shack)

Figure 15-3 A floppy disk unit for use with a Hewlett-Packard microcomputer. (Courtesy of Hewlett-Packard Company)

Microcomputer Programming

The programming process for micrcomputers is the same as for large computers. A programmer may write a program in one of the different languages available for use on microcomputers (the most common is BASIC), enter it into the system through the keyboard unit, and have the computer execute it. The computer can then store the program on a cassette or a floppy disk for recall and execution at any future time.

People who buy microcomputers for use in the home or in small business do not have to be programmers to utilize their equipment. There is an abundance of pre-written software (programs) available to accomplish everything from playing games to preparing income tax returns. Although most people who buy microcomputers will learn some programming, they usually rely on commercial software to provide their microcomputer with sophisticated capabilities. More and more software is becoming available, and as microcomputers become "friendlier," or easier, to operate, people find they do not need a technical education in order to unlock the power of these wondrous new machines.

How Will Microcomputers Be Used?

The thought of another electrical device around the home to consume energy, take up space, and worry about fixing is not very appealing to many people. When that device is a perceived "technological monster," like a computer system, no matter how small, the resistance is even greater. Though great strides have been made in making microcomputer systems easier to operate, the average individual still believes that computers are tools of mathematicians and scientists, and well beyond the understanding of the normal person. These attitudes, however, are changing as a result of many diverse factors. First, the general level of technology is increasing to the point where people are more comfortable with technological innovation; they may accept the technology better than did past generations and they make some effort to learn how to use it without much fear and apprehension. Second, electronic gadgets and microcomputers are becoming commonplace toys for youngsters, and as parents witness the level of involvement of their children with electronics, without fear, they will take a closer look at their attitudes and most likely change, too.

The third factor is that technological change is taking place anyway, and people have the choice of either accepting the technology, like it or not, or being out of step. The services offered by many commercial institutions (banks, credit card companies, etc.) are changing as technology advances, and if customers desire to take advantage of new services, they too must adapt to the technology. This, of course, may foster hard feelings about the dehumanizing effect of advanced technology; however, individual voices are likely to remain unheard in the masses.

In a different direction, one major obstacle to the widespread use of microcomputers has been the price of the equipment. Thus far, microcomputers have been used principally by small businesses that have the available capital to take advantage of the technology, and enthusiastic hobbyists. In 1978, the average micro-computer system cost 15 percent of the average worker's annual salary. By the end of the 1980s it is estimated that this cost will be down to something less than 1 per-cent with even more features and performance. (see Fig. 15.4). By then many of the young people now in lower grades will become the buying public. This group of people, who will have grown up with electronics technology, will see the computer as a friend and a natural extension of their intellect. For this generation, computer literacy will be the rule instead of the exception, as it is today.

The microcomputer will be used in the home to perform a variety of tasks, each of which we will look at in depth in the remaining sections of this chapter. Specifically, the types of uses in the home for microcomputer can be categorized into five areas.

The first is control, which relates to the ability of a microcomputer to control the operation of a wide variety of household systems. Such systems could include sprinklers, heating and air conditioning, fire, smoke, and burglar alarms. These and other systems may be controlled by dedicated microprocessors built into them, and be monitored by a larger microcomputer system. The second use for microcomputer systems will be for entertainment (see Fig. 15.5). Although today the main use of microcomputers purchased for home use is entertainment, in the future less than 10 percent of the systems purchased will be primarily for entertainment. They will, however, have entertainment as a secondary use.

A third important application in the home will be for education. People (chil-dren especially) will be able to learn about computers, or they can use the computer as a tool in learning other subjects. (see Fig. 15.6). The fourth important area for home use is data management. People will use systems to manage their own per-sonal data, including financial records, recipe file, menu planning, shopping lists, and so forth. The fifth and final area will involve the use of a home microcomputer as a communications device. People will be able to connect microcomputers to com-munications networks that will enable them to retrieve data from international infor-mation networks, receive electronic mail, and communicate with other icrocom-puters.

Figure 15-4 A Sinclair ZX 80 which costs less than $400, is a small home computer that can be used with a television set (Courtesy of Sinclair Research)

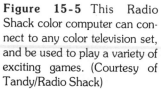

Figure 15-5 This Radio Shack color computer can connect to any color television set, and be used to play a variety of exciting games. (Courtesy of Tandy/Radio Shack)

Figure 15-6 Microcomputers can be used extensively as an educational tool. (Courtesy of Tandy/Radio Shack)

In the following sections of this chapter we explore each of these uses of micro-computer systems in more depth.

Control   One principal use of microcomputer systems in the home will be to control the variety of electrical systems that are integral parts of modern homes. With today's technology, a home would have to dedicate one complete micro system to the control function, with another system or systems used to perform tasks in one of the other areas already mentioned for home microcomputer use. In the future, how-ever, larger more powerful systems will be built for use in the home. These will be mini time-share computer systems capable of performing a wide variety of tasks almost simultaneously.

After a micro system is programmed to control various electrical systems within the home, it will be able to operate with little or no human intervention, only periodically reporting status of various in-house systems.

Most of the electrical systems in today's homes function simply by being turned on or off. There are differences, however, as to when and under what condi-tions systems are turned on and off. Assume for now that it is a simple matter to connect various home electrical systems to a microcomputer. (It will be explained how shortly.) These systems, which for now we will limit to heat, lighting, and sprinklers, have their own individual master controls that can be connected to and controlled by a microcomputer. At the simplest level, the microcomputer can be pro-grammed to respond to commands entered through a keyboard to activate or deactivate selected systems. With a speech snythesizer connected to the micro-system, the user may speak commands into the system, which will interpret them and control the apporpriate units.

On a more complex level, we can use the internal operating system capabilities within microcomputers to remove much of the human involvement in activating and deactivating household systems. A time capability can be added to most microcom-puter systems by the addition of an electronic component at a nominal cost. This component will allow the user to program the microcomputer to control household systems automatically, based on predetermined time cycles. Although for some time there have been devices that could time-control systems, they are nowhere near as flexible as a microcomputer. The microcomputer can turn systems on and off according to a fixed time schedule and, according to a program, it can also alter the time schedule itself. For example, you might connect your heater to your microcom-puter and program it to turn on heat 20 minutes before you get up, shut off an hour or so later after everyone leaves the house, turn on again a few minutes before any-one comes home in the evening, shut the systems off when everyone goes to bed, and then repeat the cycle again the next day. The system can be programmed to keep track of days of the week and automatically adjust the time schedule for Satur-days and Sundays when the family may be home all day.

The microcomputer can control lighting by turning lights on and off at desig-nated times, establishing a sequence that may give the appearance of someone being home, even if they aren't. The sequence can be altered every evening, so as not to become routine and, therefore, tip off an observer that no one is really at home.

Figure 15-7 An electronic version of the popular fantasy board game, *Dungeons and Dragons.* (Courtesy of Mattel Electronics)

The third and even more complex level of control is conditional control. In this area, the microcomputer can be programmed to control systems based on pre-determined, programmed conditions. Various analog sensors can be connected to the microcomputer through analog-to-digital converters, and the microcomputer can then continuously monitor the sensors and activate systems according to a program. Examples of sensors could be temperature sensors, or moisture sensors that would be part of a landscape sprinkler system. When a moisture sensor determines that the moisture content of the soil is too low, the microcomputer will activate the appropriate watering system.

Actually, all three of these levels of control can be incorporated into one computer, and that one computer can control many different systems simultaneously. The clock timer and control programs will be situated in the microcomputer. Sensors and actual house system activator controls will have to be wired to the microcomputer through special interface devices. In some instances, the microcomputer can be connected to a device that is added to existing house wiring. Then, as long as the systems the computer is to control are also connected to the house

Beep . . . Beep-Blip . . . Beep

Beep-Blip! I win! You lose!

You lose . . . you lose . . . you lose!

I win, hee hee! You lose . . . you lose!

You lo . . . just a moment . . . I believe you won that last match.

We are, after all, more intelligent than you think.

wiring, the computer can communicate with and control them through the existing wiring without having to "add on" any more wiring.

Entertainment The use of microcomputers in the home for control purposes is valuable and important, but it is not as glamorous and captivating an activity as using a microcomputer system for entertainment. One of the commoner uses of microcomputer systems purchased for use in the home today is for gaming. Traditionally, games and game boards have been passive, providing players with various inanimate objects with which they could interact with one another. Most such games required at least two players, and frequently became too predictable to be enjoyable. Besides the fact that few games were designed for only one player, the action in games could not be altered according to the skill levels of the opponents (see Fig. 15.7).

With the advent of microelectronics, gaming has taken on new significance for young and old. There are three categories of games that utilize computer technology: hand-held electronic games, which look like modified pocket calculators (many traditional board games are beginning to incorporate this type of device), video games, which connect a controller to a television set and allow player to manipulate graphic images on the screen with special controllers; and microcom-

305

Figure 15-8 Mattel's "Intellivision" is one of the several electronic game systems on the market which connect to a television set and enable users to play a variety of games at home. (Courtesy of Mattell Electronics)

puters, which enable players to interact with one another or the computer to play a particular game (see Fig. 15.8).

All of these games enable the player either to play a game with another individual, or to play only with the computer. Such electronic games are dynamic rather than passive, because the computer or some other electronic device becomes involved in the play, interacts with the players, keeps score, changes the playing conditions, and adjusts the difficulty level of the game to compensate for different skill levels of the players.

Some electronic games, microcomputer oriented or television hand held, are entertaining and also have an educational purpose. Many games are oriented toward development of arithmetic skills; others help children develop reading and spelling skills. Texas Instruments manufactures a product called "Speak and Spell," which uses a speech synthesizer to help children develop spelling skills. Some games that are not actually intended to be educational can be teaching tools. Special devices help players improve skills in certain games, such as chess, controlling game difficulty to the skill levels of the players. As they become more proficient, the game level can be adjusted upward.

Electronic or computer games are also designed to play certain types of board games, a variety of guessing games, or to simulate an unending array of real-life situation games. Electronics makes very elaborate and detailed simulations possible, and undoubtedly these simulations will become better developed in the future.

Most hand-held electronic games are fixed logic devices that can play one game with some variations. Television games, such as Atari and Mattel's Intellivision, utilize a variety of game cartridges to provide gaming situations (see Fig. 15.9). Microcomputers play games through programs written in BASIC or other popular languages that provide control of the game through the keyboard of the computer and display elaborate graphics on a CRT screen. Most people will not have the programming skills to develop games, but this should be of little concern because many games are available commercially at reasonable prices. One company introduced a monthly microcomputer "magazine." A subscriber receives a cassette tape occasionally which they load into their computer. A graphic "cover" is displayed on the screen along with a table of contents to the five or so computer games contained on the cassette. The cassette usually contains a computer cartoon, which looks like a mini motion picture constructed with the graphics characters available on the microcomputer.

Education   In an earlier chapter we described the role of electronics/computer technologies in education. Although the educational benefits of computers can now be brought into the home through the use of microcomputers, this type of education will be used to supplement traditional classroom instruction, not replace it.

Educational technology is undergoing a transition. Institutions have traditionally emphasized the acquisition of knowledge. Today, the focus is changing toward

Figure 15-9 Hand-held electronic games which utilize microprocessors to provide game control. (Courtesy of Mattel Electronics)

mental agility and the application of knowledge. By using sophisticated electronics devices for storing knowledge or information, people will be able to concentrate less on details or facts and more on principles. School children already have pocket calculators; before long they will have access to devices that do most of the unpleasant things, the rote work, in mathematics. Education need not concentrate on how to solve mathematical equations, but rather on how to use the results of calculations.

In the home, microcomputers will provide children with two forms of education: access to a wealth of information resources available through communications networks that are connected to the home, and computer-assisted instruction that uses the power of the computer to present material to a learner, and then provide drill and practice to reinforce it. By making more information readily available to people, not just to children, it is hoped that more people will become lifelong learners. Many persons will learn two, three, or four careers in a lifetime as telecommunications, automation, and later machine intelligence will cause entirely different work patterns. Electronics will provide both the need and the tools for lifelong learning.

Computer-assisted instruction (CAI) is an attempt to achieve interactive teaching in an automated fashion. As effective CAI materials are developed, they can be duplicated and made available to vast numbers of people, like a successful movie. The computer is ideally suited for certain types of teaching, but not for all teaching. An elaborate teaching package that can be implemented on a microcomputer at home, without the presence of a teacher, may have many branches and alternative paths. The responses to a question can elicit a variety of different actions. If correct, the main teaching routine will proceed. If partially correct or almost correct, a remedial sequence will be followed. If wrong, the instruction leading up to that question can be repeated, or an alternative, more detailed sequence followed. If the answer reveals a lack of understanding of an earlier point, the program can backtrack. If the wrong answer is the culmination of many such errors, a branch can be made to a different teaching approach (see Fig. 15.10).

Although much of the education taking place in the home today is through the use of microcomputer or video games adapted for use as educational tools, telecom-

Figure 15-10 A microprocessor-based electronic learning system. (Courtesy of Mattell Electronics)

munications links may later be used with the normal television set to gain access to what will eventually become huge libraries of computer-assisted instruction programs and data banks. Such facilities could be provided via cable television links. In the future a community with good schools may be expected to provide good computerized education via the community cable system. Children will learn and do their homework with this facility, under the direction of the local schools.

Data Management The fourth and perhaps most significant use for computer systems in the home of the future will be for data management. We may conceive of the computer initially as being an expensive way of maintaining name and address or recipe files, but in time the computer will become an indispensable tool in helping the average person to manage the abundance of information that is part of every household (see Cart. 15.2). As we take a look at the data management capabilities of microcomputers we quickly recognize that their function in this capacity is two-

I'm sorry the electricity bill got overlooked.
Must be a computer foul-up.
Do you have the account number I assigned to you?

fold: first, they can be used as a convenient facility for storing large amounts of information and providing easy access to it at a later time; and second, they can be used to manipulate information according to the wishes of the home owner. It is possible that the home computer system will even be able to connect to a communications network and utilize information available through the network to manage effectively the information stored in the home computer, and to help manage efficiently the day-to-day activities within the home.

A computer can store all important family records such as checking accounts, savings accounts, expenses, and income. Using these records, the computer can help the family plan a budget. It can also generate income tax returns and other financial reports (see Fig. 15.11). The computer also can store inventories, such as the kinds and amounts of groceries in the house, and help with meal planning. By taking into account the kinds of food in the house, nutritional requirements, family preferences, and the family budget, the computer can plan a week's meals and print out the week's shopping list at the same time.

Through the use of inexpensive word processing packages available for microcomputer systems, the home owner can prepare all sorts of routine correspondence, and even prepare documents for work or school. Mailing lists can be maintained inside the microcomputer, along with birthdates and other important information

Figure 15-11 Pocket computers, such as this one from Radio Shack, make routine analyses and calculations quickly and accurately. (Courtesy of Tandy/Radio Shack)

about relatives and acquaintances. The microcomputer can be instructed to maintain a calendar of events, providing a monthly, weekly, and daily schedule of current and upcoming events. The range of possibilities for data management in the home will be limited only by the imagination of the user.

Communications   Along with the television set and telephone, the microcomputer will provide access to a wealth of information that will be available through sophisticated communications networks. Such information will include directory listings, advertising, transportation and entertainment schedules, shopping services, and financial information. Besides acting as an access tool for information the home microcomputer can become an active part of such a communications network. It may be used for electronic mail, teleshopping, and banking. It is even possible that the microcomputer in the home, connected to communications networks, will enable people to perform work-related activities at home while remaining in touch with a distant office (see Fig. 15.12).

Other Home Systems   The use of microprocessors in consumer products has given ordinary home appliances capabilities that are well beyond those of their manually operated predecessors. Functions which once required the close supervision of a human operator now can be carried out automatically. In many instances, an easy-to-use digital control panel for providing commands to the device replaces a variety of dials, switches, and other adjustments.

Figure 15-12   An example of the wide range of equipment available for use with Apple microcomputers. (Used with permission of Apple Computer, Inc. The name Apple, Apple Computer, and the Apple symbol are registered trademarks of Apple Computer, Inc.)

A microprocessor that has been embedded into an appliance for purposes of control usually consists of four key components:

1. A microprocessor for actual control.

2. A read-only memory chip that contains the program that will actually direct the microprocessor to control the appliance.

3. A random access memory that provides space for the operator of the appliance to provide specialized control instructions.

4. Circuits for connecting the microprocessor control package to the appliance.

Though it may seem as if many of the applications of the electronics technologies mentioned here are rather trivial, providing a level of control for appliances

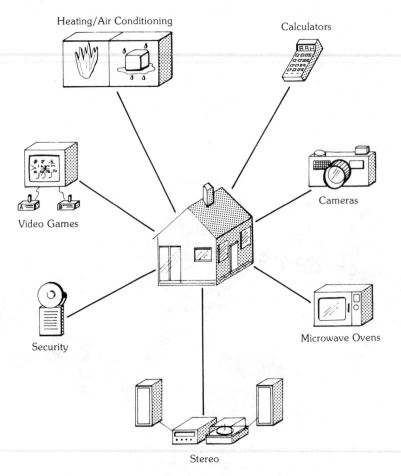

Figure 15-13 A selection of electronically controlled devices available for use in the modern home.

that could just as easily be provided by humans, they do make the operation of appliances more efficient by doing a better job and leaving less chance of human error.

Some of the wide variety of products that incorporate the use of microprocessors for control include: microwave ovens that allow the user to specify cooking time and temperature, and even adjust temperature during cooking time to accommodate several food items; washing machines and dryers that use microelectronics to provide exact control over many variables in washing and drying cycles to accommodate a variety of materials; cameras that focus automatically and set lens opening and shutter speed; telephones that store, retrieve, and automatically dial frequently called numbers; stereo components whose functions and operations can be programmed; and finally, television sets that can display time and channel number on the screen, be programmed in advance to change channels, operate a video tape recorder, display reminder messages, and even answer the telephone (see Fig. 15.13).

These are but a few of the uses of microprocessors. Many, many more will be developed in the future.

SOCIAL IMPLICATIONS

Pro Arguments

Without a doubt—and without much choice—homes of the future are going to incorporate sophisticated electronics to a much greater degree than today. Simply in the process of purchasing normal consumer products, we are going to acquire machines that are controlled by computers. Our normal, rather mundane household appliances will begin offering capabilities that will provide the home owner with more versatile service, offering a broader range of capabilities. It is expected that as electronic controls replace mechanical ones, the reliability of consumer products will increase dramatically. These products will make life easier for us, but they will not have as dramatic an effect on life styles as the microcomputer will. Household systems will operate more efficiently, and at lower cost. The vast amount of information maintained by people today will become more organized and, therefore, more useful. The microcomputer can be used to provide better financial planning, better nutrition, and better education. The capabilities of the microcomputer to manipulate information will enable people to use information to a greater advantage. As a communications tool, the microcomputer will enable people to communicate with others easier, and to gain access to the ideas of others without developing complex research skills. People will be able to perform work-related activities while at home, freeing normal commute-to-work time for other more productive activities. The microcomputer will act as an educational tool for young and old alike, allowing youngsters to drill and practice basic educational skills, and adults to continue lifelong learning in new skills or updating old ones. Microcomputers in the home may also offer a money-making opportunity for those who wish to develop software for microcomputers to be made available for sale.

Con Arguments

A recurring theme is: the more technical the machines we deal with become, fewer people will understand them. With the new electronics, fewer people will be able to do any kind of home repairs. This will be profitable for professional repairers, but it may push the cost of owning equipment higher than at any time in the past. Furthermore, there may be some resistance to another machine in the home that takes up space, uses electricity, and is considerably more difficult to operate than a television or a stereo. Although many of the machines mentioned in this chapter are designed to work together as integrated systems, there is a tremendous amount of incompatibility that will require a high degree of technical know-how to overcome. People may resist installing and utilizing sophisticated home computer systems until such time that installation and operation become simply a matter of plugging in and turning up.

Consumers now have the choice of whether to have a microcomputer in the home or not, but in the future we may be forced into having one. Certain services offered by stores, banks, and other organizations may be available only through a microcomputer system in the home. Because all of this technology costs money, the prices of the products we buy will probably be increased to compensate for the cost of the technology. After a microcomputer is in place, however, we will increase our dependance on the technology, and probably never be able to go back to doing things the "old way."

As a communications tool the computer has great potential. However, much of the communication that will take place will be between humans and machines, or between machines and other machines. There is real danger that an increased use of microcomputers for communication will decrease direct human interaction. Furthermore, as it becomes easier and easier to engage in more activities from homes, we may leave our homes less frequently, and thus cause significant changes in many social institutions. If we can perform work from our homes, it will reduce the amount of time consumed by travel to work. Many people may not be able to cope creatively with the increased leisure time, and end up wasting it.

HARDWARE

This chapter focused on two types of electronic systems that might be found in homes in the near future. The first is the use of microprocessors to control the operation of a wide range of products. Such microprocessors will be incorporated into the design of products, and used to control their operation efficiently. Some systems will incorporate microprocessors that have already been programmed to control the operation of a piece of machinery, and others will allow the owner to specify operating characteristics. Some systems within homes, such as heating, air conditioning, lighting, and intruder alarms, may be controlled with internal microprocessors, yet still be connected to a central control.

As described briefly earlier, the components of the second type of electronic system likely to be found in many homes in the future are similar to those found in larger commercial systems. Controlled by microprocessors, microcomputers use a keyboard for routine entry, and a CRT screen for display. Through special interface devices, many other electronic devices can communicate with a microcomputer, and the microcomputer can communicate with them. Speech synthesizers can be added to give the microcomputer talking capabilities. Modems and other communications equipment enable them to be connected to telephone systems. Magnetic cassette tapes can be used for storage; however, they are too slow for most applications in which a floppy disk unit, capable of storing up to 500,000 characters of information on one disk, can be used. Also available are hard, true random access disk units. However, these are very expensive at this time. More and more microcomputer systems now offer color graphics for better display of information or for more elaborate game displays. A wide variety of printers is available for use with microcomputers systems, ranging from inexpensive dot matrix printers up to expensive letter quality printers. As time goes by, more and more accessories will be available for microcomputer systems, and we hope the new equipment will become easier and easier for the nontechnician to operate.

A LOOK TOWARD THE FUTURE

Many of the capabilities of microcomputer and microprocessors are performed independent of one another. At today's level of technology, it would be necessary for a home to have several computer systems in order to accomplish all of the activities described here. Otherwise, the homeowner would be constantly manipulating one computer system, loading and unloading programs, enabling and disabling capabilities in order to perform different activities. If this were the case, while the family played games, the computer could not be controlling any of the household systems. In the future, almost all of the functions described in this chapter, and many more, will be accomplished by one central home computer system. This system will have large storage capabilities and be able to switch rapidly back and forth between tasks, almost like a time-share computer system. The computer will be connected to virtually every major system and small electrical appliance in the home. The homeowner will be able to communicate with the computer through the normal keyboard or, more likely, the microcomputer will be connected to the house intercom system and be able to receive commands and communicate with the operator by voice. Interface standards will be established so that various pieces of equipment can easily be connected together and function smoothly. Programming language will make it easier for people to tell a computer what they want it to do or, if they prefer, an endless variety of prewritten software will be available at reasonable prices.

STUDY AND REVIEW

1. How do you think people are going to react to having a computer at home?

2. Can people's resistance to having another electrical appliance in the home be overcome?

3. Describe how a microprocessor can be used for control purposes in normal home appliances.

4. What scenario can you describe for the home of the year 2000?

5. What social implications do you believe will arise from the fact that people will be able to work at home, and conduct most personal business without leaving home?

6. What are the categories of uses for microcomputers in the home? Describe a typical application in each area.

7. Describe the components and the functions of a typical microcomputer system.

8. Will the development of software by an inexperienced home computer user be a hindrance toward utilizing the capabilities of a microcomputer?

9. Summarize the positive implications of computer usage in the home.

10. Summarize the negative implications of computer usage in the home.

11. Can you foresee any other types of home applications of computer systems other than those mentioned here?

12. What do you expect the computerized home of the future to look like?

16

GOVERNMENT, LAW, AND CRIME

PERSPECTIVE

The United States government is the largest user of data processing equipment in the world. Currently more than 15,000 computers are in use, of which approximately 2,000 are data banks containing over three billion records on individuals. As indicated in the quotation below, this enormous volume of information creates problems that are well-suited for a computer solution.

> *The problems of information flow in government are common to all large organizations. Like private corporations, government bureaucracies are hierarchically structured and exhibit a spectrum of problem-solving and decision-making functions ranging from routine administrative tasks to strategic policy formation . . . Since the public interest is at stake, the needs and desires of ordinary citizens must somehow be incorporated into the decision-making environment. It is this area that computer-based information systems may make their most distinctive contribution to government administration.*
> *(Mowshowitz, 1976)*

Some of the largest users of data banks—each storing from 10 million to 500 million records—are: the Internal Revenue Service; Social Security Administration; Civil Service Commission; Department of Commerce; Department of the Army; Department of Health, Education, and Welfare; Department of the Treasury; General Services Administration; Department of Justice; and the Veterans Administration. In addition to the federal government, about 75,000 state, county, and local government units use data processing in some form or another. Rather than discuss in detail the wide variety of uses and the specifics of many noteworthy systems at the federal, state, county, and local levels, we describe only a few representative systems. However, to give a general idea of some of the major ways in which governments use computers, a brief overview of some typical applications follows.

Planning: highways, recreation areas, housing, health and educational services, zoning, environmental impact, resource allocation, simulated war strategies.

Services: medical, welfare, law enforcement, and emergency services; libraries; community information; transportation.

Financial: budgets, taxes, assessments, accounting, payroll.

Management: timely reports, statistics, record keeping.

Besides the administrative and legislative uses of computers in government, we also consider how computers are used in the judicial branch both by courts and attorneys. And closely related to the courts are ways that computers are used to commit crimes—another topic we examine in this chapter. Because our tax dollars support the uses of computers in government, it should be of interest to all of us to understand both the advantages and disadvantages of these systems. Thus, by gaining knowledge about how government computers are currently being used, we will be in a better position to anticipate how they will be used in the future. Let's see how our tax dollars are being spent.

COMPUTERS IN GOVERNMENT

There are many outstanding systems at all levels of government, yet there have been problems, mainly in efficiency and duplication of data. To better assess many requests for new computer systems in the late 1970s, the General Services Administration directed that a study be made of how efficiently computers were being used within the federal agencies. A private firm conducted extensive tests of both hardware and software and concluded that most of the systems in place were using only 60 to 70 percent of their total capability; some systems fell below 50 percent effectiveness. Consequently, many federal computer systems are being refined and streamlined for greater efficiency before they will be upgraded or replaced, and some data processing is being done outside by private service bureaus.

Some reasons for these inefficiencies are quite technical, but some less technical points should be discussed. First, government does not have to compete with other organizations; therefore, it does not have to worry about losing business or profits because of more efficient competition. For example, if a large private firm was not using its computer resources effectively its competitors could gain an advantage that might cause the firm to go out of business. Often it is difficult to detect and quantify inefficient use because the government systems are so large and unique that they cannot be easily compared with other systems in the private sector. Second, many members of Congress and the bureaucracy have no background or knowledge of data processing, so it becomes difficult for them to oversee and evaluate computer uses. Finally, many departments, bureaus, offices, and agencies have gone from filing cabinets to data banks without any significant changes in their record-keeping techniques and policies. Consequently, many of the procedures from the manual systems were carried over to the automated systems.

At least two serious problems result when this occurs, whether it be in private or government data banks. First, computer data banks tend to be viewed and used as large filing cabinets—each office wants its own! This is extremely inefficient because computers can easily be shared—even over large geographic areas—whereas filing cabinets cannot. For example, when an extensive data bank survey was made by Congress in 1974, it was discovered that some agency/department directors did not know how many data banks actually existed within their own areas of responsibility. Second, because of this "manual" approach to data banks, there is a great amount of duplicated data, all of which is subsidized by our tax dollars. It is not unusual for the federal government to have 10 to 20 files on each individual, which explains how there can be almost four billion files when there are only about 225 million people. What can be done?

Common Data Banks

One solution to this problem is to create a common data bank. This type of data bank contains only nonsensitive information that would be common to all individual data banks. Data such as name, address, age, telephone number, sex, marital status, place of employment—essentially all the information that is of public record—would be in one location only, rather than repeated in every record that is kept on a person. The idea that every agency must have its own copy of common data is a carryover from the manila folder era when information had to be physically present in the office in which it was used. With telecommunications equipment, data can be displayed at a terminal thousands of miles away in just a few seconds; no longer must every agency have its own set of common data.

There are several advantages to storing data in this manner:

- *Lower cost*—Because approximately 40 to 80 percent of the information in government files is common data, about two-thirds of all this data could be eliminated.

- *More accurate*—Because common data would be stored in just one location, coming in contact with only one agency would automatically update the common data used by all agencies, rather than requiring each agency to be updated separately.

- *Easier to access*—By contacting any agency you could have access to your common data for updating, correcting, and so forth; also, private businesses and other government agencies could easily use data because there would be no sensitive or confidential information in this data bank.

- *Better government services*—Less time would be required to fill out forms and duplicate data that already exists; also, benefit checks would be less likely to go to the wrong person or the wrong address because any errors would be easily and quickly corrected.

There are two ways in which common data banks can be used to eliminate redundancy and obtain the advantages listed above.

Horizontal Integration   When common data is consolidated at one level of organization (for example, at the county level), this is called horizontal integration. For instance, if all the common data that would appear in the records of the tax assessor, health department, education department, registrar of voters, and so forth, were to be put into one common data bank with the sensitive, confidential, or otherwise unique data for each office stored separately, this would be horizontal integration (see Fig. 16.1).

The sensitive data could be stored in the same data bank, or a separate data bank could be linked to the common data by an index and would be available only to authorized individuals within the originating agency. Many state, county, and local governments have been employing this technique for several years with substantial savings and better services for the taxpayer. One such system is called Local Government Information Control (LOGIC). This system serves Santa Clara County, California, and contains 10 subsystems dealing with health, education, welfare, courts, and general "people" information. Another impressive system is in Minnesota's Hennepin County. Dedicated to providing efficient service to more than one million citizens, several different databases are interconnected, allowing both decentralized flexibility and centralized control. Some of the major parts of this system are: the Citation Tracking System for monitoring the more than 500,000 citations issued each year; the Civil Paper Tracking System for following the status of thousands of legal complaints, summonses, writs, and court orders; the Juvenile Court Family Tracking System that follows every case from inception to disposition, and involves the family at every stage, also provides for complete security so these records do not get confused with the larger criminal justice system; and a Property Information System that consolidates data on over 300,000 real estate parcels and has the ability to produce property maps, too! Finally, a very innovative system (called the Citizen Service and Information System) in Long Beach, California, has been designed to enable residents to call a single number, get the right department and be guaranteed a response. A clerk who answers incoming calls (about 200 per day) takes the name, address, telephone number, and the inquiry. By searching information areas displayed on a computer terminal, the clerk can determine which office should handle the question. Not only is the person connected immediately,

(1) EACH DEPARTMENT HAS ITS OWN FILES (NONINTEGRATED)

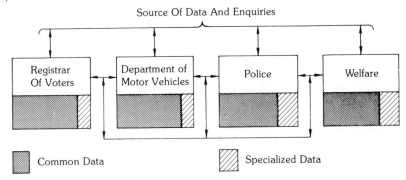

(2) COMMON DATA IN A COMMON DATA BANK (HORIZONTAL INTEGRATION)

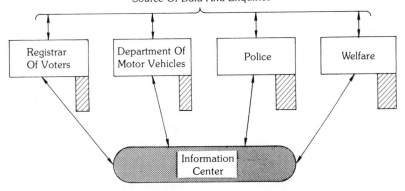

Figure 16-1 Non-integrated and horizontal integration with common data bank

but the computer prints a letter to the person thanking them for the inquiry, informs them which department is handling the request, and gives an inquiry number that can be used in case there is need or further information. Not only does this provide fast, effective service for the citizen, it also provides accurate information for the government so it can identify problem areas or where more help is needed.

Vertical Integration Even though a great amount of duplication can be eliminated through horizontal integration and common data banks, there is still much redundancy of common data when we consider the different levels of government. That is, even if a particular city were to establish a common data bank and eliminate all duplication at the city level by horizontal integration, there still would be duplication at the county, state, and federal levels. To remedy this, vertical integration is used to consolidate information and elminate redundancy in different levels of government (see Fig. 16.2). Two examples of this type of integration are briefly discussed.

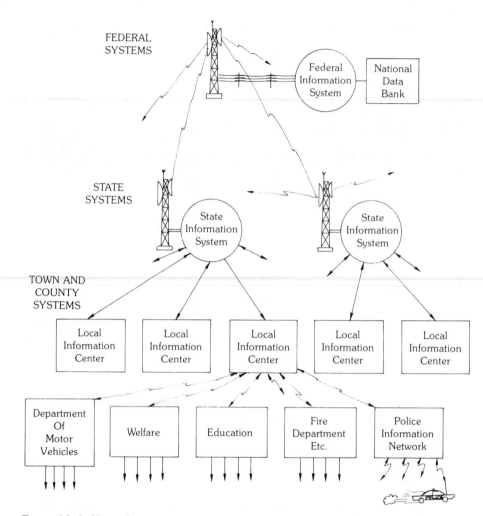

FEDERAL
SYSTEMS

STATE
SYSTEMS

TOWN AND
COUNTY
SYSTEMS

Figure 16-2 Vertical integration

Teale Data Center The Teale Center in Sacramento, California, is organized into four data banks according to the type of information stored (tax, health, education, and criminal), with all of California's local and county governments eventually being able to access and update information through this center. Theoretically, only four common data files for each individual would be needed if all agencies throughout the state used this system.

National Crime Information Center The NCIC system, operated by the FBI, is perhaps the largest vertically integrated system in existence. It stores information on wanted persons, stolen vehicles, stolen firearms, stolen securities, and other miscellaneous stolen articles. Although not designed to replace local law enforcement systems that store similar information, it does provide a central depository for vital information available to more than 6,000 law enforcement agencies. Since its inception in 1967, it has grown from 23,000 entries and 10,000 daily inquiries, to more than 8 million active records and more than 275,000 transactions per day. Because of the large geographic area covered (all of the United States, plus exchanges of data with Canada, Mexico, Great Britain, and parts of Europe) and the quick response time (usually less than a minute), over 1,000 "hits" (that is, arrests or recovered property) are made each day.

Unfortunately, NCIC cannot accurately measure the amount of deterrent it provides, though it has been established that the threat of rapid apprehension is a very strong deterrent in preventing many crimes. Nevertheless, there are many benefits from this system. These include the time saved in investigations plus an increased apprehension rate for wanted persons and increased recovery of stolen property. The most important benefit is the ability to provide accurate, timely information to a patrol officer about a vehicle and its occupants before the officer actually comes in contact with them. Local agencies can enter information into NCIC; for example, if a car is stolen and used in a robbery in New Jersey and is stopped two days later in rural Mississippi for a broken tail light, the arresting officer would be alerted. Also, property stolen in New York and recovered in California can now be identified and returned to its owner. The NCIC not only suffers from problems associated with all data banks, such as providing adequate security, maintaining the "integrity" of the data, and controlling error, it has difficulties of its own. Because so many different agencies contribute information and there is no precise way of classifying all the data, there is much duplication and problems with retrieving some types of information. Perhaps one of the more serious problems is that not all of the data is up-to-date or complete. Sometimes people are wrongfully detained or arrested because records have not been properly kept. According to studies, as much as 15 to 20 percent of the data could be incorrect at any given time (see Figure 16-3).

Political Applications

The federal government was the first major user of commercial computers in the United States and, as stated earlier, is now the largest user of computers in the world. While the primary use of computers has been for administrative and statistical purposes, computers are now being used to count votes, assist legislators, and to promote campaigns. So we now examine how the computer is being applied in these areas.

Elections Computers are an integral part of all stages of the election process now, both at federal and state levels. Prior to elections, the political party in power in each state can determine the congressional district boundaries based on the latest census figures. There are essentially no restraints on how the boundaries are drawn as long as each district has approximately the same number of voters. This process, called gerrymandering, can greatly benefit the party in power by creating political district

Figure 16-3 A police and fire dispatcher in the St. Petersburg FL, police department's communications center receives computer-developed information on two video display terminals and uses it as the basis for contacting field patrol units to answer complaints or calls for service. (Courtesy of International Business Machines Corporation)

boundaries in such a way as to increase the party's political strength. And, with the aid of a computer, thousands of possible configurations can be examined (based on voter registration, economic factors, previous voting records, and so forth), and the optimum boundaries drawn.

On the day of the election, computers can be used in two ways. In some precincts computers are used directly to tabulate ballots. There have been problems with these systems, however, mainly due to inadequate testing of the software programs and to equipment failures, which have limited their expanded use. Also many people question the security of such systems and the ability to detect errors and fraudulent practices. Until security and equipment problems can be overcome, electronic voting will probably not be widely used. But it is quite possible that electronic voting from the home will be feasible in the future—a few cities already have such systems installed for polling purposes.

The other use of computers during elections is more widespread and controversial. All of the major televison networks use elaborate computer technology to tabulate early returns and from these project or predict election results. By monitoring key precincts in several eastern states, it is possible to predict election results accurately hours before the polls close in western states. During the 1980 national election for example, TV network computers predicted Reagan's victory more than two hours before the polls closed in the west. It has been estimated that approximately one-half million voters did not vote at all because of this prediction! It is very likely that legislation will be passed in order to prevent such projection from occurring in the future.

Finally, after an election, "post-mortem" analyses are performed in order to pinpoint exactly where and why particular candidates won or lost. This information is then useful in planning for the next election campaign and for gerrymandering.

Campaigning

> *On terrorists, my position is clear. International terrorism, such as bombings and hijackings, is deplorable. Yet, the U.S. should not put itself in a position committed to meet such actions whenever and wherever they might occur. I will go to the United Nations and get an international law against terrorism.* (Computer, 1980)

This quotation, produced by a computer program, provides an indication of the extent to which computers participate in political campaigns. By collecting extensive demographic information—social, economic, religious, and ethnic data about one's constituents—a politician can use a computer to tailor-make a campaign speech to match the specific characteristics of the group being addressed. It has been estimated that about $100 million were spent during the 1980 election year for computer services, about one-tenth of the total campaign budget.

Although the Democratic party first used a computer during the Kennedy campaign, the Republican party definitely had the largest computer operation during the 1980 election. Their system, called REPNET, is representative of how computers are being used in political campaigning. Some of the major components of REPNET are: Computerized Political Accounting (CPA); Automated Donor Information System (ADONIS); Universal Correspondence and Word Processing (UNICORN); Mailing List Maintenance System (MAIL CALL); and Political Targeting and Survey Processing System (TARGET 20). The main purpose of these five systems is to identify likely voters and, through repeated computer "personalized" campaigning, get them to vote on election day. REPNET and similar systems used by the Democrats have been shown to increase voter turnout by 4 to 11 percent. Because the computer can examine so many aspects of the electorate and make very subtle distinctions within geographic areas about particular issues (called geodemographics), campaigns can no longer be conducted successfully without this technology. The main advantage of this technique is that it very accurately identifies who the likely voters are, so every dollar and every form of advertising is used effectively and efficiently.

However, a recent claim has been made that this type of computer campaigning fosters political deception by exposing only those aspects of a candidate's beliefs that are expected to be well received by the people being addressed. On another occasion before a different group, different views will be presented. One possible solution that has been suggested would be for the candidates to have on public record all of their political views on major issues, sort of an extension of the "equal time" laws, thus providing easy access to all pertinent information. But the other side of this issue is that by targeting speeches and letters to specific topics and individuals, politicians utilize funds more wisely and deliver specific information to voters who are likely to listen. What is your view on this issue?

Legislative Uses   At the state and federal levels computers are being used to assist our representatives. We now focus on how they are being used by Congress in Washington, though several states have already implemented similar systems. For approximately ten years, the House of Representatives has used a computerized voting system that allow members to vote from one of 44 terminals in the chamber. By using specially designed identification cards that are inserted into the terminals, large display screens show how each member has voted, the total number of yeas, nays, and abstentions, and the total amount of time remaining to vote on the bill.

In addition to this system, members of congress use computers to schedule activities, distribute and tabulate questionnaires, and perform other data processing tasks required by committees and individual members. There are, however, three other major systems used by Congress:

LEGIS   a bill status system that records, stores, and permits online inquiries about the current status of all bills and resolutions before Congress.

FAPRS (Federal Assistance Program Retrieval System)   provides information about federal loans and grants to assist members of Congress in deciding what funds are available for their constituents.

SOPAD (Summary Of Proceedings And Debates)   current information about activity on both the House and Senate floors.

COMPUTERS IN LEGAL SYSTEMS

In addition to the computer systems used in law enforcement, such as NCIC and other similar systems at the state and local levels, both courts and lawyers are finding the computer to be a very valuable tool. We now look at a few ways in which computers are being used in these areas.

Courts

One of the most serious problems facing federal, state, and local courts is the extremely large backlog of cases. Often, by the time a case gets into court witnesses have forgotten important details or cannot be located, innocent people without the financial resources to post bail have been unduly detained, and sometime even guilty people must be freed because they have not been given a "quick and speedy" trial. In order to combat these and related problems, many courts are employing computers to alleviate the congestion. One system that is representative of the more than 100 similar systems already in use in the United States, is Milwaukee county's JUSTIS. This system serves all of the courts, the clerks of the courts, the sheriff's department, and the district attorney's office. It handles about 40,000 cases a year and keeps all the information online for cases in progress. There are four types of files kept in JUSTIS: information regarding details of the crime; data on the defendant; information about the case and its progress; and information on participants in the case, such as victims, witnesses, police officers, attorneys, and so forth. Because all information is entered only once, there is no duplication, and regardless of which agency updates the case, it is automatically updated for all users of the information. Besides reducing court backlog, reducing errors in the records, and reducing operating costs, the system also provides detailed statistical information so bottlenecks and other problems can be quickly remedied.

Another system being developed in New Hampshire will be the nation's first statewide paperless court system. By entering all the information regarding the case into a computer, including transcripts from trials and hearings, all the data can be stored on computer output microfilm (COM), saving time, space, and money. For example, copies of large case files normally cost about eight dollars to reproduce but can be made for about six cents with this system. Other by-products of systems like these are the generation of court calendars (automatically updated so as to minimize conflicts with attorneys, witnesses, and other participants), the computer printing of transcripts, the review of cases by computer terminal, and prompt delivery of transcripts and supporting documents to the appellate courts. With word processing equipment, judges can easily and quickly distribute opinions among their colleagues so revisions can be made promptly and the final product can be printed electronically.

Finally, one other use of computers is for jury selection. By using data from the registrar of voters list, a code number can be assigned to each eligible jury candidate. Each month a list can be generated by using the code number, and from this list the necessary number of jurors can be drawn. After the code numbers of the selected jurors are entered into the computer, the summonses and other associated documents can be prepared by the computer (see Fig. 16.4).

Attorneys

Because computers affect so many areas of our lives, it is not unusual for technical computer information to be part of court cases. In fact, in the areas of copyright and patent there are numerous legal problems that are going all the way to the Supreme Court in order to be resolved. Consequently, it is becoming necessary for many attorneys to become familiar with computer technology in order to prepare these cases and to evaluate technical matters. Lawyers are also using computer tech-

Figure 16-4 Tarrant County Court Judge J. C. Duvall keeps a computer terminal on his courtroom bench and frequently asks his clerk to check the past record of a person appearing before him. The terminal is tied into the county's criminal justice information system and provides instant access to case files stored in the IBM computer. (Courtesy of International Business Machines Corporation)

nology to assist them in their research. One system called LEXIS, operated by Mead Data Central, Incorporated of Ohio, provides a legal information retrieval service to subscribers. LEXIS contains millions of case law citations and provides page number and line numbers for specific legal documents when requests about certain keywords are made. Another system, operated by West Publishing Company of Minnesota (a major publisher of law books), provides computerized summaries of thousands of cases from the last 20 years. Information from WESTLAW is accessed through online terminals that permit the summaries to be displayed in only a few seconds on a CRT, or to be printed if a permanent record is required. Systems such as LEXIS and WESTLAW permit thousands of cases to be searched in minutes, providing the most up-to-date precedents for legal research. One complaint that has been voiced regarding these types of systems is that they are relatively expensive to use and, therefore, only large law firms are able to use them, placing the smaller firms and individual lawyers at a disadvantage because it would take days or months to do comparable research.

Besides legal research, computers are being used to collect data and prepare wills, contracts, divorce papers, and other legal documents. By allowing a client to enter the required information into the computer, the program can inform the individual if any necessary data is missing and, when all the data are entered, the document can be prepared for final examination by the attorney. This greatly reduces the cost to the client and allows the attorney to use the consultation time for important matters, not just questioning the client to obtain some more information or to complete an overlooked part of the document. Programs such as this are made possible through the development of special programming languages that closely parallel the methods used in legal reasoning. It is anticipated that lawyers will soon be using computers in many areas of their practice, especially if computer services are offered through government-operated law libraries at little or no expense to the attorneys.

Closely related to law enforcement and the uses of computers in our judicial system, is the use of computers in actually committing crimes. This is the topic we discuss next.

COMPUTERS IN CRIME

Before discussing computer crime, it might be helpful to return to Chapter 3 and quickly review the main functions of an operating system. For, as we shall see, the operating system plays a pivotal role in computer crime. Can you think of some reasons why this might be so?

Definitions

For our discussion, we define computer crime as any activity in which computers or data communications are voluntarily used, resulting in actual or potential harm to a victim and actual or potential gain for the perpetrator. This definition, of course, is extremely vague in order to encompass the wide latitude of activities that actually occur. Perhaps a better term would be *computer abuse*, because many of the examples that are given here do not clearly violate laws as they are presently written. Also, many of the abuses that have taken place do not necessarily result in harm or gain as we would normally understand these terms. Nevertheless, there is great potential for both harm and gain.

The key term for clarifying the relationship between the operating system and computer abuse is *complexity*. Not only has the number of computer systems increased dramatically (more than 500,000 systems in operation in the early 1980s), but the size of the systems has grown too. Consequently, operating systems have grown proportionately for the purpose of handling the demands of very large multi-access, time-sharing systems that often support thousands of users from hundreds of locations. To compound matters, there are higher storage densities, intelligent terminals, satellite communications, and the capability to interconnect these large systems into even larger systems or networks. All of these factors contribute to the enormity and complexity of the systems, making the operating systems equally complex and vulnerable to many forms of abuse. Because the operating system is responsible for monitoring all activities—including accounting and security—the more complex the operating system becomes, the more difficult it is to detect fraudulent and unauthorized uses.

> *To cope with all eventualities in a time-sharing network, some operating systems run to hundreds of thousands of separate instructions. In the composition of something like that, hundreds of errors inevitably creep in—either oversights in the design of the safeguards or simple mistakes in the writing of instructions.*
>
> *Under certain circumstances, these errors will let data leak from one user's domain to another's or even open a way into the supposedly inviolate territory of the operating system itself.*
>
> *. . . By now, a lot of people have learned how to exploit soft-*

> *ware errors deliberately—not only to read data stored in the*
> *machine, but also to type changes in access-control safe-*
> *guards, data, and programs.*   *(Alexander, 1974)*

Though some computer crimes can be accomplished without direct penetration of an operating system, the more serious offenses usually involve bypassing or deceiving the operating system in some way. While reading the following examples of the major types of computer abuse, try to imagine ways in which the operating system might be involved in the cases under consideration.

Types of Computer Abuse

Although large, complex operating systems are vulnerable to attack, the main reason that computer crime is increasing dramatically is the high monetary gain involved in such crimes. Whereas the average noncomputer bank embezzlement is about $24,000, an average computer-related embezzlement is more than $500,000 with an estimated annual amount of from $300 million to about $2 billion. Also, it is estimated that only about 12 percent of all computer crimes are reported, only 18 percent of which result in convictions; one out of 22,000 computer criminals actually go to jail! According to reports two major areas are especially susceptible to computer crime: federal government systems and electronic funds transfer (EFT) systems. For example, of 69 crimes uncovered by the government, the losses totaled over $2 million. And a $10 million theft from the Federal Reserve System's EFT network, called Fedwire, demonstrated the inadequacy of protection for most EFT systems that are designed to transmit billions of dollars of transactions each day. The momentum and rapid progress in electronic funds transfer (discussed in Chapter 7) will no doubt be slowed down as bankers look more closely at the vulnerability of any electronic banking system. However, the high monetary gain and difficulty in detecting and preventing computer abuse will continue to be a strong motivating force in the commission of even more crimes during the 1980s.

Program and Data Theft   As you know, software is a very valuable asset in any computer system. Sometimes elaborate applications programs may take several years of labor to develop, resulting in costs often exceeding $100,000. And the data used by many programs is very expensive to collect and convert into computer-usable form, such as marketing surveys, credit reports, inventories, or difficult to collect scientific experimental data. Because the original software never disappears, legal action is extremely difficult to pursue. Not only is it difficult to know when software is stolen, but even when discovered, it is often difficult to prove theft because only a few minor alterations to a large program could make it almost unidentifiable with the original version. Nevertheless, there are documented cases where employee lists or customer lists were sold to other firms, and where programs ranging in value from $50,000 to $1.5 million were stolen.

Program and Data Alteration   In some respects, the alteration of software can be more troublesome and expensive than actual theft. For example, cases have been detected where students altered other students' grades on transcripts by changing computer stored data, sometimes charging up to $300 to alter three or four grades. A few cases have also been cited where voting results were tampered with in computerized voting systems by altering the tabulating programs. Both types of data alteration could have serious social implications because most college grades and most voting results are stored and calculated by computers. Though there are cases where changing programs and data for high monetary gain is the primary motive, these abuses are discussed under the topic of embezzlement. One form of alteration that is not motivated by money is computer vandalism. This often occurs in educational environments, for example, when students gain access to other students' or instructors' programs and change the software so that it introduces errors that are frustrating and difficult to detect and correct. Although there was some monetary gain in one case where six employees of TRW-Credit Data Corporation altered credit reports on persons who were poor credit risks and gave them good ratings, the really frightening aspect is that this company distributes credit data on more than 50 million individuals; the magnitude of these systems and the ease with which abuses are committed is causing great alarm throughout the data processing field.

Theft of Computer Time   Although this may not constitute a major monetary loss category within computer abuse, it represents one of the most frequently committed abuses. Actually, when most of the other types of abuses are carried out, more than likely the account used or method of access is unauthorized and, consequently, all the time used to commit the abuse is really stolen. Independent of this coincidental time, many crimes have been reported in which valuable CPU time has been used (which can cost more than $200 per minute). One such crime involved a 15-year-old who tapped into the University of California's computer at Berkeley. Though some programs were altered over a seven-month period, the main charge was that more than 200 hours of computer time (about 4 hours of CPU time) was stolen. The culprit used $60 worth of equipment and a telephone to commit this crime. And, in one unique case, the FBI discovered that a major midwestern bookie was using stolen computer time to calculate handicaps for his business!

Embezzlement by Computer   Using the computer to manipulate funds for one's personal gain is the most lucrative form of computer crime. This type of crime accounts for probably more than $300 million in losses per year, and it may be only a fraction of the actual amount taken. The classic computer embezzlement is the Equity Funding case, where more than two-thirds of that company's 97,000 life insurance policies were bogus—as were the death certificates—resulting in a loss of more than $2 billion.

   The range of computer embezzlements is truly fascinating—everything, including printing hundreds of false payroll checks, siphoning off money from inactive accounts, and the fairly common crime of rounding-down odd amounts and putting the remainders into one personal account. Unlike their noncomputer predecessors, computer embezzlements are often carried out by one employee because access to all records can be gained through the computer. And, because of the size of the systems, there are usually huge amounts of money available and numerous ways in which the money can be embezzled. Whereas in manual systems it would be time consuming and unprofitable to embezzle a penny or two from each account, in large-scale systems handling millions of accounts, taking a few pennies from each would be relatively easy, and in time would amount to a significant sum.

Sabotage   Although this category represents the smallest number of abuses, it is one area where many systems are particularly vulnerable. Fire, water, magnetic fields, and some chemicals can destroy millions of dollars worth of hardware and software in minutes. Software is often stored on magnetic tapes, disks, paper tapes, or punched cards—all of which can easily be destroyed or erased. If a huge defense system, police system, banking system, or airlines system were sabotaged, the effects would be disastrous. As we shall see, there are precautions that can be taken to prevent this type of abuse, but all involve expense and many systems are inadequately protected against attack.

Difficulties in Detection and Prevention

A New York bank teller with a salary of $11,000 per year used the bank's computer to embezzle more than $1 million. The crime was discovered by accident when police raided a bookie and found that the teller had been gambling $30,000 a day for several weeks!

This case is typical of computer crimes; they are usually detected by accident of some sort, which accounts for the fact that only about 12 percent are actually detected. Either someone leaks information to the police, an employee starts spending unusual amounts of money, the culprit is overly foolish (such as trying to cash 37 checks in one bank, all with the same date and amount), the computer breaks down and an altered program or procedure is detected, or perhaps the employee quits after committing the crime and leaves the evidence behind. Whatever the "accident" might be, it is rare that an audit or other form of investigation uncovers such crime. One reason so few crimes are caught by audit or other workers is that many people tend to view a computer printout as infallible or, at least, extremely accurate. Therefore, printed amounts are rarely questioned. Also, when examining manual records, an auditor or accountant can usually find some traces of an embezzlement, such as smudged figures, forged signatures, missing accounts, or other such evidence, but these "typical" signs do not appear in computer crimes.

Here are some of the main factors that hamper the detection and prevention of computer-related crimes:

Unusual Criminal Profile: Most computer criminals do not have the normal characteristics that investigators look for. They usually have college degrees, and often graduate degrees; they do not have any extreme debt or other financial problems; they are usually very motivated and intelligent, considered "good" employees; many of the criminals did not intend to commit "crimes" but viewed their activity as an intellectual "game" or challenge.

Lack of Evidence: One of the attractive features of most computer crimes is that all of the evidence can be destroyed or removed from the system without detection. Programs can be erased, operating system accounting and passwords can be by-passed. It is rare that an accomplice is required, and many crimes are committed while the computer is operating during normal working hours.

Difficulty in Prosecuting: Although laws are usually broken in the commission of computer crimes, it is sometimes difficult to apply existing laws of theft, burglary, fraud, or embezzlement to extremely complex computer crimes. However, some states have already enacted criminal statutes to deal specifically with these types of crimes. Also, when programs are stolen and altered by another user, it is very difficult to apply the laws of copyright or of patents to programs because they are not explicitly protected by law.

Undesirable Public Exposure: Many companies do not wish to prosecute for two main reasons: if a large monetary loss is detected, they might lose business, stockholders, and their public image if it is thought they did not take adequate precautions; if the case goes to court, the manner in which the crime was committed will probably be revealed, making future crimes of the same type more likely.

Cost of "Total" Prevention: Even though there are several ways in which the security of a system can be improved to prevent many crimes, there is really no way of having an unbreakable or impenetrable system. Consequently, trade-offs must be made to determine how much money will be invested in security versus the dollar amount and liklihood of potential abuses. If you are protecting a small, batch-oriented business system as opposed to a national time-sharing banking network, the risks and costs are dramatically different.

Some Possible Solutions

Computer-related crime is similar to the gun control problem. It is not productive to distinguish between computer and people problems. We should not jump to the conclusion that we need a whole new body of law and ethical standards. Remember that computers are not ethical agents. We must solve the moral and ethical problems before we can determine the legal issues. (Parker, Nycum, and Oura, 1973)

As this quotation indicates—and as we have emphasized throughout each chapter—we are dealing primarily with people in every computer context we discuss. Problems of theft, vandalism, embezzlement, and sabotage have existed for centuries; it is just that new computer technology has the ability to magnify human capabilities, for better or for worse. We must begin confronting these ethical issues by instruction and discussion in the earliest years of education, not after people have chosen their careers and are employed. One of the most disturbing facts about the typical white-collar computer criminal is his or her absense of any sense of wrongness in computer abuse activities. These criminals felt they were going only slightly beyond normal or accepted profession standards when they engaged in illicit activities. This type of attitude is not uncommon among computer "freaks"/"hackers" who spend hours trying to obtain passwords, enter unauthorized accounts, or alter a fellow worker's or fellow student's program. Because many people look on this as an intellectual challenge, they fail to see anything morally wrong or dishonest in their behavior. And, because it is sometimes difficult to detect and reprimand this deviousness in educational environments in particular, such behavior is often carried over into professional careers. Although new laws are presently being written to deal with specific, technical issues, especially in the area of telecommunications and copyright/patents, education and exemplary professional standards will play the most important role in decreasing this type of activity in the future. In the meantime, there are several measures that can be taken to reduce the vulnerability of computer systems to unauthorized use and abuse; these are discussed next.

Hierarchy of Controls   Careful analysis of the different types of computer crimes has shown that some crimes could have been prevented at essentially no extra cost, while the detection and prevention of others would have involved large sums of money. Consequently, there are many different levels of security for computer systems, with only the largest and most sensitive systems (that is, those that handle large amounts of money or support national defense and security) requiring the highest levels of protection. Here, in ascending order, are our classifications of security:

1. *Procedures.*   A large number of abuses could be prevented by merely following certain procedures that would involve little or no money to implement. For example, change passwords frequently, regulate use and storage of all systems manuals, do not let programmers operate the computer, do not let operators program, do not leave printouts containing passwords in trash baskets, and notify all users that unauthorized use of the system will result in specific penalties.

2. *Physical Security.*   Although few abuses involve breaches of physical security, cases of vandalism and sabotage often involve lax physical security. Computer room doors should be kept locked, allow only authorized personnel in the computer room, and have adequate fire protection systems and alarms, plus coded locks and/or identifying badges for larger installations.

3. *Software Techniques.*   Although most computer operating systems provide account and file protection by the use of passwords and read-write protection, usually more sophisticated techniques can be added. Extra precautions can be taken, such as data encryption, scrambling of telecommunications, programmed time locks on accounts and files, and fragmenting data and programs so they cannot be accessed through a single account.

4. *Audit Systems.* Even though a certain amount of auditing of system activity is provided by many operating systems (such as who, where, when, and for how long someone logs into the system), often more detail is required (such as what files were accessed, how many times the password was incorrectly entered, what input-output equipment was used, and how many files were added or deleted or updated). Also, it is sometimes desirable to have all audit and security procedures carried out by a separate computer that is remote from the system being protected. These types of precautions could cost almost as much as the system being protected.

As specially trained "Tiger" teams have clearly demonstrated by breaking the security on some of the most "secure" computer systems in the country in just minutes, no system is infallible. So, in the long run, education and high professional standards are the best deterrents to future computer crime.

SOCIAL IMPLICATIONS

Because we have covered such a wide variety of applications in this chapter, we now concentrate primarily on highlighting some of the major advantages and disadvantages of computers in government and law.

Pro Arguments

The major reasons for continued, or perhaps expanded, use of computers at all levels of government are that better, more responsive services would result for the public. This would be in the form of better planning, especially at the city and county government levels; more efficient administration of funds, especially in social welfare programs, resulting in less waste; and lower costs for maintaining government records by using centralized files to reduce or eliminate redundant records. In law enforcement, it is claimed that the rapid exchange of data through computer networks not only increases the rate of arrest, but presents a strong deterrent against crime. In the courts, computers are speeding up the judicial process by reducing backlogs on congested court calendars and by eliminating and streamlining the volumes of legal paperwork. In legal research, computers are providing valuable assistance to attorneys by locating important precedents quickly and in automating standardized legal instruments such as wills, divorces, and contracts.

Con Arguments

Two major complaints against the use of computers by government is that an excessive amount of information is being collected and that computers contribute to the wholesale collection of unnecessary data because it can be so easily stored and retrieved. Closely related to these is the fact that government makes inefficient use of the computers it has and that expanded use of computers will lead to more waste—at the taxpayers' expense. Furthermore, if the government wants to improve data collection and eliminate duplicated data, it might move toward a Standard Universal Indentifier (SUI) that would uniquely identify each individual from birth to death—just like methods used in some totalitarian governments. Another problem of civil liberties deals with the security and privacy of files stored in massive, centralized data banks. Many people feel they are susceptible to abuse and misuse when stored in this fashion. The major complaint about computers in legal research is that inequitable economic barriers prevent average attorneys from using this information, which places them at a disadvantage in the courtroom. The use of computers by politicians to market themselves at election time may also constitute a misuse, or even a misrepresentation, of information. Finally, the use of computers by law enforcement and domestic intelligence agencies may violate some constitutional rights if the information stored and used is inaccurate, incomplete, or used for purposes other than what was originally intended.

HARDWARE

Because most governments have medium- or large-size computers, they have not really been affected by the microcomputer revolution. Also, because so much of the data processing in government uses very large amounts of information, the use of small computers is not very practical. However, some county and city governments are using small microcomputers in individual departments for dedicated special tasks and experimental research like economic planning, resource and energy studies, and the monitoring of the environment (see Fig. 16.5).

Most applications, however, require at least a medium-size computer with a large amount of disk storage, high speed printers, and related output devices. And when governments move to timesharing and online terminals, it is almost necessary to move to a large-scale system.

Large or very large systems are the basis for most government systems, especially the data-bank variety. There is usually a great demand for business-type processing, with large amounts of input and output. Consequently, massive amounts of disk and tape storage are required, with multiple printers and maybe even computer output microfilm for the high-speed production of documents and reports. Also, because county, state, and federal agencies cover such large geographic areas, telecommunications equipment, numerous online terminals and networks are essential for the coordination of activities.

A LOOK TOWARD THE FUTURE

Despite some criticism about under-utilization of existing systems, this is perhaps due to some early misconceptions about data processing capabilities. There will be continued expansion of computers and computer use in government; however, it

Figure 16-5 A local minicomputer-based system that can tie in with larger government systems. (Courtesy of Honeywell Information Systems, Inc.)

will be mainly characterized by very efficient design and uses modeled after success-ful systems in business. There will be sophisticated uses of advanced database management systems, satellite communications for networks, and electronic mail, maybe even electronic voting from home. In the area of law enforcement, rapid apprehension will not be due to better communications alone, but also to systems that will be able to model and predict likely areas of crime before it occurs. There will also be studies so that the causes and "cures" of crime will be better understood, resulting in prevention of crime and, we hope, a much lower crime rate. The judi-ciary, especially at the level of the Supreme Court, will be resolving many cases regarding computers, such as the control and regulation of information services (net-works, electronic mail), patents, copyrights, and the merging of communications technology (television, printing, cable television). From these decisions the Congress will evolve a body of statutes to regulate and control this rapidly developing field. Finally, there will be more public participation in voting on policy issues via in-home computer response systems—perhaps a truly participatory democracy will evolve.

We hope this book has provided you with enough information so that you will want to engage actively in the shaping of our future.

STUDY AND REVIEW

1. Explain, by giving an example, the relationship between common data banks, horizontal integration, and vertical integration. What are some of the major advantages of these techniques?

2. Describe some of the ways in which computers can be used in elections and campaigns. Do you see any advantages or disadvantages to these applications?

3. Explain how computers are being used in the courts and by attorneys. What do you think are some of the benefits or problems with these uses?

4. Briefly explain four different types of computer crimes—give specific examples of each and how they were probably committed.

5. Why are computer crimes so difficult to detect? What are some of the possible ways in which computer crime can be prevented?

6. What do you think will be the long-term effects of microcomputers on government?

17

POLICY, PEOPLE, AND EMPLOYMENT

PERSPECTIVE

Throughout every chapter we have emphasized the importance of humans in the design, implementation, and use of computer technology. We also have tried to be cautious in our predictions about future social implications. The quotation that follows captures the spirit not only of this chapter but of the entire book.

> *The ultimate criterion for how computers should be used is subjective and I'm not sure that the technologist sufficiently appreicates this. Humans have always been tool builders and are not likely to stop. We will have our computers, but our subjective sense of what is right, beautiful, and consistent with a just and sustainable society, and what contributes most to human fulfillment, ought to dictate our use of these exotic tools with their enormous potential. Productivity in human terms should prevail over productivity in machine terms.*
> *(Sheridan, 1980)*

Now that we have traveled this far together, we diverge somewhat in the format of this last chapter. We will review and focus upon some previously mentioned topics, and introduce some new perspectives on the trends and recurring themes that have been discussed. The field of computers and related technologies is changing so rapidly that it is very difficult to resist speculation about the future. So, in these concluding pages, we will venture into the unknown and, in addition to discussing current trends, say a few words about some possible future trends in policy, people, and employment. Before exploring these topics, however, we will review some developments in computer systems that will, without doubt, affect policy, people, and employment.

COMPUTER SYSTEMS

In less than two decades, we have witnessed everything from multimillion dollar "maxi" computers to computers on a thin silicon chip costing less than $100. In fact, it is not uncommon to hear that a $2,000 microcomputer system today can do what a $100,000 computer system did just 10 or 12 years ago—but even faster and more efficiently! With this type of rapid advancement it will be helpful to summarize briefly some of the present accomplishments before going on to some of the likely systems developments in the future.

Current Trends

The major trend during the last several years has been to put the user in a closer relation to the computer. This has been accomplished mainly through the shift from batch to interactive time-sharing systems. Not only is programming being conducted in this way, but even data entry is moving away from the traditional keypunch techniques toward faster and quieter methods, such as key-to-tape and key-to-disk. These interactive methods save time, allow entry from many different geographic locations, save valuable paper resources, and result in quieter working environments. And with distributed processing and network telecommunications, different makes, models, and sizes of computers, from maxi to micro, can be interconnected to provide the most efficient and economic use of hardware and software. Also, the microcomputer systems are playing a larger role in business data processing and in education. Consequently, the small systems software is fast becoming a high-demand area. Finally, the advances in high-level programming languages and database management systems are making it easier and easier for humans to use and communicate with the computer. All of these factors indicate that the user, the human part of the system, is playing a larger role in influencing software and hardware developments.

Future Trends

There will be a transition from interactive to reactive systems (see Chapter 5) that will be just as significant as the change from batch to interactive processing. Whereas interactive computing in the time-sharing mode brought the user in closer communication with the computer, it did not necessarily allow the user to fully use computing power because the computer's capabilities were divided among many users. But with a powerful microcomputer that has large, high-speed, high-density memory dedicated to one user, users for the first time will experience and perhaps comprehend the magnitude of computing power in a reactive system. This means that advanced sophisticated uses of the computer will be possible, opening up entirely new horizons for engineering, design, business, and education.

Although networks will continue to play a major role in delivering computing services on a global scale, the main advancement will be intelligent networks. These are networks in which users can obtain information from many different databases by merely entering a simple request, such as "How many newspapers in Europe carried stories on pollution yesterday?" Also, intelligent networks grow and learn by allowing the user to enter certain types of information, such as responses to surveys and polls, or memos and comments that might be of interest to other users of the system.

Finally, with reactive computing and intelligent networks, advancements in artificial intelligence research will be more frequent and of a greater magnitude. These advancements, mainly in the area of software, will quickly filter down to major applications areas, such as business, engineering, education, science, government, and the home. Software will permit even more flexibility in modes of communicating, thus bringing the computer within the reach of the masses (similar to the telephone and television of today) because of the low cost and ease of use. The overall thrust of these future trends in computer systems will be to democratize the computer at the international, national, state, and individual levels. However, most important are the questions that these trends raise: Television has never lived up to its promise as an educational medium; will computers fail us too? will educators prepare children and adults to deal with this rapid change, or will there be continued alienation, confusion, and frustration? Who will give this computer revolution its direction? Will you be a leader or a follower?

POLICY

The changes in computer systems discussed in the previous section have an effect on the structure, operation, and policies of organizations. The effects are not always clear or far reaching, and they generally take place very slowly in relation to the rapid changes in technology. However, it is important to be aware of the types of policy changes that are taking place and that are likely to occur in the future. For organizations, such as large corporations and governments, exercise a great influence on our lives, both economically and politically. And when significant structural changes take place within these organizations, we can be sure our lives will be affected in one way or another.

Current Trends

With a few exceptions, the last hundred years has essentially been characterized by a centralization of power, both in corporate and government organizations. In industry there has been a constant movement toward mass production, higher efficiency, and greater productivity. In government, more services, such as health care and transportation, are being controlled and/or subsidized. These trends tend to centralize decision making and control. And, although this centralization was taking place long before the computer was introduced, batch processing and even the large time-sharing systems complemented, supported, and encouraged this type of structure. The need for large data banks, both in government and private enterprise, is another manifestation of the centralization of power. However, with the rise of mini- and microcomputers, in combination with distributed processing, there is now a possibility of decentralizing some of the power and decision-making activity. But the decision to do so is largely limited by economic factors, such as already having a large capital investment in centralized data processing equipment. The important point is: there is now at least an alternative available that will permit decentralization, and many private firms are developing policies that are moving them in this direction. It must be pointed out, however, that the choice is not really between centralization and decentralization, but rather between degrees of centralizing or decentralizing authority and control. Because there are major advantages for both centralization (economies of large-scale operations facilitate systems integration) and decentralization (fewer problems when a computer goes down, better response to user needs), the decision as to which direction to go is not easy.

Future Trends

Despite the initial difficulty in deciding whether to decentralize or not, there will be a strong trend toward decentralized systems because of the increased productivity and substantial lower costs of reactive systems and the additional services offered by intelligent networks. Because the average life expectancy for most data processing systems is about seven years, most centralized systems will be replaced with some form of distributed processing when new equipment is purchased and old equipment is phased out. And, because of the lower cost and higher productivity of manufacturing resulting from sophisticated use of microprocessor controlled equipment, there will be a trend toward custom-made products. Accompanying these hardware trends will be changes in management style, with greater attention being placed on the employee. Several studies on decreasing productivity in the United States reported that management is the main cause—not production workers on assembly lines. Perhaps we will see more of a Japanese approach toward management in the near future, with decisions being made with the consent and cooperation of the managed.

There will also be a significant rise in human engineering: the application of science to the improvement of human interaction with an environment. The environment may range from tools to office lighting, and from clean air to easy-to-use ("friendly") computer systems and equipment. As human engineering gains more knowledge of human dynamics, there will be a noticeable qualitative change toward better working and living conditions. Organizations have long known that their success depends on public acceptance, and with the understanding provided by human engineering they will be better prepared to design policies that will serve their employees and their customers. However, policies must not only be concerned with health and safety, but also with the question of the extent of computer use—how many tasks computers *should* do. Computers no longer merely perform clerical and assembly-type tasks, they also are playing a larger role in supervising and decision making. The crucial role in management and employee relations will be in determining the relationship between the employee and the computer. Although computers are capable of doing many complex activities, it is also possible that many humans could become just button pushers. Finally, on a much larger scale, careful consideration must be given to the policies relating to communications, especially the emerging technologies like television and computer networks. If the new developments in global communications are to truly serve the public interest, specifically designed policies must be implemented in order to protect our freedom and our modes of communication.

PEOPLE

One way in which computer systems, and the policies adopted by organizations that use computer systems, influence individuals is through employment patterns. As we will see in the next section (employment), the growing use of computers is creating a large number of job opportunities for different levels of work skills. Some of the more technical and higher paying positions will be found in software development/implementation and in telecommunications network design/implementation. Though there will be some job displacement because of automation, the demand for support personnel will continue to grow throughout the 1980s, particularly in the service and information areas. However, for those of you who are not clear as to what area within data processing you would like to enter, a strong recommendation would be to pursue your own interests, whatever they might be. If you are interested in business, economics, history, art, physics, architecture, music, or any other field, major in your special area of interest and minor in computer science or, at least, take two or three courses in computer science. For, no matter what field you choose, you can be sure there will be opportunities to use computers as a tool in your work. Even if you do not use the computer immediately in your work, your familiarity with computers and programming will be an asset wherever you go.

We now look at some of the ways in which people and computers affect each other (see Fig. 17.1).

Current Trends

For the most part, our population is totally overwhelmed, confused, and frustrated by the computer and its numerous uses. This results in feelings of powerlessness and alienation that lead to complete passivity. That is, most people do not un-

Figure 17-1 The focus of the '80s: Behind every computer system humans stand out as the most important factors. (Photograph courtesy of Honeywell Information Systems, Inc.)

derstand computers, and feel it would be too difficult to learn. So they cannot participate or give any direction to the computer revolution; they remain mere spectators, often fearful of what may occur in the future. Those of you who were born after 1950 have grown up in the computer age and may not feel this alienation that is characteristic of many people who were born earlier and who have had little or no exposure to computers. Fortunately, this trend is now changing as the computer receives higher visibility in the mass media, throughout all stages of education, and in many fields of employment. This is bringing about greater computer literacy, which is a necessary prerequisite if the computer is to be understood and used wisely. Also, the rapid growth of the personal computer market is allowing more people to have direct experience with "friendly" computers, rather than just through computerized bills and banking statements. Furthermore, privacy legislation, consumer ombudsman systems, and other protective and educational services are restoring confidence that individuals can exercise some control over the powerful computer. All of these factors are contributing to a demystification of the computer, thus permitting the computer for the first time to be understood, appreciated, and seen as a powerful tool that can respond to public concern.

Future Trends

Realizing that the crucial groundwork for understanding the computer has already been laid, the future should be very exciting and rewarding. The human factor, once it is understood and incorporated into the design and use of new systems, will not be forgotten or misplaced. People will become more active participants in the computer revolution when they become informed. They will be able to give direction, ask questions, receive answers, and no longer feel alienated and powerless. Through modes of communication, such as teleconferencing, electronic polls, and electronic voting, people will be able to express their views from the privacy and comfort of their homes. Government decision making will become responsive to human needs, and the possibility of a truly participatory democracy may come true. But all of this depends on two major assumptions: that the government and private organizations will open up and continue to support channels of communication so the public can express their views, and that the public will have knowledge and understanding of computers—for an uninformed participatory democracy actually would not be very different from mob rule or anarchy. It is also quite possible that individuals will gain greater insight into themselves through the use of reactive personal computers that can explore, at close to the speed of light, ideas and questions from many different perspectives. Whatever the long-range effects may be, it is very likely that people, both individually and collectively, will be playing a much larger role in shaping their destinies than in the past. However, people are very easily led. The question remains, then, "Who will lead?" Will it be understanding or fear, an enlightened public or an extremely powerful elite?

> *The computer age is here. Just as astronauts in orbit cannot return to planet earth without the computer, we have already reached the point of no return. The computer dominates major parts of our lives and will inevitably grow in its impact. . . .*
>
> *We are in urgent need of public discussion, debate, and understanding of the new technology. Let us not permit anyone to tell us that any socially relevant aspect of the computer is too complicated for us to understand. Let us revel in our ignorance, demand explanations of the unclear, and delight in our acquired ability to handle this machine and make it work for us.* (Wessel, 1974)

EMPLOYMENT

As all of the previous chapters have indicated, there have been remarkable advances in computer technology during the last 35 years. In this section we will discuss the effects of this technology on employment trends. There must be precautionary notes, however.

First, this is the most difficult topic discussed thus far. The difficulty flows from the large number of variables involved and the technicalities of interrelated issues—political, economic, social, and philosophic. This difficulty is reflected in the lack of agreement among "experts" about future employment/unemployment possibilities.

Some see the future with close to full employment while others see unemployment close to 40 or 50 percent by the end of this decade.

Second, it is impossible to isolate completely the impact of the computer, for it is so closely wedded to the larger issue of technological change and automation that it is impossible to attribute significant trends to the computer alone.

Third, just as it is impossible to separate the computer from technology, it would not be possible to discuss work without simultaneously discussing leisure. And, to fully grasp the complexity of the issues relating to work and leisure, we must also consider the values we attach to work and leisure. So we will really be looking at the interaction between values, technology, work, and leisure.

Fourth, so as not to be guilty of prophesying or gazing into a crystal ball, we must be content to talk about pictures or scenarios of what might occur. We will be considering trends as opposed to specific dates, figures, and accurate patterns of employment within different segments of our economy over short and long periods of time.

Finally, although we will be dealing with trends that may indicate general directions, we must keep in mind the volatile nature of the system under discussion. That is, employment trends can change radically in either direction due to scientific accomplishments (the colonization of space), political decisions (a new war), economic upheavals (a stockmarket crash), or the cumulative effect of several less monumental changes in these areas—all of which are unpredictable. So, with these precautions clearly before us, let us examine some of the major directions of the past and present together with some of the possible directions for the future.

Historical Overview

To understand better the present situation regarding employment trends, it is helpful to look first at some historical antecedents. There have been radical changes in employment trends during the last 100 years, but much of this is overlooked when we consider what percent of the labor force is unemployed (called *aggregate unemployment*). Generally speaking, it would be accurate to say, with the exception of the depression era, that unemployment in the United States has been about 3 to 6 percent of the available work force. However, it is more accurate to discuss *structural unemployment*—the measure of unemployment for segments of the work force, such as agriculture, women, or minorities.

But even looking at these structural parts can be misleading if we want an accurate measure of how many individuals are unemployed. Labor Department figures are based on people who are collecting unemployment benefits or who have applied for them. Consequently, they do not reflect those who are looking for their first job (mainly the young), the elderly who wish to work but who are squeezed out of the job market, women returning to the job market, and those who, out of despair, have given up looking for work. Researchers who attempt to account for these missing figures and who present a "real" unemployment figure, usually estimate that from 25 to 35 percent of the potential U.S. work force are unemployed. Finally, if we consider minority unemployment rates, particularly among Blacks, Chicanos, and Puerto Ricans, we would find this segment experiencing as high as 40 percent unemployment.

For purposes of our discussion, we will review four major sectors of our labor force: agriculture, industry, services, and information. Traditionally, only the first three sectors are measured. But, considering the current role of the information sector and its likely impact in the future, it is valuable to consider this segment separately because it already has a significant effect on the Gross National Product (GNP)—the total value of a nation's annual output of goods and services. Sometimes referred to as the "knowledge industries," the information sector is represented by those industries that sell information goods (computers and associated hardware) and services (programming, planning, consulting, data processing, and the like). It includes clerical and managerial tasks within an organization, such as personnel, research and development, planning, marketing, and other information activities that are generated and consumed internally.

In the following discussion, the period 1800-1980 has been separated into three periods to reflect significant changes in the interaction of the four segments (see Fig. 17.2).

1800-1920: Industrialization During this period the United States moved from almost an entirely agrarian economy, with approximately 85 percent employed in agriculture, 10 percent in industrial production, and 5 percent in services and in-

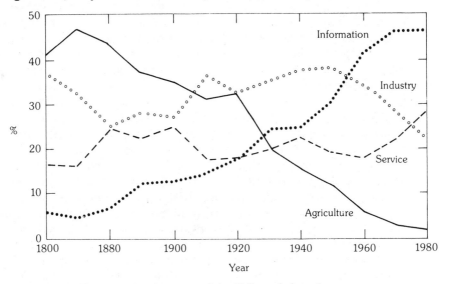

Figure 17-2 Four-sector aggregation of the U.S. work force by percent, 1860-1980, using median estimates of information workers

formation activities, into an industrial economy. By 1920, some 30 percent were employed in agriculture, an equal percentage in industry, and the remaining 40 percent in services and information. This dramatic shift evolved over 120 years and can be attributed mainly to the mechanization of farming and production, plus population shifts from rural to large metropolitan areas where factories centralize around the railroad yards. The growth of the service and knowledge segments relates to the need for clerical support, the design of new products, research, and government services for an increasing population. Note that these shifts in employment took place over a 120-year span; the remaining changes that we will discuss occurred within just 50 years.

1920-1950: Automation   In these 30 years, the most dramatic change occurred within agriculture, which shifted from employing 30 percent to about 10 percent. While the services sector remained about the same, 20 percent, there were increases in the industrial sector (30 to 40 percent) and in the information area (20 to 30 percent). Perhaps the real impact of these changes was best illustrated by remarkable increases in productivity. For example, from 1900 to 1920 productivity remained nearly the same, but from 1920 to 1950 productivity doubled in all segments of the labor force. Although there were several contributing factors to productivity, such as education, better working conditions, and changing social and political attitudes, there is no doubt that highly automated industrial processes played a crucial role in bringing about this shift in our labor force.

1950-1970: Cybernation   Considering that this is the shortest time span we have examined thus far, the changes were perhaps most revolutionary. Whereas employment in the services remained at about the same level (20 percent), and there were declines in industry (from 40 to 25 percent) and agriculture (10 to 5 percent), the most dramatic shift occurred in the information employment: an increase from 30 to 50 percent. The fact that just 30 percent of our work force can supply all the food, clothing, and product needs of our society indicates incredible increases in productivity. The key to these changes is **cybernation**—the use of computer equipment to perform routine and complex logical and decision-making tasks rapidly, often improving upon or replacing the human capacities that used to do the same jobs. For example, the Bureau of the Census required only 50 statisticians in 1960 to do the work it took 4,100 to do in 1950; increases in the Bell system volume of phone calls during this same 10-year period were more than 50 percent, yet the work force increased only 10 percent. Even more dramatic changes occurred during the period 1950-1970 in banking, insurance and the airlines industry. Finally, the U.S. is no longer in an industrial era; we are *post-industrial*. The largest portion of our work force (70 percent) is now involved in information and services, and more than two-thirds of our GNP come from these two sectors. In fact, it is correct to say that we are in an *information age*, since a large portion of both the work force and the GNP will be due to the information sector in the years to come.

Current Trends

We hope this brief overview of employment trends has shed some light on our current situation. Now, by taking a closer look at the 1970s and early 1980s, we may be in a better position to understand what may be the trends of the late 1980s and 1990s.

Perhaps one of the most significant changes during this current period is apparent in a shift in values. The period from 1800 to 1970 can be characterized as one of the Protestant or Puritan work ethic—the belief that work is good in itself and that idleness is bad, that what we do not earn through our own labor is not deserved. Since generations of Americans have been raised in accordance with this ethic, any great changes in this attitude will be slow and almost imperceptible. Significant factors are bringing about a transition, however. These include increasing unemployment held in check only by increasing inflation, larger numbers of people on welfare, college graduates being unemployed or underemployed, people retiring at earlier ages, and a steady decrease in the number of hours in the average work week (see fig. 17.3). People are beginning to place more value on leisure time and self-improvement, finding identities and purposes separate from their work. There is also an evolving conservation ethic for our natural resources. People in the 1970s were the first generation to feel the impact and understand what it means to have finite resources; it was a major step in realizing that the future does not always resemble the past.

The absence of high unemployment during the 1970s led many to believe that cybernation would never cause large-scale unemployment. This position, however, is being highly contested. Much of the current literature suggests that completely automated industrial processes are not very likely, but there will still be widespread unemployment, especially when industrial processes feel the total impact of the microprocessor. A trend of steady employment cannot continue indefinitely. Although cybernation has created many new jobs, these tend to require higher levels of education and are mainly managerial positions.

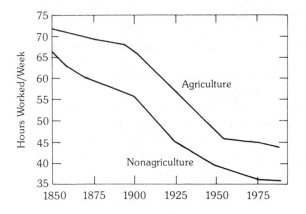

Figure 17-3 Length of work week in agriculture and in non-agricultural industries

At this point it is not uncommon for many people to start feeling resentment toward the computer, perhaps because of the fear of being displaced. This can lead to negative attitudes, but we must keep in mind that computers do not choose how they will be used: people do. As we have seen, technological advance has brought with it greater productivity of goods and services. And greater productivity leads to greater profits and higher wages. As wages increase, demand increases and prices go up—the classical wage-price spiral. However, as population growth rates slow and resources become more scarce, demand decreases. We now have the capacity to supply the industrial demand; therefore, many changes of the 1970s and early 1980s are qualitative. Cybernation is eliminating tedious, laborious, time-consuming tasks: more people are employed in service-type occupations; resources are being conserved; pollution is decreasing—the quality of life is improving in some respects. The real question for the future, particularly the remainder of the 1980s, is: With the aid of the computer, what type of future do we wish to create?

Future Trends

> The proposed reindustrialization of an economy dominated by services is an exercise in futility. Americans must unshackle themselves from the notion, dating back to Adam Smith, that goods alone constitute wealth whereas services are nonproductive and ephemeral. At the same time, they should act on Smith's understanding that the wealth of a nation depends on the skill, dexterity and knowledge of its people.   (Ginzberg and Vojta, 1981)

Anytime one begins to speculate about the future, even the very next six or twelve months, most people are somewhat skeptical of the predictions. Often we associate this type of activity with science fiction and, therefore, are not inclined to take such opinions seriously. However, in the past fifteen years or so, forecasting techniques have become more refined and more accurate. A whole new discipline called *futures research* has developed, incorporating both scientific (statistics, computer science, engineering) and social science (economics, sociology, history, psychology) forecasting methods. There are obvious difficulties with any attempt to "look" into the future and, by first considering three major problems, we will be in a better position to understand their role.

The first problem: complexity. When we attempt to isolate one aspect of society such as employment, we are confronted with the interrelatedness and dependence of this part with all other parts. What further compounds this problem is that events outside a society, on a global scale, have measurable effects on other nations. For example, we have seen that increases in oil prices or a severing of trade relations with a country can deeply affect many other countries: we are truly a global community.

The second problem: values. The techniques of measuring technological change and developments are far more accurate and reliable than forecasting changes in values. Yet values determine, both individually and collectively, what goals a society will choose to pursue. If government, via representative collective values, chose to pursue full employment regardless of inflation or cost to the tax-payer, then the results would be quite different from those of a low inflation rate policy. On an individual level, if the majority of people chose not to use automobiles as a major mode of transportation, then many segments of the economy would be affected by this choice.

The final problem: expectations. Many individuals expect a clear and accurate picture of the future, and when this does not happen (as is usually the case), they are disappointed and lose confidence in all predictions. But, as Herman Kahn and Anthony Wiener point out in their book, *The Year 2000,* forecasting offers several advantages, particularly when the scenario method is used. Here are some of the main advantages:

- Scenarios serve to call attention to the full range of future possibilities and help to overcome "carry-over" thinking, such as the idea that the future always resembles the past.

- They force the person concerned about the future to look at details and at the dynamics which might otherwise go unnoticed.

- They help to clarify the interaction of psychological, social, economic, political, cultural, and military factors.

- Even if unrealistic, they stimulate discussion and elicit evidence as to why they are unrealistic.

Generally speaking, short-term forecasts (one to ten years), particularly those dealing with technological developments, tend to overestimate significant changes, whereas long-term forecasts (greater than ten years) tend to underestimate major changes. This disparity is being diminished as techniques are improved, but it does explain why many people discredit predictions, yet are surprised by the future.

Now that you have been introduced to employment trends, the changes of the seventies and early eighties, and the difficulties of forecasting, you can appreciate the complexity of predictions about the future. Nevertheless, we will attempt to synthesize from all the disparate views about the future a core of some "probable certainties." We can be assured that productivity, with the aid of cybernation, will continue to increase gradually, while the average work week will continue to decline so that by the early 1990s it will probably be about 30 hours/week. A larger per-centage of the workforce will be employed in the service and information sectors, approximately 80 to 85 percent by the early nineties. There will be many job op-portunities, particularly in technical and computer-related fields; but, ironically, predictions of the employment rate are very uncertain. Obviously the government, through its policies, will exercise a large influence on employment. Fortunately, some workable plans of employment change have already been implemented in some countries (notably France and Japan) that allow private enterprise to have some significant impact on the situation. Realizing that people need continued education in an advancing technological age, that job markets are shifting, and that people tend to resist or resent government-created jobs, an alternative approach is developing. This new approach is similar to government tax breaks to individuals and organizations who invest money to conserve energy, develop solar power, or reduce pollution. The government may offer incentives in the form of tax reductions or exemptions on money used for activities such as work sabbaticals for retraining, on-the-job education, social service leaves, the loaning of employees to community services, improvements of working conditions to increase job satisfaction, and similar projects.

However, the ultimate question of the eighties and nineties in relation to work and unemployment is that of values and social trends. No doubt, by the nineties technology will have advanced far enough that it will not be necessary for more than 20 or 30 percent to work, as we now understand work. Perhaps there will be a gradual redefining of work so that by this time leisure will be one of our main activities. But the value we place on work will probably be the main determinant. These final remarks indicate the dilemma we face:

> The fear of joblessness and the shame attached to it die slowly in our society. (Parkman, 1972)

> Man thrives not on mindless pleasure, but on challenge. Thus, although full employment is no longer needed from a production standpoint, full participation is essential from a social standpoint. (Harman, 1976)

CONCLUSION

In our discussions throughout this book we have used the "information age," the "microcomputer revolution," and other such phrases in an attempt to describe the direction of major factors that are influencing and shaping the computer revolution and our lives. We would like the coming years to be known as the "Human Era" in computing—an era in which human values and needs are not only understood, but also respected and implemented in all uses of computers and technology. We will experience an age in which emphasis will be placed not on people for computer systems, but on computer systems for people—an age in which technological growth is not pursued for growth's sake but for significant improvements in the human condition. And, although computer systems, policy, people, and employment all interact in complex ways, it will be the individual who will then have the most important role. This is not to say that in previous years the human dimension was neglected or ignored, but only that now we have the knowledge and hardware/software to meet human needs in an economic and efficient way.

We admit that our views of the future tend to be optimistic, but our optimism is not based on blind faith. We are well aware of alternative views and possible problems that might make the future less pleasant and exciting than we have depicted it. However, throughout this book we have considered the pros and cons of most of the major applications of computers and we believe our optimism is reasonable. We have assumed that individuals are now, or are soon to be, better informed about computers than in the past, and that the public will exercise more influence over the use and design of computer systems. Upon these and similar assumptions we have based our optimism. If, however, any of our assumptions prove to be wrong, our predictions about the future will probably be incorrect. But our task was not to predict the future, but only to provide you with a basic understanding of computers, their applications, and their implications. The real work lies ahead in what you do with this information to help shape the future yourselves. We wish you success as you make the transition from the present into the future world of humans and computers. We hope that partnership will be friendly and enjoyable.

STUDY AND REVIEW

1. What do you believe to be the current trends in computer systems? Do your views differ in any way from the trends mentioned in this chapter?

2. Do you believe that individuals have much influence over the design and use of computer systems? Explain in what ways they do have influence, and in what ways they do not.

3. In what ways do computer systems (both large and small) affect corporate policy and organization? Do you think Japanese management style could be adopted in American business?

4. What do you think will be the computer's effect on employment trends by the end of this decade? Why is this such a difficult question?

5. What do you think are the most important technological developments in the past year or two? In what ways do you expect these developments to affect our lives?

A

BASIC Programming

Basic is a high-level, symbolic programming language specifically designed for people who have no prior programming experience. It is one of the easiest of all programming languages to learn. The letters B-A-S-I-C are an acronym for *Beginners All-purpose Symbolic Instruction Code*. The language was developed as an instructional language at Dartmouth College in 1963. While there are no standardized versions of the language, such as with FORTRAN and COBOL, there will probably be a standardized version of the language in the future. BASIC is a very popular language that is probably receiving its widest usage by those purchasing microcomputer systems for use in small businesses and for home uses.

BASIC is considered an "interactive" programming language, because a student can write and enter a program while sitting at the terminal of an interactive computer. Whereas most other programming languages must be written and prepared for input in some form, such as punch cards, and then fed into a computer as a complete program, BASIC instructions can be entered one-at-a-time, and the computer can check each instruction for error, which enables correction before entering the next instruction. Once a program is completely entered, it can be run by the computer or stored in auxiliary storage for use in the future.

As with the other language appendices, this is not intended to be an extensive presentation of the BASIC programming language. Instead, the elementary features of this interactive language are described, which should enable you to write some programs to solve some simple problems.

BASIC ALPHABET

The BASIC alphabet, or legal characters/symbols used in this language, consists of an extended alphabet of the 26 capital letters plus @, #, and $, the ten digits 0, 1, 2, 3, 4, 5, 6, 7, 8, 9, and the following 22 special characters:

+	plus	<	less than
−	minus	<=	less than or equal to
*	asterisk	=	equal to
/	slash	>	greater than or equal to
↑	up arrow	>=	greater than
(	left parenthesis	#	not equal to
)	right parenthesis	!	exclamation mark
'	single quote	&	ampersand
''	double quote	,	comma
.	period	;	semicolon
:	colon		blank

LANGUAGE RULES

BASIC has few rules for coding and a small set of computer instructions. The actual rules that govern the writing of a BASIC program are not as complex as those of COBOL or FORTRAN. In English, the rules of grammar are quite familiar to us: characters form words, words form sentences, sentences form paragraphs, and so on. A sentence in the English language is composed of three elements; a subject, a verb, and an object. In BASIC, the equivalent of a sentence is a *statement,* and it has three parts. The line number, which comes first in the sentence, serves as the subject. Each line of a BASIC program must have a line number, and each successive line requires a number higher than the preceding line, thus 1 to 9999 inclusive. Instructions such as READ, PRINT, LET, GO TO, are the action words of a BASIC statement and are equivalent to a verb in a sentence. The last part of the BASIC statement is the object. This is the target of the action word. The action word, READ, PRINT, GO TO, in an instruction tells the computer what to do, the object tells the computer what to do it with. The structure of a BASIC statement as presented here is summarized as follows:

40	LET	B=C*D
line number	BASIC instruction	(object)
(subject)	(verb)	

BASIC VALUES AND VARIABLE NAMES

In BASIC, no distinction is made between different types of numerical values as in FORTRAN. Variables enable programmers to write programs with calculations that contain no actual numerical values. Variables, which in BASIC are constructed using single alphabetic characters, represent the various factors in a problem. Programs that contain calculations which are constructed using variables can be used to solve one type of problem many times by substituting different numerical values for the variables as the need arises. If a programs's calculations were written using exact numerical values, then to use that program to solve a similar problem with different numerical values would require a restructuring of the program.

The variables, or variable names used in a BASIC program may be designated in one of two ways: by use of a single alphabetic character, or by use of a single alphabetic character followed by a numerical digit. Often the alphabetic character chosen to represent a factor in a problem will be the first letter of the name that represents that factor in the problem. For example, if a calculation is to be expressed that calculates the area of a rectangle, (AREA = LENGTH × WIDTH) the variables chosen could be   A = L × W.   The following characters are all valid BASIC variable names:

B   B9
X   A3

The following are *not* valid variable names:

3F   A%
D10   H#

BASIC CALCULATIONS

The BASIC arithmetic operators are + − * / and ↑, which is used for exponentiation.

Arithmetic expressions may be formed in BASIC using combinations of variable names, numerical values, and arithmetic operators. Two or more variable names separated by an arithmetic operator, preceded by the action word LET, make a BASIC arithmetic expression. More complex BASIC expressions can be formed using variable names and arithmetic operators grouped together by parenthesis.

Several examples of valid BASIC expressions are:

LET A = R * H
LET D = A + B + C
LET S = P * U + T
LET E = A + B + C / D
LET F = (P * R) /(U + O)

Expressions such as

LET B = RC * H
LET M = N / − H

are not valid because, in the first example, two variable letters are joined without being separated by an arithmetic operator. In the second example, two arithmetic operators are shown together without a variable ietter or a number between them.

PRIORITY OF OPERATIONS

In arithmetic expressions in BASIC, it is possible to perform more than one calculation. In this case, the computer executes calculations in an exact order. When writing arithmetic expressions, a programmer must consider how the computer evaluates arithmetic expressions. In a BASIC expression the computer always performs operations in the following order:

1st Operations in parentheses: ( )
2nd Exponentiation: ↑
3rd Multiplications and division * /
4th Addition and subtraction +   −

For example, the expression:
A + P / R ↑ 3
are executed in this sequence:

1. R is cubed.
2. P is divided by the value determined in step 1.
3. A is added to the answer in step 2.

In a case where operations of the same priority are contained in the same expression, they are performed from left to right.

BASIC INPUT STATEMENTS

When a program contains arithmetic expressions that use variables, the computer uses the instructions input to establish the new values for the variables used in the arithmetic expression. In BASIC there are two forms of input statements: IN-PUT, and READ. When the computer encounters an INPUT statement, it accepts values for the variables that are part of the list in the INPUT statement provided by the user at a terminal. In this example:
10   INPUT A, B, C
the computer halts execution of the program and waits for the user to enter values for variables A, B, and C. Once the user has entered these values, execution of the program continues.

The second method of input is to use the READ statement. In this case, values for the variables contained in the input list are in a DATA statement that appears farther down in the program. Thus data values for the variables are contained within the program, so that program execution is not halted when the computer needs the variable values. In this example:

10   READ A, B, C

50   DATA 100, 56, 34

when the computer executes statement number 10 it then searches the rest of the program for the "DATA" statement, to establish the values for variables A, B, and C.

BASIC ARITHMETIC STATEMENTS

An arithmetic statement in BASIC consists of: the action word LET, a variable name used to represent the answer to the problem, an equal sign, and either a second variable name, or a constant, or an arithmetic expression. The equal sign in arithmetic statements is called the *replacement symbol,* and is read "is replaced by." An arithmetic statement such as A = B is read "the value of A is replaced by the value of B."

   G = 100 is an example of using a constant in an arithmetic statement. A *constant* is any number value written into a statement. Its value does not change during execution of the program, but remains constant. The preceding statement makes variable G equal to the constant 100, thus G is replaced by 100.

   The third form of arithmetic statement uses an arithmetic expression to the right of the equal sign. An *arithmetic expression* is a sequence of constants and/or variables that are separated by arithmetic operation symbols. The operation symbols specify arithmetic computations.

   As an example, T = N + B uses the arithmetic expression N + B to specify the addition of two variables. The value of variable T is replaced by, or set equal to, the sum of N and B.

   BASIC arithmetic expressions use the five operation symbols and the grouping parenthesis designated earlier and, in expressions that contain more than one operation symbol, the computer performs the operations in the priority order: grouping, exponentiation, multiplication, division, addition, and subtraction.

BASIC CONTROL STATEMENTS

During execution of a program, the computer analyzes each statement and takes the action indicated by the program. Normally statements are executed in sequential order, just as they appear in the program. However, the power of a computer lies in its ability to change the order in which it executes a program. This change is accomplished by the use of "control" statements, which may cause the computer to "branch" to another part of the program, rather than continue in sequential order. After the computer finishes executing the branch part, the program may return to the statement after the one that caused it to branch or it may continue along some other path, depending on the instructions supplied by the programmer.

GO TO Statement

The simplest control statement is the GO TO statement. This causes the computer to transfer unconditionally to another statement in the program and continue execution from that point. In the example

```
35    GO TO  100
40    STATEMENT
```

after the program executes statement 35, rather than continue to statement 40, the computer branches to statement 100 and continues executing the program from that point, omitting 40.

IF Statement

The variables in a program can be tested for certain conditions, and then, on the basis of the results, the program proceeds. This testing process enables the computer to select alternative instructions which are included in the program. Two types of "IF" statements can be used for conditional branching in BASIC. The specific type selected may depend on the application the programmer is working on.

The first type of IF statement used for decision making is shown in the following example:

```
IF  H  =  40  THEN  100
```

When the computer encounters this statement in the program it evaluates the expression $H = 40$. If the condition in the statement exists, $(H = 40)$ then the computer transfers to statement 100. If the condition in the statement does *not* exist, then the computer does *not* branch to instruction 100, but continues executing the program in exact sequential order.

Logical IF

The second form of IF statement used in BASIC is the logical IF. Logical IF enables two values to be compared, using a logical operator. The form of this statement uses the word IF, then the first value to be compared, a logical operator, the second value that is to be compared. and the word THEN, followed by the statement number of the instruction to be executed if the comparison is true. The values being compared may be variables, constants, or arithmetic expressions. The logical operators here are: = (equal), < (less than), # (not equal), <= (less than or equal), or >= (greater than or equal).

In this example:

```
40    IF  H  >=  40  THEN  100
60    Statement
```

if H is greater than 40, then the computer executes statement 100. If H is *not* greater than 40, the computer does not execute statement 100 but continues to the next statement in sequence (60).

BASIC LOOPING

Frequently, a sequence of instructions in a BASIC program must be executed more than once, often many times. To accomplish this, BASIC has a looping procedure that enables a programmer to direct the computer to execute a specific sequence of instructions a certain number of times. This looping procedure is accomplished in BASIC by using the FOR-NEXT statements. The FOR statement sets up a variable to be used as a counter (called an index), assigns a beginning value to it, and sets an upper limit to the index value. Each time this loop is executed, an increment of value is added to the index and it is tested to determine if the index value has reached the upper limit. The form of the FOR-NEXT loop is:

```
10    FOR  X  =  F  TO  L

50    NEXT  X
```

where: X = a numeric variable to be used as an index
F = the first value of the index X
L = the upper limit of the index

NEXT X   indicates the end of the loop and the point at which the computer returns to the beginning of the loop. In this example:

```
10    FOR  X  =  1  to  10
20    Statement
30    Statement
40    Statement
50    Statement
60    NEXT  X
```

the loop begins in statement 10.   The instruction FOR   indicates that the loop is to be executed 10 times.   X is the index variable that has an initial value of 1 and continues looping between the FOR and NEXT statements until the index value equals 10. This FOR-NEXT loop just described will execute each statement from 10 through 60 ten times.

BASIC OUTPUT STATEMENT

Once the computer manipulates data, the answers must be output to be useful. BASIC uses a PRINT statement to produce output. When the computer encounters a PRINT statement, it outputs the value of the variables indicated in the PRINT statement. In the example:

    10   PRINT T, R, P

the computer will output number values for the variables T, R, P.

CONTROLLING OUTPUT SPACING

When printing output, BASIC allows the programmer to control the appearance of the output by directing the output device to skip spaces, or skip lines, or advance to new lines before continuing the printout. Computers may vary in the use of symbols or methods required to control output spacing, but most computers accept the following formats for controlling spacing:

    10   PRINT A, SPA (10), B

This statement prints the values of variables A and B separated by 10 spaces. The number of spaces selected is controlled by the expression SPA followed by the number of spaces you want enclosed in parenthesis.

    10   PRINT LIN(3)

This statement causes the output device to advance the paper 3 lines before continuing to the next statement in the program.

    10   PRINT A, LIN(5), B

This statement causes the computer output device to print the value of variable A, then space down 5 lines before printing the value of variable B.

LITERAL OUTPUT FORMAT

To improve the appearance of, and better describe the meaning of a printout, the PRINT statement may contain specifications to include alphabetic, numeric, and special symbols in the output. Within a PRINT statement, any character string that a programmer wishes output is simply included in quotation marks. In the example:

50   PRINT   LIN(2),   "YOUR NET PAY IS $",   SPA(3),   P

when printing out the numerical value for variable P,   the computer spaces down 2 lines, prints the message "YOUR NET PAY IS $", spaces 3 spaces, and then prints the numerical value of variable   P.

END STATEMENT

The   END   statement, although not executed by the computer, indicates that all statements in the program have been executed. The   END   statement must be the *last* statement in a BASIC program.

BASIC PROGRAMS

This section presents and describes three BASIC programs, using most of the techniques described here.

The first BASIC program demonstrates a single-pass execution. This program accepts one set of numerical values, calculates one employee's net pay, outputs the results, and then stops (END).

```
10    INPUT     T,  R,  R1
20    LET  G  =  T  *  R
30    LET  D  =  G  *  R1
40    LET  N  =  G  -  D
50    PRINT  "THE NET PAY FOR THIS EMPLOYEE IS $",   P
60    END
```

In this program, the computer reads the values for three variables: T, R, and R1 (TIME WORKED, RATE OF PAY and RATE OF DEDUCTIONS). T (TIME) is multiplied by R (RATE) to compute G (GROSS PAY); then G is multiplied by R1 to compute D (AMOUNT OF DEDUCTIONS). Finally, D is subtracted from G to give P (NET PAY). Last, the PRINT statement outputs the dollar results of the calculation P.

The second BASIC program uses logical operators. If an employee works more than 40 hours, then P (NET PAY) is computed differently than if hours worked were less than 40.

```
10    INPUT     T,  R,  R1
20    IF  T > 40  THEN  70
30    LET  G  =  T  *  R
40    LET  D  =  G  *  R1
50    LET  P  =  G  -  D
60    GO TO 110
70    LET  E  =  (T  -  40)  *  (R  *  1.5)
80    LET  G  =  (40  *  R)  +  E
```

```
90   LET  D  =  G  *  R1
100  LET  P  =  G  -  D
110  PRINT  "THE NET PAY FOR THIS EMPLOYEE IS  $",  P
120  END
```

Once values for the variables are read in, the IF statement determines whether the employee worked more than 40 hours. If T is greater than 40, the computer branches to statement 70 and makes the pay calculation, including overtime at 1.5 times the usual rate of pay. If the employee has not worked more than 40 hours, then the IF statement does not execute statement 70, but continues on through the calculation for an employee who worked 40 hours or less. At the end of this segment there is a GO TO 110 statement that bypasses the calculation for overtime. Based on the value of T, the computer now executes one sequence of instructions or the other, but not both. This is why the two calculation segments are separated by a GO TO statement. The output segment of the program functions the same as before.

The third BASIC program includes all of the features described in the other two examples, except that the program now accommodates more than a single set of data.

```
5    FOR X  =  1 to 500
10   INPUT  T,  R,  R1
20   IF  T  >  40  THEN  70
30   LET  G  =  T  *  R
40   LET  D  =  G  *  R1
50   LET  P  =  G  -  D
60   GO  TO  110
70   LET  E  =  (T  -  40)  *  (R  *  1.5)
80   LET  G  =  (40  *  R)  +  E
90   LET  D  =  G  *  R1
100  LET  P  =  G  -  D
110  PRINT  "THE NET PAY FOR THIS EMPLOYEE IS  $",  P
120  NEXT  X
130  END
```

All features of this program remain the same as in the other two, with the exception of the added loop. The FOR statement and the NEXT statement enable the program to be executed 500 times, computing P (NET PAY) for 500 employees using 500 different sets of data. Each time the loop returns the computer to the INPUT statement a new set of values is entered and processed.

These three BASIC programs by no means represent all that can be accomplished using BASIC language; they do demonstrate the simple techniques that can be applied to a wide variety of problems.

B

PASCAL Programming

PASCAL is a relatively new language, developed by Niklaus Wirth of Switzerland during the period 1968–1970 and named after the famous French mathematician Blaise Pascal (1623–1662). Although used initially in educational environments because of its simplicity, precision, and readability in teaching good programming techniques, it is widely used now in both business and science. Currently, PASCAL has been implemented in more than 60 different computer systems — everything from the world's largest and fastest computers to the smallest and least expensive microcomputers. Many systems in use now are batch-oriented; PASCAL is equally suited for batch and interactive use with minimal changes. In fact, interactive, terminal-executed programs would essentially be identical/compatible with the programs/statements used in the batch mode. Consequently, no distinction will be made in this appendix between batch or interactive PASCAL. One important feature of this high-level language is that it clarifies the problem-solving/programming process through its block-structured design. That is, each program consists of two parts: a heading that names the program and identifies the variables that will be used, and a body (the block) that has six specific sections. For these reasons (and others that will be explained in this appendix), PASCAL has been called 'the BASIC of the future' and 'PL/1 done right.'

PASCAL ALPHABET

The PASCAL vocabulary consists of symbols divided into three groups:

letters	A,B,C...,Z. a,b,c...,z. (all of the alphabetic characters, both upper and lower-case)
digits	0, 1, 2, 3, 4, 5, 6, 7, 8, 9
special symbols	+ − * / = ( ) [ ] ; . , : : = (plus keywords, or delimiters, such as NOT, IF, THEN, DO, WHILE; all of the relational operators; and a few more special symbols)

PASCAL DATA TYPES

Every PASCAL program must identify the type of data being used by declaring the variables to be a specific type: Integer, Real, Character (CHAR), or Boolean. The integer and real types of data have the same properties as the corresponding numeric values in FORTRAN. Examples of the four data types are:

Integer	8888	−435	+4378	12	540000
Real	888.8	−43.5	+43.78	.12	540
Character	'A'	'+'	'2348'	' '	
Boolean	true or false				

Integer and real numeric values are understood to be positive unless indicated otherwise by the programmer.

PASCAL VARIABLES

The variables or variable names used in a PASCAL program may be designated by single alphabetic characters, such as A, D, Y, or Z. For easier understanding, however, variables are more often given "word" names which describe more accurately what the variable represents. Examples of PASCAL variables are: PAY, ENTRYFEE, OVERTIME, NETPAY, FEDTAX.

In PASCAL, four rules apply to the structure of variable names:

1. The variable must begin with an alphabetic character.

2. No special symbols may be used for a variable.

3. Although the length of the variable name is not limited (except by practicality or system specifications), only the first 8 characters are significant.

4. A specific variable name may be used to represent only one factor in a problem, and the data type initially specified cannot change during the program. (For example, if TIME is declared a real variable, it must remain real throughout the program.)

Variable names in PASCAL are called *identifiers*, and are discussed further in later sections.

PASCAL CALCULATIONS

The basic PASCAL arithmetic operators for addition, subtraction, multiplication, and division are: $+$ $-$ $*$ $/$. Two additional operators can be used when both operands (values) in a division problem are non-negative integers. DIV indicates the truncated integer result, and MOD indicates the remainder. For example, 14 DIV 4 is 3 and 14 MOD 4 is 2. Also, unlike other programming languages, there is no operator for exponentiation in PASCAL such as the $**$ operator in FORTRAN and BASIC. Finally, consider what occurs when operands of different data types are used in calculations. Integers and reals are very different, yet it is not uncommon to find them intermixed in calculations, particularly if a program is fairly long. Three rules generally apply:

1. When a real value is expected, PASCAL usually accepts an integer value.

2. If an integer value is expected, PASCAL does not normally accept a real value.

3. When integer values and real values are mixed in a calculation, the result is usually real.

Several examples of correct PASCAL expressions are:

```
RATE  *  HOURS
A  +  B  +  C
PRICE  *  UNITS  +  TAX
( PIECES  *  PRICE )  /  ( UNITS  +  ORDER )
GROSSPAY  DIV  HOURS
```

Expressions such as:

```
RATE PAY / HOURS
```
or
```
RATE * + HOURS
```

are not valid because in the first instance, two variables are joined without being separated by an operator and, in the second example, two operators cannot be used together without a variable or a number between them.

PRIORITY OF OPERATIONS

Using PASCAL arithmetic expressions it is possible to perform more than one calculation. The computer executes these calculations in an exact, predetermined order. So the programmer who is writing these arithmetic expressions must consider carefully how a computer evaluates such expressions. A computer always performs operations in a PASCAL arithmetic expression in the following order:

first: expressions enclosed within parentheses   (   )
second: negation   −
third: multiplication and division   *   /   DIV   MOD
fourth: addition and subtraction   +   −

When operations of the same priority are contained in the same expression, they are performed from left to right. An expression that illustrates all of these rules is:

−A + B * C / (D − F)

which will be executed in the sequence:

first: The value of F is subtracted from the value of D.
second: The value of A is negated.
third: C is multiplied by B and the resulting value is divided by the value determined in the first step.
fourth: The value obtained in the third step is added to the value determined in the second step.

PASCAL PROGRAM FORM

Every PASCAL program may be viewed as a series of statements or rules which the computer follows in a very precise manner. Each PASCAL program contains keywords called **delimiters,** such as **DO, GO TO, BEGIN** that have predetermined meanings. (Note here that all delimiters appear in **boldface** type so they are easier to identify in the examples that follow); *identifiers,* such as GROSSPAY, and HOURS; and *other symbols,* such as *, −, := . A programmer may use as many spaces or lines to separate the words and symbols in statements as desired, but each statement *must* be separated from the next by a semicolon ; . Also, comments may be used in a PASCAL program to clarify and summarize activities that are taking place. These programmer's remarks may be enclosed in braces { } ; since many computers do not have braces, a pair of parentheses and asterisks (* *) must be used instead. A comment may be placed between two symbols anywhere in the program and may be longer than one line if necessary.

The general form of a PASCAL program is:

(* A programmer's comment that indicates the purpose of the program *)
PROGRAM name (INPUT, OUTPUT);
        Definitions and declarations ;
BEGIN
        Body of program ;
END.
        (Data cards would go here if program is executed in the batch mode)

Every PASCAL program has two main parts: the heading and the block. In the outline above the heading includes a comment (which is optional and, as with all comments, is not processed by the computer), the delimiter **PROGRAM** followed by the program name (subject to the same rules as variable names) and the mode in which the computer will communicate enclosed in parentheses (INPUT usually refers to a card reader — OUTPUT normally refers to a printer*), followed by a semicolon. Included in the heading are a complete declaration of variable names and their type along with definitions of the constants **(CONST).** The block part of the program starts at the delimiter **BEGIN** and terminates at the delimiter **END** followed by a period. Included in the block part are commands/statements that indicate what type of actions are to be performed (input data, output results, assign new values to a variable). At this time, without any further explanation, we would like you to try and determine what is taking place in the following sample program. Do not be discouraged if you have difficulty since many of the symbols and commands/action words have not yet been explained. Also, to make this experiment even more challenging, we will depart from good programming style and eliminate all comments that would normally accompany this program!

```
PROGRAM EXPERIMENT1 (INPUT, OUTPUT);
CONST SALESTAX = 1.06 ;
VAR PRICE1, PRICE2, TOTAL : REAL ;
   QUANT1, QUANT2 : INTEGER;
BEGIN
READ (PRICE1, PRICE2, QUANT1, QUANT2);
TOTAL := (PRICE1*QUANT1 + PRICE2*QUANT2) * SALESTAX;
WRITELN ('TOTAL COST FOR THIS SALE IS' , TOTAL)
END.
```

PASCAL INPUT STATEMENTS

Although all the statements that occur in the body of the program are generally classified as 'action' statements in PASCAL, there are three categories that are distinct: input, output, and control. This and the following sections discuss these specific types of actions.

As mentioned previously, PASCAL is well-suited for both batch and interactive computing systems, the main difference being that the programmer-written interactive dialogue is absent from batch-oriented programs. Consequently, no distinction will be made between batch and interactive programs in the discussion that follows. The procedure begins when the computer reads an entire program, compiles it (assuming there are no errors), and then begins executing each instruction, starting from the beginning of the program.

When a program contains expressions that are constructed using variables, the computer uses an input instruction to establish the values for the variables used in the expression. In PASCAL, the statement used for input is either a READ or a

* or terminal

READLN statement. If the statement is READ, the computer reads values from a card (or cards) in the card reader, or from another input device, and determines the values for the variables that are part of the input list in the READ statement. [These values are separated by one or more blanks (spaces) between each value]. The sequence of variables in the READ list and the order of values on the input record is extremely important; however, the position and amount of space between each value is not critical. For example, if variables A, B, C, D were declared to be of the integer type, any of the arrangements of data below (where each line represents a different card/record of data) would be compatible with the statement, READ (A, B, C, D);

[1]   12 15 967   −23
or
[2]   12   15   967
                      −23

or
[3]   12
            15
            967
            −23

However the other input statement, READLN, requires careful attention to how many values appear on each card or record. When the computer encounters a READLN statement, it automatically advances to the next card/record and begins reading from the first position and, after obtaining the values for the variables in its list, the rest of the card/record is disregarded. At the next READ or READLN statement the computer begins reading the first position of the next card/record. In the previous example, both the READ and READLN statements would accept the data as presented in the first case [1] (all value on the same card/record); however, the READLN statement could not accept cases [2] and [3] in which the values appeared on more than one card/record.

The form for both the READ and READLN input statements is the same; the variables to be input are enclosed within parentheses and they are separated by commas. Note that commas do *not* appear between data items, however, nor are commas used within numbers (that is, 22,965 would appear as 22965 in PASCAL). Examples of the READ and READLN input statements are:

        READ (HOURS, RATE, A, Z1);
        READLN (HOURS, RATE, A, Z1);

PASCAL ASSIGNMENT STATEMENTS

A variable of any type may be given a value by using the *assignment operator* (:=). This takes the form of:

variable name   :=   expression

This statement is understood to mean "take the value of the expression on the right and assign it to the variable on the left." Four examples of some of the different types of assignments that can occur in PASCAL follow:

```
NET  :=  PAY
HOURS  :=  40.0
C  :=  'DOG'
AVERAGE  :=  SUM  /  N
```

By using the assignment operator, the variable on the left can acquire different values during the execution of the program. For example, the variable NETPAY could take on a different value each time a different employee's pay is calculated.

Sometimes it is desirable to name a value that is not to change throughout the operation of a program. This requires a constant **(CONST)** declaration and this must in the heading of a program before the variable **(VAR)** declarations. Examples of this are:

```
CONST    PI  =  3.1415926536 ;
CONST    NAME1  =  'JEFF  FRATES' ;  NAME2  =  'BILL  MOLDRUP' ;
         DATE  =  'MARCH 1980' ;
```

Please note the second line here in which more than one constant is defined by separating these **three** constants with semicolons, [and that the constants being defined can extend beyond one line.] Also, be sure not to confuse the assignment operator   :=   with the constant symbol   =   .

PASCAL CONTROL DELIMITERS

During execution of a program, the computer analyzes each statement and takes the action indicated. In simple programs, statements are usually executed in consecutive order just as they appear. However, the power of a computer lies in its ability to change the order in which a program is executed. This change is accomplished by the use of "control" delimiters which cause the computer to "branch" to another part of the program, rather than continue in sequential order. After the computer finishes executing the "branch," the program may return to the statement following the one that caused it to branch, or it may continue along some other sequence, depending on the instructions in the program.

In PASCAL, as in most programming languages, there are three major types of control activity : *repetition,* (looping), *choice* (when there are only two possibilities), and *selection* (when there are many possibilities). We will now examine the PASCAL control statements that carry out these activities.

Repetition: **REPEAT - UNTIL**   When a statement or group of activity statements should be repeated until some condition is satisfied, we use **REPEAT - UNTIL** delimiters. The general form is:

REPEAT
　　　　　　statement 1;
　　　　　　statement 2;
　　　　　　statement *n*
UNTIL   expression;

The statements between the delimiters are repeated until the expression at the **UNTIL** statement becomes true. Usually the expression is a comparison between two values using one of the relational operators = (equal), < (less than), > (greater than), <> (not equal), ≤ (less than or equal), and ≥ (greater than or equal). The values being compared may be variables, constants, or arithmetic expressions. A sample illustrates this:

```
.(* ADD  INTEGERS  UNTIL  TOTAL  REACHES  500  OR  MORE  *)
PROGRAM     ADDTIL (INPUT,  OUTPUT);
VAR NUMBER,  TOTAL  :  INTEGER;
BEGIN
TOTAL  :=  0;
REPEAT
        READ  (NUMBER) ;
        TOTAL  :=  TOTAL  +  NUMBER
UNTIL    TOTAL    >=  500 ;
WRITELN    ('THE ANSWER  IS',  TOTAL)
END.
```

Repetition: **WHILE - DO**   While one activity is going on, we may wish the computer to do another activity as well. Here the **WHILE - DO** delimiters are useful. This type of repetition performs its test at the beginning of a loop. It is useful when there are conditions under which the loop should not be executed. If several statements are to be repeated within the loop (as in the next example), they should be enclosed within **BEGIN** and **END** delimiters. Note that execution of the activity statements begins *only* if the expression is true. The general form for these delimiters is:

WHILE   expression   **DO**
　　　　BEGIN
　　　　statement 1;
　　　　statement *n*
　　　　END;

The **BEGIN** and **END** delimiters here are used to group together statements into a 'compound' statement, but the program does not terminate with the **END** delimiter because **END** is not followed by a period—the use of a semicolon after **END** shows that the statement is terminated, not the program.

Repetition: **FOR - TO/DOWNTO - DO**   These delimiters are similar to the FORTRAN 'DO' and the BASIC 'FOR-NEXT' statements. That is, when one can calculate in advance how many times a repetition should be performed, the **FOR** type loop is best suited. The general form for these delimiters is:

FOR variable/identifier := expression **TO** **(DOWNTO)** expression **DO**

As in the   **WHILE - DO**   loop, the statements to be repeated are enclosed within **BEGIN** and **END** delimiters. These delimiters mean that **FOR** some initial value of a variable contained in the first expression, **DO** the statements between the **BEGIN** and **END** delimiters from a higher value **DOWNTO** a lower value (or from a lower value **TO** a higher value) which is specified in the second expression. For example, the statement:

FOR I := 1 **TO** 24 **DO**

would execute all statements between the **BEGIN** and **END** delimiters that immediately followed, for all values of I from 1 up to, and including, 24. Please note that 1) the values in the expressions should be integer, 2) the value of the initial (index) variable should not be altered within the loop, and 3) the index variable is incremented/decremented by 1 each time the loop is executed.

Choice: **IF - THEN - (ELSE)** In programs where a particular action must or must not be taken, the **IF - THEN** delimiters are well suited. Or, when there are two possible actions and one must be chosen, the **IF - THEN - ELSE** can be used. The general form of these delimiters, where the **ELSE** part is optional, is:

IF expression **THEN** statement **ELSE** statement

When the expression is true, the first statement is executed; if the expression is false, the second (when the **ELSE** form is used) statement is executed. The two examples that follow illustrate these two forms:

```
        IF  TIME  >  2400  THEN  day  :=  DAY  +  1
or      IF  ANSWER  =  1  THEN
              YES  :=  YES  +  1
        ELSE  NO    :=  NO  +  1
```

Please note that there are no semicolons after these statements, which indicates that they are *not* complete and are merely performing tests or parts of a larger activity.

Selection: **CASE - OF**   When two or more alternatives are possible, use of the **CASE - OF** delimiters makes selection easier. The general form is:

> **CASE** expression **OF**
> > case-label 1 : statement 1;
> > case-label 2 : statement 2;
> > ⋮
> > case-label *n* : statement *n*
> **END**

where the case-labels are usually integer constants (never reals), the integer expression must return a value that matches one of the case-labels in the body of the statement, and the value of the expression determines which of the corresponding case-labeled statements is selected. Also, statements can have more than one case-label (separated by commas), as long as the same case-label is not used for any other statement. For example, if the integer variable DAY always returns a value between 1 and 7, corresponding to the days of the week, the following statement could be used:

> **CASE** DAY **OF**
> > 1: WRITELN ('MONDAY');
> > 2: WRITELN ('TUESDAY');
> > 3: WRITELN ('WEDNESDAY');
> > 4: WRITELN ('THURSDAY');
> > 5: WRITELN ('FRIDAY');
> > 6, 7: WRITELN ('IT''S THE WEEKEND')
> **END**

In this example note that the apostrophe must be written twice in order to use an apostrophe in the word "it's." Note, too, that there is no period after **END** because **END** merely terminates the **CASE** here, not the program.

Miscellaneous: **GOTO**   Although **GOTO** is used frequently in other programming languages, PASCAL uses this delimiter sparingly in an attempt to eliminate much of the confusion and difficulty associated with its use. A main tenet of structured programming is to eliminate or reduce unnecessary entries and exits in a program. By using the inherent power of the five other control delimiters already discussed, the PASCAL programs become easier to read, easier to debug, and their use improves the logic of both program and programmer. Up to this point it has been unnecessary to provide any statement numbers or line numbers; however, a number reference must be given in order to use the **GOTO** delimiter in PASCAL. As in other languages, the line number (label) must be declared at the beginning of the program in a **LABEL** declaration before the constant **CONST** declarations. Usually the **GOTO** delimiter is used with the **IF - THEN** delimiters, or when it is necessary to exit from a point other than the top of a **WHILE** loop or the bottom of an **UNTIL** loop. The following short program demonstrates the use of the **GOTO** delimiter to terminate the program when the value 999 is encountered:

```
(*ADD INTEGERS UNTIL DUMMY VALUE 999 IS READ*)
PROGRAM ADDTIL2 (INPUT, OUTPUT);
LABEL 10;
VAR NUMBER, TOTAL : INTEGER;
BEGIN
TOTAL := 0;
REPEAT
        READ (NUMBER);
        IF NUMBER = 999 THEN GOTO 10;
        TOTAL := TOTAL + NUMBER
UNTIL    TOTAL >= 200000;
10:    (*CONTROL COMES HERE WHEN 999 IS READ*)
WRITELN ('THE ANSWER IS', TOTAL)
END.
```

PASCAL OUTPUT STATEMENTS

Once the computer manipulates data, the answers must be output to be useful. In the previous sample programs, you may have noticed the use of the statement WRITELN to output results. In PASCAL, two statements, **WRITE** and **WRITELN**, can be used to output results. These function similarly to READ and READLN. The general form of this statement is that WRITE or WRITELN is followed by a list of expressions (variable names, constants, literals) that are separated by commas and enclosed in parentheses. Examples are:

WRITE (HOURS, PAYRATE, TAXRATE, N, Z)
WRITELN ('YOUR PAY FOR THIS WEEK IS $, NETPAY)

To clarify the difference between WRITE and WRITELN, imagine that data to be output are stored in a temporary storage area called the "print buffer." This buffer can store enough data to fill one line of output (the length of which depends upon the system being used). When WRITE statements are used, the contents of the print buffer are not output until the line (i.e. print buffer) is full. Consequently, it is possible that more than one WRITE statement may be required in order to output a single line. For example, if the line length is 120 characters and your WRITE statements contain only 40 characters each, three WRITE statements would be needed before the print buffer would output its contents. However, the WRITELN statement can be used to empty the print buffer whether it is full or not. Remember that WRITE statements do not necessarily empty the print buffer; therefore, data from previous WRITE statements may remain in the buffer and be combined with data from other WRITE or later WRITELN statements. To avoid the possibility of leftover data intruding when using WRITE statements, a WRITELN statement (without any variables) can be inserted in your program to empty the contents (if any) of the print buffer before another WRITE or WRITELN statement is used. This takes the form:

```
FOR  I  :=  1  TO  24
          WRITE  (I);
WRITELN
```

OUTPUT SPACING CHARACTERS

When printing output, PASCAL allows the programmer to control the printer by the use of "control characters." The first *literal* term (items enclosed in single quotes) of a WRITE or WRITELN statement is the control character and it specifies the line and page instructions for the printer. In PASCAL the five standard output control characters are:

blank	advance carriage one line before printing
0 (zero)	advance carriage two lines before printing
—	advance carriage three lines before printing
+	do not advance carriage before printing (overstriking)
1	advance carriage to first line of next page

To enhance the appearance of output further, the spacing of output on each line can be adjusted so the results can be titled and easily understood. This spacing adjustment can be accomplished by becoming familiar with the amount of space PASCAL allows for different data types and then learning how this standard spacing can be adjusted. Standard line spacing is:

Integer	10 spaces, right justified
Real	22 spaces, in exponential form
Character	1 space
Boolean	10 spaces, right justified

For example, the following WRITE and WRITELN statements:

```
WRITE ('THE  TEMPERATURE  IN  ROOM',  I,'IS',  R);
WRITELN ( C )
```

produce output similar to:

```
THE TEMPERATURE IN ROOM        18  IS   7.590000000000000E+001F
```

where I is integer, R is real, and C is character. To adjust the spacing for the output item simply add a colon after the item in the WRITE or WRITELN statement followed by the space integer desired. With reals, two integers separated by colons, are used to specify the length and total number of values after the decimal point respectively. The first integer indicates the minimum number of spaces allocated: if fewer spaces are required, the item is preceded by blanks, and if more space is required, as many spaces as are needed are used.

For example, the preceding statements can be rewritten:

```
WRITE ('THE  TEMPERATURE  IN  ROOM'.  I  :  4.  '  IS'.  R  :  6  :  2  );
WRITELN  (  C  :  2  )
```

producing output similar to:

```
THE  TEMPERATURE  IN  ROOM    18  IS  77.59  F
```

Finally, the use of literals (items enclosed in single quotes) should appear in output exactly as they appear within the quotes and, if there are blank spaces within the quotes, the same number of blanks should appear on output.

END *DELIMITER*

The **END** delimiter indicates one of two conditions in PASCAL. First, when it occurs as the last delimiter in a program and is followed by a period, it signifies termination of the program. However, it is also used to terminate a group of statements that form a compound statement where the compound statement starts with **BEGIN** and terminates with **END** followed by a semicolon (as in the of the **WHILE** - **DO** example).

The next section of this appendix presents and describes three PASCAL programs that use most of the techniques described in the preceding sections. These are similar to the programs presented in the other three language appendices.

PASCAL PROGRAMS

This PASCAL program demonstrates a single-pass execution. The program accepts one set of numerical values, calculates one employee's net pay, outputs the result, and stops.

```
(*  PROGRAM  TO  CALCULATE  NET  PAY  *)
PROGRAM     NETPAY1 (INPUT.  OUTPUT) ;
VAR TIME. RATE. RDEDUC. GROSS. DEDUC. PAY : REAL ;
BEGIN
READ (TIME. RATE. RDEDUC) ;
GROSS  :=  TIME  *  RATE ;
DEDUC  :=  GROSS  *  RDEDUC ;
PAY  :=  GROSS  -  DEDUC ;
WRITELN ('1. '       '. 'THE NET PAY FOR THIS EMPLOYEE IS $'. PAY : 9 : 2)
END.
```

In this program, the computer reads the values for three variables (which have all been declared real): TIME, RATE, and RDEDUC. TIME will be multiplied by RATE to compute GROSS (gross pay): then GROSS will be multiplied by RDEDUC (rate of deductions) to compute DEDUC (amount of deductions). Finally, DEDUC will be subtracted from GROSS to give PAY (net pay). The WRITELN statement outputs the results in this form: (1) spacing to the top of a new page on the printer, (2) skipping five spaces, (3) printing the indicated characters enclosed in quotes, and then (4) printing PAY, allowing nine spaces with two to the right of the decimal point.

The second sample PASCAL program uses relational operators. If an employee works more than 40 hours, then PAY will be computed differently than if hours worked were below 40.

```
(* PROGRAM TO CALCULATE REGULAR AND OVERTIME PAY *)
PROGRAM    NETPAY2 ( INPUT, OUTPUT ) ;
VAR TIME, RATE, RDEDUC, GROSS, DEDUC, PAY, EXTRA : REAL ;
BEGIN
READ (TIME, RATE, RDEDUC) ;
IF  TIME   < = 40
       THEN  BEGIN
                GROSS  := TIME * RATE ;
                DEDUC  := GROSS * RDEDUC ;
                PAY  := GROSS  –  DEDUC
             END
       ELSE  BEGIN
                EXTRA  := (TIME  –  40.0) * (RATE * 1.5) ;
                GROSS  := (40.0 * RATE) + EXTRA ;
                DEDUC  := GROSS * RDEDUC ;
                PAY  := GROSS  –  DEDUC
             END:
       WRITELN ('1',       ', 'THE NET PAY FOR THIS EMPLOYEE IS $', PAY : 9 :
       END.
```

In this sample, once values for the variables are read in, the **IF** statement determines whether the employee worked more than 40 hours. If TIME is less than or equal to 40, the normal pay is computed as in the preceding program. However, if TIME is greater than 40, then the computer executes the statements following **ELSE** and makes the pay calculation including the overtime at 1.5 times the usual rate of pay. Please note the two sets of indented **BEGIN** and **END** delimiters that set off the two different pay calculations; the computer will execute one set of these or the other, but not both. The output segment of the program is the same as in the previous program.

The third program includes all of the features described in the first two examples, except now the program calculates more than one set of data. The inclusion of a **FOR - TO - DO** loop enables this program to handle many sets of data.

```
(* PROGRAM TO CALCULATE PAY FOR MANY EMPLOYEES *)
PROGRAM  NETPAY3 (INPUT, OUTPUT) ;
VAR TIME, RATE, RDEDUC, GROSS, DEDUC, PAY EXTRA : REAL:
BEGIN (* PROGRAM NETPAY3 *)
       FOR I := 1 TO 500 DO
       BEGIN (* PAYROLL  CALCULATIONS *)
       READ (TIME, RATE, RDEDUC) ;
       IF  TIME   < = 40
```

```
THEN  BEGIN  (*  REGULAR  PAY  PROCEDURE  *)
        GROSS  :=  TIME  *  RATE;
        DEDUC  :=  GROSS  *  RDEDUC;
        PAY  :=  GROSS  -  DEDUC
        END  (*  REGULAR  PAY  PROCEDURE  *)
ELSE  BEGIN  (*  OVERTIME  PAY  PROCEDURE  *)
        EXTRA  :=  (TIME  -  40.0)  *  (RATE  *  1.5);
        GROSS  :=  (40.0  *  RATE)  +  EXTRA;
        DEDUC  :=  GROSS  *  RDEDUC;
        PAY  :=  GROSS  -  DEDUC
      END;  (*  OVERTIME  PAY  PROCEDURE  *)
    WRITELN  ('1',                ',  'THE  NET  PAY  FOR  THIS  EMPLOYEE  IS  $,  PAY  :  9  :  2)
    END;  (*  PAYROLL  CALCULATIONS  *)
END.  (*  PROGRAM  NETPAY3  *)
```

All features of this program remain the same as in the preceding programs except the addition of the loop and the extra **BEGIN - END** delimiters that set off the statements within the loop. Note, too, the use of comments to identify the pairs of **BEGIN - END** delimiters. The **FOR - TO - DO** delimiters enable program execution 500 times, thus computing the PAY for 500 employees using 500 different sets of data. As the loop returns the computer to the READ statement each time, a new set of values is entered and processed.

These three programs demonstrate the basic techniques that can be applied to a wide variety of problems. They form a simple framework for a variety of operations that can be accomplished with the use of the PASCAL language.

BIBLIOGRAPHY

Section I: General

ARBIB, Michael, A., *Computers and The Cybernetic Society*. New York: Academic Press, 1977.

BANDURA, Albert, *Social Learning Theory,* Englewood Cliffs, NJ: Prentice-Hall, Inc., 1977.

CONDON, Roberts S., *Data Processing with Applications*. Englewood Cliffs, NJ: Prentice-Hall, Inc., 1978.

HARMAN, Willis W., *An Incomplete Guide to the Future*. New York: W. W. North & Company, Inc., 1979.

ROTHMAN, Stanley, and Charles MOSSMAN, *Computers and Society*. Chicago: Science Research Associates, Inc., 1979.

SANDERS, Donald H., *Computers and Society*. New York: McGraw-Hill., 1980.

Section II: Foundations

ADAMS, J. Mack, and HADEN, Douglas H. *Social Effects of Computer Use and Misuse, New York, John Wiley, 1976.*

BASSLER, Richard A., Applications of Computer Systems. Arlington, VA.: College Readings, Inc., 1975.

BARTEE, Thomas C., Digital Computer Fundamentals, 4th ed. New York: McGraw-Hill, 1977.

CONWAY, Richard, David GRIES, and E.C. ZIMMERMAN, A Primer on Pascal. Cambridge, MA: Winthrop Publishers, Inc., 1976.

COUGAR, J. Daniel, and McFadden, Fred R., *Introduction to Computer Based Information Systems.* New York: John Wiley, 1975.

DAHL, O. J., E. W. DIJKSTRA, and C. A. R. HOARE, *Structured Programming*. New York: Academic Press, 1976.

DOLOTTA, T. H., *Data Processing in the 1980's*. New York: John Wiley, 1976.

EDWARDS, Perry, and BROADWELL, Bruce, *Computers in Action—Data Processing. Belmont, CA: Wadsworth Publishing Co., 1981*.

KIEBURTZ, Richard B., Structured Programming and Problem-Solving with Pascal. Englewood Cliffs, NJ: Prentice-Hall, 1978.

McGLYNN, Daniel B., *Microprocessors: Technology, Architecture and Applications*. New York: John Wiley, 1976.

O'BRIEN, James A., *Computers in Business Management: An Introduction*. Homewood, IL. Richard D. Irwin, Inc., 1979.

VAN TASSEL, Dennie, *Program Style, Design, Efficiency, Debugging, and Testing*. Englewood Cliffs, NJ: Prentice-Hall, Inc., 1978.

WEINBERG, Gerald, *The Psychology of Computer Programming*. New York: Van Nostrand Reinhold Co., 1979.

Section III.   Applications

BODEN, Margaret, *Artificial Intelligence and Natural Man*. New York: Basic Books, Inc., 1977.

DREYFUS, Hubert L., *What Computers Can't Do*. New York: Harper & Row, Publishers, Inc., 1972.

DRUCKER, Peter F., *The Age of Discontinuity*. New York: Harper & Row, Publishers, Inc., 1969.

GOTLIEB, C. C., *Social Issues in Computing*. New York: Academic Press, 1978.

HOLMES, James D., and Elias M. AWAD, eds. *Perspective on Electronic Data Processing*. Englewood Cliffs NJ: Prentice-Hall, 1972.

KEMENY, John G., *Man and the Computer*. New York: Charles Scribner's Sons, 1972.

KRANZ, Stewart, *Science and Technology in the Arts*. New York: Van Nostrand Reinhold Co., 1974.

LEAVITT, Ruth, ed., *Artist and Computer*. New York: Harmony Books, 1976.

MARTIN, James, *The Wired Society*. Englewood Cliffs, NJ: Prentice-Hall, Inc., 1978.

MARTIN, James T. and Adrian NORMAN, *The Computerized Society*. Englewood Cliffs NJ: Prentice-Hall, Inc., 1970.

MEADOWS, D.L., *Limits to Growth*. New York: New American Library, 1974.

MILLER, Arthur R., *The Assault on Privacy*. Ann Arbor Mich: The University of Michigan Press, 1971.

MOWSHOWITZ, Abbe, *The Conquest of Will*. Menlo Park, CA: Addison Wesley Publishing Co., 1976.

National Information Policy.   Washington, DC: Report to the President of the United States, 1976.

NEWELL, A.,   *Human Problem Solving*. Englewood Cliffs, NJ: Prentice-Hall, Inc., 1972.

PARKER, Donn B., *Computer Abuse*. Menlo Park, CA: Stanford Research Institute. (Project ISU 2501), November 1973.

PARKMAN, R. *The Cybernetic Society*. Elmsford, NY: pergamon Press, Inc., 1972.

Personal Privacy in an Information Society. Washington DC: The Report of the Privacy Protection Study Commission. 1977.

PYLYSHYN, Z., ed.,   *Perspectives on the Computer Revolution.* Englewood Cliffs, NJ: Prentice-Hall, Inc., 1970.

RAPHAEL, Bertram,   *The Thinking Computer.* San Francisco: W.H. Freeman and Company, 1976.

SLOTNICK, Daniel L. and Joan K. SLOTNICK,   *Computers: Their Structure, Use, and Influence.* Englewood Cliffs, NJ: Prentice-Hall, 1979.

TOFFLER, Alvin, ed., *The Futurists.* New York: Random House Inc., 1970.

TOFFLER, Alvin, *Future Shock.* New York: Random House, Inc., 1972.

TOFFLER, Alvin, *The Third Wave.* New York: Random House, Inc., 1980.

VAN TASSEL, Dennie, ed., *The Compleat Computer.* Chicago: Science Research Associates, Inc., 1976.

VONNEGUT, Kurt, *Player Piano.* New York: Avon Books, 1967.

VON NEUMAN, John,   *The Computer and the Brain.*   New Haven, CN: Yale University Press, 1958.

WEIZENBAUM, Joseph, *Computer Power and Human Reason.* San Francisco: W.H. Freeman and Company, 1976.

WESSEL, Milton R., *Freedom's Edge: The Computer Threat to Society.* Reading MA: Addison Wesley Publishing Co., 1974.

WESTIN, Alan, *Information Technology in a Democracy.* Cambridge, MA: Harvard University Press, 1971.

WESTIN, Alan, *Databanks in a Free Society.* New York: Quadrangle Books/The New York Times Book Company, 1972.

WIENER, Norbert, *The Human Use of Human Beings.* New York: Avon Books, 1967.

WINSTON, Patrick Henry, *Artificial Intelligence.* Reading, MA: Addison-Wesley Publishing Company, 1977.

Section IV.   Periodicals

Much of the research for this book involved the use of current periodicals. These were used in order to ensure that the information presented in our writings would be as current and up-to-date as possible. We strongly suggest that should you do more research on your own, you consult the following periodicals:

Infoworld	Datamation
Computerworld	Byte
Popular Computing	Science
Personal Computing	Business Week
Creative Computing	Computing Decisions

INDEX